AN INTRODUCTION
to
WEB DESIGN
and
PROGRAMMING

Paul S. Wang and Sanda Katila
Kent State University

THOMSON

BROOKS/COLE

Australia • Canada • Mexico • Singapore • Spain
United Kingdom • United States

THOMSON

BROOKS/COLE

Publisher: *Bill Stenquist*
Editor: *Kallie Swanson*
Editorial Assistant: *Aarti Jayaraman*
Technology Project Manager: *Burke Taft*
Executive Marketing Director: *Tom Ziolkowski*
Marketing Assistant: *Jennifer Gee*
Advertising Project Manager: *Vicky Wan*
Project Manager, Editorial Production: *Kelsey McGee*

Print/Media Buyer: *Doreen Suruki*
Permissions Editor: *Elizabeth Zuber*
Production Service: *Matrix Productions, Inc.*
Copy Editor: *Frank Hubert*
Photo Research: *Sue C. Howard*
Cover Printing, Printing and Binding: *Webcom*
Compositor: *T$_E$X Consultants/Arthur Ogawa*

For more information about our products, contact us at:
Thomson Learning Academic Resource Center
1-800-423-0563

For permission to use material from this text,
contact us by:
Phone: 1-800-730-2214 **Fax:** 1-800-730-2215
Web: http://www.thomsonrights.com

Library of Congress Control Number: 2003111365

ISBN 0-39528-7

Brooks/Cole–Thomson Learning
10 Davis Drive
Belmont, CA 94002
USA

Asia
Thomson Learning
5 Shenton Way #01-01
UIC Building
Singapore 068808

Australia/New Zealand
Thomson Learning
102 Dodds Street
Southbank, Victoria 3006
Australia

Canada
Nelson
1120 Birchmount Road
Toronto, Ontario M1K 5G4
Canada

Europe/Middle East/Africa
Thomson Learning
High Holborn House
50/51 Bedford Row
London WC1R 4LR
United Kingdom

Latin America
Thomson Learning
Seneca, 53
Colonia Poianco
11560 Mexico D.F.
Mexico

Spain/Portugal
Paraninfo
Calle Magallanes, 25
28015 Madrid, Spain

Preface

The Web is a new communication medium that is growing rapidly. The Web will soon affect, directly or indirectly, most people's daily lives. It is already beginning to revolutionize how business, commerce, government, and education are conducted. Perhaps most important, the Web is bridging the gaps between peoples and cultures, and increasing mutual understanding and goodwill. This can only support global peace and prosperity for the human race.

The need for well-trained Web developers, already great, is on the rise. To meet demand, colleges, universities, and companies are creating curricula and training courses in this new and rapidly advancing arena. Research, development, and education in Web- and Internet-related areas will continue to increase and expand.

The market offers many books about using the Web, but few are textbooks. This college text focuses on the art and science of Web site development. It is one of the very first texts to combine computer programming with artistic design in an integrated approach. The Web may be many things, but the two most basic elements of site development remain programming technologies and visual communication design. We present theory and practice of both so that students will gain a fundamental understanding and the applicable skills at the same time.

We have worked together since the mid-1990s to develop a Web Design and Programming (WDP) curriculum at the undergraduate level at Kent State University. Kent's Department of Computer Science and the School of Visual Communication Design has fostered the collaboration. We've developed a sequence of three courses and are establishing a minor in WDP.

The nature of the Web as a medium requires both programming and artistic design. We firmly believe it is best to study Web development by being introduced to both in an integrated manner. With an overall view and understanding, an individual can then decide to specialize in one or more aspects of the whole process, and it will take more than one course to become an expert in any sub-area.

Open Technologies

The spirit of the Web and the Internet is their openness. It is a critical factor for the popularity and success of the Web. The World Wide Web Consortium (W3C) is a nonprofit organization leading the way for developing open Web standards.

This text introduces a complete set of open technologies for Web development:

- XHTML—The up-and-coming HTML standard for Web page markup.
- CSS—The standard language for controlling the presentation style of Web pages.
- JavaScript—A standard language for client-side scripting.
- DOM—The W3C document object model for cross-platform access and manipulation of Web documents.
- DHTML—Combines JavaScript, CSS, and DOM for dynamic and interactive effects on the client side.
- HTTP—The Hypertext Transfer Protocol used by the Web.
- Perl—An open scripting language for server-side programming to support HTML forms and page generation.
- CGI—The Common Gateway Interface for Web servers to interact with external programs.

We provide sufficient and well-structured coverage of these technologies. More important, we show how they combine to enable serious Web development in practice. We give an abundance of realistic examples to illustrate techniques that are applicable in many situations.

Design Principles and Methodology

Simply applying technologies will not produce good Web sites. On the contrary, incorporating programming features without a good design will produce awful sites. We cover the complete Web site creation process, from requirements and initial concepts to the deployed site. To help make a site functional, logical, easy to use, efficient, and attractive, we present concepts and principles of information architecture, visual communication design, color and graphics, fonts, layout, visual hierarchy, symmetry, balance, unity, and variation. We also describe tools for design, coding, image processing, template generation, site integration, testing, and debugging. Chapter 11, Graphics and Site Production, ties the many aspects of Web site creation together.

An Integrated Approach

Our central topic is how to develop Web sites that are highly functional and attractive. The theme is the integration of programming with artistic design. We integrate information and artistic design aspects with technological and programming contents to show how ideas and designs can be implemented and what design space the available technologies provide. Design guides, implementation, and programming help realize the design, and that's the way we wrote *Introduction to Web Design and programming*.

Perhaps not everyone can master both artistic design and computer programming. But a broad exposure at first is important. True masters of the Web medium will necessarily be those who have a good command of both design and technology.

Histories and Summaries

We also include brief history sections in many chapters in an effort to show how the different subjects presented are interrelated, have evolved through time, and are embedded in the larger picture of Web development. Chapter-ending summaries help review the material we present in each chapter and highlight the most important ideas covered. We encourage readers to pay attention to these sections because they not only put Web design and programming in context but also show where they are headed in the future.

Examples and Exercises

The text offers many interesting and realistic examples to demonstrate programming techniques and design concepts. Programming examples show how XHTML, CSS, JavaScript, and Perl/CGI constructs work individually and in combination to achieve well-defined Web site goals. XHTML and CSS examples pass W3C validation. All programming examples are ready to run and are labeled with "Ex: **ExampleName**" so they correlate easily with the online versions.

Design examples use figures and screen shots to illustrate the main points. Implementation examples show how designs, graphics, and styles are realized in code. Many examples can be applied readily in Web site development projects.

Throughout the book, examples are drawn from Web sites, providing a common thread that demonstrates how the concepts and techniques covered are applied to actual Web sites. Review questions and assignments for application of knowledge for each chapter reinforce the material covered.

Web Site

The WDP Web site www.sofpower.com/wdp provides a wealth of supplemental materials for readers of this textbook. The Web site offers reference listings, useful resources, online versions of the diagrams (in full size and color, of course), ready-to-run examples cross-referenced with in-text descriptions, hands-on experiments, and an example package ready to download. The site also offers a complete guide for conducting team projects. Information includes team organization and operation, project milestones, report preparation, and project evaluation.

ACM Curriculum Recommendations

According to the ACM *Computing Curricula 2001 Computer Science Report* (December 15, 2001):

> Today, networking and the Web have become the underpinning for much of our economy. They have become critical foundations of computer science, and it is impossible to imagine that undergraduate programs would not devote significantly more time to this topic. At the same time, the existence of the Web has changed the nature of the educational process itself. Modern networking technology enhances everyone's ability to communicate and gives people throughout the world unprecedented access to information.

We hope this textbook will make it easier to introduce a course in the Net-centric area that is fulfilling both to teach and learn. And the WDP Web site will provide the Web-enhanced education that we all hope will be more widely available.

Flexible Usage

The text is designed for a one-semester course to introduce Web design and programming. It is ideal at the undergraduate level for computer science, computer engineering, and computer technology students. Instructors of Web development are modern pioneers. It takes hard work and dedication to tackle a topic that is wide ranging and rapidly advancing. Most CS curricula lag behind despite the clear curriculum recommendation from ACM and IEEE to include Net-centric courses.

This text can be used at the undergraduate or beginning graduate level. It is also suitable for custom training courses for industry or for independent study by IT professionals. A shorter course may omit chapters 10 to 13, as appropriate. A CS instructor may elect to focus more on programming chapters and cover the art materials together with students. In an advanced course, the instructor may proceed at a faster pace, assigning Chapter 1 and parts of Chapter 2 for reading, and selecting more substantial programming projects from the exercises.

Instructors of a two-semester sequence on Web development may use this text and add some other server-side topics in the second semester.

Acknowledgments

The textbook is the result of many years of joint course development work by the authors, supported by our departments. We are grateful for the institutional support and the students who took the Web Design and Programming (WDP) courses. Special thanks goes to Jim Byrd, who read over many chapters of the initial manuscript and made corrections and suggestions; to the Spring 2003 WDP class in which the draft manuscript went through classroom trial; to Misty Tackett, secretary at the Institute for Computational Mathematics, who helped tremendously, contacting sources and obtaining necessary permissions for screen shots and other images; and to a long list of organizations who granted us permission to use their Web images. The detailed permission list can be found on the Web site. Appreciation also goes to reviewers of the manuscript: Russ Abbott of California State University—Los Angeles, Anselm Blumer of Tufts University, Mary Ann May-Pumphrey of De Anza College, Derek Oyen of Digiknow, and Al Wasco of Cuyahoga Community College—Western Campus, who provided valuable comments and suggestions.

To the entire staff of Brooks/Cole, especially Kallie Swanson, thanks for your support and able management of this project. Special thanks goes to Sue Howard for her great help in dealing with copyright and permission issues with the many figures contained in this text. We also want to thank Kelsey McGee (Brooks/Cole) and Merrill Peterson (Matrix Productions) for their able management of the production process, and Arthur Ogawa at TEX Consultants for an excellent job typesetting the manuscript and recreating the figures. We'd like to acknowledge the help and dedication of Aaron Downey at Matrix Productions for bringing everything together on schedule ready for the printer.

From Sanda   To my friend, Paul Wang for your continued inspiration and focus. Thanks for trusting me to partner with you on this exciting effort. You're amazing.

To John Buchanan, Professor, School of Visual Communication Design, Kent State University, for introducing me to Paul Wang. Thanks for playing tennis, John!

To J. Charles Walker, Director, School of Visual Communication Design, Kent State University, for giving me my favorite year. Without your support I couldn't have done this!

To my best friend, Chris Somosi, for editing the long and tedious first drafts of this book, and for the continuous encouragement and support in all ways. Thanks for taking good care of Emily and Maxim while I was staring at my computer screen. You're the best.

To my husband, John Katila, daughter, Emily, and son, Maxim. Thanks for putting up with me through the long days and nights. You're my joy, strength, and hope.

From Paul   To Sanda, it is indeed my good fortune to work together with you in this cross-disciplinary adventure. I learned so much from you.

Finally and most of all, my deep appreciation to my wife, Jennifer, and my children, Laura, Deborah, and David for their support and encouragement.

Paul S. Wang
Sanda Katila
Kent, Ohio

Contents

CHAPTER 8   Forms and Form Processing   277

CHAPTER 11   Graphics and Site Production   405

Introduction

In a few short years, the World Wide Web has grown rapidly in extent, capabilities, and applications. The global expansion of the Web has just begun. Industry, commerce, academia, government, as well as individuals are putting the Web to use in substantial ways. Many rely on it to work or perform chores in daily living. Its influence and application will only increase. And it is hard to say how the Web will shape society in the not-so-distant future.

Students in colleges and universities are naturally inquisitive about new technologies. Many are eager to learn about the Web that impacts their daily lives. In the meantime, the demand for skilled personnel for Web site development and maintenance is great and increasing. People are needed in all types of organizations to create, design, implement, and manage sites. Today, nearly all individuals filling this need have, at best, a background either in computer science/engineering or in graphical design.

But sufficient understanding of artistic design, visual communication, information architecture, color and graphics, as well as computer science and programming is needed to begin to master this new communication medium. This textbook covers the design and technology aspects of Web site development in an integrated manner. The result is a one-semester course for CS and other computer majors on Web Design and Programming (WDP). Both theoretical understanding and developmental techniques are emphasized and the focus is on the art and technology of Web site creation.

We certainly find such integration enormously exciting and beneficial. Ideally, the combined curriculum is much greater than the sum of its constituent parts, and our readers will find this book useful and enjoyable.

WEB TECHNOLOGIES

The strength of the Web lies in its openness, speed, and low cost of entry. Enabling technologies for the Web include networking protocols, data encoding formats, clients (browsers), servers, Web page markup and styling languages,

1

and client-side and server-side programming. The Web can deliver text, images, animation, audio, video, and other multimedia content. Standard and proprietary media formats, tools, and players are also part of the Web. These technologies are still developing and improving. The World Wide Web Consortium (W3C) is a nonprofit organization leading the way in developing open Web standards.

This text is about Web site development, and it focuses on a set of core Web technologies recommended by W3C:

- HTTP—The Hypertext Transfer Protocol employed by the Web.
- XHTML—The standard markup language for coding Web pages.
- CSS—Cascading style sheets, a standard language for controlling the presentation style of Web pages.
- JavaScript™—A standard scripting language for client-side programming.
- DHTML—Dynamic HTML, a technique for producing responsive and interactive Web pages through client-side programming.
- DOM—Document object model, an application programming interface (API) for access and manipulation of Web page style and content.
- CGI—The Common Gateway Interface, a standard for connecting Web servers to server-side programs to collect and process information from Web users.
- Perl—A popular language for server-side CGI programming.

In-depth and comprehensive coverage of any one of these topics can require a thick book by itself. But even after reading all such books, you still have to know how they combine and work together for Web site development.

This book provides sufficient coverage of these technologies and, more important, how they work together to enable serious Web site development. Further, we integrate technology with artistic design to achieve effective and attractive Web design. It is our hope that after getting to know the overall landscape of Web development, you will find motivation for in-depth study of some of these individual technologies.

DESIGN PRINCIPLES

Simply applying technologies does not produce good Web sites. A Web developer must learn how to make the site serve its intended purposes, how to structure and organize the content of the site for effective and efficient delivery, and how to make the site convenient, pleasing, functional, and attractive.

To help achieve these goals, the text presents concepts and principles of information architecture, visual communication design, color and graphics, fonts, layout, visual hierarchy, symmetry, balance, unity, and variation. Understanding these design topics is essential for a Web developer to create highly functional and attractive sites.

WEB SITE DEVELOPMENT

The central topic of this book is how to develop Web sites that are highly functional and attractive. The theme is integration of programming with artistic design.

The reader will first get an overview of the Web and Internet, the Web site development process, and the technologies, techniques, and tasks involved. Then, different topics are presented in a logical sequence following the Web site development process. The material balances theory, concepts, tools, and practices to provide both fundamental understanding and developmental abilities.

Even though many subjects are discussed, the core of Web site development remains *visual communication design* and *programming*. Throughout the book, these two aspects are covered in an integrated manner to provide a solid background for the reader as a Web developer.

A Web site production process puts both aspects together for a team-based approach. The text also suggests ways to streamline the cooperation between designers and programmers in the entire site development process.

THE WDP WEB SITE

This book has a Web site that offers reference listings (in lieu of appendixes), useful resources, online versions of the figures (in full size and color), ready-to-run examples cross-referenced to in-text descriptions, hands-on experiments to enhance learning, and an example package ready to download. Examples are labeled with "Ex: **ExampleName**" so they correlate easily with the online versions. The Web site is:

www.sofpower.com/wdp

In the text, we refer to this Web site as the *WDP site*. The site itself applies the concepts and technologies we cover. All pages pass the strict XHTML validation test, and all styling is CSS based. Thus, it provides a rich source of examples and a common thread through all the chapters as a Web site development project.

INTENDED USE

The text is designed for a one-semester course to introduce Web Design and Programming. It is ideal at the undergraduate level for computer science, computer engineering, and computer technology students. It can be used at the beginning graduate level in other departments. Familiarity with programming and the computer as an operating environment is required. A lab-oriented class format is recommended.

The text is also suitable for custom training courses for industry or self-study by information technology (IT) professionals. A shorter course may omit Chapters 11 to 13, as appropriate. An advanced course may proceed at a faster pace, assign one or two chapters for reading, and select more substantial programming projects from the exercises.

Students should have basic computer skills and some programming experience. The materials are diverse enough to remain interesting and challenging even for people with some experience in Web development.

CHAPTER 1

Web Basics and Overview

The Web is an Internet-based distributed information system. Anyone with a computer connected to the Internet can easily retrieve information by giving a Web address or by clicking a mouse button. The Web is a great way to disseminate information and make it available 24/7. Information can also be collected from Web users and customers through online forms. Maintainers and administrators can control and update Web content from anywhere on the Web. All of these features make the Web a powerful tool for mass communication, e-business, and e-commerce.

Compared with TV, radio, newspapers, and magazines, putting the word out on the Web is relatively simple and inexpensive. But a Web site is much more than a one-way communication medium. It can be a virtual office or store that is always open and supported by workers from anywhere.

Web service companies offer free Web space and tools to generate simple personal or business Web pages. But well-designed and professionally implemented Web sites are much more involved. Even then, expertly produced sites are still much more cost-effective than other means of mass communication. For business and commerce, the cost of a Web site is negligible when compared to building and operating a brick-and-mortar office or store. Once in place, a Web site is a store that never closes, and that is very attractive. People take great pains in building an office or store to project the right image and to serve the needs of customers. Likewise, well-informed businesses will insist on professionally architected, designed, and implemented Web sites. Nothing less will do.

As a communication medium, the Web consists of these major components

- Networks—The local area and wide area networks that connect computers worldwide and form the Internet.
- Clients—Web browsers that enable users to access the Web.
- Servers—Constantly running programs that serve information to the Web.
- Documents—Web pages, mostly coded in HTML, that supply information on the Web.

- Protocols—The Hypertext Transfer Protocol (HTTP) that Web clients and servers use to talk to one another and the TCP/IP (Transmission Control Protocol/Internet Protocol) on which HTTP depends.

A basic understanding of these components and how they work together lays a good foundation for web design and programming. Let's begin by taking a look at networking.

1.1 ABOUT NETWORKING

A *computer network* is a high-speed communications medium connecting many, possibly dissimilar, computers, or *hosts*. A network is a combination of computer and telecommunication hardware and software. The purpose is to provide fast and reliable information exchange among the hosts and between *processes*, or executing programs, on different hosts. The Web is one of the most widely used Internet services. Others include email, file transfer, audio/video streaming, and log on to remote hosts, just to name a few. The Web also provides convenient ways to tap into these other Internet services.

A network greatly extends the powers of the connected hosts. Modern computers and networks are so integrated it is hard to tell where the computer ends and where the network begins. The view that "the network is the computer" is more valid than ever before, and companies slow to adopt this view are scrambling to implement network-centric solutions to their corporate needs. A Web site can work wonders for companies, organizations, governments, and individuals.

Networking Protocols

For programs and computers from different vendors, under different operating systems, to communicate on a network, a detailed set of rules and conventions must be established for all parties to follow. Such rules are known as *networking protocols*. Protocols govern such details as:

- address format of hosts and processes
- data format
- manner of data transmission
- sequencing and addressing of messages
- initiating and terminating connections
- establishing remote services
- accessing remote services
- network security

Thus, for a process on one host to communicate with another process on a different host, both processes must follow the same protocol. A protocol is usually viewed as having logical layers that come between the process and the networking hardware. The corresponding layers on different hosts perform complementary tasks to make the connection between the communicating processes.

Among common networking protocols, the Internet Protocol (IP) suite[1] is the most widely used. IP is the basic protocol for the Internet (Section 1.2), which is by far the most predominant worldwide network. The Web is a service that uses HTTP (the Hypertext Transfer Protocol), which is based on Internet protocols.

Networking protocols are no mystery. Think about the protocol for making a telephone call. You (a client process) must pick up the phone, listen for the dial tone, dial a valid telephone number, and wait for the other side (the server process) to pick up the phone. Then you must say "hello," identify yourself, and so on. This is a protocol from which you can't deviate if you want the call to be made successfully through the telephone network. And it is clear why such a protocol is needed. The same is true of a computer program attempting to talk to another through a computer network. The design of efficient and effective networking protocols for different network services is an important area in computer science.

If your computer system is on a network, chances are that you are already connected to the Internet. This means you have the ability to reach, almost instantaneously, across great distances to obtain information, exchange messages, retrieve data, interact with others, do literature searches, and much more without leaving the seat in front of your workstation. If your computer is not directly connected to a network but has a telephone or cable modem, then you can reach the Internet through an Internet service provider (ISP).

1.2 THE INTERNET

The Internet is a global network that connects IP networks. The linking of computer networks is called *internetworking*, hence the name Internet. The Internet links all kinds of organizations around the world: universities, government offices, corporations, libraries, supercomputer centers, research labs, and individual homes. The number of connections on the Internet is large and growing rapidly.

---

[1]Including TCP, UDP, and others.

The Internet evolved from the ARPANET,[2] a U.S. Department of Defense Advanced Research Projects Agency (DARPA) sponsored network that developed the IP as well as the higher level TCP and UDP (User Datagram Protocol) networking protocols. The architecture and protocol were designed to support a reliable and flexible network that can endure wartime attacks.

The transition of ARPANET to the Internet took place in the late 1980s as NSFnet, the U.S. National Science Foundation's network of universities and supercomputing centers, helped create an explosive number of IP-based local and regional networks and connections. The NSFnet remains an important component of the Internet. The Internet is so dominant now that it has virtually eliminated all historical rivals such as BITNET and DECnet.

The Internet Corporation for Assigned Names and Numbers (ICANN; www.icann.org) is a nonprofit organization responsible for IP address space allocation, protocol parameter assignment, domain name system management, and root server system management functions.

Network Addresses

An address to a host computer is like a phone number to a telephone. Every host on the Internet has a unique network address that identifies the host for communication purposes. The addressing technique is an important part of a network and its protocol. For the Internet, each host has a unique IP address represented by 4 bytes in a 32-bit quantity. For example, monkey, a host at Kent State, has the IP address 131.123.35.92 (Figure 1.1). This *dot notation* (or *quad notation*) gives the decimal value (0 to 255) of each byte.[3] The IP address is similar to a telephone number in another way: The leading digits are like area codes and the trailing digits are like local numbers.

Because of their numerical nature, the dot notation is easy on machines but hard on users. Therefore, each host also has a unique *domain-based name* composed of words, rather like a postal address. For example, the domain name for monkey is monkey.cs.kent.edu (at Department of Computer Science,

Figure 1.1 IP ADDRESS

---

[2]The ARPANET was started in the late 1960s as an experimental facility for reliable military networking.

[3]To accommodate the explosive growth of the Internet, the next generation IP (IPv6) will support 128-bit addresses.

Kent State University). With the domain names, the entire Internet host name space is recursively divided into disjoint domains. The address for monkey puts it in the kent subdomain within edu, the *top-level domain* (TLD) for educational institutions. Other TLDs include org (nonprofit organizations), gov (government offices), mil (military installations), com (commercial outfits), net (network service providers), uk, (United Kingdom), cn (China), and so forth. Within a local domain (e.g., cs.kent.edu), you can refer to machines by their host name alone (e.g., monkey, dragon, tiger), but the full address must be used for machines outside. Further information on Internet domain names can be found in Section 1.10.

The ICANN accredits *domain name registrars*, which register domain names for clients so they stay unique. All network applications accept a host address given either as a domain name or an IP address. In fact, a domain name is first translated to a numerical IP address before being used.

Packet Switching

Data on the Internet are sent and received in *packets*. A packet envelops transmitted data with address information so the data can be routed through intermediate computers on the network. Because there are multiple routes from the source to the destination host, the Internet is very reliable and can operate even if parts of the network are down.

Client and Server

Most commonly, a network application involves a server and a client (Figure 1.2):

- A *server* process provides a specific service on a host machine that offers such a service. Example services are remote host access (Telnet), file transfer (FTP), and the World Wide Web (HTTP). Each Internet standard service has its own unique port number that is identical across all hosts. The port number together with the Internet address of a host identifies a particular server (Figure 1.2) anywhere on the network. For example, FTP has port number 21, Telnet 23, and HTTP 80.
- A *client* process on a host connects with a server on another host to obtain its service. Thus, a client program is the agent through which a particular network service can be obtained. Different agents are usually required for different services.

A Web browser such as Netscape is an HTTP client. It runs on your computer to access Web servers on any Internet hosts.

Figure 1.2 CLIENT AND SERVER

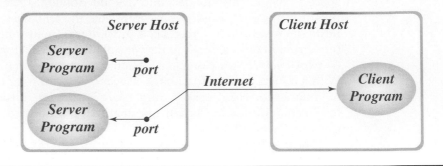

1.3 THE DOMAIN NAME SYSTEM

As stated in Section 1.2, every host on the Internet has a unique IP address and a domain name. The *network name space* is the set of all host names and changes dynamically with time due to the addition and deletion of hosts, regrouping of local work groups, reconfiguration of subparts of the network, maintenance of systems and networks, and so on. Thus, new domain names, new IP addresses, and new domain-to-IP associations can be introduced in the name space at any time without central control. The *domain name system* (DNS) provides a distributed database service that supports dynamic update and retrieval of information contained in the name space (Figure 1.3). A network client program (e.g., the Netscape Navigator browser) will normally use the DNS to obtain address information for a target host before making contact with a server. The dynamic DNS also supplies a general mechanism for retrieving many kinds of information about hosts and individual users.

Here are points to note about the DNS name space:

- The DNS organizes the entire Internet name space into a big tree structure. Each node of the tree has a label and a list of resources.
- Labels are character strings (currently not case sensitive), and sibling labels must be distinct. The root is labeled by the empty string. Immediately below the root are the top-level domains: edu, com, gov, net, org, and so on. TLDs also include country names such as at

Figure 1.3 DOMAIN TO IP

Figure 1.4   THE DOMAIN NAME HIERARCHY

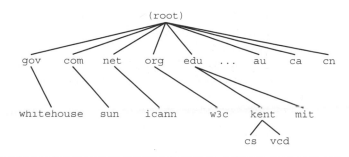

(Austria), ca (Canada), and cn (China). Under edu, for example, there are subdomains berkeley, kent, mit, uiuc, and so on (Figure 1.4).

- A full domain name of a node is a dot-separated list of labels leading from the node to the root (e.g., cs.kent.edu.).

- A relative domain name is a prefix of a full domain name indicating a node relative to a domain of origin. Thus, cs.kent.edu is actually a name relative to the root.

- A label is the formal or canonical name of a domain. Alternative names, called *aliases*, are also allowed. For example, the main Web server host info has the alias www, so it is also known as www.cs.kent.edu. To move the Web server to a different host, a local system manager reassigns the alias to another host.

See Section 1.10 for more information on the DNS and name servers.

1.4   THE WEB

There is no central control or administration of the Web. Anyone can potentially put material on the Web and retrieve information from it. The Web consists of a vast collection of documents that are located on computers throughout the world. These documents are created by academic, professional, governmental, and commercial organizations as well as by individuals. The documents are prepared in special formats and retrieved through *server programs* on each computer that provides Web service. Each Web document can contain (potentially many) links to other documents served by different servers in other locations and therefore become part of a *web* that spans the entire globe. New materials are put on the Web continuously, and instant access to this collection of information can be enormously advantageous. As the Web grows explosively, MIT of the United States and INRIA (the French National Institute for Research in Computer Science and Control) have agreed to become joint hosts of the *W3 Consortium*, which is supported by industry and will further develop Web-related standards, protocols, and services.

A *Web browser* is a program that helps users obtain information from the Web. Given the location of a target document, a browser connects to the correct Web server and retrieves and displays the desired document. You can click *links* in a document to obtain other documents. Using a browser, you can retrieve information provided by *Web servers* anywhere on the Internet.

Many different Web browsers are available. Mosaic, developed at the U.S. National Center for Supercomputing Applications (NCSA), is the original browser with a convenient graphical user interface. Today, widely used Web browsers are Netscape's Netscape Navigator (NN) and Microsoft's Internet Explorer (IE). RealOne is an audio/video media player and Web browser from RealNetworks. Other browsers include IBM's WebExplorer, JavaSoft's HotJava, and W3C's Amaya, Mozilla, and Opera, just to name a few. Web browsers compete to offer speed and convenience for the user and are evolving with time.

Typically, a browser supports the display of HTML files and images in standard formats. Helper applications or plug-ins can augment a browser to treat pages with multimedia contents such as audio, video, animation, and mathematical formulas.

Hypertext

A Web browser communicates with a Web server through an efficient Hypertext Transfer Protocol (HTTP) designed to work with hypertext and hypermedia documents that may contain regular text, images, audio, and video. Native Web pages are written in the Hypertext Markup Language (HTML) and usually saved in files with the .html (or .htm) suffix.

HTML organizes Web page contents (text, graphics, and other media data) and allows *hyperlinks* to other pages anywhere on the Web. Clicking such a link causes your Web browser to follow it and retrieve another page. The Web employs an open addressing scheme that allows links to objects and services provided by Web, email, file transfer, audio/video, and newsgroup servers. Thus, the Web space is a superset of many popular Internet services. Consequently, a Web browser provides the ability to access a wide variety of information and services on the Internet.

URLs

The Web uses *Uniform Resource Locators* (URLs) to identify (locate) resources (files and services) available on the Internet. A URL may identify a host, a server port, and the target file stored on that host. URLs are used, for example, by browsers to retrieve information and by HTML to link to other resources.

A full URL usually has the form

scheme://*server*:*port*/*pathname*

The *scheme* part indicates the information service type and therefore the protocol to use. Common schemes include the following:

- http—Service is Web. The file located is retrieved by the Web-defined Hypertext Transfer Protocol (HTTP).
- ftp—Service is FTP. The URL locates a file, a directory, or an FTP server. For example,

  ftp://ftp1.mcom.com/netscape/

  The protocol is the *file transfer protocol*.
- file—Service is the local file system. The URL locates a file on the same host.
- mailto—Service is email. The URL is simplified and identifies an email address to send email via the Internet.
- telnet—Service is Telnet. The URL names a target host for remote logon.
- news—The URL locates a Usenet newsgroup.

Many other schemes can be found at www.w3.org/addressing/schemes.

The *server* identifies a host and a server program. The optional port number is needed only if the server does not use the default port (e.g., 21 for FTP and 80 for HTTP). The remainder of the URL, when given, is a *file pathname*. If this pathname has a trailing / character, it represents a directory rather than a data file. The suffix (.html, .txt, .jpg, etc.) of a data file indicates the file type. The pathname can also lead to an executable program that dynamically produces an HTML or other valid file to return.

Within an HTML document, you can link to another document served by the same Web server by giving only the *pathname* part of the URL. Such URLs are *partially specified*. A partial URL with a / prefix (e.g., /file_xyz.html) refers to a file under the *server root*, the top-level directory controlled by the Web server. A partial URL without a leading / points to a file relative to the location of the document that contains the URL in question. Thus, a simple file_abc.html refers to that file in the same directory as the current document. When building a Web site, it is advisable to use a URL relative to the current page as much as possible.

Accessing Information on the Web

You can directly access any Web document, directory, or service by giving its URL in the Location box of a browser. When given a URL that specifies a directory, a Web server usually returns an *index file* (typically, index.html) for that directory. Otherwise, it may return a list of the file names in that directory.

The Web contains a vast amount of useful information in a loosely organized fashion. However, locating sites with something related to what you are
looking for may not be simple. Fortunately, there are *search engines* that collect
information available on the Web and establish easy-to-search databases. These
search engines continuously update their databases and can be enormously
helpful in locating information. Newly established Web sites usually submit
their URLs to popular search engines so the new sites will be included in the
search databases.

Yahoo! (www.yahoo.com) is among the first such engines. Here are some
others:

www.google.com   www.lycos.com
www.excite.com   www.askjeeves.com

1.5 CONTENT TYPES

On the Web, files of different *media types* can be placed and retrieved. The Web
server and Web browser use standard *content type* designations to indicate the
media type of files in order to process them correctly.

The Web borrowed the content type designations from the Intenet email
system and uses the same MIME (Multipurpose Internet Mail Extensions)
defined content types. There are hundreds of content types in use today. Many
popular types are associated with standard file extensions. Table 1.1 gives some
examples.

When a Web server returns a document to a browser, the content type
is indicated. The content type information allows browsers to decide how to
process the incoming content. Normally, HTML, text, GIF, JPEG, PNG, and so

Table 1.1   CONTENT TYPES AND FILE SUFFIXES

Content Type	File Suffix
text/html	html htm
image/jpeg	jpeg jpg jpe
audio/basic	au snd
audio/mpeg	mpeg mp2 mp3
audio/x-realaudio	ra
audio/x-wav	wav
video/mpeg	mpeg mpg mpe
video/quicktime	qt mov

forth. are handled by the browser directly. Others types such as QuickTime, PDF, audio, and video are handled by plug-ins or helper programs.

1.6   PUTTING INFORMATION ON THE WEB

Now let's turn our attention to how information is supplied on the Web. The understanding sheds more light on how the Web works and what it takes to serve up information.

The Web puts the power of publishing in the hands of anyone with a computer connected to the Internet. All you need is to run a Web server on this machine and establish files for it to service. Major computer vendors offer commercial Web servers with their computer systems. Examples are Windows 2000 (Microsoft), Solaris/iPlanet (Sun Microsystems), and NetWare (Novell). Apache is a very popular UNIX-based Web server freely available from www.apache.org (the Apache Software Foundation).

Once a Web server is up and running on your machine, all types of files can be served (Figure 1.5), including hypertext (.html), plain text (.txt), graphical image (e.g., .gif), sound (e.g., .wav), video (e.g., .mov), and so on.

On a typical UNIX system, follow these simple steps to make your personal Web page:

1. Make a file directory in your home directory (~*userid*/public_html) to contain your files for the Web. This is your *personal Web directory*. Make this directory publicly accessible:

    chmod o+x ~*userid*/public_html

    When in doubt, ask your system managers about the exact name to use for your personal Web directory.

2. In your Web directory, establish a home page, usually index.html, in HTML. The home page usually functions as an annotated table of contents. Make this file readable:

    chmod a+r ~*userid*/public_html/index.html

Figure 1.5   WEB SERVER FUNCTION

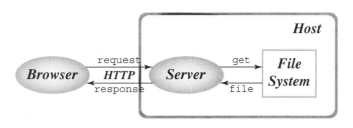

3. Place files and directories containing desired information in your Web directory. Make each directory and each file accessible as before. Refer to these files with links in the home page and other pages.

4. Let people know the URL of your home page, which is typically

```
http://your-sever/~your-userid/
```

In a Web page, you refer to another file in the same directory with a simple link containing a partial URL (`<a href="filename">`), where *filename* can be either a simple file name or a pathname relative to the current document.

Among the Web file formats, hypertext is critical because it provides a means for a document to link to other documents.

1.7 WHAT IS HTML?

A document written in HTML contains ordinary text interspersed with *markup tags* and uses the `.html` filename extension. The tags mark portions of the text as title, section header, paragraph, reference to other documents, and so on. Thus, an HTML file consists of two kinds of information: contents and HTML tags. A browser follows the HTML tags to layout the page content for display. Because of this, line breaks and extra white space between words in the content are mostly ignored. In addition to structuring and formatting contents, HTML tags can also reference graphics images, link to other documents, mark reference points, generate forms or questionnaires, and invoke certain programs. Various visual editors or *page makers* are available that provide a graphical user interface (GUI) environment for creating and designing HTML documents. For substantial Web site creation projects, it will be helpful to use *integrated development environments* such as Macromedia Dreamweaver (Chapter 11). If you don't have ready access to such tools, a regular text editor can create or edit Web pages. An HTML tag takes the form `<tag>`. A *begin tag* such as `<h1>` (level-one section header) is paired with an *end tag*, `</h1>` in this case, to mark content in between. Table 1.2 lists some frequently used tags.

The following is a sample HTML page (Ex: **Fruits**):

```
<html>
<head> <title>A Basic Web Page</title> </head>
<body>
   <h1>Big on Fruits</h1>
   <p>Fruits are good tasting and good for you ...</p>
   <p> There are many varieties, ...
   and here is a short list: </p>
   <ol>
      <li> Apples </li>
      <li> Bananas </li>
      <li> Cherries </li>
```

Table 1.2   SOME HTML TAGS

Marked As	HTML Tags
Entire Document	`<html>...</html>`
Header part of document	`<head>...</head>`
Document Title	`<title>...</title>`
Document Content	`<body>...</body>`
Level n Heading	`<hn>...</hn>`
Paragraph	`<p>...</p>`
Unnumbered List	`<ul>...</ul>`
Numbered List	`<ol>...</ol>`
List Item	`<li>...</li>`
Comment	`<!--...-->`

```
    </ol>
</body></html>
```

Figure 1.6 shows the big on fruits page displayed by Netscape. We begin in-depth coverage of HTML in Chapter 2.

Figure 1.6   A SAMPLE WEB PAGE

1.8 WEB HOSTING

Web hosting is a service to store and serve ready-made files and programs so they are accessible on the Web. Hence, publishing on the Web involves

1. designing and constructing the pages and writing the programs for a Web site
2. placing the completed site with a hosting service

Colleges and universities host personal and educational sites for students and faculty without charge. Web hosting companies provide the service for a fee.

Commercial Web hosting can provide secure data centers (buildings), fast and reliable Internet connections, specially tuned Web hosting computers, server programs and utilities, network and system security, daily backup, and technical support. Each hosting account provides an amount of disk space, a monthly network traffic allowance, email accounts, Web-based site management and maintenance tools, and other access such as FTP and SSH (secure login).

To host a site under a given domain name, a hosting service associates that domain name to an IP number assigned to the hosted site. The domain-to-IP association is made through domain name servers (DNS) managed by the hosting service.

For truly global Web sites, hosting services such as those provided by AKAMAI can distribute a site in multiple countries for much faster access from anywhere in the world.

1.9 DOMAIN REGISTRATION

To obtain a domain name, you need the service of a *domain name registrar*. Most will be happy to register your new domain name for a very modest yearly fee. Once registered, the domain name is property that belongs to the *registrant*. No one else can register for that particular domain name as long as the current registrant keeps the registration in good order.

ICANN accredits commercial registrars for common TLDs, including `.com`, `.net`, `.org`. New TLDs being added include `.biz`, `.info`, `.pro`, `.aero`, `.name`, and `.museum`. Some registrars, such as VeriSign (formerly Network Solutions), also register `.edu` domains. Other restricted domains (e.g., `.gov` and `.us`) are handled by special registries (e.g., `nic.gov` and `nic.us`). Country-code TLDs are normally handled by registries in their respective countries.

Accessing Domain Registration Data

The registration record of a domain name is publicly available. The standard Internet *whois* service allows easy access to this information. On UNIX systems, easy access to whois is provided by the **whois** command

whois *domain_name*

which lists the domain registration record kept at a major *network information center* (nic). For example (Ex: **Whois**),

whois kent.edu

produces the following information

```
Domain Name: KENT.EDU
Registrar: NETWORK SOLUTIONS, INC.
Whois Server: whois.networksolutions.com
Referral URL: http://www.networksolutions.com
Name Server: NS1.OAR.NET
Name Server: NS.MCS.KENT.EDU
Name Server: DHCP.NET.KENT.EDU
Name Server: NS.NET.KENT.EDU
Updated Date: 13-jun-2003
```

This record is in summary form. By querying the particular registrar's whois server, a more detailed domain name registration record can be obtained. For example, depending on the computer system used, one of the commands

whois -h whois.networksolutions.com kent.edu
whois kent.edu@whois.networksolutions.com

will produce the detailed domain record for kent.edu:

```
[whois.networksolutions.com]

Registrant:
    Kent State University (KENT-DOM)
    125 Library
    Kent, OH 44242
    US

    Domain Name: KENT.EDU

    Administrative Contact, Technical Contact, Billing Contact:
        Yoho, Ransel  (RY678)  ransel@NET.KENT.EDU
        Kent State University
        120 Library
        Kent, Ohio 44242
        330-672-9576 (FAX) 330-672-9593
```

```
Record last updated on 21-Jul-2002.
Record created on 19-Feb-1987.
Database last updated on 9-Oct-2003 10:48:00 EDT.

Domain servers in listed order:

NS.NET.KENT.EDU            131.123.1.1
NS.MCS.KENT.EDU           131.123.2.130
DHCP.NET.KENT.EDU         131.123.252.2
NS1.OAR.NET               192.88.193.144
```

On Linux systems, the whois command is sometimes called **fwhois**.

On Mac OS X, some neat networking tools can be found in the NetProbe package including Ping, DNS Lookup, Trace IP Route, WhoIs, and Finger.

On Windows systems, there is no built-in whois program. But you can easily find a freeware whois program on the Web (just search for "whois for Windows"), as you can for other common Internet tools.

On-Web whois searches are also available (e.g., www.crsnic.net at VeriSign).

1.10   WHAT ARE NAME SERVERS?

Name servers are the programs that provide the domain-to-IP mapping information on the Internet. We mentioned that DNS provides a distributed database service that supports dynamic retrieval of information contained in the name space. Web browsers and other Internet client applications will normally use the DNS to obtain the IP of a target host before making contact with a server.

There are three elements to the DNS: the name space (Section 1.2), the name servers, and the resolvers.

- *Name servers*: Information in the distributed DNS is divided into *zones*, and each zone is supported by one or more name servers running on different hosts. A zone is associated with a node on the domain tree and covers all or part of the subtree at that node. A name server that has complete information for a particular zone is said to be an *authority* for that zone. Authoritative information is automatically distributed to other name servers that provide redundant service for the same zone. A server relies on lower level servers for other information within its subdomain and on external servers for other zones in the domain tree. A server associated with the root node of the domain tree is a *root server* and can lead to information anywhere in the DNS. An authoritative server uses local files to store information, to locate key servers within and without its domain, and to cache query results from other servers. A boot file, usually /etc/named.boot, configures a name server and its data files.

The management of each zone is also free to designate the hosts that run the name servers and to make changes in its authoritative database. For example, the host `a.root-servers.net` runs a root name server. The host `cssrv1.cs.kent.edu` may run a name server for the domain `cs.kent.edu`.

A server answers queries from resolvers and provides either definitive answers or referrals to other name servers. The DNS database is set up to handle network address, mail exchange, host configuration, and other types of queries, some yet to be implemented.

- *Resolvers*: A DNS resolver is a program that sends queries to name servers and obtains replies from them. On UNIX systems, a resolver usually takes the form of a C library function. A resolver can access at least one name server and use that name server's information to answer a query directly or pursue the query using referrals to other name servers.

  Resolvers, in the form of networking library routines, are used to translate domain names into actual IP addresses. These library routines in turn ask prescribed name servers to resolve the domain names. The name servers to use for any particular host are normally specified in the file `/etc/resolv.conf` or `/usr/etc/resolv.conf`.

The ICANN and others maintain *root name servers* associated with the root node of the DNS tree. Domain name registrars, corporations, organizations, Web hosting companies, and other Internet service providers (ISPs) run name servers to associate IPs to domain names in their particular zones. All name servers on the Internet cooperate to perform domain-to-IP mappings on the fly.

1.11 LOOKING UP HOST INFORMATION

On UNIX and MS/Windows systems, the **host**, **dig**, and **nslookup** commands provide direct user access to the DNS. These commands are similar, but **dig** is designed to replace **nslookup**. You may find that one or all three work on your system. We'll see how **nslookup** works because it provides simpler output. The form

nslookup *host*

submits a name server query and obtains a domain name, IP address, and alias information for the given host. For example,

nslookup `www.kent.edu`

gives

```
Server:   clmboh1-dns3.columbus.rr.com
Address:  65.24.0.166
```

```
Non-authoritative answer:
Name:    info.cs.kent.edu
Address: 131.123.32.129
Aliases: www.cs.kent.edu
```

The desired information together with the identity of the name server (from RoadRunner in Columbus, Ohio) that provided the data is displayed. As this example shows, the name www is typically a DNS alias for a host whose real domain name is something else.

Nslookup is very handy for verifying the existence of hosts and finding the IP address or domain name aliases of hosts. Once the name of a host is known, you can also test if the host is up and running, as far as networking is concerned, with the **ping** command.

ping *host*

This sends a message to the given remote host requesting it to respond with an echo if it is alive and well. If this command is not on your command search path, try the command **/etc/ping** or **/usr/etc/ping** instead.

1.12   THE WEB DEVELOPMENT PROCESS

With this background information, we now turn to our main subject: Web design and programming (WDP). WDP involves conceptualizing, architecting, designing, organizing, implementing, maintaining, and improving Web sites for functionally effective and aesthetically attractive information delivery and exchange.

The Web is a new mass communication medium. To create a well-designed and effective Web site is a challenge. It takes expertise in information architecture, visual communication design, mass communication, computer programming, business administration, and consumer psychology, just to name some areas. It usually involves teamwork.

The heart of the enterprise is a combination of artistic design and computer programming. In this text, we cover these two areas in an integrated fashion.

Many tasks are involved in creating a Web site. The overall *Web site development process* can be summarized here. Subsequent chapters provide in-depth coverage of these tasks.

Requirement Analysis and Development Plan—What are the requirements for the finished site? What exactly will your finished Web site achieve for the client? What problems does your client want you to solve? Who are the target audiences of the Web site? Can you realistically help the client? What is the scope and nature of the work? What design and programming tasks are involved? What resources and information will be needed and what problems do you foresee? Who will provide content information for the site and in what formats? What resources are needed or available: textual content, photos, imagery, audio, video, logos, corporate identity standards, copyrights, credits, footers, and insignia?

Answer the preceding questions and make a plan. Create and group content, functional, and look and feel requirements and set clear goals and milestones for building and developing the site.

Site Architecture—Decide on an appropriate architecture for the site. The site architecture is influenced by the nature of the information being served and the means of delivery. Ordinary sites involve static pages with text, images, and online forms. Specialized sites may involve audio, video, streaming media, and dynamically generated information or access to databases.

Website *information architecture* (IA) deals with the structuring, the relationship, the connectivity, the logical organization, and the dynamic interactions among the constituent parts of a Web site.

Within each Web page, consider the placement, layout, visual effect, font and text style, and so forth. These are also important but may be more "interior decoration" than architecture. However, architecture and interior/exterior decoration are intimately related.

The site architecture phase produces a blueprint for building the Web site. The blueprint is a specification of the components and their contents, functionalities, relations, connectivity, and interactions. Web site implementation will follow the architecture closely.

An important aspect of site architecture is the navigation system for visitors to travel in your site. The goal is to establish sitewide (primary), intrasection (secondary), and intrapage (tertiary) navigation schemes that are easy and clear.

Content-only Site Framework—Follow these steps to prepare a skeletal site as a foundation for making adjustments and for further work to complete the site.

- Content: Create a content list or inventory; prepare content files ready to be included in Web pages.

- Site map: Draw a relationship diagram of all pages to be created for the site, give each page appropriate titles, show page groupings and on-site and off-site links, distinguish static from dynamic pages, identify forms and server-side support. Major subsections of the site can have there own submaps.

- Skeletal site: Conceive an entry page, home page, typical subpages and sub-subpages, textual contents (can be in summary form), HTML forms with textual layout and descriptions of server-side support, structure of the file hierarchy for the site, and well-defined HTML coding standards for pages.

- Navigation: Follow the site architecture and site map to link the pages, use textual navigation links with rough placements (top, left, right, or bottom), avoid dead-end pages, and avoid confusing the user.

Visual Communication and Artistic Design

- Design concepts: features, characteristics, and look and feel of the site; the design must reflect client identity and site purpose.
- Storyboards: simple layout sketches based on content-only site for typical pages, HTML forms, and HTML form response pages; header, footer, margins, navigation bar, logo, and other graphical elements to support the delivery of content; client feedback and approval of storyboards.
- Page layout (for pages at all levels): content hierarchy and grouping; grids, alignments, constants, and variables on the page; placement and size of charts, graphs, illustrations, and photos; creative use of space and variations of font, grid, and color; style options and variations.
- Home page/entry page: visuals to support the unique function and purpose of entry to the site and home page as required by site architecture.

Site Production

- Page templates: Create templates for typical pages at all levels. Templates are skeleton files used to make finished pages by inserting text, graphics, and other content at marked places in the templates. In other words, a template is a page frame with the desired design, layout, and graphics ready to receive text, links, photos, and other content. A template page may provide HTML, style sheets, JavaScript, `head`, `body`, `meta`, `link`, and `script` tags as well as marked places for page content. Templates enable everyone on the project team to complete pages for the site. Advanced templates may involve dynamic server-side features.
- Prototype pages: Use the templates to complete typical pages in prototype form, test and examine page prototypes, present prototype pages to the client and obtain feedback and approval. Make sure that the layout system has been designed with enough versatility and flexibility to accommodate potential changes in content.
- Client-side programming: Write scripts for browsers and possibly other Web clients that will be delivered together with Web pages to the client side. These scripts may include style sheets and JavaScripts. Client-side programs can make Web pages more interactive and responsive.
- Server-side programming: Write programs for form processing, dynamic page generation, database access, e-business, and e-commerce features. Make sure these follow the site architecture, user orientation, and visual design.
- Finished pages: Following page prototypes, add text, graphics, photos, animations, audio, and video to templates to produce all pages needed; make final adjustments and fine-tuning.

Error Checking and Validation—Apply page checking tools or services to finished pages to remove spelling errors, broken links, and HTML coding problems. Check page loading times.

Testing—Put the site through its paces, try different browsers from different access locations, debug, fine-tune, and check against architecture and requirements.

Deploying—Release the site on the Web, make its URL known, and register the site with search engines.

Documentation—Write a description of the Web site, its design and functionalities, its file structure, locations for source files of art and programming, and a site maintenance guide.

Maintenance—Devote time to the continued operation and evolution of the Web site.

1.13   DYNAMIC GENERATION OF WEB PAGES

Documents available on the Web are usually prepared and set in advance to supply some fixed content, either in HTML or in some other format such as plain text, GIF, or JPEG. These fixed documents are *static*. A Web server can also generate documents on the fly that bring these and other advantages:

- customizing a document depending on when, where, who, and what program is retrieving it
- collecting user input (with HTML forms) and providing responses to the incoming information
- enforcing certain policies for outgoing documents
- supplying contents such as game scores and stock quotes, which are changing by nature

Dynamic Web pages are no magic. Instead of retrieving a fixed file, a Web server calls another program to compute the document to be returned. As you may have guessed, not every program can be used by a Web server in this manner. There are two ways to add server-side programming:

- Load programs directly into the Web server to be used whenever the need arises.
- Call an external program from the server passing arguments to it and receive the results thus generated. Such a program must conform to the Common Gateway Interface (CGI) specifications governing how the Web server and the external program interact (Figure 1.7).

Figure 1.7   COMMON GATEWAY INTERFACE

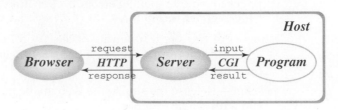

Dynamic Server Pages

The dynamic generation of pages is made simpler and more integrated with Web page design and construction by allowing a Web page to contain active parts that are treated by the Web server and transformed into desired content on the fly as the page is retrieved and returned to a client browser.

The active parts in a page are written in some kind of notation to distinguish them from the static parts of a page. The ASP (Active Server Pages from Microsoft), JSP (Java Server Page), and the popular PHP (Hypertext Preprocessor) are examples.

Because active pages are treated by modules loaded into the Web server, the processing is faster and more efficient compared to CGI programs. Active pages also provide form processing, HTTP sessions, and easy access to databases. Therefore, they offer complete server-side support for dynamic Web pages.

Both CGI and server pages can be used to support HTML forms (Chapter 8), the familiar fill-out forms you often see on the Web.

1.14   HTTP BRIEFLY

On the Web, browser-server communication follows the HTTP protocol. It is good for a Web developer to have a basic understanding of HTTP. Here is the framework of an HTTP transaction:

1. *Connection*—A browser (client) opens a connection to a server.
2. *Query*—The client requests a resource controlled by the server.
3. *Processing*—The server receives and processes the request.
4. *Response*—The server sends the requested resource back to the client.
5. *Termination*—The transaction is finished and the connection is closed unless another transaction will take place immediately between the client and server.

HTTP governs the format of the query and response messages (Figure 1.8). The header part is textual, and each line in the header should end in RETURN and NEWLINE, but it may end in just NEWLINE.

Figure 1.8   HTTP QUERY AND RESPONSE FORMATS

```
initial line                 (different for query and response)
HeaderKey1: value1           (zero or more header fields)
HeaderKey2: value2
HeaderKey3: value3

                             (an empty line with no characters)
Optional message body contains query or response
data. The amount and type of data in the body are
specified in the headers.
```

The initial line identifies the message as a query or a response:

- A query line has three parts separated by spaces: a *query method* name, a local path of the requested resource, and an HTTP version number. For example,

```
GET   /path/to/file/index.html   HTTP/1.1
```

or

```
POST   /path/script.cgi   HTTP/1.1
```

The GET method requests the specified resource and does not allow a message body. A GET method can invoke a server-side program by specifying the CGI or active-page path, a question mark, and then a *query string*:

```
GET /cgi-bin/newaddr?name=value1&email=value2   HTTP/1.0
```

Unlike GET, the POST method allows a message body and is designed to work with HTML forms (Chapter 8).

- A response (or status) line also has three parts separated by spaces: an HTTP version number, a status code, and a textual description of the status. Typical status lines are:

```
HTTP/1.0   200   OK
```

for a successful query, or

```
HTTP/1.0   404   Not Found
```

when the requested resource cannot be found.

- The HTTP response sends the requested file together with its content type (Section 1.5) and length (optional) so the client will know how to process it.

1.15 SUMMARY

The Web is a versatile and all-encompassing distributed information system. Web servers and clients use the HTTP protocol, which is based on TCP/IP.

Web resources are identified by URLs. The *host* part of the URL identifies a host computer either by its IP address or by its domain name.

Web pages are usually written in HTML, which can markup content and supply hyperlinks using partial and full URLs. Web pages are placed under Web servers and become available on the Web. Commercial hosting companies provide hosts and servers to serve Web pages online.

Generating simple Web pages is very easy. But well-designed and implemented Web sites take skill and training to build. The *Web design and development process* described in Section 1.12 shows the scope and depth of efforts needed for a professionally developed site.

It takes technical understanding, talent, and teamwork to build Web sites. The most central aspects are design and programming. This book covers both the artistic design and programming of WDP in the subsequent chapters.

EXERCISES

Review Questions

1. What is a computer network? Name the major components in a computer network.

2. What is a networking client? A networking server? A networking protocol?

3. What addressing scheme does the Internet use? What is the format of an IP address? What is the quad notation?

4. Consider the IP address:

    `123.234.345.456`

    Is there anything wrong with it? Please explain.

5. What is DNS? Why do we need it? How are TLDs registered?

6. What do name servers do? Why do we need them?

7. What is the relation between the Web and the Internet? What is the relation between HTTP and TCP/IP?

8. What are the major components of the Web? Why is HTML central to the Web?

9. What is the difference between a Web server and a Web browser? Is the Web server a piece of hardware or software? Explain.

10. How does a Web page get from where it is to the computer screen of a user?

11. What is a URL? What is the general form of a URL? Explain the different URL schemes.

12. What are content types? How are they useful?

13. What are the major tasks in the overall Web site development process? What knowledge and skills do you expect to learn to participate in this process?

14. What is the difference between a static Web page and a generated Web page?

15. What is an HTTP transaction? A query? A response?

Assignments

1. Take the domain name `sofpower.com` and write the full URL that will access its Web site. Use that URL to visit the site. Find this book's Web site there.

2. Take the domain name `sofpower.com` and find its IP address. Use this IP address instead of the domain name to visit the site. Write the bit pattern for this IP address.

3. Search on the Web for the Internet Corporation for Assigned Names and Numbers. Visit the site and discover its mission and services.

4. Find the domain record for `sofpower.com`. Who is the owner of this domain name? Who are the administrative and technical contacts?

5. Type the following URL in the Location window of your browser:

   `telnet://HostDomainName`

   where `HostDomainName` identifies a computer where you have an account and are allowed to logon. You should be able to proceed and logon.

6. This assignment gives you a real experience with HTTP. Assume that

   `http://targetHost/index.html`

   is a valid URL and the page exists.

   a. Start the Telnet application on your computer.

   b. From the Terminal menu, start logging on to a file, say, `savedfile.html`.

   c. Connect to `targetHost` at port 80.

    d. Type on the keyboard exactly and without delay (you won't see your typing on the screen! Do not copy and paste):

```
GET /index.html HTTP/1.0
```

and press ENTER or RETURN twice. The Telnet application will terminate and close automatically.

    e. View `savedfile.html` now with a text editor. What do you get? Remove the HTTP header and save the modified file as a well-formed HTML file.

    f. Now view the `savedfile.html` with a Web browser. What do you get?

Can you explain what you have done? (Tip: See Section 1.14.)

CHAPTER 2

Creating Web Pages: XHTML

A Web page is a document, identified by a URL, that can be retrieved on the Web. Typically, a Web page is written in HTML, the Hypertext Markup Language. When a Web browser receives an HTML document, it can format and render the content for viewing, listening, or printing. The user can also follow embedded hyperlinks, or simply links, to visit other Web pages.

HTML enables you to structure and organize text, graphics, pictures, sound, video, and other media content for processing and display by browsers. HTML supports headings, paragraphs, lists, tables, links, images, forms, frames, and so on. The major part of a Web site is usually a set of HTML documents. Learning and understanding HTML are fundamental to Web design and programming.

To create HTML files, you may use any standard text editor such as vi, emacs, Word (MS/Windows), or SimpleText (Mac/OS). Specialized tools for creating and editing HTML pages are also widely available. After creating an HTML file and saving it in a file, you can open that file (by double-clicking the file or using the browser File>Open File menu option) and look at the page.

XHTML (Extensible Hypertext Markup Language) is a modern version of HTML that is recommended for creating new Web pages. Having evolved from Version 2.0 to 4.01, HTML now gets reformulated in XML (Extensible Markup Language) and becomes XHTML 1.0. XML-conforming documents follow strict XML syntax rules and therefore become easily manipulated by programs of all kinds, which is a great advantage. XHTML 1.0 is the basis for the further evolution of HTML. The HTML codes in this book follow XHTML 1.0. Unless noted otherwise, we shall use the terms HTML and XHTML interchangeably.

The basics of HTML are introduced in this chapter. Chapter 3 continues to cover more advanced aspects of HTML. The two chapters combine to provide a comprehensive and in-depth introduction to HTML. Other aspects of HTML are described when needed in later chapters.

2.1 HTML BASICS

HTML is a *markup language* that provides *tags* to organize information for the Web. By inserting HTML tags into a page of text and other content, you mark which part of the page is what to provide structure to the document. Following the structure, user agents such as browsers can perform on-screen rendering or other processing. Thus, browsers process and present HTML documents based on the marked-up structure. The exact rendering is defined by the browser and may differ for different browsers. For example, common visual browsers such as Internet Explorer (IE) and Netscape Navigator (NN) render Web pages on screen. A browser for the blind, on the other hand, will voice the content according to its markup.

Hence, a Web page in HTML contains two parts: *markup tags* and *content*. HTML tags are always enclosed in angle brackets (< >). This way, they are easily distinguished from the contents of the page.

It is recommended that you create Web pages with XHTML 1.0, the current version of HTML. An XHTML document in English[1] has the following basic form:

```
<?xml version="1.0" encoding="UTF-8"?>
<!DOCTYPE html PUBLIC "-//W3C//DTD XHTML 1.0 Strict//EN"
    "http://www.w3.org/TR/xhtml1/DTD/xhtml1-strict.dtd">

<html xmlns="http://www.w3.org/1999/xhtml"
      xml:lang="en" lang="en">
<head>
<title>Company XYZ: home page</title>
</head>
<body>  <!-- page content begin -->
   . . .
   . . .
<!-- page content end -->  </body>
</html>
```

The xml line specifies the version of XML and the character encoding used (Section 3.1). The DOCTYPE line indicates the version of XHTML used, XHTML 1.0 Strict in this case. Next comes the html line which indicates the default XML name space used. An important advantage of XHTML is the ability to use tags defined in other name spaces. These three initial lines tell browsers how to process the document. In most situations, you can use the preceding template verbatim for creating your HTML files. You place the page content between the <body> and </body> tags. Comments in HTML source begin with <!-- and end with -->.

---

[1]See Section 3.20 for Web pages in other languages.

In Chapter 1, you saw some simple HTML code in Figure 1.6. Generally, HTML tags come in pairs: a *start tag* and an *end tag*. They work just like open and close parentheses. Add a SLASH (/) prefix to a start tag name to get the end tag name. A pair of start and end tags delimits an *HTML element*. Some tags have end tags, but others don't. For browser compatibility, it is best to use the suffix SPACE/> for any element without an end tag. For example, write the "line break" element in the form <br />.

The head element contains informational elements for the entire document. For example, the title element (always required) specifies a page title that is

1. displayed in the *title bar* of the browser window
2. used in making a bookmark for the page

The body element organizes the content of the document.

2.2   CREATING YOUR FIRST WEB PAGE

Let's create a very simple Web page (Ex: **FirstPage**)[2] following the template from Section 2.1. Using your favorite editor, type the following:

```
<?xml version="1.0" encoding="UTF-8"?>
<!DOCTYPE html PUBLIC "-//W3C//DTD XHTML 1.0 Strict//EN"
    "http://www.w3.org/TR/xhtml1/DTD/xhtml1-strict.dtd">
<html xmlns="http://www.w3.org/1999/xhtml" xml:lang="en" lang="en">
<head>
<title>My First Web Page</title>
</head>
<body style="background-color: cyan">
<p>Hello everyone!</p>
<p>My Name is (put your name here) and today is (put in the date).
    </p>
<p>HTML is cool.</p>
</body>
</html>
```

Save it into a file named firstpage.html. The content of body consists of three short paragraphs given by the p element. The page background color is set to cyan.

From your favorite browser, select the Open File option on the File menu and open the file firstpage.html. Now you should see the display of your first Web page (Figure 2.1). For more complicated Web pages, all you need to know is more HTML elements and practice in how to use them.

---

[2]Examples available online are labeled like this for easy cross-reference.

Figure 2.1   FIRST WEB PAGE

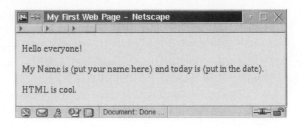

2.3 ELEMENTS AND ENTITIES

HTML provides more than 90 different elements. Generally, they fall into these categories:

Top-level elements: html, head, and body.

Head elements: elements placed inside head, including title (page title), style (rendering style), link (related documents), meta (data about the document), base (URL of the document), and script (client-side scripting).

Block-level elements: elements behaving like paragraphs, including h1–h6 (headings), p (paragraph), pre (preformatted text), div (designated block), ul, ol, dl (lists), table (tabulation), and form (user-input forms). When displayed, a block-level (or simply block) element always starts on a new line, and any element immediately after the block element also begins on a new line.

Inline elements: elements behaving like words, characters, or phrases within a block, including a (anchor or hyperlink), br (line break), img (picture or graphics), em (emphasis), strong (strong emphasis), sub (subscript), sup (superscript), code (computer code), var (variable name), kbd (text for user input), samp (sample output), and span (designated inline scope).

When an element is placed inside another, the containing element is the *parent* and the contained element is the *child*.

Comments in an HTML page are given as `<!-- a sample comment -->`. Text and HTML elements inside a comment tag are ignored by browsers. Be sure not to put two consecutive dashes (--) inside a comment. It is good practice to include comments in HTML pages as notes, reminders, or documentation to make maintenance easier.

In an HTML document, certain characters, such as < and &, are used for markup and must be escaped to appear literally. Other characters you may need are not available on the keyboard. HTML provides *entities* (escape sequences) to introduce such characters into a Web page. For example, the entity <

gives < and ÷ gives ÷. Section 3.2 describes characters and entities in more detail.

2.4   A BRIEF HISTORY OF HTML

In 1989, Tim Berners-Lee at the European Laboratory for Particle Physics (CERN) defined a very simple version of HTML based on SGML, Standard Generalized Markup Language, as part of his effort to create a network-based system to share documents via text-only browsers. The simplicity of HTML makes it easy to learn and publish. It caught on. In 1992–1993, a group at NCSA (National Center for Supercomputing Applications, U.S.) developed the Mosaic visual/graphical browser. Mosaic added support for images, nested lists, and forms, and it fueled the explosive growth of the Web. Several people from the Mosaic project helped start Netscape in 1994. At the same time, the W3 Consortium (W3C) was formed and housed at MIT as an industry-supported organization for the standardization and development of the Web.

The first common standard for HTML is HTML 3.2 (1997). HTML 4.01 became a W3C recommendation in December 1999. HTML 4.01 begins to clearly separate the document structure and document presentation aspects of HTML and specifies a clear relationship between HTML and client-side scripting (JavaScript).

HTML 4 comes in three flavors: Strict, Transitional, and Frameset. The latter two flavors help Web authors move to the strict standard that emphasizes structure over presentation and designates most presentational elements and attributes as *deprecated* (soon to be abandoned). The WDP Web site lists deprecated elements and attributes.

Starting with HTML 4, you can specify the presentation style of individual elements and also attach presentation styles to different element types with *style sheets* (Chapter 6).

HTML 4.01 is great but not based on XML, a popular and standardized way to define additional tags and use them in documents. Making HTML follow the strict syntax of XML brings important advantages:

- XHTML elements can be used together with other elements defined by XML.
- XHTML pages can be processed easily by any XML tools.

In January 2000, W3C released XHTML 1.0 as an XML reformulation of HTML 4.01. XHTML 1.0 is basically HTML 4.01 written under the strict XML syntax. To support the three HTML 4 flavors, XHTML 1.0 provides three DTDs (document type definitions) indicated by the three DOCTYPE declarations:

```
<!DOCTYPE html PUBLIC "-//W3C//DTD XHTML 1.0 Strict//EN"
   "http://www.w3.org/TR/xhtml1/DTD/xhtml1-strict.dtd">
```

```
<!DOCTYPE html PUBLIC "-//W3C//DTD XHTML 1.0 Transitional//EN"
    "http://www.w3.org/TR/xhtml1/DTD/xhtml1-transitional.dtd">

<!DOCTYPE html PUBLIC "-//W3C//DTD XHTML 1.0 Frameset//EN"
    "http://www.w3.org/TR/xhtml1/DTD/xhtml1-frameset.dtd">
```

Deprecated elements and attributes, frames, or link targets are not allowed in HTML 4 or XHTML Strict. You can use Transitional for a page containing deprecated features. Use Frameset for a frameset page (Section 3.18). However, NN, IE, and other popular browsers will often render a page successfully even if the page contains elements or attributes not allowed by the DOCTYPE declaration.

In April 2001, W3C released the *Modularization of XHTML* recommendation to group related XHTML elements into modules defined by XML *DTD Fragments*. The modular organization makes XHTML more flexible and extensible. XHTML 2.0 is a working draft (August 2002) that updates XHTML modules, drops support for deprecated elements, and forms a base for the future evolution of XHTML.

2.5 XHTML SYNTAX

The *syntax*, or grammar, of HTML (XHTML) is defined using SGML (Standard Generalized Markup Language). SGML is an ISO (International Organization for Standardization) standard formal language for defining markup languages. HTML is defined with an SGML DTD that specifies available *elements* such as head, body, h1, p, and so on. By revising and extending the DTD, HTML can be evolved with relative ease. The three flavors of XHTML 1.0 are supported by different DTDs (Section 2.4).

The following general syntax rules will help you use XHTML:

- All tags begin with < and end with >. The *tag name* is given immediately following the leading <. Make sure the tag is spelled correctly. Unrecognized tags are ignored by browsers. Any *attributes* are given following the tag name in the form:

  $<tag\ attribute_1 = "value"\quad attribute_2 = "value"\ \dots >$

- Tag and attribute names are given in lowercase. Attributes are always given in the form

  `attribute_name="value"`

  where the value is case sensitive.

- Unrecognized tags and attributes are ignored by browsers.

- Most elements involve opening and closing tags. Other elements, such as <br /> and <img ... /> (inline image), do not have closing tags and are known as *empty elements*. Note the use of the extra SPACE in front of '/>' for empty elements.

- Elements must be *well-formed*. This means no missing opening or closing tags and no improper element nesting. For example,

```
<p>Learning <strong>XHTML</p></strong>
```

overlaps the tags and is not properly nested. Existing browsers may tolerate such ill-formed code. The correct nesting is

```
<p>Learning <strong>XHTML</strong></p>
```

- Attributes can be required or optional and can be given in any order. If an attribute is not given, its default value, if any, is used.

- Extra white space and line breaks are allowed between the tag name and attributes and around the = sign inside an attribute. Line breaks and white space within attribute values are also allowed but should be avoided because they may be treated inconsistently by browsers.

- The body element may contain only block-level HTML elements. Freestanding text (not enclosed in block elements) or inline elements are not allowed directly in the body element.

Certain tags are only allowed within their permitted context. For example, a `<tr>` (table row) element can only be given inside a `<table>` element. Learning XHTML involves knowing the elements, their attributes, where they can be placed, and the elements they can contain.

2.6   CORE ATTRIBUTES

All XHTML elements admit the following *core attributes*:

- `id`—Uniquely identifies the element in a page. All `id`s in a document must be distinct. Among other uses, a URL ending in #*some_id* can lead directly to an element inside a document.

- `style`—Gives presentation styles for the individual element. For example, the code used in Ex: **FirstPage** (Section 2.2)

```
<body style="background-color: cyan">
```

gives the color value cyan to the style property background-color for this element. Several style properties separated by semicolons can be given. The style attribute is a direct but inflexible way to specify presentation style. Although this attribute is sometimes necessary, better and much more versatile methods for assigning styles can be found in Chapter 6.

- class—Specifies the *style class* for the element. Thus, you may place HTML elements in different classes and associate presentation styles to all elements belonging to the same class (Chapter 6).
- title—Provides a title for the element. This may be used for tool-tip displays by browsers.

2.7   HEADINGS AND PARAGRAPHS

Typically, textual contents are organized into paragraphs and placed in sections under appropriate headings. HTML offers six *heading elements*, h1 through h6, for level-one to level-six section headings. Headings are block elements that are usually displayed with a bolder font followed by a blank line (Ex: **Heading**). Use h1 for top-level section headings, and h2 for subsections within top-level sections, and so on. Unless otherwise specified, browsers use increasingly larger fonts to render higher level headings (Figure 2.2). It is advisable to use h1 for the most prominent heading, such as the headline of an article. The following (Ex: **Phoenix**) is an example (Figure 2.3):

```
<h1>The Phoenix Project</h1>
<h2>Project Background</h2> <!-- 1st section -->
    <p>Put first paragraph here</p>
    <p>Put second paragraph here</p>
<h3>A Successful Past</h3><!-- subsection -->
    <p>Another paragraph here</p>
<h2>Current Status of Phoenix</h2><!-- 2nd section -->
    <p>Another paragraph here</p>
<h2>Future Goals</h2><!-- 3rd section -->
```

The block element p (a paragraph) may contain text and inline elements but not any block elements. It is typically displayed with a leading and a trailing

Figure 2.2   HTML HEADING ELEMENTS

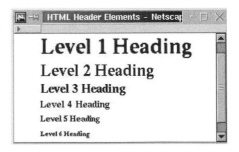

Figure 2.3   SECTIONS AND PARAGRAPHS

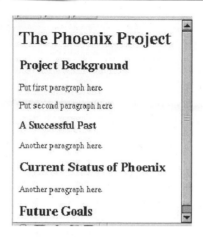

blank line. The paragraph content will be formatted to fit the available width.[3] Line breaks are inserted automatically (*line wrapping*) where needed to render the paragraph. Extraneous white spaces between words and lines within the source text of the paragraph are normally ignored (*white-space collapsing*). If you need a line break at a specific point in the text or page, you can use the `<br />` tag to call for a line break. Inside a paragraph, you can place other inline elements such as q, em, strong (see next subsections) and img (Section 2.17). Remember always to use the tag `</p>` to end a paragraph.

By default, browsers usually display headings and paragraphs left-aligned and without indenting the lead line. You may use line-break elements (`<br />`) to call for a line break between inline elements.

The ` ` entity is a nonbreaking space. Use it instead of a regular SPACE character between two words that must be kept together on one line or use several nonbreaking spaces to add more horizontal spacing between two words.

Quotations

The block element `blockquote` contains one or more block elements, typically paragraphs, that are quoted from other sources. The optional attribute `cite` can specify a URL leading to the source.

Browsers usually display a quoted block with increased left and right margins. In other words, quoted material is normally indented on the left and right (Figure 2.4).

---

[3]On the computer screen, width is horizontal and height is vertical.

Figure 2.4   BLOCK QUOTE

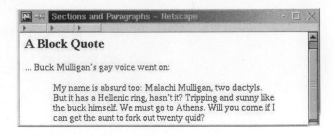

Inline quotations can be structured with the q element. For example (Ex: **Quote**):

```
<p>According to the <em>Pittsburgh Post Gazette</em>:
<q lang="en">The number of Web users in the US
has reached 50 million in just four years.</q></p>
```

Browsers display inline quotations by supplying language-appropriate quotation marks (Figure 2.5). Nested quotations are handled correctly as well.

Horizontal Rules

The block element hr gives you a horizontal rule to separate sections in a document. A horizontal rule provides a strong, but crude, visual indication of the start of contents of a different nature.

It is normally not necessary to place any rules between paragraphs or sections of an article. But used appropriately in selected situations, horizontal rules can increase the clarity of a page.

The tag <hr /> is empty and contains no elements. There is no end tag. For hr, browsers usually render a narrow full-width horizontal line. In XHTML, the <hr /> element admits nothing other than core attributes (Section 2.5). The

Figure 2.5   INLINE QUOTE

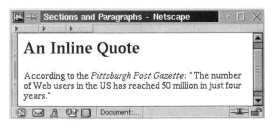

style attribute is used to control the length, width, color, border, and other display styles for the horizontal rule. For example (Ex: **Hrule**),

```
<hr style="height: 4px; width: 60%;
    margin-left: auto; margin-right: auto" />
```

gives a centered rule 4 pixels thick. Add the property background-color: blue to get a solid blue rule. Use margin-left:0 (margin-right:0) for left- (right-) adjusted alignment. The hr element comes in handy when you need an invisible spacer or filler in your page layout (Section 11.9).

The border property gives control and flexibility for drawing lines on any of the four sides of hr or other elements (Section 6.12).

2.8   WHITE SPACE AND LINE WRAPPING

In HTML, *white space* separates text into words, and user agents such as browsers can flow the words onto a rendered page in a format appropriate to the language of the document. HTML regards the following as white-space characters:

- SPACE: ASCII 32 (entity)
- TAB: ASCII 9 (entity 	)
- FORMFEED: ASCII 12 (entity )
- Zero-width space: a non-ASCII character (entity )

Words can be separated by one or more white-space characters but will only result in at most one rendered interword space. Hence, browsers perform *white-space collapsing*.

In addition, a RETURN (ASCII 13), NEWLINE (ASCII 10), or a RETURN-NEWLINE pair is considered white space. These are line breaks in the HTML source code, but they have no relation with the displayed line breaks in a Web page. An important function browsers perform is to flow text into lines, fit lines in the available display space, and wrap lines around when necessary. Line wrapping can only happen at word boundaries. Thus, no word will be chopped across lines. When the display window is resized, the text lines are reflowed to fit.

Only white space separates words. Tags don't. Thus, it is safe to use code such as

```
<p>The E<strong>x</strong>tensible HTML.</p>
```

```
<p>Visit <a href="...">our store</a>, and you'll
find what you need.</p>
```

You can manage line breaks as follows:

- To force a line break, use the <br /> tag.

- To keep two words on the same line, use the nonbreaking space (entity ` `) instead of a regular SPACE.

- To indicate where a long word can be broken across lines, use the *soft hyphen* (entity `&shy;`), which is rendered as a HYPHEN (-) only at the end of a line. Browsers generally do not break a word that is hyphenated in the source code.

Preformatted Text

Sometimes text lines are *preformatted* with spacing and line breaks. By enclosing such material in the `pre` element, the existing spacing and line breaks will be preserved. For example (Ex: **Pre**):

```
<body style="background-color: cyan">
<pre>
          North


   West             East


          South
</pre></body>
```

results in the display shown in Figure 2.6. Without the enclosing `pre` tags, the four words would be displayed on a single line with only a single space between any two words. By default, browsers use a constant-width font, such as Courier, to display `pre` contents. But the font used can be controlled by setting the font properties (see next subsection) of `pre`.

The `xmp`[4] element goes one step further: It makes everything enclosed literal. This makes it very convenient to display HTML and other code in a Web page.

Figure 2.6   PREFORMATTED TEXT

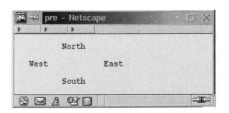

_____

[4]xmp is considered obsolete but still widely supported by browsers.

2.9   INLINE ELEMENTS

Frequently useful inline elements include

a: hyperlink or named anchor (Section 2.16)

br: line break; keep in mind that <br /> cannot be given where inline elements are disallowed

em: emphasis, usually displayed in italics

strong: strong emphasis, usually displayed in boldface

code: computer code, usually displayed in a monospaced font

sub: subscript (e.g., x₀)

sup: superscript (e.g., x<sup>2</sub>)

samp: sample output

span: an inline element that can contain other inline elements, providing a simple way to attach presentation styles to enclosed elements; for example

```
<span style="font-weight: bold; color: blue">Important point
</span>
```

2.10   CONTROLLING PRESENTATION STYLES

Browsers follow built-in default presentation styles and styles based on user preferences to render Web pages. It is usually important for the Web developer to control the presentation style to achieve well-designed visual effects.

You control document presentation by attaching *style rules* to elements. There are three ways to attach style rules:

1. Place style rules for individual and groups of elements in separate *style sheets* and then attach them to HTML documents with <link ... /> in the head element (Chapter 6).
2. Include <style> elements in the head element.
3. Define the style attribute for an individual element.

For example,

```
<h1 style="color: blue">The Phoenix Project</h1>
```

renders the heading in blue. All three ways of attaching style rules can be used in the same page. The style attribute takes precedence over styles in the <style> element, which takes precedence over those specified in separate style sheets.

In our coverage of XHTML, we use the simpler and most basic style attribute approach. The style knowledge gained here will be directly applicable in Chapter 6 when we present style sheets.

A style attribute is given in the general form:

style="*property*$_1$:*value*$_1$; *property*$_2$:*value*$_2$; ... "

Use the color (background-color) property to indicate the foreground (background) color for an element.

Text Alignment

The text-align style property controls how text lines within a block are aligned.

text-align: left—lines are left justified

text-align: right—lines are right justified

text-align: center—lines are centered

text-align: justify—lines are justified left and right

For example (Ex: **CenterText**),

```
<h1 style="text-align: center; color: blue">The Phoenix Project</h1>
```

centers the headline and renders it in blue. The code

```
<p style="text-align: center; font-weight: bold">
...
</p>
```

centers all lines in the paragraph. For many lines, this is seldom useful unless you are rendering a poem. But it is an effective way to center a short line or an inline image (Section 2.18).

To specify the style for a number of consecutive elements that form part of a page, you can wrap those elements in a div element and attach the style to the div element. For example (Ex: **FontSize**), to include some fine print, you can use:

```
<div style="font-size: x-small">
<p> ... </p>
...
<p> ... </p>
</div>
```

The div is a block element that can contain block and inline elements. It provides a simple way to attach presentation styles to a set of enclosed elements.

An indentation for the first line in a block can be specified by the style property text-indent. For example (Ex: **IndentFirst**),

```
<p style="text-indent: 3em"> ... </p>
```

will indent the first line of the paragraph by a length of three ems (one em equals the width of M in the current font). To indent entire paragraphs, use the style properties:

```
margin-left: length
margin-right: length
```

For example,

```
<div style="margin-left: 5em; margin-right: 5em">
<p> ... </p>
<p> ... </p>
</div>
```

2.11 LENGTH UNITS

In style properties, a length value consists of an optional sign (+ or −), a number, and a unit. Relative length units are:

- `em`—size of M in current font
- `ex`—size of x in current font
- `px`—pixels based on resolution of the rendering device

Absolute length units are: `in` (inches), `cm` (centimeters), `mm` (millimeters), `pt` (points; 1 pt = 1/72 in.), `pc` (picas; 1 pc = 12 pt). Absolute lengths are not sensitive to changes in font size or screen resolution, while relative length units are.

2.12 COLORS

Color values in style properties can be color names from the Windows VGA palette (Figure 2.7 and Ex: **`Colors`**) or given in RGB (red-green-blue) with the following notations:

1. `#`*`rrggbb`*—where the first two, middle two, and last two of the six hexadecimal digits specify red, green, and blue values, respectively (e.g., `#0ace9f`). This is 24-bit color.

Figure 2.7 COLOR NAMES

aqua	black	blue	fuchsia	gray	green	lime	maroon
navy	olive	purple	red	silver	teal	white	yellow

2. #*rgb*—shorthand for the above notation when the first two, middle two, and last two digits are the same (e.g., #03c stands for #0033cc). This is 12-bit color.

3. rgb(*r*, *g*, *b*)—where base-10 integers between 0 and 255 inclusive are used (e.g., rgb(0,204,108)). This is the decimal equivalent of notation 1.

4. rgb(*r*%, *g*%, *b*%)—where integral percentages are used for the three color components.

It takes dividing or multiplying by 16 to convert between decimal and hex notations for RGB color values. Hex calculators allow you to take decimal RGB values and convert to hex automatically. On the Mac, you can download a good calculator by going to

ftp://ftp.amug.org/pub/mirrors/info-mac/sci/calc/calculator-ii-15.hqx.

Personal computer users have a built-in calculator located under Start>Accessories. Select the hex option and enter the decimal RGB numbers.

Although the Web uses the RGB color codes described here, there are other ways to specify color (Section 7.10). Setting colors is easy, but choosing colors that combine to make a site functional and attractive is another matter entirely. Chapter 7 explains colors and their usage.

2.13   TEXT FONTS

One of the most important design aspects of a Web site is its readability (Section 5.11). The textual content of the site must be easily readable, and the designer's understanding of what factors enhance readability is absolutely essential to Web development. The font type (Figure 2.8), style, and leading (line separation) can affect the readability and the look and feel of the entire site.

You can specify style properties for font family, style, variant, weight, and size for HTML elements. For example (Ex: **FontFamily**),

```
font-family: Times
font-family: Arial, Helvetica, sans-serif
```

You may list more than one name, in order of preference, for the font-family property. In this example, if the browser does not have Arial, it will check for Helvetica and so on.

It is a good idea to list a generic font family at the end of your preference list. The following generic font families are known:

- serif—for example, Times
- sans-serif—for example, Arial or Helvetica
- cursive—for example, Zapf-Chancery

Figure 2.8 **SOME FONTS**

times   arial

`courier`   monospace

- `fantasy`—for example, `Western`
- `monospace`—for example, `Courier`

Multiword font family names must be enclosed in single or double quotation marks.

The `font-style` property can be set to `normal` (the default), `italic`, or `oblique` (slanted). The `font-variant` can be set to `normal` (default) or `small-caps` (SMALL CAPITALS).

The `font-weight` property controls how heavy (bold) the font type is. For example,

```
font-weight: normal
font-weight: bold
font-weight: bolder
font-weight: lighter
```

The setting `bolder` (`lighter`) increases (decreases) the boldness relative to the current setting. The absolute weights $100, 200, \ldots, 900$ can also be used. The exact meaning of these weights are browser and font dependent.

The `font-size` property can be set to a predefined size (Figure 2.9)

```
xx-small    x-small     small
medium      large       x-large     xx-large
```

or a specific size given in

pt (points; 1 pt $= 1/72$ in.)

pc (picas; 1 pc $= 12$ pt)

For example, `font-size: 16pt`.

Alternatively, you can set font size to a value relative to the current font size of the parent element.

`smaller`

`larger`

`xx%` (a percentage of the current font size)

It is advisable to set the basic font size in body to a predefined size that is correct for different browsers running on different display devices. Inside body, headings and fine print can use percentages to get a larger or smaller font size.

Figure 2.9 FONT SIZES

ᴴᴴ⁻small ˣ⁻small small medium large x-large xx-large

The vertical spacing between text lines can be important for readability. Browsers have default settings for vertical spacing depending on the font size. You can control line spacing by setting the line-height style property to a *number*, a *percentage*, or a fixed length.

The number and percentage specify a multiple of the current font size. Few places call for a fixed line height independent of the font size. The WDP site uses line-height: 150% for 1.5 line spacing.

One point to keep in mind is that users can increase or decrease the text size with browser settings. Thus, it is not possible to assume that your page will be displayed in a predetermined font size. The Web designer must take this into account when laying out a page.

An important Web site design consideration is what font and sizes to use for headers, running text, links, and fine print. Once the font and sizes have been determined, ensure they are consistently applied throughout the pages in your site. Any deviation must be for a specific design purpose. Otherwise, the unity of the site will suffer.

Section 5.7 provides a more comprehensive introduction to fonts, and Section 6.2 discusses the use of fonts with style sheets.

2.14 LISTS

In addition to headings and paragraphs, lists can organize and present information for easy reading. Web users like to find information quickly and will usually not have the patience to read long-winded passages. Itemized lists can highlight important points and send visitors in the right directions.

Three block-level list elements are available:

- Bulleted list: The ul element provides an *unordered list* where the ordering of the items is unimportant. A ul is usually presented as a set of bulleted items.

- Ordered list: The ol element offers a *numbered list* where the ordering of the items is important. An ol is typically displayed as a sequence of enumerated items.

- Definition list: The dl element is handy for a *definition list* where each term (<dt>) is given a definition or description (<dd>).

List elements may only contain list items. List items in ol and ul are given as li elements, which can contain other block elements such as headings, paragraphs, and lists. List items are usually displayed indented. A list given inside an li is nested in another list and is further indented. Here is a simple example (Ex: **List**):

```
<ul>
<li>Fruits
    <ol><li>Apple</li><li>Banana</li><li>Cherry</li></ol>
</li>
<li>Cereals
    <ol><li>Barley</li> <li>Rice</li> <li>Wheat</li> </ol>
</li>
<li>Meats
    <ol><li>Beef</li> <li>Chicken</li> <li>Pork</li> </ol>
</li></ul>
```

A version of this list is shown in Figure 2.10.

List items in a definition list (dl) are terms and descriptions.

```
<dl>
  <dt style="font-style: italic">HTML</dt>
  <dd>Hypertext Markup Language</dd>
  <dt style="font-style: italic">HTTP</dt>
  <dd>Hypertext Transfer Protocol</dd>
  <dt style="font-style: italic">CSS</dt>
  <dd>Cascading Style Sheets</dd>
</dl>
```

Figure 2.10   LISTS

Figure 2.11   DEFINITION LIST

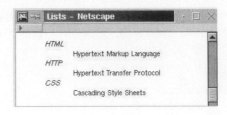

The definition term (dt) contains inline elements, and the definition description (dd) can contain inline and block elements. There is normally no automatic indentation for definition list items (Figure 2.11).

2.15   LIST STYLES

The default *list item marker* for ul and ol is defined by the browser. Switching item markers for nested lists is also done automatically. But you can take control of the list item marker by the list-style-type property. For example (Ex: **BulletType**),

```
<ul style="list-style-type: circle"> ...  </ul>
<ol style="list-style-type: upper-alpha"> ...  </ol>
```

specify the marker type for the entire list. Specifying list-style-type for li allows you to control the item marker for each item separately.

Available list style types (Figure 2.12) are disc (solid circle), circle (open circle), square, none (no marker), decimal (Arabic numerals), lower-roman (lowercase Roman numerals), upper-roman (uppercase Roman numerals), lower-alpha (lowercase English alphabet), upper-alpha (uppercase English alphabet). By giving an inappropriate style type, you can actually display a ul with numbered markers or an ol with bullets.

Figure 2.12   LIST ITEM MARKERS

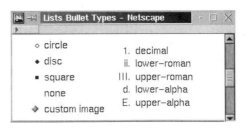

Figure 2.13   MARKER COLORING AND POSITIONING

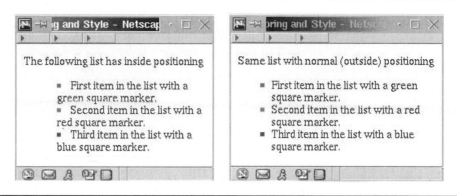

Use the property list-style-image: url(*imageURL*) for any custom list marker image identified by the *imageURL*. It overrides nonimage list markers. The list-style-position property takes the value outside (the default) or inside. The latter makes the list marker part of the first line of each list item (Figure 2.13).

You can also change the color of the item markers with the color style property. For example, the following code (Ex: **MarkerStyle**)

```
<p>The following list has inside positioning</p>
<ul style="list-style-position:inside">
  <li style="list-style-type: square; color: green">
    <span style="color: black">First item in the list with a
        green square marker.</span></li>
  <li style="list-style-type: square;  color: red">
    <span style="color: black">Second item in the list with a
        red square marker.</span></li>
  <li style="list-style-type: square; color: blue">
    <span style="color: black">Third item in the list with a
        blue square marker.</span></li>
</ul>
```

results in the display shown to the left in Figure 2.13.

2.16 HYPERLINKS

Anchor elements (<a> ... </a>) can specify *hypertext references* (or *hyperlinks*) to other documents on the Web/Internet. A hyperlink can be attached (anchored) to an inline element such as text or image. A link can also be attached to a specific part of an image via an image map (Section 2.19).

A hyperlink is given in the form

```
<a href="URL">anchor</a>
```

The enclosed inline element(s) *anchor* is linked to a resource located with the given *URL*. The URL can link to any document or service allowable. For example,

```
<a href="bio.html">Brief Bio</a>
```

links the text *Brief Bio* to the document bio.html. Links to remote documents should be specified with full URLs, and links to local documents should be given by partial URLs (Section 1.4).

Here are some sample links:

```
<a href="http://www.w3c.org/">The W3C Consortium</a>
<a href="../pic/dragonfly.jpg"                          (1)
   title="dragonfly.jpg">Picture of Dragonfly</a>       (2)
<a href="sound/cthd.mp3" type="audio/mpeg">             (3)
   Tan Dun, Yo Yo Ma - Crouching Tiger,
   Hidden Dragon - Theme</a>
```

The notation ../ leads to the parent directory (folder) of the current document (line 1). The title attribute (line 2) supplies text that a browser can use as a ToolTip display. The type attribute (line 3) helps inform the browser of the MIME type of the target resource. Here the link is to an mpeg audio file (Chapter 12) in MP3 format. It is usually not necessary to specify the type because when the file is retrieved by the browser, it will come with the correct MIME type information.

It is also possible to link directly to a specific point within the same document or another document. To do this, the target element in the destination document must have an id.

```
<h3 id="products">Our Quality Products</h3>
```

A link in the form

```
<a href="URL#products"> ... </a>
```

leads to the point labeled by products in the document given by the *URL*. If the *URL* part is omitted, the link leads to a point labeled products in the same HTML document.

Web pages often take advantage of this feature to give a set of links at the beginning of a long article to serve as an active table of contents. For example,

```
<ul>
<li><a href="#products" title="Web Products">Products</a></li>
<li><a href="#services" title="Web Services">Services</a></li>
<li><a href="#resources" title="Web Resources">Resources</a></li>
<li><a href="#news" title="Web News">News</a></li>
</ul>
```

```
...

<h3 id="products">Our Quality Products</h3>

...

<h3 id="services">Web Services</h3>
...
```

HTML allows #*xyz* to lead to any element whose id is *xyz*. In XHTML, the id attribute uniquely identifies (labels) an element in a page. For older browsers, you may still need to place a *named anchor* (<a> with a name attribute):

```
<h3 id="products"><a name="products">Our Quality Products</a></h3>
```

as a label for hyperlinks to follow.

URL Encoding

According to the URL specification (RFC1738), only alphanumerics [0-9a-zA-Z], the special characters

```
$  -  _  .  +  !  *  '  (  )  ,
```

and reserved characters

```
;  /  ?  :  @  =  &
```

used for their reserved purposes (supporting the URL syntax) may be included unencoded within a URL. Other characters are *unsafe* and ought to be encoded. To include unsafe ASCII characters, such as spaces and control characters they must be URL encoded.

To URL encode an unsafe ASCII character, replace it with the three-character sequence %*hh* where *hh* is its ASCII code in hexadecimal. For example, ~ is %7E and SPACE is %20. Thus, a link to the file "chapter one.html" becomes

```
<a href="chapter%20one.html">First Chapter</a>
```

The UNIX command

man ASCII

displays the ASCII table in octal, decimal, and hex. Hex codes for ISO Latin can be found on the Web.

To include non-ASCII characters in a URL, each such character is first UTF-8 encoded (Section 3.1) into two or more bytes. Each unsafe byte is then %*hh* encoded.

Internal and External Links

In building a Web site, hyperlinks are used for two major purposes: to organize pages within the site (internal links) and to reach resources on the Web (external links).

Following an internal link, a visitor stays within a site and its navigation system. By clicking an external link, the visitor goes to another site. Hence, a well-designed site should make a clear distinction between these two types of links.

It is recommended that each external link

- is clearly indicated as going off site
- is displayed in a new window so the visitor can come back by closing or iconifying that new window

A simple way is to use the attribute `target="_blank"` to cause the referenced page to display in a new window:

```
<a href="http://www.w3c.org/" target="_blank">The W3C Consortium</a>
```

But the `target` attribute is not supported by XHTML Strict. Thus, strictly speaking, any page using the `target` construct for external links must use XHTML Traditonal instead of XHTML Strict (Section 2.4). Major browsers are usually more tolerant.

Alternatively, you can use JavaScript to open new browser windows (Section 9.12).

Site Organization

Now let's consider using hyperlinks to organize pages within a Web site for www.enterprise.com.

- Organize the pages for a site into a hierarchy of files and directories (folders) stored on the hard disk of the server host. Avoid nonalphanumeric characters in file and directory names. Otherwise, the file name must be URL encoded before becoming part of a URL.
- Place the site entry page (usually, `index.html`) in the *server root* directory.
- Use subdirectories such as `images/`, `products/`, `services/`, `contractors/`, `members/`, and `affiliates/` to organize the site. The `index.html` page within each subdirectory is usually the lead page for that part of the site.
- Keep the organization simple and avoid using more than three levels of subdirectory nesting.
- Design a navigation system that is clear, easy to use, and effective in getting visitors where they want to go in your site.

- Use partial URLs exclusively for linking within the site and make sure the link is in one of these forms:

  1. relative to the *host page* itself (`href="file"` or `href="dir/file"`)
  2. relative to the server root (`href="/path-to-file"`)

If all links are of the first kind, then the pages of the site can be moved as a group to a different location in the file system or to a different hosting computer without change. If you have both types of relative links, then the pages can be moved to the server root on another host without change.

In creating the content-only site, consider establishing pages with these parts:

1. *Major navigation*—Links to the main page, major first-level pages, site map, and/or site search page(s). Indicate if a page will have a logo of the business and ensure the logo image will be a link to the main page as well. Remember, a site may or may not have an entry page that is fancy or animated. The page the entry leads to is the main page.
2. *Minor navigation*—Links to subpages of this page and links to directly related sibling pages.
3. *In-page navigation*—Links to parts of this page when appropriate.
4. *Draft page content*—Includes text, pictures, and other media types.

Page Relocation

Consider downloading a remote Web page to your local file system (or desktop). The downloaded page and all its links and images can still work correctly if the following `base` element is included inside the `head`:

```
<base href="full url of original page location" />
```

The `base` element tells any browser processing the page to regard it as coming from the given URL. However, in building a Web site, it is not a good idea to include the `base` element in every page because this makes relocating and reorganizing the site more difficult.

Linking to Services

Besides document references, other frequently used types of links in practice are:

- Email links—A link in the form

  ```
  <a href="mailto:email-address?SUBJECT=line">
  ```

tells the browser to launch a program to send email to the given address using the indicated subject line. The subject line (from ? on) is optional. For example,

```
<a href=
 "mailto:pwang@cs.kent.edu?SUBJECT=Web%20Design%20and%20Programming"
contact Paul</a>
```

Note spaces (%20) and other nonalphanumeric characters should be URL encoded.

Generally, the `mailto`[5] URL may have zero or more & separated *header*=*value* pairs. Useful headers include `to` (additional recipient address), `cc`, and `body` (message body). For example,

```
<a href=
    "mailto:wdpgroup-request@cs.kent.edu?SUBJECT=join&BODY=subscribe"
Joint web design and programming email listserv group</a>
```

provides an easy way to join a listserv.

- Download links—A link in the form

```
<a href="ftp:host:port/path-to-file">
```

tells the browser to launch an FTP program to connect to the given *host* and to download the specified *file* by anonymous FTP. This is useful for downloading large files such as programs and compressed (ZIP or GZIP) files. If *port* is not given, then the standard port 21 for FTP is assumed. For example,

```
Download <a href="ftp://monkey.cs.kent.edu/package.zip">
        <code>package.zip</code></a> (35439 bytes).
```

An FTP URL can also supply username, password, and file location information for file retrieval (see www.w3.org/Addressing/schemes).

- Logon links—A link in the form

```
<a href="telnet://host:port">
```

tells the browser to launch a Telnet program connected to the given *host* at the specified *port* for remote logon. If *port* is not given, the standard port 23 for Telnet is assumed. For example,

```
<a href="telnet://monkey.cs.kent.edu">login to Monkey</a>
at the CS Department, Kent State University.
```

---

[5]See RFC2368 for more information on the `mailto` URL scheme.

Display Style for Hyperlinks

Visual browsers pay special attention to the presentation of hyperlinks. Usually, different display styles (Section 6.5) are used for textual hyperlinks to indicate whether the link is not visited yet, under the mouse (hover), being clicked (active), or visited already (visited). A link is usually underlined in blue. As you click the link, it turns red. A visited link becomes reddish-purple. The user can control these colors through browser preference settings. An image anchoring a link will by default be displayed with a distinct border.

Web users are accustomed to seeing links underlined. Therefore, avoid underlining regular text because it can cause confusion. Image links, on the other hand, are almost always presented without the default border (Section 2.17). Web users understand that clicking an image often leads to another page.

A consistent set of link styles and colors is important for site design. Style sheets give you much control over the styling of links (Section 6.2).

2.17   IMAGES

With a hyperlink such as `<a href="cat.gif">My cat<a>`, you display a stand-alone image in a separate page. To include an image within a page together with other content, use the *inline image* element `img`

```
<img src="URL" width="..."  height="..."  alt="..." />
```

where *URL* points to an image file usually in GIF, JPEG, or PNG (Portable Network Graphics) format. The *raster image formats* store a fine grid of *pixels*, or picture elements, to represent the image. They also employ data compression to reduce the size of the file with little or no sacrifice in image quality.

The inline element `img` can be placed in any block or inline element except `pre`. Attributes of `img` include:

- `alt="text"`: Required alternative text to use for nonvisual browsers and when the image file is not available.
- `height="ht", width="wd"`: Height and width of display area for the image. This size information, `wd` and `ht` in number of pixels, allows browsers to reserve the correct room for the image and continues to render the page without waiting for the image to load. For a page with multiple images, this can make the page appear on the screen much faster. Hence, it is recommended that the exact image size in pixels always be specified. A size different from the original image can be given, and the image will be scaled up or down to fit the specified area. Both `height` and `width` are optional.

- longdesc="*URL*": A text file providing a verbal description of the image. For example, this gives browsers for the blind a way to explain the image to the user.

We recommend that you always include the alt, width, and height attributes for img. To find the width and height of an image, use any image processing tool such as Photoshop or Paintshop. On Linux systems, the command

xview -verbose *file*.jpg

shows the size of the given image. Opening the file with a browser also works.

Graphical Links

Pictures, logos, and icons are often used as navigation and/or information links. This is done by putting an image inside <a href="*URL*">...</a>. Usually, browsers will place a border around the image as a visual clue that the image is a link. To eliminate the image border, use the "border: none" style:

<a href="page2.html"><img src="next.gif" style="border: none" /></a>

In this example, the next.gif icon is clearly a link, and an added border is not needed or wanted. The "border: 0px" style also works because it sets all the border widths to zero (Section 6.12).

The WDP Web site uses a set of images to provide visual identification for major sections. Figure 2.14 is an example for the Hands-on Experiments section. Such an image, when placed on a subpage, is conveniently linked to the top page of the section to aid site navigation.

For pictures that are large and time consuming to load, a smaller "thumbnail" image (often in GIF) can be created as a link to a page containing the full image. Use your favorite image processing tool to crop and/or scale down the picture to create a thumbnail. An online photo gallery or portfolio usually lays out arrays of thumbnails linking to collections of images.

Figure 2.14   PAGE IDENTIFICATION: WDP SITE HANDS-ON EXPERIMENTS

© Photodisc/
Getty Images

Text around Images

To cause text to flow around an image (Ex: **Float**), you *float* the image to the left or right margin and add appropriate spacing between the image and text. For example,

```
<p>Monarch butterfly eggs are somewhat difficult to find in the    (1)
<img src="monarch.jpg" alt="Monarch Butterfly" width="200"         (2)
     height="133" style="float: left; margin-right: 1em;
            margin-bottom: 8px; margin-top: 8px" />
wild. Since it ... milkweed plants.</p><p>A female will ... </p> (3)
```

The image of a monarch butterfly (line 2) is floated to the left side of the page with text in paragraphs (lines 1 and 3) flowing around the image. The image margins provide room between the image and the surrounding text. The display is shown in Figure 2.15. The style properties `float: right`, `margin-left`, and `margin-top` are also available (Section 6.9).

Floating alows you to place text alongside an image or some other floating element such as a table. Sometimes you need to put just a short caption or legend alongside a floating element, stop wrapping, and start a new paragraph beyond the floating element. To end the wraparound before it is completed and start a new element below the floating element, use the `clear` style property: `clear:left` (clear float on the left), `clear:right` (clear float on the right), or `clear:both` (clear float on both the left and right). Here, *clear* means "move beyond."

For example (Ex: **FloatClear**), if we were to revise line 3 in Ex: **Float** to

```
...</p>
<p style="clear: left">A female will ... </p>     (3 with clear left)
```

then the display would change to that shown in Figure 2.16.

Figure 2.15   TEXT AROUND AN IMAGE

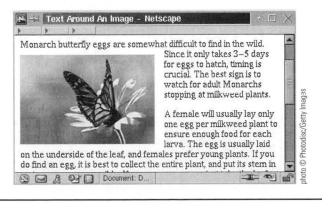

Figure 2.16 **TEXT CLEARING IMAGE**

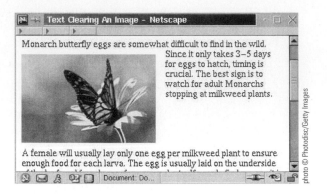

2.18 POSITIONING INLINE IMAGES

When a text line includes images, the relative vertical position of an image with respect to the text can be controlled by setting the vertical-align style property. For example,

```
Here is some text and an
image <img src="URL" style="vertical-align: baseline" />
```

aligns the baseline of the image with the baseline of preceding text. This is usually the default alignment. In general, the vertical-align style property applies to any inline element. Settings that align to the preceding text include (Ex: **ImageAlign**):

- vertical-align: baseline—Aligns baselines of image and text.
- vertical-align: middle—Aligns middle of image with middle of x character in preceding text.
- vertical-align: text-top—Aligns top of image with font top of preceding text.
- vertical-align: text-bottom—Aligns bottom of image with font bottom of preceding text.
- vertical-align: xx%—Raises the bottom of image xx percent of the text *line height*.

Figure 2.17 shows these vertical alignments using images from the navigation bar of the WDP Web site.

In case a line contains elements of several different heights, you can also align an image with respect to the entire line using:

Figure 2.17   INLINE ALIGNMENTS

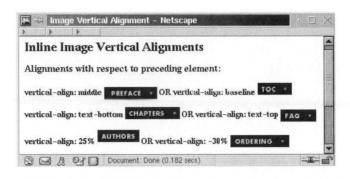

- `vertical-align: top`—Aligns top of image to tallest element on the line, which could be another image or some other tall element in the same line.
- `vertical-align: bottom`—Aligns bottom of image to lowest element on the line, which could be another image or some other element in the same line.

Figure 2.18 shows how the image PREFACE is aligned with the top of an image further down the line and how the FEEDBACK image is aligned with the bottom of a previous image in the same line. The HTML code is:

```
<h3 style="color: blue">Alignments with respect
to the whole line:</h3>
<p><span style=
"color:blue">vertical-align: top</span>
<img alt="preface" src="u_preface.gif"
     style="vertical-align: top" /> in a line with
another <img alt="loon.gif" src="loon.gif"
style="vertical-align: baseline" /> image.</p>
```

Figure 2.18   WHOLE-LINE ALIGNMENTS

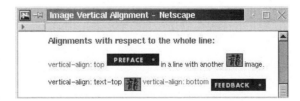

To center an image (see Ex: **Center**) horizontally on a line, use

```
<p style="text-align: center"><img ... /></p>
```

2.19 IMAGE MAPS

An *image map* is an image with *active areas* that, when clicked, lead to designated URLs. For example, you may use a picture of a number of products, a county map of a state, or a group picture of classmates to make an image map.

To create an image map, you associate a map element to an image. A map element contains one or more area elements that define active areas within an image and connect each to a hyperlink. The required name attribute of a map is used to associate it with an image. The map code can be placed in any block element (but not directly in body) and is itself not displayed by browsers.

An area element can define a rectangle, a circle, or a polygon using co-ordinates in pixels (or infrequently, in percentages). The upper left corner of an image is (0, 0) following the coordinate system for computer graphics (Figure 2.19).

```
<map name="samplemap">
 <area shape="rect" coords="0,0,100,150"        (corners of rectangle)
     href="some-url" alt="item 1" />
 <area shape="poly" coords="0,0,10,32,98,200"  (vertices of polygon)
     href="some-url" alt="item 2" />
 <area shape="circle" coords="0,0,100" (center and radius of circle)
     href="some-url" alt="item 3" />
 <area shape="default"                           (rest of image)
     href="some-url" alt="item otherwise" />
</map>
```

Like images, an area requires the alt attribute. The special shape default stands for the rest of the image not included in the otherwise marked regions. The special nohref attribute can be given instead of href to indicate no link for

Figure 2.19   IMAGE COORDINATES

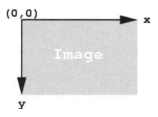

an `area`. For regions of irregular shapes, the polygon, given as x_0, y_0, x_1, y_1, ..., is the most useful.

To obtain the coordinates, you can open the image in question in any image processing tool (e.g., Paintshop, Photoshop, ImageMagick) or use an image map editor. On the Web, the Poor Person's Image Mapper is a free service. A completed `map` is placed within the `head` element and associated with an inline image with the `usemap` attribute of the `img` element:

```
<img src="img-url" usemap="#map-name" />        (an image map)
```

Here is a map for Mount Rushmore (Ex: **ImageMap**) that links to pages on four U.S. presidents: Washington, Jefferson, Roosevelt, and Lincoln.

```
<head>
<title>Mount Rushmore</title>
<map name="rushmore">                                    (1)
  <area shape="poly"
     coords="23,19,8,55,18,83,39,98,84,92
            ,101,59,82,19,61,4"
     href="presidents/washington.html"
     alt="George Washington" />


  ...


  <area shape="poly"
     coords="243,89,252,173,322,185,319,62">
     href="presidents/roosevelt.html"
     alt="Theodore Roosevelt" />
  <area shape="default"                                  (2)
     href="presidents/index.html"
     alt="List of US Presidents" />
</map>
</head>
<body><div style="text-align: center">
<h2>Mount Rushmore</h2>
<img src="rushmore.gif"
     usemap="#rushmore" style="border: none" />    (3)
<p>Click on the head of each president to see a
portrait and biography.</p>
<p>Click otherwise in the picture to get a
list of all US presidents.</p>
</div></body>
```

The required `name` attribute of the `map` is set to `rushmore` (line 1).

Figure 2.20 shows the image with the polygon for Washington outlined in green (see color insert). The `default` shape (line 2) provides a link for any click on the image map that does not fall in one of the defined areas. The image

Figure 2.20   MOUNT RUSHMORE IMAGE MAP

rushmore.gif (line 3) is associated with the map with the usemap attribute. The complete example (Ex: **Rushmore**) can be found at the WDP site.

Note, since HTML 4, W3C has recommended a new style image map that is friendlier to nonimage browsers and more flexible in usage. You can, for example, define a text-based navigation bar along with the image map. However, support by browsers is still lacking. Please refer to the WDP Web site for a link to more details.

2.20   EDITING HTML

To work with HTML or any other programming language, a good editor is essential. Something simple like the Notepad on Windows may be easy at the beginning but is not powerful enough for serious site creation or maintenance work. For programmers familiar with HTML syntax and semantics, a general text editor such as vi or emacs works well for simple sites. These editors come with UNIX systems and are available, as freeware or shareware, for Windows and Macs. Learning these editors will help not only HTML coding but any other type of text editing. After creating or modifying an HTML file, you can view it with a browser through the File>Open File menu option.

Word processing software such as Microsoft Word usually can export native formats to HTML. Files thus generated may require hand-tuning or transformation through a code checking tool before being placed on a Web site.

Netscape Composer is a convenient visual HTML editor that comes with the freely available Netscape Navigator browser. Start Composer through the Tasks>Composer menu option. The Composer window (Figure 2.21) shows the tools and options immediately available. With this type of visual editor, you can create and format a Web page visually just like word processing. In the normal mode, you do not see the HTML tags being created, just the resulting content display. But you can switch among normal, show tags, show source,

Figure 2.21   NETSCAPE COMPOSER

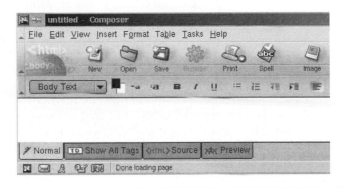

and `preview` modes at any time. You can request specific HTML elements for images, links, anchors, lists, tables, and so forth. Text alignments and font changes are also easily made. At this time, Netscape Composer is generating HTML 4 code, not XHTML code. Ideally, this will improve soon.

Amaya from W3C is a complete Web browsing and authoring environment that comes with a WYSIWYG-style (What You See Is What You Get) interface similar to popular commercial browsers. With Amaya, users can easily generate HTML and XHTML pages and cascading style sheets. Amaya is available for most computer platforms. See www.w3.org/Amaya/ for information and downloading.

HTML-Kit is an integrated development environment (IDE) designed to help HTML, XHTML, CSS (Chapter 6), and script (Chapter 9) authors to edit, format, validate, preview, and publish Web pages. This tool also provides easy help and reference for HTML coding. HTML-Kit offers numerous tools that make the processes of inserting and editing HTML tags easier. In contrast to many WYSIWYG editors, HTML-Kit gives complete control over the HTML development and editing process. HTML-Kit let's you use templates and will point out errors and suggest how to comply with standards. The HTML-Kit (for Windows) can be downloaded free from www.chami.com/html-kit/.

Coffee Cup is a popular, free WYSIWYG HTML editor available for all major platforms, including Linux. It has all the usual features and some extras. You can obtain it from www.coffeecup.com/software. This tool produces HTML 4 code and does not yet support XHTML.

Commercial HTML editors and IDEs abound. HomeSite and Dreamweaver MX (for Windows and Macs) from Macromedia are large and comprehensive tools popular with Web developers. Both support open standards and generate files compatible with other tools. FrontPage from Microsoft is also powerful and easy to use. But the pages it generates are nonstandard and not compatible with other tools. It is best to use tools compliant with open standards. HoT-MetaL Pro, available for UNIX, Windows, and Macs, includes site management tools, graphical editors, HTML validation, and global search and replace across a Web site.

The WDP site resource page contains links to many HTML editors and other tools. Be aware that automatically generated HTML may be very verbose, may not follow the latest coding standards, and may be incorrect. Check the generated code over and hand-tune it where necessary.

If you use an HTML tool that does not generate XHTML code or are working on existing code that is not fully XHTML compliant, you can run the HTML files through the free tool TIDY to check and correct errors and to reformat the source code. TIDY is available for all major platforms and can be downloaded free from www.w3.org/People/Raggett/tidy.

Normally, you run TIDY from the command line:

```
tidy in.html out.html
tidy -m in.html                    (modifies file in-place)
tidy -f errfile in.html out.html   (records errors in given file)
```

Through command-line options and configuration files, you can control the many features of TIDY, including:

- --char-encoding ascii—Converts all characters above 127 to HTML entities.
- --char-encoding latin1—Converts all characters above 255 to HTML entities.
- --output-xhtml yes—Outputs XHTML code.
- --fix-backslash yes—Changes BACKSLASH in URLs to *slash*.

Many other options (configuration settings) are available. See the documentation on the TIDY download page.

All of the aforementioned tools are not completely XHTML Strict oriented. Until such tools become available, you need to hand-tune the code produced for XHTML compliance. You will find the HTML validator at W3C handy to check your HTML code.

HTML pages are often produced on one platform and deployed and maintained on another. Web pages (HTML files) are text files, and text files on UNIX, Windows, and Mac use different *line termination conventions*. On UNIX, the NEWLINE character terminates a line. For Windows (DOS), the pair RETURN and NEWLINE does the same, whereas Macintosh uses RETURN for line termination (Table 2.1). When an HTML file is transfered from one platform to another, it may work perfectly as a Web page, but native text editors may either lack line breaks or have an extra RETURN at the end of each line. On UNIX, the **mtools** help deal with UNIX-DOS text file conversion. Many Windows and Macintosh tools can deal with text files in all three formats and can save text into files of a chosen format for transporting to another system. Just remember to put the files in the right format before FTPing them.

Table 2.1   TEXT FILE LINE TERMINATORS

Operating System	Line Terminator
UNIX	NEWLINE
Windows (DOS)	RETURN + NEWLINE
Macintosh	RETURN

2.21   SUMMARY

New Web pages should be written in XHTML to confirm to the new W3C-recommended standard. XHTML documents are XML compatible and therefore can be treated by XML tools and can be easily mixed with other XML-defined tags such as MathML. XHMTL is based on HTML 4.01 and offers three modes: Strict, Traditional, and Frameset. Make your pages conform to the Strict standard when possible.

In XHTML, all tag names and attributes are in lowercase and all attribute values must be enclosed in double quotation marks. All end tags must be used. Empty elements must end in SPACE/>. Each element defines available attributes and elements allowed as child or parent. Core attributes applicable to all elements are id, style, class, and title.

Block-level and inline elements are placed in body to provide document content. White-space characters separate words and extra white spaces are collapsed. Text flows to fill lines that can be left adjusted, centered, or right adjusted. Three different lists help organize and present information. Images can be placed inline with text and aligned vertically in multiple ways.

HTML elements and their attributes are primarily used to provide structure to documents. Presentation styles can be attached to elements with the style attribute. In Chapter 6, you'll see more flexible ways to specify style and how to separate style from structure even more completely.

Use h1-h6 for section headings, p for paragraphs, br for line breaks, q and blockquote for inline and block quotations, hr for horizontal rules, ul for unordered lists, ol for ordered lists, dl for definition lists (containing dt and dd), img for inline images, map for image maps (containing areas), a for hyperlinks, and span (div) for attaching style properties.

Style properties are assigned to HTML elements to control page presentation. Style properties mentioned in this chapter include font-family, font-size, font-weight, text-align, color, background-color, vertical-align, list-style-type, text-indent, height, width, border, and margin. Chapter 6 covers styles more comprehensively.

Hyperlinks may use text or image as an anchor, and areas inside an image can lead to different URLs in an image map. URLs for links may contain a restricted set of ASCII characters. Other characters must be URL encoded before being placed in a URL. In addition to Web pages, URLs may link to Internet services such as FTP, Telnet, and email.

A good text editor can be used to build Web pages. Tools specially designed for editing HTML make the job a lot easier. Generated HTML code often needs hand-tuning to do what you want. The HTML TIDY tool can be useful in checking and formatting XHTML files.

EXERCISES

Review Questions

1. Where is the information given by the `title` element displayed?

2. What does overlapping tags mean? How do you suppose you can guard against such mistakes?

3. What is the proper form of an element without an end tag? Give three examples of elements without end tags.

4. What is the difference between block-level elements and inline elements?

5. How are comments given in HTML files?

6. What is the relation between HTML 4.01 and XHTML 1.0?

7. List and explain the core attributes for XHTML.

8. What role does white space play in an HTML file? What constitutes white space in an HTML document?

9. How is a header, a short line, or a paragraph centered horizontally in a page?

10. How are length units specified in a style declaration?

11. How are colors specified in a style declaration?

12. Name and describe the three different types of list elements in HTML. How do you control the bullet style for lists?

13. Explain how a hyperlink for sending email is done.

14. Explain how a hyperlink for remote logon is done.

15. What is a full URL? A relative URL? What are the two types of relative URLs?

16. What is the form of a URL that links to a local file on the hard disk?

17. What image formats are usually used on the Web? Why is the `img` element an inline element?

18. Can an image anchor a hyperlink? What effect will a link have on the image?

19. Which attributes are required for `<img>`?

20. What is an image map? How is it useful? Where is an image map placed in an HTML file? How is an image associated with its map?

21. What is the benefit of organizing a Web site using document-relative URLs?

Assignments

1. Take the "big on fruits" page from Section 1.7 and make it XHTML using the template given in Section 2.1.

2. Take the first Web page you created in Section 2.2 and deploy it in your personal Web directory in Section 1.6.

3. Take the first Web page you deployed in the previous assignment and make it into a simple personal home page. Introduce yourself to the world, make your résumé available, add a picture of yours, list your interests, talents, and so on.

4. Take the first Web page and experiment with font family, font size, and line height settings. View the page with different browsers and different user-selected font size preferences.

5. Specify `width` and `length` for an image differently from the image's original size and see the display effects.

6. Put `id` on some tags in a page and link to these locations inside the page from another page. Will the links work?

7. Take the butterfly image (Figure 2.15) and float it to the right of the page.

8. Complete the Mount Rushmore image map (Figure 2.20) and test it.

9. Download TIDY (Section 2.20) and run some of your pages through it.

Advanced XHTML

HTML is the language for authoring Web pages. Chapter 2 introduced HTML/XHTML and covered many basic topics. With that foundation, we are ready to explore more advanced features of HTML.

The Web is international. Web pages may be written in the Universal Character Set (the Unicode characters) that covers most known languages in use. HTML also provides ways to enter these characters from ASCII keyboards.

A major HTML topic is tables. HTML tables are useful for presenting information and for creating page layouts. The many aspects of table formatting and style control require careful presentation and patient experimentation to learn and master. Many practical examples are provided to help you.

Frames are a controversial construct. The pros and cons of frames are discussed at length so you can pick the right situations for their use.

Various elements, such as `meta` and `base`, given exclusively inside the `head` element provide critical functions for Web pages. You'll become familiar with them in this chapter.

The chapter concludes by showing how to avoid common Web page errors and how to check and validate pages.

3.1 CHARACTER ENCODING

The ASCII character set contains only 128 characters. HTML uses the much more complete Universal Character Set (UCS), or Unicode[1] character set, defined in ISO10646. UCS contains characters from most known languages. Characters in UCS are put into a linear sequence, and each character has a code position. The ASCII characters are given the code positions 0–127.

An HTML document containing UCS characters can be encoded in different ways when stored as a file or transmitted over the Internet. UTF-8 is

---

[1]www.unicode.org

a byte-oriented Unicode transformation format that is popular because of its ASCII preserving quality. UTF-8 represents:

- ASCII characters (code positions 0–127) with the lower 7 bits of 1 byte (single-byte code)
- code positions 128–2047 with 2 bytes
- code positions 2048–65536 with 3 bytes

UTF-8 sets the most significant bit of every byte to 1 for multibyte codes to distinguish them from single-byte codes. Some bits of the leading byte are used as a byte count. In contrast, UTF-16 encoding uses 2 bytes to represent each Unicode character.

An XHTML document specifies its character encoding via a line in the form

```
<?xml version="1.0" encoding="UTF-8" ?>
```

which usually comes first in a document file.

3.2   SPECIAL SYMBOLS AND HTML ENTITIES

On ASCII-oriented computers, it may not be easy to enter characters not directly available on the keyboard into a document. HTML provides a character-set-independent way to enter Unicode characters.

A *numeric character reference* specifies the code position with the notation

```
&#decimal;   or   &#xhex;
```

where *decimal* is a decimal integer and *hex* is a hexadecimal integer. A correctly configured browser seamlessly displays entities together with ASCII characters. The Chinese characters displayed in Figure 3.1 are 王 士 弘, the Chinese name of Paul S. Wang (Ex: **Chinese**).

To make characters easier to use, HTML *character entities* provide mnemonic names for them. An *entity* is a short sequence of characters beginning with an ampersand (&) and ending with a semicolon (;). Figure 3.2 shows the browser presentation of some entities for often-used commercial symbols. See the Ex: **Symbols** example for the source code.

Figure 3.1   **DISPLAYING CHARACTER REFERENCES**

Paul S. Wang 王士弘

Figure 3.2   ENTITIES FOR COMMERCIAL SYMBOLS

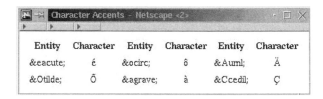

Figure 3.3   CHARACTER ACCENTS

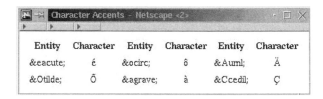

HTML entities form a subset of UCS and include Latin-1 characters, mathematical symbols, Greek letters, characters with accents, and other special characters. Figure 3.3 shows how character accents are specified (Ex: **Accents**). Other special symbols (Ex: **S**pecial) useful in HTML codes are shown in Figure 3.4.

Greek characters are also easy to specify. They are frequently used in mathematical notations. Figure 3.5 shows how to form entities for Greek characters and how to add superscripts or subscripts to them (Ex: **Greek**). Good tables for HTML entities are available on the Web, and links can be found at the WDP site.

Figure 3.4   SPECIAL SYMBOLS

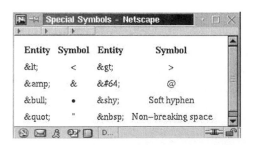

Figure 3.5 GREEK CHARACTERS

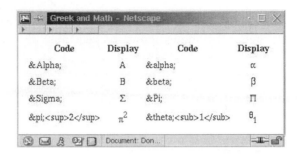

MathML is a markup language specifically designed to put mathematical formulas on the Web. More information on MathML can be found at the W3C site.

3.3 TABLES

Tables let us display information in a clear and concise fashion. The block element `table` organizes and presents information in neatly aligned rows and columns. It is often used to

- present tabular data
- layout Web pages by aligning content and graphics in horizontal and vertical grids (Section 5.12) to achieve visual communication designs
- organize entries in fill-out forms for user input

In general, a table involves many aspects: rows, columns, data cells, headings, lines separating cells, a caption, spacing within and among cells, and vertical and horizontal alignments of cell contents. The rows and columns can be separated into groupings. A cell can also span several columns or rows. Thus, `table` is a complicated HTML construct that takes some effort to understand and master. But the ability to use `table` effectively is critical for HTML programming.

HTML Table Basics

In its most basic form, a `table` has a number of rows, each containing the same number of table entries (or cells). The following is a table (Ex: **SimpleTable**) with two rows, two columns, and a caption:

```
<table border="1">                              (A)
<caption>Four Seasons</caption>
```

```
    <tr> <td>Spring</td> <td>Summer</td> </tr>      (B)
    <tr> <td>Fall</td>    <td>Winter</td> </tr>      (C)
</table>
```

Figure 3.6 shows the displayed table along with HTML codes for its parts (Ex: **Tablestructure**).

The `tr` element gives you a table row. We have two rows in this example (lines B and C). You may only place table cells inside a table row.

A table cell is either a `td` or a `th` element. Use `th` for a cell that contains a header for a column or a row. Usually, a header will automatically appear in boldface. A `td` (`th`) may contain any inline and block elements, including `table`. Hence, you can put table(s) into a table.

The table caption (`caption`) is optional. Attributes and style rules for table elements control the visual presentation of tables. In this example, the `border="1"` attribute in the `table` element (line A) gives the width of the table border and the rules between the cells. With `border="0"` (the default), the same table would be without a border or separating lines, as shown by the first table in Figure 3.7.

For more spacing between table cells, set the `table` `cellspacing` attribute. For example, the code

```
<table border="1" cellspacing="10">
```

Figure 3.6   TABLE STRUCTURE

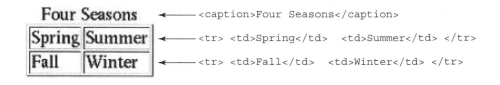

Figure 3.7   TABLE STYLES

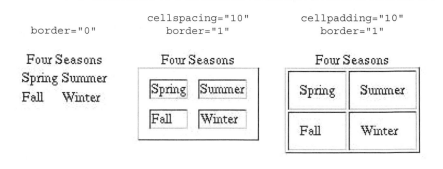

produces the second table in Figure 3.7. To give cell contents more breathing room inside cells, set the `cellpadding` attribute. For example, the code

```
<table border="1" cellpadding="10">
```

produces the third table in Figure 3.7. Notice that the contents are left aligned in the three tables of Figure 3.7. Let's turn our attention to cell content alignment.

3.4 CELL CONTENT ALIGNMENT

By default, content in a cell is `left` aligned horizontally and `middle` aligned vertically inside the space for the cell.

The `align` (horizontal alignment) and `valign` (vertical alignment) attributes of `tr` specify content alignment for all cells in a row. Possible values for `align` are `left`, `right`, `center`, `justify` (left and right justify lines in a cell), and `char`. The `align="char"` attribute can, for example, line up the decimal points in a column of numbers. But this feature is poorly supported by browsers.

Possible values for `valign` are `top` (top of cell), `middle` (middle of cell), `bottom` (bottom of cell), and `baseline` (align baseline of first line of each cell in a table row).

The `align` and `valign` attributes can be placed in a `td` (defaults: `left` and `middle`) or `th` (defaults: `center` and `middle`) to control the content alignment for a single cell. Let's use an HTML table (four rows and four columns) to demonstrate cell content alignments. The source code for the table shown in Figure 3.8 is as follows:

```
<table style="background-color: #def" border="1">
<tr><th></th>                                              (D)
    <th><code>align="left"</code></th>
    <th><code>align="center"</code></th>
    <th><code>align="right"</code></th> </tr>
```

Figure 3.8   CELL CONTENT ALIGNMENTS

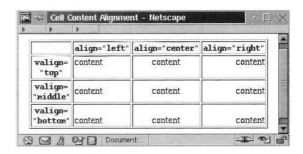

```
<tr><th><code>valign=<br />"top"</code></th>                     (E)
    <td align="left" valign="top">content</td>
    <td align="center" valign="top">content</td>
    <td align="right" valign="top">content</td> </tr>
<tr><th><code>valign=<br />"middle"</code></th>                  (F)
    <td align="left">content</td>
    <td align="center">content</td>
    <td align="right">content</td> </tr>
<tr><th><code>valign=<br />"bottom"</code></th>                  (G)
    <td align="left" valign="bottom">content</td>
    <td align="center" valign="bottom">content</td>
    <td align="right" valign="bottom">content</td> </tr>
</table>
```

The first row supplies headers (line D) indicating the horizontal alignment for cells in each column. The second row (line E) uses valign=top, the third row (line F) uses the default valign=middle, and the fourth row (line G) uses valign=bottom.

3.5   DISPLAYING TABLES

Because tables are inherently presentational, it is important to learn how to use element attributes and style properties to achieve the desired display in practice.

Let's first look at a realistic example (Ex: **Cart**) in which a shopping cart is displayed as a table of purchased items (Figure 3.9):

```
<table cellspacing="0" cellpadding="1" border="1">   (1)
<thead>                                               (2)
 <tr align="center" style="background-color:#fc0">   (3)
   <th>Item</th> <th>Code</th> <th>Price</th>
   <th>Quantity</th> <th>Amount</th>
 </tr>
```

Figure 3.9   SAMPLE TABLE

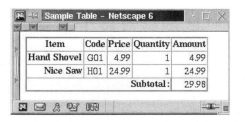

```
</thead>                                          (4)
<tbody>                                           (5)
 <tr valign="middle" align="right"
     style="background-color:#f0f0f0">            (6)
   <th> Hand Shovel</th>
   <td align="center">G01</td> <td>4.99</td>       (7)
   <td>1</td> <td>4.99</td>
 </tr>
 <tr valign="middle" align="right"               (8)
     style="background-color:#f0f0f0">
   <th>Nice Saw</th>
   <td align="center">H01</td> <td>24.99</td>
   <td>1</td> <td>24.99</td>
 </tr>
 <tr>
   <th colspan="4" align="right">Subtotal:</th>   (9)
   <td align="right">29.98</td>
 </tr>
</tbody>                                           (10)
</table>
```

This example gives a table more structure by putting the header row in a `thead` element (lines 2-4) and the rest of the rows in a `tbody` element (lines 5-10). It is possible for a table to have several `thead` and `tbody` elements, each containing one or more rows (Section 3.9).

To control the presentation of a table, you use `table` attributes for the whole table, `tr` attributes for a whole row, and `td` or `th` attributes for a single table cell.

The next sections continue to explain this example.

3.6   FORMATTING TABLES

Attributes for the `table` element control various formatting options for the table.

- `border`—Specifies the width in pixels of the border around a table (line 1). A nonzero `border` setting also implies horizontal and vertical rules, and a zero value also implies no rules.

- `rules`—Specifies the thin 1-pixel rules separating table cells: `none` (no rules), `groups` (rules between row groups and column groups only), `rows` (rules between rows only), `cols` (rules between columns only), and `all` (rules between all cells). The default is `none` if `border` is not set (set to 0), and the default is `all` if `border` is set. This attribute is poorly supported by browsers.

Figure 3.10   TABLE FEATURES

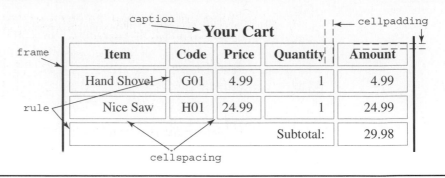

- frame—Specifies the visible sides of the table's outer border: void (no side), above/below (top/bottom), vsides/hsides (left+right or top+bottom), lhs/rhs (left or right), border (all sides).
- cellspacing—Specifies the amount of space between table cells (line 1). The default cellpacing is usually 1 pixel.
- cellpadding—Defines the amount of space between the cell border and cell contents (line 1). The default cellpadding is usually 1 pixel.
- summary—Text describing the purpose and content of the table for nonvisual browsers.

Figure 3.10 shows a table declared as

```
<table cellspacing="4" cellpadding="8" border="2" frame="vsides">
```

Because of its flexibility, you may find it convenient to use the border style property (Section 6.12) to display table rules, borders, and frames.

At the WDP Web site, the Ex: **TableStyle** example shows various table attribute settings. Note that the rules and frame attributes are poorly supported by many browsers.

3.7 POSITIONING TABLES

A table is normally positioned left adjusted by itself on the page. To center a table (or any block element) horizontally on the page, you can use the margin style properties (Ex: **CenteredTable**):

```
<table style="margin-left: auto; margin-right: auto">
```

Figure 3.11   **TEXT AROUND TABLE**

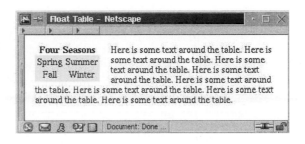

Add this code to Ex: **Cart** and see how it centers. If a table has a caption, you may need to add the automargin style to the caption element as well.[2] You can also set the caption-side style property to top or bottom to place the caption above or below the table.

These margin properties can also take on a length or a percentage to control the horizontal placement of any element.

A table can also be positioned left or right adjusted with text flowing around it (just like text around images; Section 2.17). Figure 3.11 shows a table (Ex: **FloatTable**) coded as follows:

```
<table style="float: left; margin-right: 1em;
              background-color: #def">
<caption style="font-weight:bold">Four Seasons</caption>
<tr align="center">
<td>Spring</td> <td>Summer</td> </tr>
<tr align="center">
<td>Fall</td> <td>Winter</td> </tr>
</table>
<p>Here are some text around the table ...  </p>
```

Again, just as for floating images (Section 2.17), the clear property can be used to place an element clear after a floating table.

3.8   TABLE WIDTH AND HEIGHT

The width and height of a table are automatically computed to accommodate the contents in the table cells. You may also explicitly suggest a width using the width attribute of table.

---

[2]Older browsers such as IE 6 do not support automargins, and you may have to resort to the deprecated center element.

The attribute `width="wd"` specifies the overall width of the table in pixels (`width="400"`) or as a percentage (`width="100%"`) of the available horizontal space. Use a percentage rather than a fixed length whenever possible.

If the suggested width is insufficient, the table will be made wider automatically. If the suggested width is wider than necessary, the excess width is distributed evenly into the columns of the table. The height of a table is determined automatically by the accumulated height of cells and cannot be specified.

By default, all cells in the same table column have the same width. The width of the widest cell becomes the column width. Similarly, all cells in the same row have the same height. The height of the tallest cell becomes the row height. The width and height of each table cell are normally computed automatically to accommodate the cell content.

But you can also suggest a desired dimension for a table cell with the style properties `width` and `height`:[3]

- `style="width: wd"`—Sets the width of the element to *wd*, which can be a fixed length or a percentage of the available horizontal space.
- `style="height: ht"`—Sets the height of the element to a fixed length *ht*.

Incidentally, the `width` and `height` style properties apply in general to any block element and replaced element. A *replaced element* is an inline element, such as an image, that is loaded from a given URL.

For example (Ex: **TableWidth**), the following is a table taking up 60 percent of the available width, with no cell padding or spacing (line A), centered horizontally (line B), and having a light blue background (line C). The four columns take up 10, 20, 30, and 40 percent of the table width, respectively (lines E-F). Cell contents are centered horizontally (line D). Figure 3.12 displays this table with two rows.

```
<table width="60%" border="1" cellspacing="0" cellpadding="0"    (A)
       style="margin-left:auto; margin-right:auto;               (B)
              background-color: #def">                            (C)
<tr align="center" >                                             (D)
<td style="width:10%">10%</td> <td style="width:20%">20%</td>    (E)
```

Figure 3.12 TABLE AND CELL WIDTH

10%	20%	30%	40%
10%	20%	30%	40%

---

[3]The `width` and `height` attributes for the `td` element have been deprecated.

```
<td style="width:30%">30%</td> <td style="width:40%">40%</td>    (F)
</tr>
</table>
```

The height of a table cell is the minimum height required to accommodate the cell content. The cell height can be set with its `height` style property (`height: 60px`) but will always be large enough for the cell content.

If a table becomes wider than the display window, a horizontal scroll bar will appear, and the user must perform horizontal scrolling to view the entire table. Because horizontal scrolling is one of the most unpleasant tasks for users, it is important to make sure your table fits well in a page and adjusts its width in response to different window sizes.

In summary, you set the `width` attribute of `table` and the `width` style properties for `td`s to control table width. Note that the attribute `width="300"` and the style declaration `width: 300px` use different notations. Unlike HTML attributes, length values for style properties must be given with units (Section 2.11). The `height` style property of `td` can only be set to fixed lengths. Width and height control are useful when applying tables to implement a layout grid for a page (Section 3.11).

Row and Column Spans

A table cell can span multiple rows and/or columns. You use the `rowspan` (`colspan`) attribute to specify the number of rows (columns) a table cell spans.

We have already seen the use of `colspan` (line 9 of the first code in Section 3.5). For a more complete example (Ex: **Spans**), let's look at how the table in Figure 3.13 is coded.

```
<table width="120">                                    (i)
<tr align="center">
 <td colspan="2"
    style="background-color: red; height: 40px">A</td>    (ii)
 <td rowspan="2" style="background-color: cyan">B</td>    (iii)
</tr>
<tr align="center">
```

Figure 3.13   ROW AND COLUMN SPANS

```
<td rowspan="2"
    style="background-color: yellow">C</td>                    (iv)
<td style="background-color: green;
    color: white; height: 40px">D</td>                         (v)
</tr>
<tr align="center">
 <td colspan="2"
    style="background-color: blue;
    color: white; height: 40px">E</td>                         (vi)
</tr>
</table>
```

The table has a total width of 120 pixels (line i). On the first row, cell A, which spans two columns (line ii), is followed by cell B, which spans two rows (line iii). Thus, the table has a total of three columns. On the second row, cell C, which spans two rows (line iv), is followed by cell D, which stays in a single row and column (line v). We don't specify the third cell for row 2 because that cell has already been taken. On the third row, cell E spans columns 2 and 3 (line vi), and that completes the table.

This example again shows control of the background color (lines ii and iv) and the foreground color (lines v and vi) for individual cells.

You can practice row and column spanning by making the mirror image of Figure 3.13 at the WDP Web site.

Rules between Cells

The rules attribute of table is not supported well by browsers. But you can still manage to place horizontal and vertical rules in tables without setting border="1". The frame="box" attribute puts a simple box around the table. The border style properties (Section 6.12) on individual cells can be used to piece together desired rules in a table.

For example (Ex: **Rules**), the table

```
<table width="150" cellspacing="0" frame="box">
<tr>
<td style="border-bottom: thin #000 solid">A</td>
<td style="border-bottom: thin #000 solid">B</td>
<td style="border-bottom: thin #000 solid"
    align="right">25.00</td>
</tr><tr>
  ...
</tr><tr>
  ...
</tr></table>
```

Figure 3.14   TABLE WITH HORIZONTAL RULES

A	B	25.00
C	D	35.00
E	F	45.00

with three rows coded entirely the same way results in the display shown in Figure 3.14.

3.9   GROUPING ROWS AND COLUMNS

Rows can be grouped by thead (a group of header rows), tbody (a group of table rows), or tfoot (a group of footer rows to be displayed at the end of the table). For example (Ex: **RowGroup**),

```
<table width="200">
<thead align="center" style="color: blue">
  <tr><th>Item</th><th>Description</th><th>Price</th></tr>
</thead>
<tbody align="center" style="color: green">
  <tr><td>Fr-01</td><td>Banana</td><td align="right">0.65</td></tr>
  <tr><td>Fr-19</td><td>Pineapple</td><td align="right">1.25</td>
  </tr>
</tbody>
</table>
```

has a blue thead row group and a green tbody row group (Figure 3.15). Thus, row grouping allows you to specify alignment and style attributes for a group of rows at once.

Figure 3.15   ROW GROUPING

Column grouping is also possible with the `colgroup` and `col` elements. Column groupings are given right after any table caption and before everything else in a table. With column grouping, width and alignment settings can be done for all cells in one or more columns at once. But support for column grouping varies among browsers.

For example (Ex: **ColGroup**),

```
<table border="1" width="300">
<colgroup span="2" width="40%" />              (I)
<colgroup span="1" width="20%" />              (II)
<tr> <td>A</td><td>B</td><td >25.00</td></tr>
<tr> <td>C</td><td>D</td><td >35.00</td></tr>
<tr> <td>E</td><td>F</td><td >45.00</td></tr>
</table>
```

specifies `40%` width (line `I`) for the first two columns and `20%` width (line `II`) for the third column (Figure 3.16).

The `colgroup width` gives the width for each column in the group. The value is a pixel number, a percentage of the table width, or a relative length expressed as n*, where n is an integer. A width `"2*"` is twice as wide as `"1*"`. The width `0*` specifies the minimum width needed by the column content. For example,

```
<table>
<colgroup span="4" width="2*" />              (III)
<colgroup span="3" width="1*" />              (IV)
<tbody>
    . . .
</tbody></table>
```

specifies each of the first four columns (line `III`) to be twice as wide as each of the next three columns (line `IV`).

You may also use the closing tag `</colgroup>` and enclose zero or more `col` elements within. A `col` element supplies alignment and width attributes for one or a span of columns.

Figure 3.16   COLUMN GROUPING

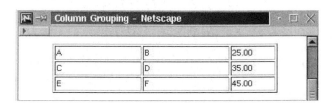

Table Structure

A `table` element follows a well-defined structure. It contains an optional `caption`, followed by zero or more `col` and `colgroup` elements, followed by an optional `thead`, an optional `tfoot`, and then one or more `tbody`. The `tbody` tags are optional when a table has one `tbody` and no `thead` or `tfoot`.

3.10   NESTING TABLES

You can put one table inside another easily. All you do is enclose a table in a `td` element of another table. All the complicated formatting and positioning will be done automatically.

Figure 3.17 shows a table (Ex: **Nest**) with one row containing two cells: a picture and an information table. The superstructure of the nested table is:

```
<table frame="box" cellpadding="0">
<tr valign="top">                                           (A)
<td><img src="honda.jpg" alt="honda odyssey"
        width="240" height="155" /></td>
<td>
   <!-- place the nested table here -->
</td></tr>
</table>
```

Note the vertical alignment used (line A) to ensure the image and the inner table will be placed correctly.

And the table nested inside is just another table structure:

```
<table  cellspacing="5">
  <caption style="font-size: larger; font-weight: bold">
      2004 Honda Odyssey EX</caption>
  <tr valign="top">
     <th align="left">MSRP</th><td>$27,210</td></tr>
```

Figure 3.17   TABLE NESTING

	2004 Honda Odyssey EX
MSRP	$27,210
TYPE	Front–engine, FW drive, 7–passenger minivan
ENGINE	3.5–liter, single overhead cam V6
MILEAGE	18 mpg (city), 25 mpg (highway)
TOP SPEED	NA. LENGTH: 201.2in
WHEELBASE	118.1in, Curb WT. 4398lb

© Paul Wang

```
<tr valign="top">
   <th align="left">TYPE</th>
   <td>Front-engine, FW drive,
      7-passenger minivan</td></tr>
<tr valign="top">
   <th align="left">ENGINE</th>
   <td style="white-space: nowrap">3.5-liter,      (B)
      single overhead cam V6</td></tr>
<tr valign="top">
   <th align="left">MILEAGE</th>
   <td>18 mpg (city), 25 mpg (highway)</td></tr>
<tr valign="top">
   <th align="left">TOP SPEED</th>
   <td>NA. LENGTH: 201.2in</td></tr>
<tr valign="top">
   <th align="left">WHEELBASE</th>
   <td>118.1in Curb WT 4398lb</td></tr>
<tr valign="top">
   <th align="left">CURB WT.</th>
   <td>4,398 pounds</td></tr>
</table>
```

Note the top vertical alignment for rows and left alignment for th. We also want to prevent line wrapping and preserve enough table width for the inner table. We can do this by using the nowrap declaration on a long line (line B).

3.11 USING TABLES FOR PAGE LAYOUT

A clear and attractive Web page usually follows an underlying *layout grid* (Section 5.12) to position various visual components in the page. The table element offers a practical way to create the underlying grid and to make it work for variable window sizes and screen resolutions. The ability to nest tables makes even complicated page layout easy to implement. Figure 3.18 shows a sample page layout with top and bottom banners, left navigation bar, links, spacing, and right margin. Follow these rules to define table-based alignment grids:

- Use width="100%" to ensure a table takes up all the available horizontal space.
- Use style="width:xx%" for all cells in some selected row so the column widths follow a designed proportion (Section 6.15). Pick a row that has the least row spanning. Don't provide widths in more than one row to avoid inconsistent settings.

Figure 3.18   A SAMPLE LAYOUT

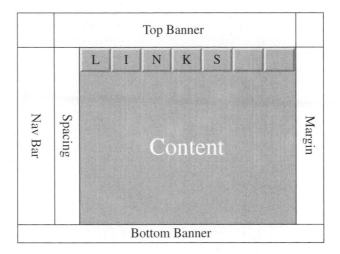

- Use attributes `border="0"`, `cellpadding="0"`, and `cellspacing="0"` to ensure that the underlying grid stays unseen.
- Use `valign="top"` so contents in cells on a table row align along the top edge of the row.
- Do not make the grid into one big table when using nested tables can simplify the overall structure.
- Mark the beginning and end of different parts with HTML comments such as

```
<!-- Top Banner Begin -->
<!-- Top Banner End -->
<!-- Content Begin -->
<!-- Content End -->
```

to make revising the page much easier.
- When piecing together a bigger picture with images in neighboring cells of a layout table, intervening gaps must be eliminated (Section 6.17).

To implement the grid shown in Figure 3.18, we can use a table of three rows and four columns. The third cell of the second row can contain another table for the cyan part (see color insert). The bottom banner may span all four columns.

3.12 PAGEWIDE STYLE WITH body

The body element contains the content of an HTML page. To organize page content, you place block elements inside the body container.

Style properties attached to the body tag affect the presentation of the entire page. For example

```
<body style="color:navy; background-color: white"}
```

asks for navy characters over white background for all child elements in body. A child element can override parent style settings by specifying its own style properties, as we have seen in the preceding sections and in Chapter 2.

An image can also serve as the page or element background. Usually, the background image is automatically repeated horizontally and vertically (like floor tiles) to cover the entire page. The background image may be stationary or scroll with the content. Use these style properties to manage the background image:

- background-image: *URL*—the *URL* links to an image (GIF, JPG, PNG)
- background-attachment: *how*—scroll or fixed
- background-repeat: *how*—repeat-x (horizontally), repeat-y (vertically), repeat (both ways), no-repeat

A search on the Web will turn up many sites with background image collections. Use background images only as part of the site's visual design to enhance communication, to increase readability, or to complement functionality. Make sure background-color is set to a color similar to the background image in case a browser does not support images.

To set page margins, use the style properties:

```
margin-top: length
margin-bottom: length
margin-left: length
margin-right: length
```

Similar to a printed page, margins give the content breathing room and are important page layout considerations. It is a good idea to use appropriate margins consistently for all pages in a site. For example, Ex: **BodyStyle**,

```
<body style="color:navy; background-color: white;
             margin-top: 40px; margin-bottom: 40px;
             margin-left:50px; margin-right: 50px">
```

sets the left and right margins to 50 pixels and the top and bottom margins to 40 pixels.

Other body style properties to set in practice include font-family, font-size, color, and hyperlink styles.

Consistently setting the style of the body element (Section 6.2) is important for the design unity (Section 4.5) of a site.

3.13   HEAD ELEMENTS

So far, we have focused on elements you place inside body to create page content. But HTML also allows you to attach administrative information, or *metadata*, for a page within the head element. The head element is required for each page, and it encloses administrative elements for a page. Let's now turn our attention to these elements.

The head must contain exactly one title element and zero or more optional elements:

- base—for page location (Section 3.16)
- style—for in-page style sheet (Chapter 6)
- link—for links to related documents such as favicons (Section 3.17) or external style sheets (Chapter 6)
- script—for in-page or external scripts such as a JavaScript program (Chapter 9).
- meta—for various page-related information (Sections 3.14 and 3.15)

The meta element has the general form

```
<meta name="some_name" content="some_text" />
```

and the values for *some_name* and *some_text* can be arbitrary. Well-established conventions for using meta are included in this chapter. The meta element is also used to place HTTP header information inside a page as illustrated by the page forwarding mechanism in Section 3.15.

3.14   SEARCH ENGINE READY PAGES

Search engines use *robots* to continuously visit sites on the Web to collect and organize information into indexed and easily searchable databases. This gives users a quicker and easier way to find sites they want. To attract the right visitors to your site, it is important to provide search engines with the correct information about your site. There are a few simple but important steps you can take to ensure your site is effectively and correctly processed by search engines.

Use these elements inside the head element to make your Web page search engine ready:

- `<title> ... </title>`—Supplies a precise and descriptive title.
- `<meta name="description" content=" ... " />`—Gives a short and concise description of the content of the page.
- `<meta name="keywords" content="word1, word2,  " />`—Lists keywords that a person looking for such information may use in a search.

- `<meta name="robots" content="key1, ..." />`—Tells visiting robots what to do: index (index this page), noindex (do not index this page), follow (follow links in this page), nofollow (do not follow links in this page), all (same as index, follow), none (same as noindex, nofollow).

  For a regular page, you invite the robot to collect information from the page and follow links to recursively index all subpages with

  ```
  <meta name="robots" content="index, follow" />
  ```

For a page such as terms and conditions of service, copyright notices, advertisements for others, and so on that you do not want indexed as content of your site, use

```
<meta name="robots" content="noindex, nofollow" />
```

to prevent such extraneous information from being indexed as representative of the type of information supplied by your site.

To further help visiting robots, you can place a robots.txt file at the *document root* directory of your domain. In the robots.txt file you can indicate that certain parts of your server are off-limits to some or all robots. Commonly the file is in the form

```
User-agent: *
Disallow: server-root-URL-of-dir1
Disallow: server-root-URL-of-dir2
```

List the URL relative to the server root of any directory that is useless for a robot to index (/pictures/, for example). Such a directory may be for images, CGI scripts, administration of your site, internal documentation, password-restricted files, and so forth.

The full details on the Standard for Robot Exclusion can be found at

www.robotstxt.org/wc/norobots.html

3.15 FORWARDING PAGES

Web pages sometimes must move to different locations. But visitors may have bookmarked the old location, or search engines may still have the old location in their search database. When moving Web pages, it is prudent to leave a forwarding page at the original URL, at least temporarily.

A forwarding page may display information and redirect the visitor to the new location automatically. Use the meta tag

```
<meta http-equiv="Refresh" content="8; url=newUrl" />
```

The http-equiv meta tag provides an equivalent HTTP response header (Section 1.14) for the page. The preceding meta element gives the response header

```
Refresh     8; url=newUrl
```

The effect is to display the page and load the *newUrl* after 8 seconds.

Here is a sample forwarding page:

```
<head><title>Page Moved</title>
<meta http-equiv="Refresh" content="8; url=target_url" />
</head><body>
<h3>This Page Has Moved</h3>
<p>New Web location is: ... </p>
<p>You will be forwarded to the new location
    automatically.</p>
</body></html>
```

The Refresh response header (meta tag) can be used to refresh a page periodically to send updated information to the user. This can be useful for displaying changing information such as sports scores and stock quotes. Set the refresh target URL to the page itself so the browser will automatically retrieve the page again after the preset time period. In this way, the updated page, containing the same meta refresh tag, will be shown to the user.

3.16   PORTABLE PAGES

Sometimes a page is downloaded from the Web and saved on your computer. But in all likelihood, the saved page won't display correctly in a browser because it needs images and other files that now can't be found. This happens because the hyperlinks to the needed images and files are relative to the original location of the page.

You can fix this easily by adding the base element in the header:

```
<base href="Full_URL_of_original_location" />
```

The base provides a browser with an explicit base upon which to interpret all relative URLs in the page. Now your saved page works as if it were in its original location.

If a site expects certain pages to be used after being downloaded, then those pages should have the base tag in place already.

Pages generated dynamically by CGI scripts can also use this technique to easily use images and links independent of the program location (Section 13.15).

3.17   WEB SITE ICONS

A Web site may define a small icon, such as a tiny logo or graphic, that is displayed by browsers in the URL location box. It is called a *favicon* and is also used in bookmarks and favorite-site listings. Figure 3.19 shows the favicon of the CNN site.

Figure 3.19 **LOCATION BOX SHOWING FAVICON**

Favicons can help brand a site and distinguish its bookmarks. To install a favicon on your site, follow these two steps.

1. Create a `favicon.ico` file for the icon and place it in the document root directory of your Web server. If the document root is not accessible to your site, then place `favicon.ico` at the top directory of your site.

2. Add a header element, for example

    ```
    <link rel="shortcut icon" href="favicon.ico" />
    ```

    in the `head` element for all `index.html` and other key pages on your site. It tells browsers where the favicon is located if it is not in the document root. It also allows different pages to use different favicons, although this is seldom done. You do not need to insert the `shortcut` link tag in pages if you are able to place the favicon in the document root.

To create the `favicon` file, you may use any raster graphics editor to get a 16-color 32 by 32 graphic. Then save it as an ICO (Microsoft icon format) file. Tools are available to convert `.bmp`, `.gif`, and other image formats to `.ico`.

3.18 FRAMES

Normally, a browser window displays one Web page. The `frameset` element, used instead of `body`, allows you to divide a window into rectangular regions, called *frames*, and display a different page in each frame. The identification, size, and scroll ability of each frame can be configured by attributes as well. Hyperlinks in one frame can change the displayed content in another frame.

Frequently, frames are used to divide a window into fixed-display and variable-content regions. Constant materials, such as a top banner, a table of contents, a logo, a navigation bar, and a copyright notice, can be placed in their own frames and made always visible. Clicking a link in a fixed frame can update the information displayed in the content-display frame. This situation is not new. Look at the top and bottom of your browser window. The title bar, the menu bar, the tool bar, and the status bar are always visible.

Frames can give a page a "broken-up" or a monotonous look. When the content frame shows a page not designed to display together with the fixed frames, the page can look terrible. Most style experts will tell you to avoid frames, and others will even say "misuse of frames is one of the ten worst problems on the Web today."

Frames can be effective in certain situations. But they should be used carefully and they are not for every situation. Be sure to use the correct XHTML DOCTYPE declaration

```
<!DOCTYPE html PUBLIC "-//W3C//DTD XHTML 1.0 Frameset//EN"
    "http://www.w3.org/TR/xhtml1/DTD/xhtml1-frameset.dtd">
```

for any frameset page. In such a page, the body element is not allowed. XHTML Strict, the future of HTML, does not support frames.

Using Frames

Use the rows and cols attributes of <frameset> to subdivide the browser window into frames. For example,

```
cols="25%,75%"    (first column width 25 percent, second column 75 percent)
rows="100,*"      (first row height 100 pixels, second row the rest)
```

The cols values specify the width of each column from left to right. The rows values give the height of each row from top to bottom. If both rows and cols are specified, a grid filled in row-major order is defined.

The value for rows (cols) is a comma-separated list of lengths in pixels (e.g., 100), percentages of the available window height (width), or relative units (e.g., 3*). For instance, cols="*, 3*, 200" gives 200 pixels to the third column and three fourths of what's left to the second column.

If a row or column is given a dimension of zero, for example,

```
rows="0,*"    (first row is hidden)
```

then it is hidden. If you also get rid of frame borders (see next subsection), then even a page that looks like a single window can be a frameset.

Within a frameset, you may place frame and frameset elements to fill the defined grid in row-major order. For example,

```
<?xml version="1.0" encoding="UTF-8" ?>
<!DOCTYPE html PUBLIC "-//W3C//DTD XHTML 1.0 Frameset//EN"
    "DTD/xhtml1-frameset.dtd">
<html xmlns="http://www.w3.org/1999/xhtml"
      xml:lang="en" lang="en">
<head>
   <title>A frameset example</title>
</head>
<frameset cols="*,*,*">                              (1)
  <frameset rows="*,200">                            (2)
    <frame name="frame1" src="a.html" />
    <frame name="frame2" src="graphics.gif" />
```

```
        </frameset>                                          (3)
        <frame name ="frame3" src="b.html" />                (4)
        <frame name ="frame4" src="c.html" />                (5)
    </frameset>                                              (6)
    </html>
```

The outer `frameset` (line 1) gets you three equal columns. The first column (lines 2-3) is occupied by an inner `frameset` that has two rows. The second column (line 4) is filled by frame3, and the third column (line 5) is filled by frame4 (Figure 3.20).

Note that the `frameset` is used instead of a body in an HTML document. The ‹noframes›...‹/noframes› element (placed between lines 5 and 6) can be used to supply alternative body for browsers that do not support frames. For example,

```
<noframes>
<body>
<p>This page uses frames, but your browser doesn't support them.
Here is a <a href="regular.html">no-frames version</a>. </p>
</body>
</noframes>
```

Frame Borders

Frames in a frameset are usually separated by borders that can be used to resize the frames. But in certain applications, you need to remove the borders around frames. This means not drawing the frame borders and eliminating the space between the frames. According to HTML, all you need to do is to set

```
frameborder="0"
```

Figure 3.20   FRAMES

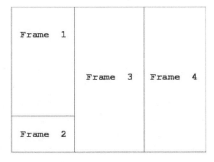

for all frames involved. Unfortunately, this is not enough for the current NN or IE. You also need to include the nonstandard `frameset` attributes:

```
<frameset  ...
    border="0"              (for NN)
    frameborder="0"         (for IE)
    framespacing="0"        (for IE)
>
```

The `frame` Element

The `frame` is an element to supply attributes. Neither end tag nor content is allowed.

- `name="id"`—Identifies the frame.
- `src="URL"`—Supplies content.
- `frameborder="flag"`—Enables or disables frame border; `flag` is 1 or 0.
- `marginwidth="pixels"`—Sets left and right margin width.
- `marginheight="pixels"`—Sets top and bottom margin height.
- `noresize`—Disables frame resizing.
- `scrolling="flag"`—Controls the display of scroll bars (`flag` is yes, no, or auto). The auto setting displays a scroll bar only when necessary.

The frame name must begin with a letter. The name allows you to specify a target frame for any element involving an `href` attribute—that is, a, area, base, form, or link.

Targets

The `target` attribute can be used in any element that provides a hyperlink. If the target is the name of a frame, then the referenced information is destined to that frame. Thus, in frame1, the link

```
<a href="index.html" target="frame3">homepage</a>
```

displays index.html in frame3 when clicked.

When displaying frames, the browser Location box shows the URL of the frameset document, not the URL of any page contained in any of its frames. Right clicking a frame and selecting Frame Info in the pop-up menu shows you the title and URL of the page in that frame. The browser Back and Forward buttons work on a linear history of pages visited. In the context of frames, the history includes the frame targets of the pages as well as their URLs. Thus, these buttons always work with or without frames.

Without an explicit `target`, the default target for a hyperlink is the frame containing the link. The `target` attribute in the `base` element can set the default target for all untargeted links in a page.

In addition to named frames, there are also *known targets*:

- `_blank`—a new, unnamed top-level window
- `_self`—the same frame containing the link, overriding any base-specified target
- `_parent`—the immediate frameset parent of the current frame
- `_top`—the full, original window (thus canceling all other frames)

The `_blank` target is often useful for displaying links external to a site. If you do use these targets, be sure the page is declared XHTML Transitional.

Frames: Pros and Cons

Although frames are tempting, their use does present a series of problems for a Web site. The combined weight of these problems is serious enough for many to consider frames to be the number one mistake in site implementation.

Here are the top-10 reasons.

1. A significant number of browsers do not support frames. Having to create the noframes version of the pages essentially negates the convenience frames offer. If the noframes versions are not provided, nonframe browsers will display a blank page.

2. Because a frameset uses a different navigation model than the generally understood hyperlink, many Web surfers can get confused by the behavior of frames.

3. The strength of the Web is hyperlinks. But an outside link to an internal page of a frame-based site does not work. The link leads to a page without its associated frames, making it an incomplete page.

4. When visiting a frames site, the browser Location box does not indicate the displayed page, just the frameset. When you visit different pages in such a site, the Location box stays the same.

5. Bookmarking internal pages of a frames site is difficult, and the saved links do not work due to reason number 3.

6. Links from a frames page to off-site pages always require a new top-level window. Otherwise, the outside page will be framed in the wrong context.

7. Search engines have trouble with frames because they don't know what composites of frames to include as navigation units in their index.

8. Browsers are likely to have page printing problems with a frames page. For example, each part on the screen that belongs to a different frame may be printed on a separate page.

9. Links to file types such as PDF that use browser plug-ins may have problems or be limited to a small area of the window.

10. Applications of frames use them primarily for banners and navigation bars. Such design gives a very ordinary and boxy look with one rectangle on top and one rectangle on the left. From a design standpoint, this is far from innovative or attractive. Fixed banners and navigation bars can be achieved with CSS positioning (Section 6.20), which is more flexible and does not limit you to the boxy look. Besides, the CSS approach has no frames-induced problems.

The frames construct does have its advantages. It updates only the contents, making pages appear more quickly. The different frames can be resizable and scrollable, making very lengthy navigation bars possible. Viewers can also reduce the decorative top banner to give more screen space to the content. Certain self-contained sites may wish to discourage outside links into the middle of the site. In this case, a frames organization can really help. There are situations that call for the use of frames. But a Web designer must think twice before deciding on a frame-based design.

3.19   SERVER-SIDE INCLUDES

The basic idea of *server-side includes* (SSI) is simple: You put special instructions, called *SSI directives*, inside a Web page for the Web server to include files or other information in the page. The page delivered to the client side results after the inclusions have been made.

To use SSI, you usually need to give the file the suffix .shtml or make the .html file executable:

chmod +x page.html

It depends on your server configuration, and you need to check with your server administrator.

SSI directives are placed inside HTML comments. For example,

```
<!--#echo var="DATE_LOCAL" -->        (Server-side date and time)
<!--#echo var="LAST_MODIFIED" -->     (Last modified time of page)
```

can be handy for including such changing information in a page. Make sure there is no space before the # character.

To include another file, use either of these two directives:

```
<!--#include file="relative-path" -->
<!--#include virtual="local-URL" -->
```

The *relative-path* is a file pathname relative to the directory containing the page. The local-URL is a URL relative to the page or to the server root (e.g., /footer or /cgi-bin/prog.cgi).

A Web site will often have many pages that share a common front part and perhaps also a back part. It is convenient to keep them in header and footer files included in pages with SSI (Figure 3.21). In this way, any changes in the header or footer will be very easy to make.

Modern hosting services also support PHP, a much more powerful server-side include and programming language that can be used for including files. Typically, PHP directives can be placed in regular .html files. This is an advantage over SSI because you don't have to use a different file suffix or add execution permission.

It is beyond the scope of this text to discuss PHP, but we do need to cover a few points. PHP directives are given in a Web page as follows.

```
<?php  . . . ?>      (Full syntax)
<?   . . . ?>        (Shorthand)
```

To include another file with PHP, use

```
<? include("filename"); ?>
```

The shorthand PHP syntax conflicts with the very first line required by an XHTML file

```
<?xml version="1.0" encoding="UTF-8"?>
```

which will cause a PHP syntax error. To server XHTML pages from a server that supports PHP, you need to send the first line this way

```
<? print('<?xml version="1.0" encoding="UTF-8"?>');   ?>
```

which instructs PHP to produce the first line verbatim.

Figure 3.21   FILE INCLUSION

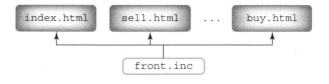

3.20   INTERNATIONALIZATION

The Web is international, and XHTML documents allow all ISO10646 (Unicode) characters (Section 3.2). The primary language for an HTML file is set by the `lang` attribute of the `html` tag (Section 2.1)

```
<html    ...       lang="language">
```

where *language* is a two-character (case insensitive) language code specified by the International Organization for Standardization (ISO) Code for the Representation of Names of Languages (ISO 639). Table 3.1 shows the two-letter codes of some languages. The `lang` attribute can be included with any element to indicate a language that may be different from the primary language of the page. Support for the `lang` attribute from browsers is increasing. The `dir` attribute specifies the base direction of *directionally neutral text*—that is, text without an inherent directionality as defined in Unicode or the directionality of tables: `dir="LTR"` (left-to-right) or `dir="RTL"` (right-to-left). A `RTL` table has its first column on the right of the table.

An international page may also use a different character set encoding. To specify the character encoding for a document, use both the encoding attribute specification on the `xml` declaration and a `meta http-equiv` element. For example,

```
<?xml version="1.0" encoding="gb2312"?>
```

and the `meta` element

```
<meta http-equiv="Content-Type"
   content="text/html; charset=gb2312"/>
```

indicate the simplified Chinese gb2312 character set (Figure 3.22). The two values should be the same. If they are different, the encoding setting in the `xml` declaration takes precedence.

Table 3.1   SOME TWO-LETTER LANGUAGE CODES

Code	Language	Code	Language
AR	Arabic	DE	German
ES	Spanish	EN	English
FR	French	IT	Italian
IW	Hebrew	JA	Japanese
RU	Russian	ZH	Chinese

Figure 3.22   A PAGE IN ARABIC, CHINESE, AND ENGLISH

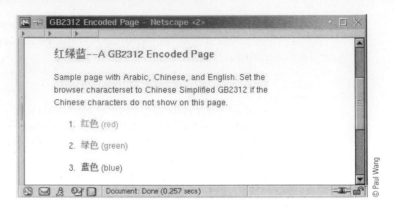

Examples of other charset settings are:

charset=utf-8   (Unicode)
charset=big5   (Traditional Chinese)

You can see many examples in the character set option menu of your Web browser.

3.21   COMMON PAGE ERRORS

Before publishing a Web page, we must check and ensure it is free of errors. Testing a page with a browser is a start. Of course, it is best to avoid errors in the first place.

We list some common Web page errors here to help you avoid them:

- Missing or extra end tags—If you use a regular editor, insert and delete the begin and end tags of each element at the same time. In this way, open and close tags always come and go in pairs.
- Missing / for elements without end tags—Always use the three-character " />" to close elements without end tags.
- Overlapping tags—For example, `<li><p>...</li></p>` is overlapping and incorrect. If you insert begin and end tags together, you can largely avoid tag overlapping as well.
- Missing quotation marks for attributes—For example, width=50 or width="50 is incorrect. Remember always to use quotation marks for attribute values. Insert both beginning and ending quotation marks at the same time to avoid missing them.

- Uppercase tag and attribute names—XHTML requires all tag and attribute names to be in lowercase.

- Incorrect element placement—Placing an inline element where only block elements are allowed, or vice versa, is largely tolerated by browsers but not allowed in XHTML. For example, br or img can't be placed as a direct child of body, and a list can't be a direct child of another list.

- Table rows with a different number of cells—This error is hard to detect. When constructing a table with multiple rows, consider duplicating the first row a number of times and then edit the rows for content and formatting. In this way, at least the cell count will be correct for all rows.

- Missing required attributes—For example, alt (for img and area), and name (for map) are required.

- Missing, incorrect, or useless title—The title element is required. Use a correct and descriptive title for each page. Keep in mind that browser bookmarks are named with page titles. Titles such as "Home Page" are useless.

- Broken links—Check for incorrectly entered links or links to pages that have been moved.

- Spelling and grammar errors—Proofread, copyedit, and use a spelling checker.

- Misspelled entities—These result in strange characters on the page. Make sure your entities are correctly typed and that pages don't contain extraneous characters from copy and paste or file transfer.

- Illegal characters—Characters such as < and & are not allowed directly. Use < only to start a tag. Use & only to start an entity. Everywhere else, use entities to introduce such characters.

3.22   PAGE CHECKING AND VALIDATION

After creating or extensively editing a page, you should first pass it through a spelling checker. The Netscape Composer has a spelling checker that understands HTML. On a personal computer, word processors such as Microsoft Word can be used to check spelling.

On UNIX systems, **spell** is usually available to check spelling. The **aspell** checker has an HTML mode, so it will ignore tags and focus on textual content.

The UNIX command

```
aspell -l -H < file.html > output-file
```

will produce a list of suspect words.

To see if your XHTML code meets standards, you can use the free HTML/ XHTML code validator available at W3C:

http://validator.w3.org/

You pick a document type and enter the URL of the page you wish to check. It is that easy. The result of the check lists any errors, their location in the source code, and their possible causes. The source code line numbers are also displayed to aid debugging. If the page to check does not have a URL, then you can use the "check uploaded file" feature to check files on your local hard drive. The WDP Web site offers hands-on experiments to guide you through the page validating process. Other validators are also available on the Web. Make sure you choose one that understands XHTML.

When validating your XHTML pages, it is necessary to keep in mind that there are three XHTML standards: Strict, Traditional, and Frameset. Each has its own DOCTYPE declaration (Section 2.4). If the page contains any deprecated tags (e.g., center or font) or disallowed attributes (e.g., bgcolor, topmargin, background, and target), then your DOCTYPE is XHTML Traditional. If the page uses frameset, then the DOCTYPE needs to indicate Frameset. Only when a page is free of such constructs can it have a chance to validate successfully under XHTML Strict.

Comprehensive page checkers examine many aspects of a Web page, including spelling, broken links, coding errors, coding improvements, and load time. They then suggest improvements. Commercial versions are available at places such as DoctorHTML

www2.imagiware.com/RxHTML/

and NetMechanic

netmechanic.com/toolbox/html-code.htm

Typically, these Web sites also offer to check your pages as a trial for their software or services. It is a good idea to check your pages thoroughly before placing them on the Web.

3.23 FOR MORE INFORMATION

XHTML 1.0 is stable, but XHTML is evolving. The W3C site (www.w3c.org) has up-to-date and complete specifications of XHTML recommendations.

The following Web sites are good references:

- XHTML 1.0 Recommendation: www.w3.org/TR/xhtml1/
- HTML 4 Elements: www.w3.org/TR/html4/index/elements.html
- HTML 4 Element Attributes:
  www.w3.org/TR/html4/index/attributes.html

• HTML 4 Reference at WDG: www.htmlhelp.com/reference/html40/

The WDP Web site has additional resources for HTML.

3.24   SUMMARY

HTML documents are international and may contain characters from a specified character set using a designated encoding. HTML entities use ASCII character sequences to represent non-ASCII characters. They make it easy to enter non-ASCII characters from ASCII keyboards.

The `table` element can be used for presenting information in tabular form and to provide page layout grids that contain cells for the placement of graphics and textual contents.

The full table superstructure looks like this:

```
<table>
<caption> ... </caption>                    (0 or 1)
<colgroup> ... </colgroup>                  (0 or more)
<col />                                     (0 or more)
<thead> <tr> ... </tr>   ... </thead>       (0 or 1)
<tfoot> <tr> ... </tr>   ... </tfoot>       (0 or 1)
<tbody> <tr> ... </tr>   ... </tbody>       (0 or more)
</table>
```

Table rows (`tr`) contain cells (`td` or `th`). A cell can span multiple rows and/or columns. Each cell has a padding and a spacing from neighboring cells. The table may have an outside frame as well.

Table cell contents can be aligned vertically (`top`, `middle`, `bottom`, `baseline`) and horizontally (`left`, `center`, `right`, `justify`, `char`) and have individual styles. A `td` may contain inline and block elements, including a `table`. Thus, tables can be nested. By default, a table is left aligned. However, it can easily be centered (`margin-left: auto; margin-right: auto`), floated to the left/right (`float: left`), or otherwise positioned on a page.

The `body` element provides a place to define pagewide styles such as margins, background and foreground colors. fonts, and background images.

Elements for the `head` can be used for page refreshing, page forwarding, favicon provision, and for making a page search engine ready. Other head elements attach style sheets and JavaScript programs to a page, as you'll see in later chapters.

Frames present several Web pages in designated areas in the browser window. They represent a departure from the window-per-page navigation model and can be confusing to users. The pros and cons discussed in this chapter allow you to choose the right situations to apply frames.

SSI (`<!--#...-->`) or PHP (`<?...?>`) codes enable you to include other files in an HTML file, making it easy to share common parts of pages on your site. This can be important for the site maintainability.

Avoid common HTML coding mistakes listed in this chapter and check/validate your pages before putting them on the Web.

EXERCISES

Review Questions

1. Which part of an XHTML file specifies the document language? The document character set? The document character encoding? Show the XHTML code.

2. Consider UTF-8 and UTF-16 character encodings. Why do we say UTF-8 is ASCII preserving?

3. UTF-8 seems to use more bits than UTF-16 for character at higher code positions. What advantage does UTF-8 have over UTF-16?

4. Name four ways to enter the Greek character π in a Web page.

5. Consider HTML tables. How do you center a table? Float a table to the left or right?

6. Are there situations when a correctly specified `table` has rows containing different numbers of `td` elements? Explain.

7. What attributes are available for `table`? `tr`? `td`?

8. Is it possible to specify the height of a table? The height of a table cell? How?

9. Consider frames. Why is it difficult to link to an internal page of a frames site?

10. List the elements and information you need to place in a page to make it search engine ready.

11. List some common HTML coding errors not listed in Section 3.21.

Assignments

1. Enter the mathematical formula $\sin(\pi^2)$ into a Web page and display the results.

2. College sororities and fraternities often have names with Greek letters. Enter your favorite sorority or fraternity name into a page.

3. Take a simple table with a caption and center the table. Does the caption automatically go with the table or do you need to center the caption separately? Experiment with different browsers and discover for yourself.

4. Consider specifying table cell `width` with percentages. What happens if the total adds up to more than `100%`? What happens if one or more cells have no `width` specified while others have percentages? Experiment and find out.

5. By using background colors for the table and the cells, you can make thin rules appear between cells that are sometimes more appealing than what you get with settings such as `border="1"`. Experiment.

6. Consider `cellspacing` and `cellpadding`. Is it true that they are set to zero if you do not set them? Explain.

7. When centering a block element such as `table`, what is the difference between

    `style="margin-left: auto; margin-right: auto"`

    and

    `style="margin-left: 20%; margin-right: 20%"`

    Experiment and explain.

8. Practice row and column spanning by creating an HTML table to present the mirror image of Figure 3.13.

9. Access the W3C XHTML validator and use it on some of your pages. Look at the results and fix any problems.

CHAPTER 4

Design Basics

HTML is a language for authoring Web pages. Together with CSS, HTML allows you to structure content and define presentation. But without a good design, no amount of coding will produce an effective and attractive Web site. There is no formula to creating good designs for Web sites or anything else. However, an understanding of design principles and what makes good and bad designs will go a long way to help you create better sites.

Web design is further complicated by changes from many directions. Technology is one major factor, and tools are another. As various political and economic winds continue to play a part in how we view and use the Web, it is safe to say that change on the Web may be the only constant. In an environment of perpetual flux, it may be difficult to find the constants that one can rely on. Luckily, the basic design principles are one of those constants, and they have not changed since their inception. The way designers have interpreted them has changed, and certainly styles continue to change, but tested and true design principles apply to the Web as well as to other media.

Since design is a mix of art and communication, many people think that "good taste," coupled with basic image processing skills and a little HTML, will equal a Web site—and to some extent, this is true. Unfortunately, being able to create and publish a Web site does not necessarily make it good. In fact, the old adage "a little knowledge is dangerous" can be applied here. For many novices who want to post their site to communicate with friends and family, this knowledge is fairly innocuous, although one may argue that this is the very reason for so many unattractive Web sites. However, professional sites, created for clients as part of an overall business or marketing plan, involve specific goals, messages, and products. They must go well beyond the simpleminded approach to be effective.

Many principles introduced in this chapter originated in print design and have long been used by designers, layout artists, production artists, art directors, and others working in the design profession. Their effectiveness has been tested in newspaper designs, annual reports, billboards, television graphics, movie title sequences, animation graphics, and multimedia. Each medium has influenced the other, creating a myriad of complex cultural icons and generating popular vernacular, which defines our culture. This rich heritage, stemming from their well-established print cousins, can and should be applied to Web design.

This chapter introduces basic design principles and explains how they apply to Web site design. The two-dimensional design concepts discussed include unity and variety, emphasis, focal point, hierarchy, symmetry, asymmetry, and contrast. Examples show how design principles apply to the Web for creating aesthetically pleasing sites.

4.1   WHAT IS DESIGN?

Design is the process of communicating and editing ideas in the visual arts. The designers' task is to convey an idea and communicate a message on behalf of their clients. For that idea and message to emerge, designers must rely on creativity and perception, as well as the basic principles and elements of two-dimensional form. These principles, such as figure-ground, contrast, grouping, proximity, similarity, continuation, and unity, provide the structure for elements such as point, line, and plane, or shape, color, texture, and space. The primary goal of design is to combine all these components into a harmonious whole to achieve unity.

4.2   DESIGN AND PERCEPTION

As designers, we have to be aware of many factors involved in communicating with our audience. These factors may sometimes be simple, such as regional and demographic information, whereas other factors, such as the emotional response of a target audience, may not be quite as easily determined.

Although most designers are not formally trained in psychology, there are a number of fundamental principles designers call upon to explain the working of visual perception. One such theory is *gestalt* theory, which states that the whole is greater than the sum of its parts. In other words, people perceive an object as a complete unit before they become aware of the individual components that comprise it. For example, a person looking at a poster of a child on a bicycle would not notice that the bicycle has 12 spokes on the wheels, that the child is wearing a button-down sweater with a coarse texture, or that the bicycle is positioned on a grassy path. The viewer would see a child on a bicycle first.

This theory of basic perception acknowledges the human mind's ability to organize, simplify, and unify what it sees. It is how we perceive and understand everything around us. Given that wholeness is something a mind seeks in order to perceive, it stands to reason that the designer's primary objective is to create unity. Figure 4.1 shows how we perceive the cross in the center before we see anything else.

Figure 4.1   **VIEWER SEES THE CROSS FIRST: A GESTALT**

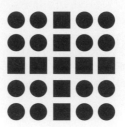

4.3   BRIEF HISTORY OF DESIGN ON THE WEB

Graphic design has been around for as long as people have tried to give structural order and visual form to ideas. Early graphic designers can be traced back to the Sumerian scribes who invented writing, Egyptian artisans who combined words and images on papyrus manuscripts, Chinese block printers, medieval illuminators, and 15th-century printers and compositors who printed early European books.

The emergence of a new medium, such as the Web, is not a new phenomenon. In 1760, the Industrial Revolution ushered in the machine age, creating an upheaval in technological processes and opening doors to mass communication. People at that time wondered how their lives would change in this brave new world just like they do today.

In 1990, the first Web browser or browser/editor called WorldWideWeb was designed by Tim Berners-Lee, working at CERN, the European Laboratory for Particle Physics, in Switzerland. It ran on the NeXT computer, allowing us to see simple Web pages for the first time. Other browsers soon followed. For example, Lynx is a text-only browser for UNIX that is still in use today.

Mosaic, an early browser, was developed to run on UNIX X11 workstations, Macintoshes, and Microsoft Windows personal computers. Web pages had essentially the same appearance on all computers, and the browser operated in very much the same way on all computers. Thus, WWW applications became independent of the computing platform used. Another thing that contributed to the popularity of Mosaic was that anyone could download it from the National Center for Supercomputing Applications (NCSA) server at no cost.

While the WWW was useful, the great explosion of the Web was a result of the development of the graphical user interface browser "Mosaic for X" (Marc Andreessen 1993) at NCSA at the University of Illinois at Urbana-Champaign.

Early Web designers were scientists and programmers who, out of necessity, had to play the multiple roles of researchers, writers, and designers. Then there were the techies who were the first designers because they knew how to use the medium, and their efforts were commendable. Scientists and programmers created many of the so-called first-generation Web sites. Many of these sites went online around 1995 and 1996.

Designers, or visual design communicators, as they are referred to in the profession, got on board the Web medium rather late and, in their initial efforts, created many "online brochures." Most did not embrace the medium, failing to see its potential and feeling limited by the restrictions that left them disappointed when compared to their beloved print media. With their large, slow loading images and graphical text, they tried to control the very things that made the medium unique. Many clients were happy with this solution, content just to be online.

The second generation of Web sites was slightly more sophisticated visually than the first. Many corporations realized that Web presence wasn't enough to actually do business on the Web, so they redesigned most of their first-generation sites. With the second-generation sites, we began to see more interactivity, the addition of Web forums, live chat rooms, more online forms, and mailing lists. Designers were challenged with organizing different types of information such as e-forms, using print forms as a model. That was a good place to start.

In December 1996, FutureWave Software sold FutureSplash Animator to Macromedia, and it became Macromedia Flash 1.0. By 2001, Flash underwent five versions as it evolved from a simple Web drawing and animation tool to a complete multimedia development package. Today, more than 325 million Web users have downloaded the Flash Player. This addition to the Web has changed the way many approach their design on the Web. With increased freedom to market their sites to Flash audiences, the Web has become a much more visually diverse environment.

In 1998, W3C recommended that CSS2 become a Web standard. This decision further opened doors to creativity with more precise typography and layout control. The ability to set kerning and leading will result in more refined text for clients who understood the value of clean, readable pages.

We've come a long way from the once static gray screen. In less than a decade, we have seen a fabulous metamorphosis. The future of Web design is bright and exciting.

4.4   ELEMENTS OF DESIGN

Design elements are the forms such as logos, icons, text blocks, and photos included in a composition. The elements must be grouped and organized to create meaning in a given two-dimensional space. Most designers group these elements or forms according to a set of guidelines for two-dimensional design known as the *design principles*. Thus, elements are the objects, and principles are the guidelines for placing the objects in a layout or a particular arrangement of elements, known as the composition. Together, they can produce many different visual effects that are discussed in this chapter such as contrast, hierarchy, focal points, unity, and visual balance. These principles are said to be the "tools" of visual designers. But as in any discipline, it is not enough to follow the rules mechanically. A designer needs to know how to create meaningful compositions. Understanding design principles is only the first step. The real learning begins when you immerse yourself in the design discipline and begin to see the world through different eyes.

One good way to learn about design is to examine how other designers have solved similar visual problems. What makes one particular design successful? Is it the way the colors are combined? Is it that concept and form work well together to communicate a powerful message? What is it about this particular design that you find intriguing? Begin to analyze successful designers' works. You will find many good examples in periodicals such as *Communication Arts*, *Graphics*, *How Magazine*, and *Print* magazine. These periodicals have been in circulation for many years and focus primarily on printed matter; however, in recent years, they have begun to feature Web design. Be sure to read about clients and their project objectives while you examine the final product to see how a designer arrived at a particular solution. Once you begin to get a sense of form and aesthetics, you will discover that your own ideas are beginning to take flight. And as you go further on this journey, you will begin to take more chances with your work and find solutions to problems that will become quite sophisticated. As with any process of creative discovery, design can sometimes be frustrating, but if you persevere, the outcome will be well worth it.

Point, Line, and Plane

Before we can discuss such elements as space, grid, value, shape, or color, we need to understand the fundamental building blocks of form: point, line, and plane. A *point* is the smallest element on the page regardless of its shape. It can be a letter, figure, word, or shape. A *line* is a mark whose length is considerably greater than its width. When a line is too thick to indicate movement, it has crossed the boundary and becomes a *plane*, or area (Figure 4.2).

Figure 4.3 shows point, line, and plane translation where all compositions can be broken down into these simple elements. This kind of an exercise is meaningful in demonstrating that all forms, no matter how complex in structure, can be broken down into these elements. Once you see this breakdown and the relationship between these elements, you will understand structure and the principles of design at work.

Figure 4.5, a simple line drawing translated from the photograph[1] in Figure 4.4, illustrates an arrangement of points, lines, and planes. The arrangement is created and controlled by the designer for a specific effect. Someone else may interpret this ship in a harbor differently with different line widths and lengths

---

[1] Work by Rick Zhang, graduate student, Kent State University.

Figure 4.2 **A LINE BECOMES A PLANE**

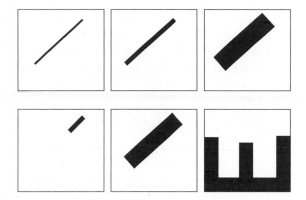

Figure 4.3 **DIGIKNOW HOME PAGE REDUCED TO POINT, LINE, AND PLANE**

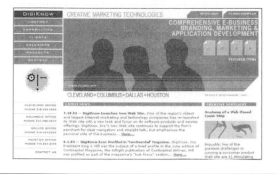
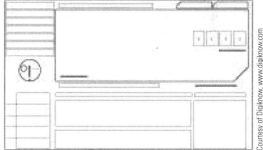

that emphasize different forms. By purposeful placement of basic design elements, an abstract image of a ship in a harbor can be created. There is beauty in this simple arrangement of elements—a concept that is often referred to as "aesthetics."

Space

Space in two-dimensional design refers to both the illusion of depth as well as the physical space in which designers manipulate compositions. Illusion of depth in space can be a powerful and dynamic device, inviting the viewer deep inside a composition. In any two-dimensional design, photography, or abstract design, size is the simplest way to create depth perception. In Figure 4.6, we see how the smallest squares appear to recede to the back, and the larger squares appear to be in the front of the composition.

Figure 4.4   SHIP IN HARBOR PHOTOGRAPH

Figure 4.5   LINE DRAWING OF SHIP IN HARBOR PHOTOGRAPH

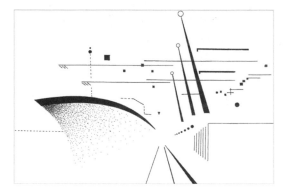

Figure 4.7, from fitch.com, is a good example of an existing Web site that employs size and value to create an illusion of space.

Overlapping is another device used to create the illusion of depth of space (Ex: **Depth**). One way this can be achieved is by the simple overlapping of elements shown in Figure 4.8 (left). Transparency and overlapping two forms can sometimes create an illusion of space; however, it is a more ambiguous way of dealing with depth. As illustrated in Figure 4.8 (right), it isn't completely clear which forms are on the top and which are on the bottom. Despite the unpredictability of the outcome, many designers have opted to use this device for creating depth, especially on the screen. Software tools such as Adobe Photoshop have become popular choices for designers who create depth on the screen as part of their vision. This effect is easily achieved and can be

Figure 4.6   **ILLUSION OF ELEMENTS RECESSION IN SPACE**

Figure 4.7   **SPACE BY SIZE AND VALUE**

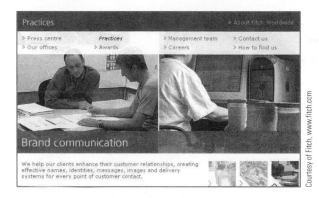

effective when used in moderation. An example of this transparency on the Web is shown at the top of Figure 4.9.

Space on the Web is unique because it is on a computer screen with its associated properties, such as the common 4:3 aspect ratio (Section 5.13) and variable color characteristics (Section 7.8). Furthermore, a Web page is displayed in a browser window whose dimensions and font sizes can be changed interactively by the user. These factors can be both disappointing and challenging for a designer. Knowing how to manipulate screen space in creative ways can be a valuable skill when designing layouts for the Web. It may mean cropping your photos in a new way or perhaps not cropping them at all. Figure 4.10 (www.pointinspace.com/www/hosting/enspace/), for example, shows the illusion of space created with horizontal format and sparsely placed images.

Figure 4.11 (from enspace.com) demonstrates an interesting crop technique (left) and creating depth through size, transparency, and overlap (right).

Figure 4.8 OVERLAPPING OF ELEMENTS AND ILLUSION OF TRANSPARENCY

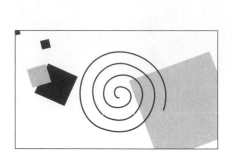

Figure 4.9 CONVENTION AND VISITOR'S BUREAU OF GREATER CLEVELAND: PROTOTYPE HOME PAGE

International Exposition Center, Cleveland, Ohio

Instead of taking the "techno" approach to everything new and innovative, why not try to make it seem more understated? Instead of drawing on the same old images from stock photo CDs, why not commission a photographer to take a unique photograph? Images do not always have to derive from photos. Look up a good illustrator whose style fits your concept and see your design solution in a whole new light (ronchan.com). The idea of transforming space on the screen is an illusion. We can never make screens into posters or sculptures, but as Web designers, we can push the limits of two-dimensional space, create fantastic illusions, and stretch our creative ideas into endless possibilities.

Figure 4.10   SPACE BY FORMAT AND LAYOUT

Figure 4.11   INTERESTING PHOTO CROP AND DEPTH CREATION

4.5   UNITY AND VARIETY

Unity is the presentation of a unified image. Elements such as type, graphics, and shapes agree with one another and are perceived in a congruent relationship. This relationship is often described as harmonious. The opposite holds true if these various elements are not harmonious or related, forming incongruent relationships and creating a vague or chaotic perception for the viewer.

The chess pieces shown in Figure 4.12 illustrate this idea using similar, but not identical, shapes. Even though each figure is different, it appears to be in harmony with the other chess pieces. The result is visual unity.

Ways to Achieve Unity

Unity can be achieved through

- proximity
- repetition
- continuation

Figure 4.12 VISUAL UNITY: CHESS PIECES SIMILAR BUT NOT IDENTICAL

© Photodisc./Getty Images

An important aspect of visual unity is that the whole must predominate over the parts; you must first see the whole pattern before you notice the individual elements. Figure 4.13 (left) has no unity (Ex: `NoUnity`). It appears as a series of squares thrown on a white surface. However, the center and right of Figure 4.13 both illustrate control of elements in a logical order.

Figures 4.13 (center) and 4.13 (right) are both examples that use a grid to align elements creating proximity and continuity. The viewer moves from top to bottom and from side to side in the composition. To further illustrate this point, let's examine a concrete example, like the kind you might see on the Web (Figure 4.14). This page from the Macromedia site (macromedia.com) uses a familiar Web layout consisting of top navigation bar, large image, rows of text with icons, and logo at the top left. Unlike many pages that use this layout, Macromedia designers adhere to a specific grid that consistently respects margins, alleys (space between text), and internal alignment like the kind you see between logo placement and headline.

Figure 4.13 UN-UNIFIED AND UNIFIED COMPOSITIONS

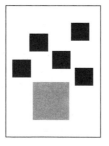 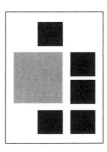 

Figure 4.14   **PROXIMITY AND SIMILARITY UNIFY A DESIGN**

Courtesy of Macromedia, Inc., www.macromedia.com

Continuation is the planned arrangement of various forms so that their edges are lined up; hence, forms are "continuous" from one to another within a design. A grid determines page margins and divides the format into areas used on successive layouts. Unlike intellectual unity, which can be understood as a collection of unified ideas that share a common theme but may not necessarily produce unity, visual unity is the construction of physical elements deliberately combined and observable to the eye. Figure 4.14 is an example of a well-designed grid, effectively used to align text and images, leading the eye in a logical motion from one point to the next. Notice the subtle relationship between logo placement and margins.

In addition to unifying elements within a page, we also need to unify different pages in a Web site. Thus, pages from the same site follow certain well-defined design rules and become easily recognized as part of the same site. Whether you're designing a site for entertainment, news, business, commerce, or education, the principle of unity is the same. But unity can manifest itself in many different ways (Ex: **WaysUnity**). Global brand and design consultancy Fitch:Worldwide have achieved unity in their Web site (Figure 4.15) through the use of large geometric shapes and colors. The focal point of the site is the image. Large, bold rectangles anchor the layout inside a prominent grid. The logo is downplayed inside and throughout the site. The IBM site (Figure 4.16) is unified through color, a strong use of horizontal lines and a defined grid. The IBM logo is clearly positioned in the left corner of the site, with plenty of contrast to distinguish it from the dark background.

Proximity, repetition, and continuation are all evidence of unity on the enspace site (Figures 4.10 and 4.11). The black horizontal bar, repeated throughout the site, serves both as a repetitive form tying the site together, as well as the main navigation bar. Carefully placed headlines, logo, and text are in logical visual proximity to one another, creating unity throughout the site. This is a good example of form following function.

Figure 4.15 UNITY THROUGH REPETITION OF SHAPES AND COLORS

Figure 4.16 UNITY THROUGH COLOR, HORIZONTAL LINES, AND LAYOUT GRID

Other elements important for site unity include font size and style, background color of pages, placement of navigational elements, style of hyperlinks, and consistency of layout formats.

It is a design objective to achieve unity but not total uniformity. There has to be a measure of variety to add interest and avoid monotony. So what is the right recipe for design? How much unity? How much variety? How is a designer to know? If design was as simple as following a recipe with a certain dash of this and a spoonful of that, we could quickly distribute those recipes, and there would be no reason to read the rest of this book. Unfortunately or fortunately, design is a creative process of discovery by which a solution emerges and designers embark on a journey every time they create a layout for a brochure, a book, or a Web site. The best designers often make this process look "easy" and deceptively simple.

Despite our need for unity in design, human beings are often drawn to images that are ambiguous, disturbing, puzzling, or unsolved. Consequently, designers are often compelled to create compositions that invite viewers to solve, re-create, or complete their design, thereby enticing viewers to participate in this creative process.

4.6   EMPHASIS, FOCAL POINT, AND HIERARCHY

An audience must have a place to begin when viewing a design and will select a starting point to begin to make sense of the visuals. It is the designer's responsibility to see that the viewer begins at a specific location on the page. That starting point in design is called a focal point, and it is the most prominent place in the hierarchical order or design. Following are examples of three simple devices designers use to create a focal point: isolation, size, and value.

In Figure 4.17, the first two compositions are un-unified. The third arrangement, however, uses the darkest square (value) to draw the eye to that square, which is positioned outside the established alignment pattern (isolation). This is an example of both value and isolation emphasis. Because that square is the darkest and the most isolated, it demands that we focus there first.

The three compositions in Figure 4.18 show the effect of size and proximity (Ex: **FocusSP**). In the left composition, the three different shapes are about the

Figure 4.17   FOCUS BY VALUE AND ISOLATION

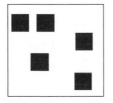 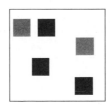 

Figure 4.18   SIZES AND FOCUS

same size. Therefore, all three shapes demand equal attention. Because of their grouping and position in the square, the three shapes are perceived as a unit. In the middle arrangement, the smallest circle, a point element, is the focal point because of its location. Even though the two other shapes are larger, they are positioned to be secondary in the composition. In the right composition, the circle is the largest element and the most isolated. This composition clearly shows the use of size and shape for a focal point.

A focal point may be different things depending on your message. It may be a logo, a headline, or an image that says something directly about the content of the page. In most commercial sites, the focal point tends to be a headline, company name, logo, or some other image that leads viewers into the text. Hierarchy is the order in which you see things. It is determined by the importance of each element and the primary message you want to convey. In Figure 4.19, we see the large photo as the focal point. In Figure 4.20, the headline is the focal point. In Figure 4.21, hierarchy begins with navigation, followed by content.

Although navigation is a critical component of any Web site, it shouldn't be the emphasis of each page. Think of navigation as a set of signs on the highway. They should be clearly visible and effectively communicate where to go, yet they should not overpower the landscape or the road.

Figure 4.19   UNLEASHED MEDIA: IMAGE AS FOCAL POINT

Courtesy of Unleashed Media, www.unleashedmedia.com

Figure 4.20   HOUSE INDUSTRIES HOME PAGE: HEADLINE AS FOCAL POINT

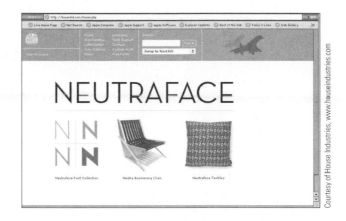

Figure 4.21   HOUSE INDUSTRIES: NAVIGATION AND CONTENT AS FOCAL POINTS

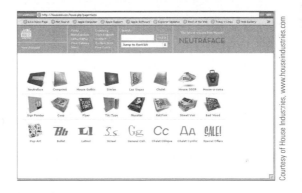

4.7 CONTRAST

We all learned about contrast very early in our lives. We came to realize that up was the opposite of down and that night was the opposite of day and that backward was the opposite of forward. In design, contrast can convey opposites, such as black and white, thick and thin, small and large. Very simply, contrast in design is visual opposition: taking the elements of design such as line, point, and plane or shape, color, texture, space, mass, and volume and giving them diverse treatment in one composition.

One of the fundamental components of contrast is the figure-ground relationship, often referred to as "positive and negative space." The figure-ground relationship also helps create depth in a two-dimensional space. In Figure 4.22 on the left, we quickly recognize that a black circle is on a white field (not a

Figure 4.22   DEPTH BY FIGURE-GROUND RELATIONSHIP

white space with a hole in it), and on the right, the black circle appears to be in front of the gray circle. We say the black circle is in the *foreground*, and the gray circle is in the *background*. The contrast between foreground and background helps people perceive depth, even though there is no actual depth on these two-dimensional surfaces.

What Is the Purpose of Contrast?

The basic purpose of contrast is to introduce visual variety into a composition and heighten the overall visual effect. Creating simple contrast is easy. Any mark made on a piece of paper or screen creates contrast by interrupting the white space. A single mark disrupts the surface and organizes the space in which it appears (Figure 4.23). However, to create a harmonious, unified, cohesive design, the successful designer must know how to manipulate contrast in many ways and in many complex situations.

The purpose of contrast on screen is to help the viewer distinguish between elements. Contrast creates depth and tension between elements. Contrast can create drama, and it can increase readability. Contrast can also speak loudly or softly to the audience.

Figure 4.23   ANY MARK DISTURBS THE PAGE AND CREATES CONTRAST

How Much Contrast Is Enough?

Although we cannot answer all these questions in this book, it's important to remember, when considering contrast, that a composition can quickly change from monotony to contrast and then back to monotony in a few easy steps. The challenge comes in knowing when and how much contrast to apply to each element. Figure 4.24 illustrates this point, but keep in mind that the concept also applies to more sophisticated design.

Contrast of Size

Size is the most basic and most frequently used form of contrast in design. The sheer size of a shape is almost always the first thing noticed. For example, a large screen, a large photograph, or a large boat is captivating first because of its size. Equally captivating is something very small, like a small sculpture or a painting with complex detail. Again, with a small object such as the middle example of Figure 4.25, the fist thing we tend to notice is its miniature quality. Extreme sizes are almost always captivating, and they demand our attention. For that reason, size is an important part of our overall visual awareness.

The size of an object is often regarded as small or large in comparison to the size of the human figure. Size, just like value, is relative. For example, if an ant is placed near a human figure, the ant would appear very small. On the other hand, if an ant stood next to a grain of sand, it would seem rather large. When an element is so small that its shape appears secondary, we call it

Figure 4.24 **PROGRESSION OF CONTRAST**

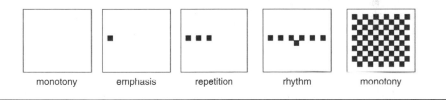

| monotony | emphasis | repetition | rhythm | monotony |

Figure 4.25 **CONTRAST OF SIZE**

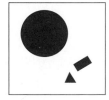

a "point." A few examples of how large and small elements can achieve size contrast in a comparison appear in Figure 4.25.

Herbert Matter's 1935 poster design for a Swiss ski resort is a good example of how extreme size changes the overall dramatic effect of a composition. In Figure 4.26, Matter could have created a size contrast between the skier and the man's face by making the two elements slightly bigger. However, he chose to push the size contrast to an extreme for a maximum visual impact.

To see how size affects contrast and in what quantities, let's look at one possible evolution of Matter's composition. Figure 4.27 illustrates what happens to the smallest element when it progressively increases in size. Starting with the original design and moving to the right, we see that relative contrast between the elements does exist in the second example, but it isn't quite as

Figure 4.26   HERBERT MATTER'S 1935 SWISS SKI RESORT POSTER

Courtesy of Staley & Wise Gallery, New York

Figure 4.27   MATTER'S SIZE CONTRAST PROGRESSION

dramatic as in the original. In the last example, the two elements begin to compete for space, and as a result, contrast virtually disappears.

Figure 4.28 shows how the progression works in reverse; when the largest element decreases in size, the same diminishing of contrast occurs. The two elements become equal, and contrast diminishes. Knowing when to increase or decrease the size of the elements in a composition is not an exact science; it is a design decision.

As we experiment with principles and develop a sense of space and form, decisions on the formal aspects of composition will become easier and more successful. One way you can develop this sense is by enlarging a single element in the layout. Seeing all parts of the layout in a new arrangement may stimulate different thinking, and new ideas may emerge. Think about how different your living room would look from another vantage point. For example, a crawling baby may see nothing but legs, shoes, and bottoms of furniture from his vantage point. For him, space is arranged very differently than for adults. Just get down on your hands and knees and see what a different world it is! A giant looking at the same room may see tops of heads, small moving creatures, and tiny objects for creatures to sit on. Changing your vantage point may change your thinking about form, and looking at extremes is sometimes a good place to start.

On the Web, an example of contrast of shape can be seen in the *Communication Arts Magazine* site (Figure 4.29). The strong, rigid, geometric forms contrast well with the soft, organic image of an eye. Adding further to the drama is the contrast of dark and light values in two shades of blue (see color insert).

Contrast of Value

Value is another vehicle for controlling contrast. It refers to the relative darkness or brightness of an object. At one extreme is white and at the other is black. All the tones of gray fall between these two poles. Value is often referred to in relation to color, but for our purposes, we focus on black and white. In traditional

Figure 4.28   MATTER'S SIZE CONTRAST PROGRESSION IN REVERSE

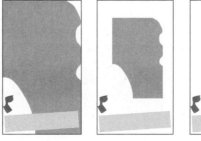

Figure 4.29 *CA MAGAZINE:* **CONTRAST OF SHAPE**

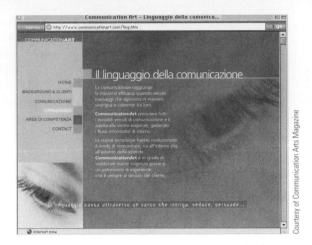

Courtesy of Communication Arts Magazine

fine art, value is used to model three-dimensional forms and to indicate light sources. Designers, on the other hand, use value almost exclusively to indicate lightness or darkness on flat shapes.

Depending on the composition, contrast in value can range from dramatic black and white to various shades of gray for more subtle contrasts. A designer must understand the control of value because it means control of contrast and, hence, control of the impact of the overall design. Many times, black and white alone may not be enough to create the interest you want. Gray tones can be an excellent choice for adding a wide range of values and richness to the composition.

All elements in design affect one another. Dark values affect light values, and white creates tension against black, but value actually changes according to its surroundings. For example, in Figure 4.30, you can see how the middle

Figure 4.30 **SIMULTANEOUS CONTRAST**

value gray appears darker on a light gray background but appears lighter on a darker background. This is called *simultaneous contrast*.

Simultaneous contrast is important because it urges us to make careful choice in the placement of elements and to be sensitive to the subtleties in value. Contrast in value is critical on the Web, especially between foreground and background, because if there isn't enough contrast, the viewer will not be able to distinguish between elements, and design will appear "flat," or lacking in impact. Figure 4.31 is a good example of "flat" design. All the elements such as the headline, links, feather image, and background are about the same size and all demand equal attention, which results in lack of hierarchy. The poor choice of background pattern creates difficulty in reading.

Contrast of Shape

To understand contrast through shape, we must first understand the concept of shape. *Shape* is a word that defines two-dimensional design as an area created by an enclosing boundary defined by outer edges. The boundary can be a line, a color, or a value change. Value refers to the relative lightness or darkness of an object. The word *shape* describes two-dimensional visual elements. In a three-dimensional mass, sometimes called *volume*, the word *form* is used instead. It's important to remember that every three-dimensional form has a counterpart shape in a two-dimensional space. For example, a cube has an abstract counterpart we call a square. The existence of such counterparts allows us to treat three-dimensional forms as abstract elements in a two-dimensional space. This book will deal primarily with simple, abstract, geometric shapes in two-dimensional design; however, the concepts investigated here may be applied to any form or shape in any environment.

Contrast of shape can be achieved by comparing one type of shape to another, but the most dramatic contrast occurs when one shape is compared to

Figure 4.31   LACK OF VALUE AND SIZE CONTRAST

© Sanda Katila

Figure 4.32   CONTRAST OF SHAPE

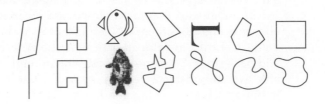

Figure 4.33   SAN FRANCISCO MOMA: CONTRAST OF SHAPE 1

© San Francisco Museum of Modern Art

Figure 4.34   SAN FRANCISCO MOMA: CONTRAST OF SHAPE 2

© San Francisco Museum of Modern Art

a completely opposite shape. Examples include a curvilinear shape contrasted with an angular shape, a geometric shape contrasted with an organic shape, or even an abstract shape contrasted with a representative shape (Figure 4.32).

In a design with two or more elements of the same size and approximately the same shape, not only is the contrast minimal, but the visual impact also tends to be confusing. On the other hand, when shapes are distinctly different from one another, contrast is easier to achieve.

Figures 4.33 and 4.34 are good examples of this shape contrast on the Web. The San Francisco MOMA (Museum of Modern Art) does an effective job of contrasting a simple, open line graphic at the bottom of the page with a large, flat shape containing an image. In this case, the image is curvilinear, which makes for an even more striking contrast. Figure 4.34 is another good example of this shape contrast where the large rectangular photo containing a strong organic shape is contrasted with the three circles on the left. The combination of different shapes ranging from capital letters to the rectangular logo (right) to the small circular icon (bottom left) offers a range of shapes providing contrast of shape on the page.

4.8 VISUAL BALANCE

All compositions, whether in fine art or graphic design, are composed of structures that appear to have visual weight. That perceived visual weight can be seen in clusters of elements which, when grouped together, are perceived as "heavier" than the isolated elements. Large, dark areas may also be perceived as heavier than their lighter, smaller counterparts. When a composition appears unified and has a seemingly comfortable amount of visual weight throughout a space, it is said to be in balance.

Two of the most common visual balances in design are known as *symmetrical* and *asymmetrical*. Symmetrical balance, often seen as more formal balance, is achieved by juxtaposing elements in equal amounts to achieve a mirrorlike balance. Symmetry can appear quite pleasing in many compositions. For example, one of the most common types of symmetry is the traditional wedding invitation with its centered axis and text placed on the page, centered from left to right.

Asymmetrical balance is markedly different because it is not as obvious or as easily detected as symmetrical balance. An example of this kind of balance can be seen in Figure 4.35, where the small dark element is directly juxtaposed to the large light element creating a visual balance that is not exact, yet somehow both halves seem in balance.

Asymmetrical design is often more difficult to achieve because it requires designers to go beyond the obvious and create a more sophisticated, less predictable solution. A less predictable solution may be more desirable because it involves the viewer with content for a longer period of time. Visual balance

Figure 4.35 **SYMMETRY AND ASYMMETRY**

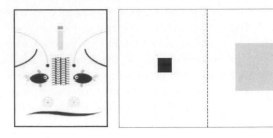

© Sanda Katila

Figure 4.36 **SYMMETRICAL BALANCE**

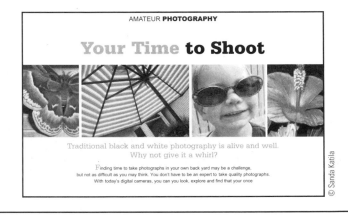

© Sanda Katila

Figure 4.37 **ASYMMETRICAL BALANCE**

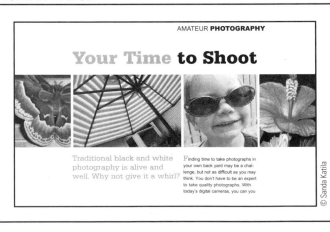

© Sanda Katila

Figure 4.38   **DIGIKNOW (ORIGINAL) HOME PAGE**

Figure 4.39   **DIGIKNOW (ORIGINAL) WEB SITE INSIDE PAGES**

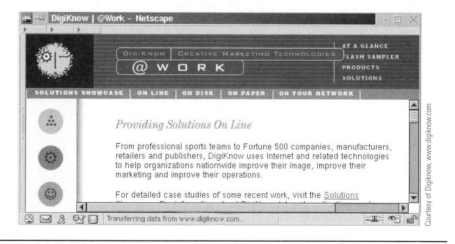

can be adjusted in every layout depending on the effect one is trying to achieve, as illustrated in Figures 4.36 and 4.37.

Figures 4.36 and 4.37 use identical headlines, subheads, text, and images, but Figure 4.36 is symmetrical, and Figure 4.37 is asymmetrical. Although neither design is exceptionally exciting, many people would say that the asymmetrical design is slightly more interesting and maybe less predictable than its symmetrical counterpart.

Figure 4.40   SYMMETRICAL BALANCE

Most commercial Web sites have asymmetrically balanced internal layouts such as DigiKnow's original site. Even though the entry to the site was symmetrical (Figure 4.38), the subsequent pages were asymmetrical (Figure 4.39).

Although this rule may be applied to many sites, let's not forget that alignment alone can't make good design. There are symmetrical layouts on the Web (www.mattmercer.com) that are dynamic and quite powerful (Figure 4.40).

Although most designers would not mix asymmetry with symmetry in the same layout, it can be done. Figure 4.41 (www.stephenjshuman.com) shows examples of this kind of combined balance working effectively in this situation. When deciding on visual balance, remember your message, your voice, and the big picture you're trying to convey.

Figure 4.41   SYMMETRY PLUS ASYMMETRY OF TYPE

4.9 SUMMARY

Design is a process that involves creating and communicating ideas or concepts through form. Designers' primary role is to create perception in their viewer's mind through form. This perception is based on the gestalt theory, which states that the whole is greater than the sum of its parts, meaning that viewers perceive the entire design before they notice the details that make up the whole.

We were introduced to the principles of design such as hierarchy, contrast, focal point, and visual balance such as asymmetry and symmetry. We also learned ways to achieve these principles in a two-dimensional space.

Designers use a variety of elements to create forms. These elements can all be distilled into point, line, and plane in a given space. We have learned several ways to manipulate that space through devices such as overlapping, transparency, and perspective. Understanding basic elements and principles alone will not make you a good designer, but it is the first step in understanding how form can be manipulated to create perception and communicate ideas.

Unity in design is desirable and is something designers seek to achieve in a two-dimensional space, as well as on the computer screen. Unity alone may become monotonous and requires variety to temper design. And a combination of unity and variety achieves aesthetically pleasing design and visual balance.

Because the authors consider contrast to be one of the most important design principles, this chapter focused on three important kinds of contrasts: contrast of size, value, and shape. Design styles, variations in aesthetics, and popular culture have had a significant impact on style in the last century, but basic design principles have remained constant. Emphasis, focal point, hierarchy, and contrast continue to play a significant role in Web design.

EXERCISES

Review Questions

1. One good way to learn about design is to examine how other designers have solved similar visual problems. Select a Web site that you think is aesthetically pleasing and well designed. Applying the principles that you have learned, list specific things that make this design successful. Here are a few suggestions on what to look for:

   - What about this particular design do you find intriguing?
   - Why do you think this design is successful?
   - What is your perception of this design? Why?
   - Describe how the design is unified.
   - Is the visual balance symmetrical or asymmetrical?
   - What is the focal point of the design?

- What is the hierarchy? Describe what you read first, second, third, and so on.
- What kind of contrast does it use: size, shape, value, or all three?
- Does the design use a grid? Find it and show how it was used.
- How does the crop of the photos or other images impact the overall design?
- Did they use perspective or other depth creating devices to draw you into the image?

Assignments

1. Creating simple unity: Figures 4.13 (center) and 4.13 (right), were created from Figure 4.13 (left). Using the exact same elements found in Figure 4.13 (left), create a variation of this design. Test your skill in arranging and organizing elements in a simple space by adding order to disorganized elements. Strive to create visual unity.

2. Using the grid: Refer to the DigiKnow page (Figure 4.3). Using the exact same grid shown there, create a variation on that design. Consider rearranging the various elements in this design to see how it affects the visual impact.

   - Change the focal point by enlarging or reducing images.
   - Enlarge and reduce the type.
   - Switch to a different color.
   - Reposition graphics and type on another part of the grid.

3. Creating asymmetry: Refer to Figure 4.36. Find one symmetrical layout of your choice on the Web. Change it to an asymmetrical design. Try to create as many variations on that design as you can.

4. Cropping photos: Choose a particular company for your hypothetical Web site. Say you choose a computer store. What images do you want to show on your site? Most people have seen images of computers, software, monitors, keyboards, and so on. What can you do with a photo crop to make these products exciting? How can you make the image dynamic and fresh? Can you effectively reveal the product and still make it unpredictable? Find as many images as you can and crop them in a more dynamic way.

5. Creating contrast: Find two pages on the Web, each from different sites. Page 1 uses good contrast of size, shape, or value, but page 2 does not. Compare and contrast the two sites. Why is the first one successful? How was this achieved? What devices did the designer use on page 1? What devices did the designer use on page 2? What can be done to page 2 to improve it? Try to redesign page 2 to more successfully use contrast of size, shape, value, or all three.

6. Object translation—point, line, and plane (problem developed for the Intro-
    duction to Graphic Design course at Kent State University, School of Visual
    Communication Design): Use the examples in Figures 4.4 and 4.5 to construct
    the following:

    (a) Begin by choosing a black-and-white photo or copy in black and white a
        color photo.
    (b) Paste the photograph on Bristol board and cover it with three layers of
        tracing paper.
    (c) Isolate the points on one layer of tracing paper, isolate the lines on the
        second, and isolate the planes on the third. Be sure to select as many of
        these elements as possible.
    (d) Take another piece of tissue paper and begin constructing an asymmetrical
        design using the elements collected in step c.
    (e) Your objective is to come up with an aesthetically pleasing composition
        that uses the following principles of design: contrast of size, value, and
        shape, hierarchy, and asymmetry.
    (f) Once you have decided on the final design, transfer it from tracing paper
        to the Bristol board. Using a thin, black marker and ruler, draft the final
        composition onto the Bristol board.
    (g) Critique the work after placing everyone's project on the wall.

## CHAPTER 5

Information Architecture, Page Layout, and Typography

Design refers to the overall process of communicating and editing ideas in the visual arts. *Layout*, however, is the actual arrangement and placement of textual contents and images in a two-dimensional space. Chapter 4 introduced basic design principles that provide a basis for creating page design. This chapter takes those principles and applies them to page layouts.

Many, regardless of their background, can easily grasp the design principles. They can critique Web sites, pointing out the successes and flaws, using the correct concepts. A more difficult task is to create aesthetically pleasing layouts that communicate effectively. Materials presented here can help you get started with creating effective and attractive layouts.

Layouts deal with visual presentation of information. But we must first collect and organize the information for a Web site and design a logical information structure for effective delivery to the intended audience. How the information is broken into manageable segments and how the segments are interconnected are important considerations for a Web site. This is information architecture (IA), and it must be addressed before the page layout stage.

This chapter serves as a primer, an overview for layout creation, with practical tips on how to get started. Keep in mind that almost every topic discussed here, such as IA, typography, perspective, spacing, readability, and layout grids, are broad topics that are in themselves complete areas of study. Supplemental materials and suggested readings can be found on the WDP site.

5.1 LAYOUT OVERVIEW

The Starting Point

Layouts, or the formal arrangements of elements, emerge after you have developed the overall design for the project. This means that you already have the design concepts or ideas at hand. To create page layouts for a Web site, you begin with defining its *information architecture* (IA), a blueprint for the site's information delivery, organization, and functionality. The visual communication design of a site must follow and enhance its IA. We recommend going through a sequence of steps in developing the IA and creating the actual layout visuals.

Layout tasks include: *brainstorming*, *thumbnails*, *comp*, and *graphics production*. These are explained briefly in this section, leaving in-depth coverage for later sections.

Let's begin with brainstorming. Brainstorming means generating as many ideas as possible and then writing them down. Try not to edit while thinking, regardless of how implausible or outlandish an idea it may at first appear. Once the list is completed, go back and consider all viable options. Fine-tune your ideas later.

The next step is the so-called thumbnails in which the same process is repeated, but this time, designers draw small, postage-stamp layouts that visually represent ideas. These thumbnails are drawn quickly in pencil or black marker on white layout paper (Figure 5.1).

It is not unreasonable to do as many as 10 to 20 different thumbnails before choosing a final direction. Again, try not to edit unreasonable ideas because this stifles the creative flow. Implausible ideas may often lead to good concepts later.

After completing the thumbnails, you then go on to the comp, or the comprehensive layout stage (Figures 5.2 and 5.3). This is a revised, more complete layout that can be created at half or full size in full color. In this stage, a designer determines margins, organizes space, determines grids (Section 5.12), and considers proportions, colors, and logo positions. Finally, you add color, photos, and whatever other elements may be necessary to complete the final comprehensive layout, which will then be presented to the client (Figure 5.4).

Clients will often make changes in copy, colors, size of photos, size of logos, and so forth. Be sure to show key pages in the site such as the home page, main menu page, main section pages, order forms, and site map. After

Figure 5.1   THUMBNAILS: SMALL, QUICK DRAWINGS

Figure 5.2 CVB COMPREHENSIVE LAYOUT 1

Figure 5.3 CVB COMPREHENSIVE LAYOUT 2

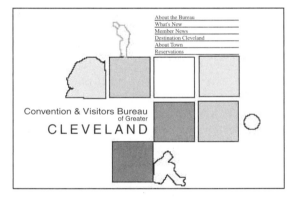

client approval, which may take several revisions or more, designers can begin constructing graphics, page layout, and page templates for the site. This production process will be discussed in Chapter 11.

5.2 WEB SITE ARCHITECTURES

A Web site is the storefront of a business or an organization on the the information superhighway. Just as different brick-and-mortar stores have different architectures, so should different Web sites. The information architecture must be designed effectively to achieve the mission of the site.

Figure 5.4   CVB FULL-COLOR COMPS

International Exposition Center, Cleveland, Ohio

© Photodisc/Getty Images

Web site architecture deals with the structuring, the relationship, the connectivity, the logical organization, and the dynamic interactions among the constituent parts of a site.

Within each Web page, the placement, layout, visual effect, font, and style of *copy* (content) are also important but may be considered more "interior decoration" rather than architecture. However, architecture and interior/exterior decoration are intimately related.

When a Web site architecture replicates familiar real-life architectures, orientation and navigation become obvious and intuitive. Web site architecture considers:

- organization to support Web site goals and requirements
- attractive and interesting presentation for the target audience
- structure and components in competing sites
- convenient navigation and customer orientation
- logical and efficient arrangement of components
- structure to support easy site maintenance
- requirements and techniques for implementation

There are many familiar information architectures that can be good models for structuring a Web site:

- A *book model* with table of contents, chapters, sections, and so on.
- A *newspaper model* with front page, headlines, sections, and quick index.
- An *organizational model* to reflect the departments and administrative hierarchy of a company or business: manager, customer service, marketing, sales, personnel, and so on.

- A *museum model* that has an entrance, a waiting/ticketing area, main exhibits, and exit.

- A *department store model* with an entry directory of goods and services and departments; each department has its own specific items and directional signs.

- A *hierarchical model* in which information is organized into a "family-tree structure."

- A *central dispatching model* or a *star topology* in which a main contact point directs visitors to different parts of the site.

- A *connected graph model* that has no particular defined entry into the site and all pages lead naturally to all other pages.

- A *linear model* in which information is organized in a sequence of previous and next pages.

- A *circular model* in which each page leads to the next, but the last page also leads to the first.

- A *distributed model* in which a site consists of subsites independent of one another and maintained by different departments of an organization.

- An *audience-oriented model* in which different types of site visitors are immediately directed to different parts of the site. The most common business of the customers is prominently displayed for easy access.

- A *catalog model* in which an extensive listing under different categories is available. An index and a search function help users find the items or information desired.

- A *library model* with circulation desk, card catalog, and downloading of extensive information on specific topics.

- A *map model* that has information connected to parts of a diagram or map for intuitive navigation.

A site can use a combination of models to achieve the most effective and logical organization.

5.3   INFORMATION ARCHITECTURE

A common mistake is to begin creating Web pages before doing sufficient groundwork on the information blueprint for a site. You first need to create the site's information architecture, or IA. The six concrete steps to IA are: (a) define goals, (b) define audience, (c) create and organize content, (d) formulate visual presentation concepts, (e) develop site map and navigation, and (f) design and produce visual forms.

We discuss these steps in this section and then apply them in a case study for the Convention & Visitors Bureau of Greater Cleveland (CVB) Web site (Section 5.4).

Step 1: Define Goals

The first step involves surveying key people to get a clear idea of what should appear on the site. Create questions to determine the site's mission and purpose by involving everyone in the creative process. Next, you should define the scale of your project and time frame for completion. How do you obtain these goals? Call meetings with key players; prepare an agenda and questions; talk to client employees one on one and record their responses; find out their thoughts, ideas, and opinions; get approval from key people.

Here are sample questions that may help you reveal the true objectives of the site:

1. What is the mission or purpose of the organization? Read the mission statements and business plans. Review the client's literature. Remember that the client's mission may change with time.

2. What are the short- and long-term goals of the site? Key people may not be thinking in the long term. Their immediate need may be to get the site up and running. Look toward the future; accommodate growth and change.

3. Who are the intended audiences? Inadequate analysis in this area is the number one mistake made in designing sites.

4. Why will people come to the site? For the first time? For repeat visits?

5. Does the site provide a well-defined service or sell specific products?

6. Does your client have an existing site? Find this out now.

Be sure to write down all answers and prioritize objectives in order of importance. Group goals into categories and have people rank the importance of each category separately. By doing this step, you will establish a clear set of goals that will be used to design the site. Be sure to share these with your client and the employees involved in key decisions in the company.

Step 2: Define Audience

The purpose of this step is to determine who your users are and what their goals and objectives are. This means that you need to define user experience and understand how users will react with the site. It is helpful to write scenarios for all intended audiences. Scenarios are stories that describe the steps someone may take in using the site. Scenarios define the users' experience and enable designers to better visualize and connect with their audience. A good scenario depicts the activities, moves, and experiences of a possible visitor to the site.

Writing scenarios may seem like a frivolous task, but be assured, it is no such thing. In fact, it may be the single biggest factor in defining the user experience.

You may be uncertain how to begin. Here are some simple guidelines to follow. Refer to the audience list gathered in IA step 1. Create a set of users who represent the majority of visitors. Depending on the size of the site as well as the audience, determine how many user scenarios are needed. Write a scenario for each user: name, background, and task to accomplish; use a task from your list of audience needs and goals. Discuss the scenarios with your team members and with potential visitors. Once you have good scenarios, use them to define content and functional requirements. Next, prioritize each audience group, compile results, and share them with key people. Get approvals from the client.

The last step in defining your audience is knowing your competition. To be aware of what your competition is doing, list your competitors. Some criteria for judging competition may include download time, page size, design, and "feel" of site. To conclude this step, you may write a summary of the target audience and include it in your report for steps 1 and 2.

Step 3: Create and Organize Content

Most of the time, programmers and designers are not responsible for creating content for clients. Content, in this case, refers to written text and images that appear on the site. Text is usually written by marketing people, copywriters, or public relations staff on your team or the client's team. Images may be supplied by the client or generated by designers. There is more on generating images in Section 11.3.

It is your job as a designer to organize content into major sections. In the initial stages of development, you need to answer two questions regarding content: What content does the site need? What functionality will be required? Then, you need to create a content and functional requirements list on which you label and group content.

Here is a list of sample questions that may help you determine the functional requirements for the site:

1. Which pages will be static and which dynamic?
2. What will be the function of these pages?
3. What transactions will users perform?
4. What about copyright notices and privacy statements?
5. What about membership rules, member logon pages, sign-up pages for email newsletters, and other pages involving forms or transactions?

Complete and prioritize the content and functional requirements list. Rank the importance of each item and ask yourself: Do I have the technology and the skills to meet each requirement? Do I have the time and money to buy or build the functionality? You may have to drop some items to meet your deadlines.

Organize site content by grouping and labeling the content items you have gathered. The content organization will help define the site architecture. Try organizing content in different ways. After grouping items, give each group a descriptive name. Discuss grouping and labeling within the team and with other key people to see if they match expectations and functional requirements. Final groupings and labels will be used to define sections of the site. Consider major sections as transient; their names and content may change in the next stage of the IA process. Get client approval. Revise if necessary.

By completing this step, you will inventory, group, and label the content into major sections and determine what sort of functionality will be required. This content and functionality will be the basis of your site.

Step 4: Formulate Visual Presentation Concepts

Concept may be defined as a visual direction, an idea, or a theme for the site. Concept is the idea you want to communicate and present (discussed in Section 4.1). Form is how you express that idea. Concept and form combine in one design.

It is important to keep concepts simple. Our rule regarding concepts is this: Articulate your concept in one or two sentences. If you have to write two paragraphs to explain your concept, you're probably trying to say too much. Remember that you can't be everything at once, even though the client may insist that you can. If you try to be everything to everyone, your design will be a mess that lacks focus and says nothing. By trying to be everything, you will confuse your visitors. You need to prioritize your objectives and then proceed accordingly. As with other aspects of design, knowing what to leave out is just as important as knowing what to include. The old adage "less is more" is especially true in Web site design.

So how do we get started with creating concepts? The following process is a simple method for creating concepts that will lead to ideas for your site. These ideas can then be translated into visuals.

Word associations—Make a list of words associated with a particular subject or idea. Write them all down. Don't edit your ideas at this point; rather, write all words or phrases associated with the subject and try to write as many as possible.

Word links—Connect the words and phrases on the list with each other. Be sure to do this randomly. Choose combinations that have the most promising possibilities. Don't necessarily rule out odd or implausible solutions; they may lead to interesting concepts later.

Written rough—In this stage, you try to write down a few random thoughts that may later become visuals. At this point, you are still only writing and not sketching your ideas. Be sure to explore a wide range of possibilities and not just ones you think you can find or draw yourself. You should approach this problem as if you have a whole staff of illustrators, photographers, and production artists at your disposal. This way, you won't limit your thinking.

List a few alternative site design concepts with justifications and explanations. Consult your client for their preferences.

Step 5: Develop Site Map and Navigation

The site map is a comprehensive, diagramed layout of the site that describes its organizational structure. Site maps are synonymous with site structure, and at their best, they map out major sections of a site and construct pattern in layers and levels. At their worst, site maps can be confusing and fail to indicate key sections and subsections. Sometimes they may be incomplete and not include vital cross-links or depth levels within the site. Some site maps are chaotic and difficult to read. These errors can lead to lots of frustration for clients as well as internal miscommunication about the site's requirements. It is vital that site maps provide a clear road map to all sections of the site, that clients understand and approve them, and that everyone on the design and programming team understands exactly what is going to appear on the site and where it will appear. An example of this can be seen in Figure 5.5, which is a partial site map for the CVB.

This site map shows four levels of a single section of the site. In this case, the "Things to Do" section was chosen to illustrate this point. Each one of the sections you see under the home page should have the same level of detail included as "Things to Do." If done correctly, the site map should also indicate cross-links, which are links that can take you to more than one section within the same site.

Figure 5.5   CVB SITE MAP

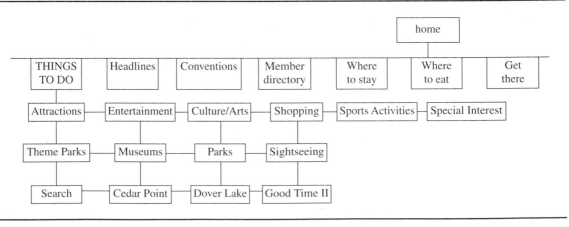

A good site map should provide viewers with all key site sections as well as descending levels in the site. Site maps should:

- provide cross-links that indicate all ways to get from point A to point B
- provide major sections, or "roots," of structure listings
- map out the organization of each section with items from content inventory
- have a legend that defines how on-site and off-site links work
- distinguish function, transaction, and dynamically generated pages from simple text pages
- make provisions for large sites by making several maps starting with a generalized overview followed by all subsequent subsections

Navigation is a method of informing the viewer about three pieces of information: Where am I? Where have I been? Where can I go from here? If these three points are clearly indicated, you are halfway there (Figure 5.6).

Here are some other points to consider when designing an interface that employs effective navigation:

- How will users use the site?
- How will they get from one place to another?
- How do you prevent them from getting lost?
- Make sure that major sections are included in the global navigation system.
- Local navigation should include a list of topics, a menu, and a list of a few related items.
- Use a section's title as a link to that section.

Figure 5.6   INTERFACE DESIGN FOR THE CVB SITE

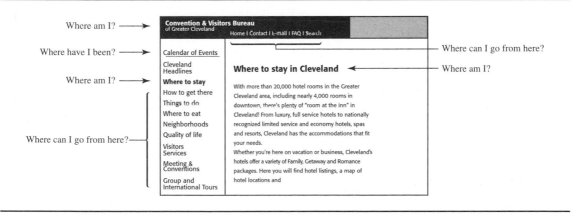

- Identify each page of your site (logo, name of company, symbol, etc.).
- Accurately describe each page that will appear in the browser bar for effective bookmarking.
- Be sure to orient the viewer to your site as well as to the Web as a whole.
- Be aware that users prefer to control where they want to go. Confining viewers to certain sections does not promote friendly usability.
- Design for flexibility of movement.

In completing this step, write down the logical organization of the site, the structure of links in the site, and the way the site can be navigated. Decide the organization of file folders, subfolders, and files.

So far, you have successfully combined reasons for the site and target audience; you have categorized content; and in this fifth step, you have created a site structure that will provide a valuable foundation for the forms that will be created in the next step.

Step 6: Design and Produce Visual Forms

Visual form is the way your site looks. It refers to all things visual on the site such as layout, type, graphics, colors, logos, charts, photos, and illustrations. Visual form is created when all previous steps have been completed. It is the part of your site design that requires your creative ability as well as formal training. It is the part of your site that identifies the client, creates a brand, creates the look and feel of the site, and sets the mood for all you say about your client's goods and services.

Visual form often begins with mapping contents in a given space. To map contents onto Web pages, you need to consider a number of things.

Uniformly organize pages in different sections. Be sure to examine the best ways to display text; itemize bullet points for easy scanning. Although there are no steadfast rules for this, usability testing shows that readers prefer 20 percent of the page designated for navigation and 80 percent for content. Block out space for global and local navigation; integrate other aspects of the site that may not be part of the site structure. A company's brand identification should be present on each page. Examine your structure listing and make a list of all possible page types. History page, mission statement, ordering information, and employee section are examples of different kinds of content that may need to be laid out differently, yet all must appear related to one another. Individual pages within sections should be formally consistent to preserve visual unity. Review content inventory and develop two or three generic page types. Consider branding, advertising and sponsorship, navigation, page titles, header graphics, and footers, including copyrights. Incorporate advertising and sponsorship: Do you put it at the top? Do you put it under the title of each page? How do you integrate sponsorship? Is sponsorship integrated into the graphic headers on each page? Is there a small sponsorship logo at the bottom of each page? Global navigation must be consistent across every page of your site, although local navigation systems can change depending on the content. Be as consistent as possible. Create page mock-ups representing the actual site and integrate design sketches with layout grids. Use design sketches as temporary graphics.

In completing this step, you have created your first visual mock-up, which you can present to the client. You will generate the actual graphics and fine-tune copy later.

5.4   IA CASE STUDY: CVB

Now let's see how the IA steps discussed in Section 5.3 can be applied in a real Web project: a Web site for the Convention & Visitors Bureau of Greater Cleveland (CVB).

Step 1:   The goal of the CVB site is to attract families and professionals to visit Cleveland and corporations to hold conventions in Cleveland. The site also provides information and services to all who visit Cleveland.

Step 2:   The target audience of the CVB site includes:

- out-of-town visitors looking for events in Cleveland
- local visitors looking for events in Cleveland
- convention planners looking for events, lodging, restaurants, and so on
- out-of-towners looking for visitor's services
- media and public relations professionals looking for press services, facts and figures, sources, archives, photos
- people relocating to Cleveland who need neighborhood information
- anyone wishing to know how to reach different locations in the city
- anyone looking for a calendar of events
- users searching for other information

All of these possible site visitors may share common needs and have different needs. Their site visit scenarios will help guide the IA of the site. A complete scenario may look like this:

Convention planner Christine needs to find a suitable city for her marketing associations. She needs to schedule flights and lodging for 100 people. She needs to make restaurant reservations for Friday and Saturday. The convention will take place in February, and she needs to ensure that restaurants and hotels are not booked for Valentine's Day and that there are at least three scheduled membership activities for Saturday, all within walking distance of the hotel she chooses. Christine is also concerned about nightly activities for Friday and Saturday and is hoping to find a few fun spots for the association's members. This is her first job, and she wants to impress her bosses with just the right location, hotels, and activities. She wants the occasion to be memorable and the visitors to be comfortable and happy with the convention.

Step 3:   Next we create the contents and define their organization for the CVB site.

Major sections of the site include:

- Calendar of events
- Where to stay, hotel location map, hotel packages, book online, overnight stay
- What to do
- Where to eat
- Neighborhoods
- Services for visitors
- Meetings and conventions
- Media center
- Multicultural heritage
- Career opportunities
- CVB information and membership

Consider the "where to stay" section as an example. It may contain the following information:

- Listing of downtown and University Circle hotels—The information includes rates, locations, reservation information, facilities, and downtown attractions.
- Other lodging—This may include bed and breakfast, apartments, and temporary housing.
- Travel information—This may include a city map of downtown Cleveland, a street map of University Circle, departure flights from Cleveland, driving times and distances between Cleveland and major cities.
- Site search of local lodging—Visitors may find lodging by type, geographic location, and hotel name.
- Book a room online—The booking page is linked from appropriate places.

Step 4:   Based on the site content and organization, we can now proceed to explore the visual design concepts for the CVB site.

It would be extremely difficult, and highly impractical, to say, "Cleveland is the coolest city in the midwest. We have everything for your family and professional needs. We can accommodate any visitor in any situation. We have exciting activities during the day, and we have everything you want to do at night. We're in a great location on Lake Erie. We're economically sound and inexpensive. We have the Great Lakes Science Center and the Rock 'n' Roll Hall of Fame. We have the Cleveland Orchestra, many terrific museums, and sports arenas. We have brand new hotels. We have golf courses for the whole family." Keep the message simple. Remember our one to two sentence rule when describing the concept. We may come up with these word associations:

interesting, family vacations

cultural, museums, Rock 'n' Roll Hall of Fame, science center

professional, golf and other sports

late meetings, high-rise buildings, sleek dinner

corporation, playground games, formal attire

theater, dinners, money

ball parks, corporation, cultural

Then the concept for the site may be, "Cleveland is an interesting old city with fresh new sophistication for professionals and families alike. Come and see us!" The key words are "sophistication, professionals, families."

- Sophistication: interesting, cultural, theater, music, sculpture, formal attire
- Professionals: corporation, blue suits, sleek, high-rise buildings, money, golf, late meetings
- Families: children, playgrounds, family vacations, ball parks, having fun, games, dinners

Now we can take the terms grouped under the three key words and combine them randomly: interesting, high-rise, family vacations; cultural, sleek, games; theater, high-rise, having fun; sculpture, playgrounds, dinner; formal attire, golf, family vacations. Some combinations will obviously work better than others. For our example, we came up with these visuals: families on vacation having fun, images of golfers, late meetings, nighttime scenes, dinners, cultural centers, children in playgrounds, company sponsored family days at ball parks, high-rise buildings, images that project a corporate, money, black-tie feel (see Figure 5.4).

Step 5:   Figure 5.5 shows CVB site map and navigation plan.

Step 6:   With these steps, we are ready to design the visual forms for the CVB site.

5.5 CLIENT IDENTITY

What Is Client Identity?

Client identity is the image or perception that a company projects to the world through various media. Most people think of logos or trademarks as a client's corporate identity, but that is only one small part of it. Client identity includes the "look" of annual reports, the style of advertising, and the specific color palette used on visual materials such as company brochures, labels, and even signage. Corporate identities are most often created by design firms, corporate identity specialists, advertising agencies, marketing communication firms, or public relations firms. In recent years, corporate identity has evolved to something known as *branding*, which means that the image of the brand, or the perceived style or "attitude" of a particular "branded" product or service, becomes linked with the company that makes the product. Think of Disney or Volvo or Mercedes. Try to recall images that create a perception or the viewers' image of these companies. If a branding campaign has been successful, you should quickly recall a perception or image of that company. Mercedes stands for quality, Disney stands for magic, and Volvo stands for safety. Every commercial, every brochure, and every element in visual communication can be traced back to these simple concepts.

How to Maintain Client Identity

When you design Web sites, you need to understand your client's corporate identity. In many cases, companies will provide you with a corporate identity manual that specifies logo sizes, positions, and usage, lists font usage, and in some cases, provides sample layouts for brochures or other *collateral* (corporate pamphlets, brochures, annual reports) materials. If you are not given a manual, you need to get this information from your client. Here are some typical questions to ask clients regarding corporate identity:

- Can your logo be used in color? If so, what colors?
- Can your logo be reversed? (Can it be printed white on a dark background?)
- Do you have a tag line that goes with the logo and does it have to appear with the logo?
- What are your corporate colors?
- Do you have a company mission statement?
- What image do you want to project on your Web site?
- Is the image different from your corporate identity for print?

Corporate identity must be considered in your overall concept for the site. For example, Cool Car Corporation's brand image in traditional print, radio,

Figure 5.7   WILLIAMS-SONOMA IDENTITY

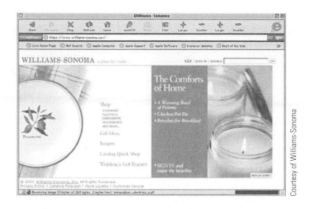

and TV advertisements may be "Safety first," but the concept for the site may be "How to have fun driving our cars for audiences 45 and over!" In this case, you will need to consider how to craft a concept and look that blends both the traditional brand image with the visual objectives for the site.

Figure 5.7 is a good example of a successful integration of print and online marketing. The look and feel of all their visual communication pieces look like they belong in one family. Williams-Sonoma has a distinct color palette of subtle pastels that they use to indicate section divisions. Large, beautifully arranged photos on all their materials are captivating. A clear organization of photos, copy, and graphics on every page is possible because the designer used a flexible grid. The contrast of sizes between very small and large elements creates depth on the page. The consistent use of colors and fonts, logo placement, and clear navigation also contribute to the overall unity of the site.

5.6   ORGANIZATIONAL FRAMEWORK

What Is Organizational Framework?

An *organizational framework* is the visual system for placement of graphics, photos, copy, headlines, headers, footers, and all other elements in your site. You begin by determining *groupings* that establish *unit relationships* and a *hierarchy*. In other words, look at your content and decide what is the most important thing on each page and where it should go. What is the second most important thing on this page and where should it go? How will you organize the space? Where are the margins? Are you going to have one wide column of copy, two narrow columns, or both? Maybe you need three. What about sidebar information? Where will it go? Will all the information be laid out this way on every

Figure 5.8   WILLIAMS-SONOMA GRID SYSTEM

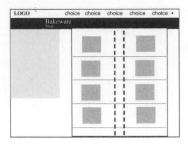
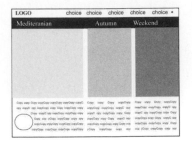
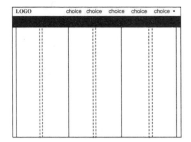
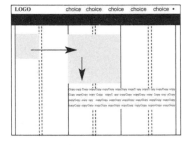

Figure 5.9   WILLIAMS-SONOMA FLEXIBLE GRID SYSTEM

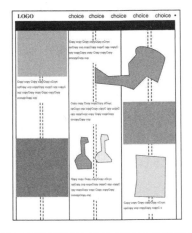

Relationships/Alignments/Unity

page or will it be different because the mission statement and forms pages are different? What will unify this design? How can I keep it interesting and different on every page and yet keep it consistent with the corporate identity? How will each section be different from the others? All these questions are answered in this stage of development, which results in the final layout. Templates and style sheets will later be applied to this system, so consistency can easily be maintained and updated when necessary.

How to Create an Organizational Framework

Now that you know what organizational framework is and what it does, how do you create it? Perhaps the best way to begin is by seeing a few examples of systems that were created for successful sites. Referring back to the Williams-Sonoma site, here is an example of how a designer created a grid structure

Figure 5.10   WILLIAMS-SONOMA GRID OPTIONS

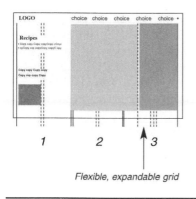  

Flexible, expandable grid

for the site. The Williams-Sonoma grid system (Figure 5.8) consists of the following: margins; flexible grid accommodating one, two, and three columns for text or image; header position; logo placement; and global navigation bar.

Figure 5.9 and 5.10 are good examples of using an expandable grid to construct a modular system for positioning all elements. The grid provides a starting point for placement and alignment of elements to create unity throughout the site.

5.7 TYPOGRAPHY BASICS

Type, Typeface, and Fonts

Of all design components, typography seems to be the most neglected and least understood. It is often mishandled by amateurs and professionals alike.

The words *type*, *typeface*, and *font* are almost always used indiscriminately, and we should clarify these terms before moving forward. Font and typeface generally mean the same thing. A font is a set of characters set in one style and one variation of weight, width, and posture. A typeface refers to one font or an entire family of fonts from the same style with similar attributes. A typeface is defined as a collection of fonts having the same type style by varying weights, widths, and postures. Type in print is measured in points, which are a printer's unit of measurement. One point is equivalent to 0.3528 millimeters, or 0.01389 of an inch (1/72 inch). The point is usually combined with a larger scale unit, the pica. One pica is equivalent to 12 points. Type on the screen may be measured in picas or pixels. When choosing type in Photoshop, the type window will display points or pixels.

In the past, many designers found typography on the Web to be fairly limited compared to print, but with the advent of style sheets, many of these limitations are changing. Web designers now have the option to control type-faces, type size, and the biggest improvement of all, leading. *Leading* is the space between lines of type. As with images, the ultimate power of type display remains with viewers and their personal browsers. Why do most Web designers select Times in many of their documents? The answer is simple: Times and Courier, along with a few other fonts, ship with most operating systems, and most browsers offer these options as the default text.

Here is a limited set of fonts that ships with major operating systems:

- Macintosh: Courier, Times, Charcoal, Chicago, Geneva, Helvetica, Monaco, New York, Palatino, Symbol
- Windows 95/98: Arial, Courier New, Times New Roman, Wingdings, Symbol
- Free Web Fonts/Internet Explorer: Arial Black, Comic Sans, Georgia, Impact, Trebuchet MS, Verdana, Webdings

Anatomy of Type

Whether we're discussing fonts or typefaces, the basic component of type is the character. Sets of characters are sold by type foundries under familiar names such as Helvetica, Times, and so on. First, let's investigate the underlying structure of these characters by examining their characteristics (Figure 5.11).

Arm—The horizontal stroke that is free on one end, as on the uppercase E.

Ascender—Part of the lowercase letter that extends above the x-height, as in the lowercase b, h, and l. The distance from the top of the x-height to the top of the ascender height characters, such as the b, h, and l.

Baseline—The imaginary line upon which all characters in a font rest or align.

Bowl—The rounded or elliptical forms that make up the basic shape of letters, such as the uppercase C and O and the lowercase b, o, and p.

Cap height—The height of the uppercase letters. The cap height is usually a bit shorter than the height of the ascenders.

Counter—The partially or fully enclosed parts of a letter, such as the defined space within the uppercase H and lowercase n and u.

Crossbar—The straight horizontal stroke extending across two vertical or diagonal stems. This is seen in the uppercase H.

Descender—Part of the lowercase letter that extends below the baseline, as with the lowercase g, j, p, and q. The distance from the baseline to the bottom of a descender character such as the lowercase g, j, p, and q.

Ear—The small extension that projects from the top right of the lowercase g.

Figure—The distance from the baseline to the top of the figures (numerals). This height is usually the equivalent of the cap height.

Figure 5.11 ANATOMY OF TYPE

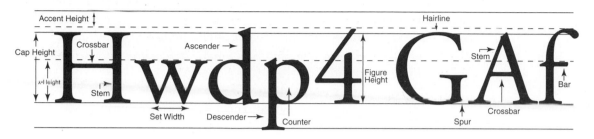

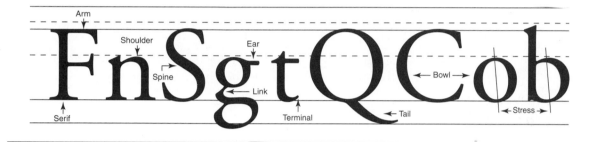

Hairline—The thin horizontal stroke located at the top and bottom of round characters such as the uppercase and lowercase o, c, and s.

Kern—The negative letterspacing that is applied between specific character combinations to reduce the space between them.

Link—A stroke joining the upper and lower body of the lowercase g.

Point size—Type is measured in units with the same name as the traditional printer's unit of measurement, the point. In desktop publishing, the point is equivalent to 0.3528 millimeters, or 0.01389 of an inch (1/72 inch). This is a measurement used in typewriter technology. The traditional point, still used by most British and North American printers, is 0.351 millimeters, or 0.01383 of an inch (1/72.27 inch). The point is usually combined with a larger scale unit, the pica. The pica is equivalent to 12 points.

Serif—The beginning and/or finishing strokes on a stem drawn at a right (or oblique if the style is italic) angle to the stem. The serif guides the eye from one letter to the next. The use of serifs in a text typeface makes it much easier to read.

Set width—The total width of the character, including the white space on either side. This does not include kern.

Shoulder—The curved stroke between two vertical stems, such as on the lowercase h, m, and n. Its weight may taper as it leaves one stem and connects to the other.

Spine—The main diagonal stroke on an upper- and lowercase s.

Stem—The straight vertical strokes of a letter, such as the uppercase I and T and lowercase l and r.

Stress—The orientation, measured in degrees, upon which the thin and thick strokes of a character are aligned. This is most noticeable in closed characters such as the lowercase b, o, and p, but it is reflected in all the characters within a typeface.

Tail—The descending stroke of an uppercase Q or the diagonal stroke of the uppercase R. The tail usually extends below the baseline.

Terminal—The end of a stroke that is not finished with a serif, as on the lowercase t and e.

x-height—The height of the lowercase letter from the baseline. This does not include the ascender or descender heights.

Font Designs

In the last decade, the design industry has gone through a virtual explosion of new fonts. It seems that all designers at some point need to create a font of their own. However unique, all fonts (with the exception of the symbol or picture fonts) have variations in weight, width, and posture. These variations create font styles.

Weight refers to the words you see at the end of the font name such as light, bold, extrabold, and so on. The standard levels of type weight are extralight, light, semilight, regular, medium, semibold, bold, extrabold, and ultrabold or black. The most common weight in Roman is referred to as normal or plain weight. Bold style faces, often used for emphasis, came into existence in the 20th century. They are used to draw readers to headlines, advertising, or any place where type needs to make an impact, although one can argue that light type surrounded by dark elements for contrast can make the same kind of impact.

Bold and Light   Bold type (Figure 5.12) can be extremely effective alone or with images. Its primary function is to call out certain words or phrases to

Figure 5.12   FRUTIGER FONT WEIGHTS

Frutiger 65, LIGHT, **BOLD, BLACK, ULTRA**

indicate their importance. Bold type should be used sparingly because it can quickly interrupt a line's reading flow. Italics are better suited for this task.

Light-weight type (Figure 5.12) tends to be airy and delicate. When used correctly, it can be quite beautiful. But when used in small sizes, say 6, 7, 8, or 9 points depending on the font, the light-weight type can fall apart on the screen. Light fonts can also look attractive as body text, but most are used for display purposes only.

Width   Width refers to the amount of horizontal space the type style uses (Figure 5.13). Condensed or compressed characters are narrower or tighter than Roman (normal or plain weight). Expanded or extended fonts have wider widths than Roman characters.

Posture   Posture refers to the angle of characters. Character strokes can be straight (referred to as Roman) or tilted to the left or the right in posture. Left-slanted italics are rare, and their use is generally discouraged because of their odd posture and unfamiliarity to the eye.

Most *italic* characters (Figure 5.14) slant to the right and are based on the cursive handwriting style. This style is used to complement the Roman weight and to emphasize, introduce, and indicate words and phrases.

Oblique fonts are basically Roman fonts tilted to the right. Oblique and italic look similar, but they are easy to distinguish because oblique fonts are usually not cursive.

Figure 5.13   FONT WIDTH: COMPRESSION AND EXTENSION

Franklin Gothic, CONDENSED, EXTRA CONDENSED
Eurostyle EXTENDED, **BOLD EXTENDED**

Figure 5.14   FONT POSTURE: ITALIC AND OBLIQUE

Figure 5.15   SCRIPT AND DECORATIVE FONTS

Nuptual Script   *Present*   **Arnold Boecklin**

Scripts   Script typefaces (Figure 5.15) are based on handwriting and are often quite elegant and beautiful. Scripts are intended to link to one another and look best with tight letter spacing. For this reason, setting scripts in all uppercase looks very bad and should be avoided at all times. For the best results, do not set long lines of text in script. They can be difficult to read. Script types are frequently used as a decorative style for menus, formal invitations, and titling.

Decorative Type   Decorative typefaces (Figure 5.15) are just that—decorative—and consequently, should not be used with large amounts of text. You will often see decorative type on posters, menus, titling, and signage. They are also used in advertising headlines and logos.

Other Type Differentiations

The terms text and display are not considered classifications—they are type categories defined by their usage. The terms are typically referred to as text size and display size.

Text Size   *Text fonts* (Figure 5.16; *The Waking*, a poem by Theodore Roethke, 1953) are intended to be used in small sizes such as 8, 9, 10, 11, and 12 points. These fonts are designed to flow with a rhythm that keeps the eye moving along a reader's line. Many publications are frequently set in serif type faces because some designers claim these typefaces are less taxing on the eye. However, studies show that readers gravitate toward text they are most accustomed to seeing and don't necessarily prefer to read serif or sans serifs fonts.

Figure 5.16   PALATINO ROMAN, 9/11, –10 TRACK

I wake to sleep, and take my waking slow
I feel my fate in what I cannot fear,
I learn by going where I have to go.

We think by feeling. What is there to know?
I hear my being dance from ear to ear.
I wake to sleep, and take my waking slow.

"The Waking," copyright 1953 by Theodore Roethke, from *The Collected Poems of Theodore Roethke* by Theodore Roethke. Used by permission of Doubleday, a division of Random House, Inc.

Figure 5.17   DISPLAY FONTS

Fur Extra Rounded Light   Industria Inline A

Display Style   *Display typefaces* (Figure 5.17) are used to catch the reader's attention, and they can sometimes be quite ornate. They can be effective for use in titling, advertising, posters, or any other place where type needs to be eye catching. Display fonts usually start with 14 points and go higher. They are not designed for prolonged reading in text.

5.8   TYPE FAMILIES

Type foundries have often constructed their own systems for classifying type, which can vary widely. However, categorizing type is not as critical as understanding basic type styles and their origins. In this book, you will be introduced to five basic type families, which represent many of the fonts you will see in print and on the Web. It will be useful for you to get to know these type styles because each has individual characteristics that make it unique. Recognizing these styles will give you a good basis to understand basic type classification.

Old Style

Old style type was inspired by Roman inscriptional letterforms and was developed during the Italian Renaissance. This typeface is modeled after the medieval manuscript writing style of the 15th century. A famous typeface designer, Claude Garamond, a punchcutter working in Paris, created many beautiful typefaces, including Garamond (Figure 5.18), which is an outstanding example of old style type.

Figure 5.18   OLD STYLE, TRANSITIONAL, AND MODERN

Garamond Light
New Baskerville Roman
Bodoni Regular

Old style type is characterized by a large x-height and shortened ascenders as well as marked differences between thick and thin strokes. Its graceful proportions make it ideal for extensive reading text in publications such as books, newsletters, and manuals. Old style type is quite versatile, performing well in small and large sizes in heading, signage, and general text. On the screen, old style faces generally work well in large and medium sizes. Sizes 9 points and smaller tend not to work well on low-resolution monitors.

Transitional

Transitional typefaces are based on designs from the late 17th and 18th centuries, which were considered a period of typographic evolution. This is often referred to as the neoclassical period. The name *transitional* reflects this historical classification because the typeface was developed between the old style and modern periods.

Transitional typefaces are marked by a gradual increase of contrast between thick and thin strokes and sharper, more horizontal serifs. Structurally, they are less complex and more mathematical in their appearance. Geometric serifs tend to be symmetrical and almost businesslike. The differences in heights between uppercase and lowercase are much less pronounced than in old style characters. This makes it a better choice for low-resolution screens. The simplicity and understated elegance of transitional typefaces are evident in John Baskerville's typeface shown in Figure 5.18.

Modern

During the 1700s, we continue to see a shift from writing and calligraphy to the more mechanical construction of letterforms. This push toward refined, more exaggerated forms defines the modern typeface. It is marked by extreme contrast between thick and thin strokes (Figure 5.18). This exaggerated contrast may be the reason the faces were referred to as "hairline serifs." Although quite elegant, modern type is difficult to read in small point sizes on the screen. The serifs tend to disappear, especially when reversed out of backgrounds. Despite this handicap, modern type has been used extensively in 19th-century book typography and continues to be very popular in 21st-century design.

Slab Serifs or Egyptian

Slab serifs (Figure 5.19) were developed in the 19th century for use as display faces, and they became very popular. They were referred to as Egyptian faces because they were given Egyptian-sounding names, such as Cairo and Kernak, to capitalize on the public's fascination with ancient Egyptian artifacts. Their bold, machinelike qualities were an expression of the industrial age, when letterpress printers used them to give their message graphic impact.

Figure 5.19   **SLAB SERIFS FONT**

Lubalin Graph Book

Figure 5.20   **SANS SERIF FONT**

Univers 55 Regular

Their characters are marked by rectangular serifs and an almost uniform stroke width, which have a bold abstract quality. Their right-angle joinery is unmistakably found in faces such as the Clarendon, Century, and Cheltenham type families. Strong, confident, and very readable, these faces are often used in logotype and corporate identity. Slab serifs blend well with both grotesque and geometric sans serifs. Type historians have speculated that the first sans serif typefaces may have been created by removing the serifs from slab-serif designs. For example, ITC Lubalin Graph was designed by adding serifs to the geometric sans serif type family Avant Garde Gothic.

Sans Serif

Sans serif (Figure 5.20) typefaces appeared early in the 19th century, and their use became increasingly popular during the 1920s. It was referred to as the new functional style for a rational era. Asymmetrically balanced on a grid system, its functional simplicity was seen as the ideal typographic expression of both a scientific and a technological century. Its graphic unity enabled typographic designers to use all 21 fonts together in an integrated typographic system. This remarkable "form follows function" principle is evident in faces like Univers and Helvetica, both designed in the 1950s as a contemporary redesign of Akzidenz Grotesque, a German turn-of-the-century sans serif.

5.9   CHOOSING TYPE

One function of design is to support content and resonate the message. Your choice of type can either support or hinder that message. Type helps express our written message the same way photographs or well-written headlines speak to our hearts and minds. Type is another element to choose when creating layouts, much like choosing colors. And just like colors, type tends to be subjective. Nevertheless, there are some basic guidelines for choosing type.

Type should convey the mood of whatever you are expressing through similarity or contrast to the subject. It should give dimension to the words on the screen and harmoniously support the overall feeling of whatever you're expressing. Type in itself can make or break design. Poor type choices stand out like sore thumbs and shout to your readers how little you know about this basic form. Poor type can detract from your message and undermine the perception of reliability for your client.

When choosing type, in general, it is best to work with fewer fonts when you're just getting started. Certainly no more than three in the entire site. Starting out with one serif and one sans serif face may be a good choice for several reasons. You have instant unity and variation between headline and text. Figure 5.21 shows a choice of fonts. It is simple to have only two choices. Try to avoid using a pair of styles that are too close in weight. Figure 5.22 shows the use of a Berkeley Book headline over Franklin Gothic text. This produces confusion, and it may not create enough contrast between headlines and text.

Type should support your message and not get in the way of reading. If it becomes too noticeable, you've probably made the wrong choice. Think about your content. Is the nature of your message conservative? Is it serious or dramatic? If so, you may choose a more traditional serif font such as Century or Galliard. Times Roman also fits that description but tends to be overused in

---

Figure 5.21 CHOICE OF FONTS

Choosing Type

When choosing type, in general, it is best to work with fewer fonts when you're just getting started. Certainly no more than three in the entire site. Starting out with one serif and one sans serif face may be a good choice for several reasons. You have instant unity and variation between headline and text. You have two choices. Try to avoid using a pair of styles that are too close in weight. This produces confusion, and it may not create enough contrast between headlines and text.

Figure 5.22 TYPEFACES LACKING CONTRAST AND READABILITY

Choosing Type

When choosing type, in general, it is best to work with fewer fonts when you're just getting started. Certainly no more than three in the entire site. Starting out with one serif and one sans serif face may be a good choice for several reasons. You have instant unity and variation between headline and text. You have two choices. Try to avoid using a pair of styles that are too close in weight. This produces confusion, and it may not create enough contrast between headlines and text.

Web design. Content with more edge or a more radical message may require a sans serif type with geometric angles and more technical appeal.

Try to avoid headline and subhead type styles that literally "illustrate" the meaning of something. In many cases, this will overshadow your message rather than support it (Figure 5.23).

Typography is part of a "bigger picture" in design; it has to work with other elements in a space to contribute in a meaningful way. For example, if you were going to decorate a room, you would want all of the elements to work together. You would choose wall color or texture, furniture, floor coverings, and accessories that all looked good together because it is the whole room that you're addressing, not just one aspect of it. So if you've been saving that 10-foot by 10-foot dude ranch mural for something special, you may want to give it to a friend because it probably won't look good in your simple Shaker-style apartment. The first line in Figure 5.23 may appear to be a good choice for headlines and suheads, but it may prove to be a poor choice. It would be difficult to read every headline and every subhead in this type family, though it supports the obvious message.

Dos and Don'ts in Choosing Type

- A typeface with a larger x-height is likely to be more legible.
- Limit using white type on black or dark colored backgrounds for longer text because it generally tires the eyes and it may print poorly.
- Text in all uppercase needs more horizontal space or leading to ensure each letter is clearly read.

Figure 5.23   EXAMPLES OF ILLUSTRATIVE TYPE

THE BEST RUST PREVENTION YOU CAN BUY!

The Best Rust Prevention You Can Buy!

The Best Rust Prevention You Can Buy!

The Best Rust Prevention You Can Buy!

- Lines of copy that are too long, too short, or too close together make finding the next line difficult. This slows readability.
- Do not mix body copy styles such as Times and Stone Serif. You will interrupt the reading flow. If you have to introduce a highlight point, use bold or italic of the same face.
- Use script faces sparingly and don't set the type in long widths. Script faces often work well on invitations, menus, titling, or formal occasions. They look best with greater letter spacing.
- Don't ever set script faces in all uppercase characters. This breaks the connection of characters and defeats the purpose of using a script style.
- Decorative type should be used for headlines and subheads but never for text. Use this style of type sparingly.
- Text fonts are used in body copy that must be readable and legible at 7–14 points.
- Display type is only used in 14 points or larger, and it is designed to catch a reader's attention.
- Choose typefaces that have varying styles and widths for the most flexibility.

Finding Web Fonts

Now that you know some things about choosing fonts, how do you know if they will look good on the Web? Print fonts don't necessarily look good on the screen, and you should be aware of that when making type choices. As the Web continues to evolve, the need for greater type choices has increased, as has the availability of type for the Web.

There are a number of digital type foundries that have worked together to bring us viable fonts for the Web. Galapagos Design Group, the Font Bureau, Emigre, Agfa, Bitstream, Monotype, and Microsoft have specifically developed fonts that look good on low-resolution screens.

The following is a list of Web fonts from Microsoft and Galapagos:

- Baltra GD, Impact, Maiandra GD
- Comic Sans, Comic Sans Bold
- Georgia, Georgia Bold, Georgia Italic, Georgia Bold Italic
- Verdona, Verdona Bold, Verdona Italic, Verdona Bold Italic
- Trebuchet, Trebuchet Bold, Trebuchet Italic, Trebuchet Bold Italic

The following is a personal favorites list from Emigre, which ranges from very readable faces to script to display faces to symbols that can be applied in your Web design. They are available for download (www.emigre.com/) in PostScript or TrueType format for the Mac or personal computer: Citizen, Dogma, Exocet, Filosophia, Glyphic, Journal, Keedy, Mason, Matrix Emigre,

Matrix Script, Modula, Mrs. Eaves, Outwest, Platelet, Quartet, Remedy, Senator Tall, Suburban, Tirplex, Totally Gothic, and Whirligig.

The WDP site lists URLs to other type foundries that make high-quality fonts for the Web.

5.10 SPACING TYPE

Vertical Spacing

Line height is the distance from the baseline of one line of type to the baseline of the next. The term *leading* sometimes means the amount of space added between lines of text to make the document legible, but at other times, leading may mean line height. The term *leading* originally referred to the thin lead spacers printers used to physically increase space between lines of metal type. Most applications automatically apply standard leading of 120 percent of the font's point size. For example, 10-point type is set on 12-point leading. This is done not only for readability but also for appearance. When characters are surrounded by limited or small amounts of vertical space above and below the ascenders and descenders, lines of type will look crowded. Although this distance varies considerably with each typeface, the general rule of 120 percent leading applies.

In Figure 5.24, the left side is set in 10-point Helvetica on 2 points of leading (10/12), or 120 percent. The right side is set in the same size, but with 3 points of leading (10/13), or 130 percent, making it a little easier to read and more aesthetically pleasing. It may be a subtle difference, but it's one worth noting.

Typefaces with larger x-heights require more leading because tall x-height takes up more space around the character. Small x-height characters will look good with 120 percent leading due to the vertical space above it. This is not a formula, but only a rule of thumb.

In general, when setting body copy, leading should increase proportionally as line length increases. However, headlines, being shorter and using larger fonts, are often set with less leading to reduce the vertical space. This is done

---

Figure 5.24   EFFECT OF FONT SIZE AND LEADING ON READABILITY

Typefaces with larger x-height require more leading because tall x-height takes up more space around the character. Small x-height characters will look good with 2 points of leading due to the vertical space above it.	Typefaces with larger x-height require more leading because tall x-height takes up more space around the character. Small x-height characters will look good with 2 points of leading due to the vertical space above it.

to enhance the appearance of grouped words on the page. Advertisers often use this treatment on headlines with several lines of type. This reduction of leading also uses less space in the overall ad space. The top part of Figure 5.25 shows headlines in 16 point type with 2 points of leading (16/18). With all-uppercase type, the headlines may look better with less vertical spacing (lower part of Figure 5.25). The headlines read a little faster and take less page space. The lower part of Figure 5.25 is actually using negative leading. (16/16 is no leading, 16/14 is negative-2 leading.) In this case, it is a more aesthetically desirable option.

Body text can tolerate more leading, but be careful: This flexibility can look awkward when pushed beyond a reasonable point. Many readability crimes are committed for the sake of filling space or pushing aesthetic limits, especially by novice designers. Nothing quite says "Don't read me" like lines of poorly leaded type.

Horizontal Spacing

Horizontal spacing is controlled through *tracking*, or *word spacing*. Tracking refers to space between words in a paragraph. *Kerning* refers to space between letters. Word spacing should remain consistent through paragraphs and create a rhythm that aids in reading. The general rule for word spacing is that if words are set to read in sequence, they should always be closely spaced. This produces a tight gray value on the page or screen and aids in reading. The most important tip about word spacing is this: If you can see word spacing, it is usually not done well. The whole idea of word spacing is that it allows the reader to focus on reading and not on white spaces between words. Take a look at your local newspaper or the newsletters you receive in the mail. Many of these publications are poorly designed and have what designers refer to as "white rivers" cascading through the text, looking all too obvious and distracting.

Figure 5.25 FRUTIGER HEADLINE TYPE

FRUTIGER ROMAN
SET ON 16/18.
THIS IS TOO MUCH SPACE.

FRUTIGER ROMAN
SET ON 16/14.
THIS IS BETTER SPACING.

On the other hand, if words are set too closely together, they create one long line of indistinguishable gray that no one can read. On the screen, in general, words appear closer than they do in print. This must be taken into consideration when laying out pages and choosing fonts.

Printing

Users may want to print a Web page. The main point to keep in mind when designing pages for printing is printer limitations. Some table cell colors may print well, but others may not. Background colors and images sometimes look good, whereas other times, they may cause readability problems. Pages created in Flash are virtually unpredictable when it comes to printing. Many sites are designed only to view on the screen, and printing on an 8.5-by-11-inch page is added as an afterthought.

Identify the importance of page printing early in your Web project. That can guide your design of the site. It is perhaps always good to pick a design that is easy on a printer. Testing in the early stages of development is the key. Using cascading style sheets to adjust your text, layout, and colors for the screen and the printer is another very good option (Section 6.21).

Figure 5.26   LIGHT GRAY TYPE ON GRAY BACKGROUNDS

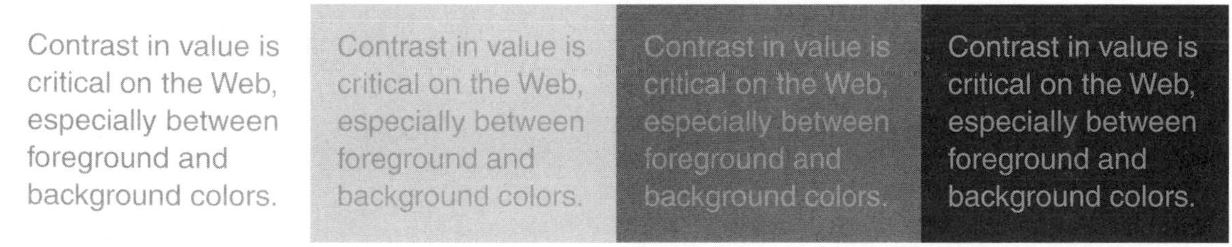

| Contrast in value is critical on the Web, especially between foreground and background colors. | Contrast in value is critical on the Web, especially between foreground and background colors. | Contrast in value is critical on the Web, especially between foreground and background colors. | Contrast in value is critical on the Web, especially between foreground and background colors. |

Figure 5.27   DARK GRAY TYPE ON COLOR BACKGROUNDS

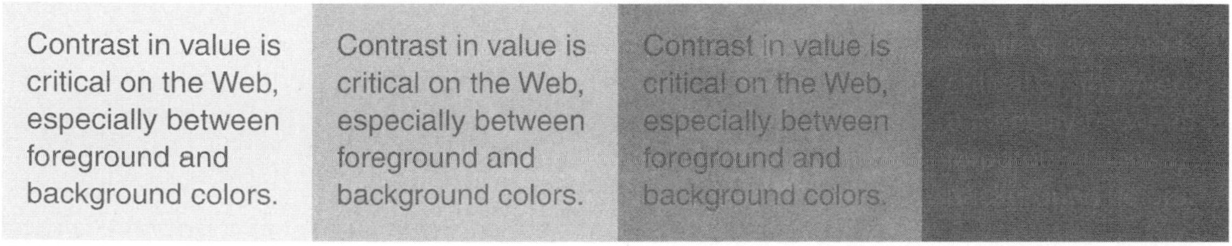

| Contrast in value is critical on the Web, especially between foreground and background colors. | Contrast in value is critical on the Web, especially between foreground and background colors. | Contrast in value is critical on the Web, especially between foreground and background colors. | |

Type and Cascading Style Sheets

For a Web page, leading, font size, and other text display properties are controlled through *cascading style sheets* (CSS) (Chapter 6). Now that you know a little more about type, you can begin to apply that knowledge to creating great looking, smart type on Web sites. Here is a list of features that can be controlled through a CSS (see Chapters 2 and 6).

- font color, size, and weight
- style, such as normal, oblique, or italic
- uppercase, lowercase, or small caps
- font family in order of preference, separated by commas
- line height or leading, letter spacing, and word spacing
- text color, background color, background image
- white-space properties
- text indent, alignment, underlining, and more

Font Family, Color, Size, Weight, Style, and Variant

Fonts of different designs belong to different *font families*. Within each font family, you can set the font color, size, weight (boldness), style (italic, slant), and variant (small cap or normal). The CSS properties font-family, color, font-size, font-weight, font-style, and font-variant are used to set these styles (Section 2.10).

A well-selected set of fonts is an important part of site design. Since not everyone has the same set of fonts on their computer, it is a good idea always to specify at least two font choices. You may use very specific font names like Berkeley bold italic. If unsure of the second choice, you can always fall back on one of the following generic font names: sans serif, cursive, fantasy, or monospace.

If the viewer doesn't have the font specified in a designer's italic face, the browser will display text in oblique. Italic tags can be added and removed depending on the text you're formatting (Palatino italic or Berkeley italic, or you can just say Palatino and then choose italic depending on how much italic text you have and how often you want to change it). Also consider removing italic as a way to emphasize a term inside italicized text.

Line Height and Leading

The style property line-height (Section 2.13) can be set to control the vertical separation of lines. For on-screen readability, it is recommended that you use plenty of vertical separation, such as setting line height to 1.5 the font size.

In CSS, leading precisely refers to the difference between line height and font size:

$$\text{leading} = \text{line height} - \text{font size}$$

See Section 2.13 for how to set values for the style property `line-height`.

Tracking and Kerning

Both tracking and kerning can be controlled through CSS, as can indents for the first line of a paragraph. To specify tracking, type `word-spacing:`*`length`*, where *`length`* is a numeric value in pixels, point, ems, and so forth. To specify kerning, type `letter-spacing:`*`length`*, where *`length`* is a numeric value in pixels, point, ems, and so forth. To add indents, type `text-indent:`, where the number is an absolute value or a percentage. There are several points you need to keep in mind when working with kerning and tracking values. You may specify negative values for word and letter spacing, but be careful because the display of these features always depends on the browser's capabilities. In addition, word and letter spacing values may be affected by your choice of alignment. When justifying text, it is best to use a zero value for letter spacing to avoiding large open holes. If you want to use default letter and word spacing, be sure to set the value to normal.

Aligning Text

To align text, type `text-align` and then write any of the following four choices:

- `left`—Aligns the text to the left.
- `right`—Aligns the text to the right.

Figure 5.28   JUSTIFIED TYPE

Justified type tries to align all text so that it is perfectly flush on left and right sides. This usually results in odd word and letter spacing which is not aesthetically pleasing and is difficult to read. We do not recommend that you use this option.

- center—Aligns the text on center.
- justify—Aligns the text on both the right and left (Figure 5.28).

As a general rule, justified text tends to look awkward on the screen. Word spacing and letter spacing may be adversely affected. Justify text with caution and only when absolutely necessary.

Underlining Text

Underlining text is generally unpopular with many designers and for good reasons. Underlined text tends to be distracting and often looks "dated," evoking images of old Smith Corona typewriters of times long past. Nevertheless, if you must underline, CSS lets you underline and remove underlining easily throughout your document.

To underline text, type text-decoration: underline. For a line above the text, type overline. And for strike through text, type line-through. To remove underlining, overlining, or strike through text, type text-decoration: none.

If you don't wish to use underlining to indicate links, you can type the none option for text-decoration. In this case, be sure to also eliminate underlining under visited links, active links, and transitional links. However, be careful with this option; you still have to visually clue your viewers to the links on the page. Consider changing text color or changing background behind the text.

Legibility and Readability

Legibility refers to how well your typeface supports fluent reading. The typeface you choose may help or hinder that process. For example, if you choose a typeface that is too small, the characters may run together and make the words difficult to read. The foreground and background contrast is important for readability (Figures 5.26 and 5.27). Reversing white type out of a black background can also be difficult to read because the brightness and glare of white against black blur or run words together, making them difficult to distinguish from one another. Text set in all uppercase letters needs more word spacing to ensure that each word can be read. Type that has no vertical spacing or leading may fuse together and appear as one large gray block. Adding at least 2 points (or 20 percent in your style sheet) of leading will alleviate this problem.

Readability refers to the ease of reading type blocks rather than the typeface itself. In other words, you can choose a perfectly legible typeface for your layout, but if the style and design of your layout are poor, viewers may find your text difficult to read.

Type as Graphic

Early Web designers didn't have the flexibility to choose fonts beyond the standard Times and Helvetica. They didn't have the option, as they do now in style sheets, to specify leading or indents for running text or even create drop caps and raised caps (Figure 5.29) (Section 6.14). The treatment of the initial letter in a paragraph can be used to break up the monotony in chapters, articles, or large amounts of text. Instead, early Web designers relied on type images created with photo manipulation programs such as Photoshop to add artistic touches to type. The technique is still valid today. There are certain advantages to treating type in this fashion. First, you can choose any font, any color, any size, any leading, and any tracking you wish and embed it as a graphic wherever you wish. You can control the look of your headlines and ensure corporate identity type standards as well as overall aesthetics. Second, you can manipulate, stretch, gradate, and apply filters to express virtually any idea with type, adding creative possibilities that can't be created in any other way. To most designers, even with the advent of style sheets, this prospect looks very appealing. However, the argument for not using type as a graphic throughout your site is compelling, and it should be considered in the design process.

There are four primary reasons for using this type treatment sparingly or, in some cases, omitting it altogether. First, embedded graphics are not searchable by search engines, which may make it difficult to find your site. Prospective visitors may find this to be a problem. Second, embedded type graphics can't be read in text-only browsers such as those used in speech devices on most ADA-compliant sites, so visitors who rely on those devices (U.S. figures show 20 percent of the population have some sort of disability) are not going to be able to hear your site. Third, graphics add more weight to your site and increase download speed. It may not be noticeable on smaller sites, but on bigger sites (e.g., 1,000 pages or more), extra graphics can really bog down the speed significantly. Fourth, type created as a graphic takes more time to edit. For example, on sites that are updated several times a day, this can

Figure 5.29   DROP AND RAISED CAPS

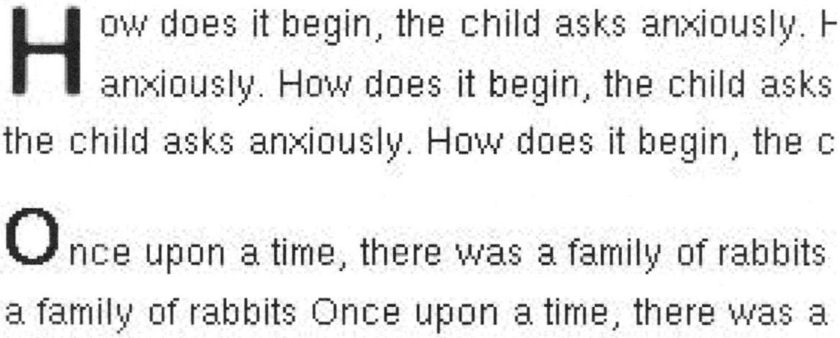

How does it begin, the child asks anxiously. H anxiously. How does it begin, the child asks the child asks anxiously. How does it begin, the c

Once upon a time, there was a family of rabbits a family of rabbits Once upon a time, there was a

significantly slow down maintenance and create lots of extra updating work for the Webmaster or designer.

The text formatting ideas discussed here are further reinforced in Section 6.14, where CSS coding and examples are covered.

5.11 READING TYPE ON THE WEB

When designers first began to work with type on the Web, many tried to force print rules onto the new medium and many have failed. The reason for the failure is due to basic control issues. Many of the features that make text successful in print fail on the Web. Such factors as kerning character pairs and ligatures, for example, just aren't practical for most text. Ligatures are special combined characters, such as "fi," "fl," "ff," and "ffi." They were first designed for metal type because these character combinations could not be kerned closely enough together, so they were instead combined on a single piece of metal. Letting go of hanging punctuation or set widths is also necessary. Trying to control browser windows, in most cases, frustrates many viewers who would prefer that your text works in their window and not yours. Print and CD-ROMs are fixed media and, thus, allow and encourage fine control. Text on the Web must be a dynamic marriage of efficient editing and aesthetically pleasing communication. Design with respect for your viewers and capitalize on the strength of the medium.

Ways of Making Type Readable on the Screen

Applying common sense may be the best advice when working with text. The two key points to making type readable on the screen are size and space, which are more challenging than they appear at first glance. On-screen type is contingent upon resolutions, platforms, and browser rendering capabilities. These variables make it difficult to say it is best always to use 10- or 12-point Times. The best way to get consistent cross-platform results when choosing type sizes is to specify a standard font size, such as `medium` or `small` (Section 2.13), and pair that with sufficient leading.

Proportional relationships (or sizes) between type are important because they establish a hierarchy for headers, body text, photo captions, copyrights, and other legal text. You have control over this aspect of type, so take advantage of it. This hierarchy is one way to prioritize information, which is one of the designer's most essential functions.

One easy way to make type more readable is line length. The optimal length of a line of text should be between 40 and 70 characters long. Shorter lines tend to disrupt reading flow. With longer lines, viewers have a hard time finding the next line, and it slows reading. When using the default browser font, a good rule is that your text blocks should be about 400 pixels wide.

Another good rule for making type readable is to keep the background simple. This means eliminating extraneous textures or patterns that may make reading difficult. Textured backgrounds may be interesting when viewed on their own, but often they do nothing but add noise behind the text.

When using CSS, it is easy to change letter spacing and word spacing. Avoid placing the letters too closely. Too little space between words can lead to words touching on the screen, and individual letters have to be clearly distinguishable for type to be readable.

Designing for "scannability" is also very important when working with text on the Web. In this case, scanning means looking at the page quickly to pick key words or phrases of interest. Shorter paragraphs and quick reading subheads may help viewers spot the items rather than seeing one large page of gray type. Breaking up the page into smaller portions may also help viewers get to their topics more quickly. Given that people read text online 10 percent slower than print, this becomes very important. Make it easy for people to read your message.

Leading, or space between lines, is another aspect of type that can improve readability. Leading allows a viewer to see lines of type more clearly without interference from the lines above and below. When using CSS, be sure to increase leading to 15 or 16 points or 130 percent.

So, with all that said, what fonts are more readable on the screen? First, the bad news: The fonts that are used the most on the Web, Times and Courier, are not especially good for readability. Although Times is excellent for newspapers, it isn't particularly good for the screen. The original version of Times was designed to squeeze as many letters as possible on a printed page and still remain legible. The print version is narrow, with medium x-height and sharp, small serifs. Its small ascenders and descenders make it very economical because they reduce the need for leading, enabling the typesetter to set more lines per page.

The bitmapped version of Times does not translate the subtleties of the print version because the smallest possible unit on the screen is a pixel. Half pixels don't exist to accommodate the details of many typefaces, and even anti-aliasing does not help this problem. Unfortunately, most screen fonts were designed to resemble their printer fonts at 72 pixels per inch in QuarkXPress and were not designed to be legible on the screen.

The good news is that many more fonts are being optimized for on-screen reading. Products like Microsoft's Fontpack and Adobe's Webtype contain fonts that have been designed to fit into a square pixel grid. The fonts have a more open face, wider letters, increased x-height, and more letter spacing.

The WDP site uses the following CSS rules for running body text and headings. For example,

```
body
{    font-family: Verdana, Geneva, Arial, helvetica, sans-serif;
     font-size: small;            /* one notch below medium size */
```

```
        line-height: 150%;          /* 1.5 spacing                */
    }
```

See Sections 2.13 and 6.2 for CSS information on fonts and text styling. Be sure to check your pages using various browser versions on different platforms (personal computers, Macs, and UNIX).

5.12 LAYOUT GRIDS

A layout grid is a set of invisible vertical and horizontal lines to guide content placement. It is the primary way designers organize elements in a two-dimensional space. A grid aligns page elements vertically and horizontally, marks margins, and sets start and end points for element placement. A well-designed grid makes a page visually clear and pleasing; it results in increased usability and effective content delivery. A consistent page layout also helps to create unity throughout the site (Section 4.5).

Grids are certainly not a new invention. They have been used for centuries as the basis for ornamental design (Figure 5.30; ornamental grid design) in screens, textiles, quilt design (Figure 5.31), posters, and architecture. In the 20th century, the grid itself became popular as designers began using the shapes themselves as art. Bauhaus architects in particular used the grid in a way that showed in both the inside and outside of building architecture (Figure 5.32). Layouts with strong grid structures can be traced to the de Stijl movement where artists like Van Doesburg and Mondrian began dividing their canvases into symmetrical patterns. Swiss designer J. Muller-Brockmann had an important impact on defining and shaping two-dimensional design though the use of the grid in everything from photography and architecture

Figure 5.30   AN ORNAMENTAL GRID DESIGN

Figure 5.31   HANDMADE QUILT

© Jonathon Blair/CORBIS

Figure 5.32   GRIDS IN ARCHITECTURE

© CORBIS/Sygma

to logo designs. His legacy still remains in much of today's popular culture, permeating our computer screens and printed materials with "Swiss design."

5.13   WEB PAGE LAYOUT GRIDS

Grids in Web design are substantially different from grids in print. Print pages have fixed and known dimensions, whereas Web pages are displayed on monitors of different sizes and resolutions and in resizable browser windows.

Major layout challenges for a Web designer include:

- Most CRT monitors and LCD screens have a 4×3 aspect ratio and settable resolutions: 640×480, 800×600, 1024×768, 1400×1050, and higher. Sometimes you'll find irregular screen sizes such as 1280×1024. Different resolutions can make pages look smaller or larger. With the move to HDTV, computer screens may soon have the 16×9 aspect ratio.

- The maximum available display area for Web pages is the screen size minus the space taken up by borders and toolbars of the browser used. For example, on an 800×600 monitor, the usable area may become 750×425.

- Browsers can use different default font sizes according to user preferences.

- Browser windows can change size dynamically.

- Some users may surf the Web on TV screens, palmtops, text-only devices, or Braille readers.

- Users may want to produce hard copies of pages on a printer. The typical 8.5-by-11-inch paper is very different in size from monitor screens.

Designers generally have used these basic layout strategies:

- Left-justified layout—A fixed-width grid is used and the page starts at the left margin. This design can leave an annoying white space on the right side for larger resolution screens.

- Centered layout—A fixed-width grid is centered horizontally in the browser window.

- Full-width fluid layout—The grid is *scalable* and fills the width of the browser window and responds to browser resizing dynamically. For larger screens, text lines can become too long for easy reading.

- Centered fluid layout—This layout uses fluid but equal left and right margins and a fluid centered grid.

Surveys show that users strongly dislike having to scroll horizontally. Fixed-width pages run the risk of causing horizontal scroll for entire pages. According to the Software Usability Research Laboratory of Wichita State University:

> Fluid layouts are significantly preferred to both centered and left-justified layouts. In a study by Bernard and Larsen (Winter/2001) participants indicated they perceived the fluid layout . . . as being the best suited for reading and finding information, as well as having a layout that is most appropriate for the screen size (for both small and large screens). They also indicated that the fluid layout looked the most professional, and consequently preferred it to the other layout conditions. Conversely, the consistently least preferred condition was the left-justified layout.

Achieving fluid layout with a scalable grid is a design challenge (Sections 6.15 and 6.22). The principal technique is to use relative proportions for the grid columns and margins instead of fixed widths. Images and font sizes normally will not automatically scale up or down with window size. By creative use of multiple columns, spacing, centering, and automatic reflow of text content, a fluid page can be made to look good under most viewing conditions. A scalable page offers more flexibility and freedom for the user to resize the browser window and can fit on printer paper as a side effect.

The main objective of your design is to create aesthetically pleasing layouts, regardless of the window size. Proportion of elements to one another becomes the key factor in scalable page layouts. In other words, create contrast between elements, consider groupings, determine hierarchy, and so on as they relate to each element. Make the page look ideal for the most popular window sizes and then make it scale well to smaller and larger window areas.

Specific techniques to make a grid fluid will be discussed in the next subsection. But be sure to test a fluid layout at all different sizes in initial design stages so that final results are pleasing. A general suggestion for well-designed, proportional layouts in any size is to adhere to basic principles of design. Use contrast to establish hierarchy, strive to design the negative space to be as interesting as the positive, and be sure to create a focal point and dynamic relationships between elements (see Section 4.1).

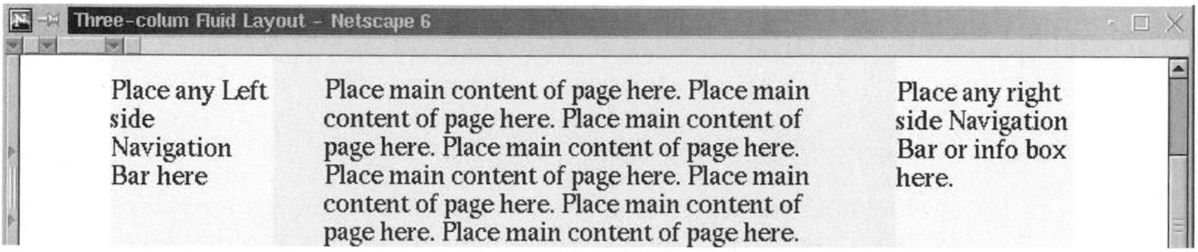

Fluid layout can be achieved with cascading style sheets (CSS) techniques (Chapter 6) or with scalable HTML tables. The two techniques can also be combined. The `<table>` element is flexible and widely used to implement layout grids. We will look at grids with tables next.

A Fluid Table Grid

As an example, let's look at a three-column grid (Figure 5.33) centered horizontally in the browser window, leaving comfortable left, right, and bottom margins.

Figure 5.33   A THREE-COLUMN FLUID GRID

Let's look at the HTML code (Ex: **Grid3**) for the grid ready to receive page content and graphics:

```
<?xml version="1.0" encoding="UTF-8" ?>
<!DOCTYPE html PUBLIC "-//W3C//DTD XHTML 1.0 Strict//EN"
    "DTD/xhtml1-strict.dtd">
<html xmlns="http://www.w3.org/1999/xhtml"
      xml:lang="en" lang="en">
<head><title>Three-column Fluid Layout</title>
</head> <body style="margin-top:0px; margin-right:8%;
            margin-bottom:50px; margin-left:8%">          (1)
<table width="100%" cellpadding="0" cellspacing="0">     (2)
<tr valign="top"> <td style="width:14%">                 (3)
<!-- Left Navbar Begin-->
<!-- Left Navbar End-->
</td>
<td> <div style="margin-left:8%; margin-right:8%;">       (4)
<!-- Main page content begin -->
<!-- Main page content end --> </div> </td>
<td style="width:14%">
<!-- Right Box Begin-->
<!-- Right Box End--> </td>                               (5)
</tr></table></body></html>
```

The body element specifies a bottom margin of 50 pixels. It is important to leave some bottom margin and not run the text to the very bottom edge of a page (line 1). The body style also reserves 8% each for scalable left and right margins. A full-width table with cell padding and spacing both set to zero is used for the three-column layout grid (line 2). The leftmost column, receiving 14% of the table width, is a good place for a navigation bar whose graphical images with matching background color can make this a decorative and functional part of the page (line 3). The same percentage table width is also given to the third column for placing any informational boxes, news items, or links to pages external to the site (line 5). The center column, receiving the remaining 72% of the table width, displays the main content of the page (line 4). To give the contents breathing room, we add a left and right margin each of 8% of the center column width.

Follow the same proportion principles in this example to design your own grids using tables.

Tips for Creating Fixed and Scalable Grids with Tables

It would be unreasonable to say that you should design for all screen resolutions, by always making tables scalable to ensure resolution-independent design. This kind of approach applied across the board could unnecessarily limit your design. You have to design for your target audience.

Whenever possible, try to avoid using fixed sizes and specify layout as percentages of the available space. For example, when attempting to put as much information as possible on the home page, as in newspaper/magazine style format, it may be more dynamic to use scalable tables, but the complicated nature of these layouts may make construction more difficult and time consuming.

Pages that are designed to display in fixed width may look poor when printed. Either they come out as a thin stripe wasting loads of paper, or they are cut off because they are too wide for the printer. Be sure to include separate documents or styles for printing.

Even a 600-pixel-wide layout that works on most normal computer monitors (although not on WebTV and small-screen devices) will be 8.3 inches wide when printed at the standard resolution of 72 pixels to the inch.

If you're trying to design for desktop computers as well as small-screen devices or television sets, you may be better off creating three different style sheets that customize your site for optimal viewing on all devices. It may be more time consuming and expensive to do this, but at least you'll be assured that your entire viewing audience will see your site.

When it is possible to design with a scalable browser window in mind, here are a few points to consider:

- In general, sites that have lots of running copy seem better suited to take advantage of scalable pages. Pages that are copy light can look odd when stretched to full screen width.

- Making good use of screen real estate is smart, but be careful when creating layouts with lines of text that go on and on across the screen. Such long lines are very hard to read.

- Using a two- to four-column approach is a good place to start to avoid long lines of text, but also consider what will happen to the layout when the browser window is reduced to a narrower width.

- Using tables, and in some cases using tables and frames, you can combine fixed-width columns with columns that stretch and reflow with the browser window; controlling part of the layout while other elements reflow may help combine both approaches.

- Page headers or headlines created as graphics, as opposed to straight HTML, can help prevent variable column widths from collapsing when a browser width is reduced. Images in a line can be placed inside a `div` to prevent them from flowing into multiple lines when the browser window narrows. Text and images can also be kept on the same line by setting the `white-space` style property to `pre` or `nowrap`.

- Standardizing the sizes of inline graphics (e.g., photographs associated with a story) can help make text reflow more manageable; it's easier than using many different sizes of inline images.

- Treat the inline graphic as a thumbnail that pops up a detail (larger) view image in a new window.

5.14 DESIGNING LAYOUT GRID SYSTEMS

Once you have grouped and prioritized content, you are ready to design a layout. A layout can be defined as a grouped set of elements arranged to create aesthetically pleasing balance and proportion in a two-dimensional space. Unfortunately, there isn't a mathematical formula for creating layouts. Layouts are a product of sensitive eyes using dynamic arrangements and contrasts to lead viewers' eyes in a specific way that reveals a specific message. So, which do you create first, the layout or the grid? There are no steadfast rules; there are only suggestions for possible methods on how to begin. To construct a grid first is to force elements into a specific arrangement that may not make sense for the subject. To create a whole layout without first considering the grid is equally impractical because the grid will serve as the basis for structure. Perhaps the best way to begin is to refer back to your thumbnail sketches. Look at where you have indicated text, logo, photographs, and illustrations. Don't look only at the home page, but review a series of thumbnails throughout the site. This will give you an idea of what grid would make the most sense.

The layout for a site will most likely be implemented by HTML tables (Section 3.11), perhaps with the help of style sheets (Chapter 6). The code can be generated by a tool such as Dreamweaver and used as a template (Section 11.12) for creating actual pages for your site.

The key point to remember when constructing a grid is flexibility. Remember that one grid will be used for the entire site. You don't want to construct a limited one-column grid that will only give you one option for placement. With a one-column grid, you can only place graphics into one width. A two-column grid is a little more versatile because it allows you to place elements into one or two columns (Figure 5.34). A four-column grid is more versatile yet, allowing

Figure 5.34   TWO- AND FOUR-COLUMN GRIDS

table cells to span from one to four columns (Figures 5.34 and 5.35). With a six-column grid, you normally won't use all columns for text. Some columns can provide negative space before, between, or after columns for page content. Text placed in an overly narrow column becomes difficult to read due to poor and frequent line breaks.

You can get very elaborate with your grid design, and if that kind of complexity makes sense for your design, that's great. In the case of the San Francisco Museum of Modern Art (Figure 5.36), this kind of solution made perfect sense. The six-column grid was versatile enough to support many different kinds of information ranging from an exhibit section to general museum information to a gift shop, creating a unique look for the museum. The unusual, stationary

Figure 5.35   FOUR-COLUMN GRID (DIGIKNOW)

Courtesy of DigiKnow, www.digiknow.com

Figure 5.36 SIX-COLUMN GRID: SFMOMA

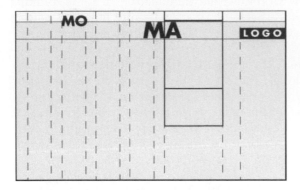

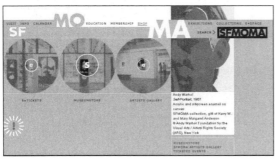

fifth column was designed to support additional links for membership and donor information. This grid was used through most of the site.

5.15 GRIDS ON THE WEB: A CRITIQUE

Now that you know a little more about grids, let's examine several sites to see how they designed their grids and what makes them successful.

One site that uses a strong, interesting grid is Sapient (sapient.com). If you examine Figure 5.37, you will see that each page uses the same grid, yet the permutations on each page vary depending on the sections. *Permutations*, in this case, mean variations or rearrangements that make a set of elements such as type, photographs, and graphics appear differently.

At their best, grids should not make every page look exactly alike. It's true that designers strive for unity, but there is a fine line between unity and monotony. Unless you're laying out a telephone directory or another totally uniform document, each section of your site should vary somewhat. Why

Figure 5.37   GRIDS OF THE SAPIENT SITE

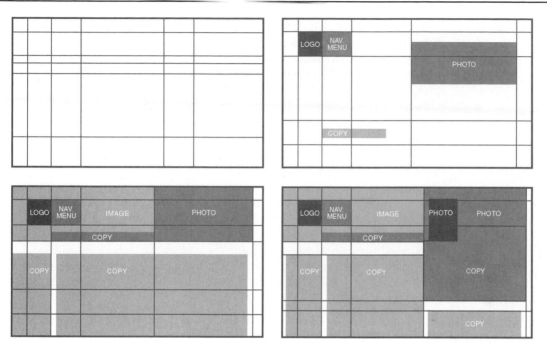

should it vary? The simple reason is the nature of the content may vary. You would not use the exact same layout on a home page as you would on a site map page, for example. And you probably would not use the exact same layout on the page for ordering merchandise. The information on each of the major sections is different; therefore, the arrangement of the elements should reflect that. The inspiration for the variations in form is content. If you begin with that premise, all of your formal arrangements will make sense. So, consider the layout needs of the entire site with its different sections and contents and then design a grid system that can be used flexibly. A flexible grid allows you to vary the basic layout by combining columns (or rows) to form a wider column (or row) and to divide a column (or row) into smaller ones. The variation is done while preserving certain unifying features of the basic grid and page style.

Now, let's examine the Sapient grid more closely. The home page (Figure 5.37) is divided into halves, introducing a thin white line that will later be used to organize type and images. Main navigation appears on the red and white rectangle floating on top of the photograph here and throughout the site. Further subnavigation appears on the far right side on a vertical, an alignment choice that usually does not work on the Web. In this case, it happens to fit into the design, and it is not difficult to read. Other sections on this site use a two-column grid for text and single column on the left for navigation.

Resize the window on the Sapient site entry and you'll find a fluid grid that responds well to different window sizes. The vertical navigation bar on the right side stays visible while the middle parts of the page give up space. All the pictures on the site entry are background images. The rightmost table column, which displays the vertical navigation bar, has `"width: 1%"` while the buffer columns are left without `width` specifications. Thus, the HTML table uses background images and cells with black background in the center columns to act as buffers for changes in window size (Section 6.18).

Grids don't have to be complicated or clever to be effective. The Museum of Modern Art (moma.org) in New York uses a simple grid for most of its pages. The home page grid is exactly like all the other grids in the site (Figure 5.38). Large, horizontal space at the top allows for the display of exhibit photos, and the area below introduces a simple three-column structure for navigation and text.

Dotted horizontal rules organize the navigation bar type, and solid rules organize the body text. We should also add that the sensitivity to type, choice of color, and generous use of negative space make this site aesthetically pleasing.

Figure 5.38   GRIDS OF THE NEW YORK MOMA SITE

The Museum of Modern Art, New York, Web site: MoMA Splash page, www.moma.org. Design by Allegra Burnette, programming by Tanya Beeharilall and George Hunka, May 2002, © 2003 The Museum of Modern Art, New York

The Museum of Modern Art, New York, Web site: www.moma.org/about_moma/index.html. Design by Allegra Burnette, programming by Tanya Beeharilall and George Hunka, May 2002, © 2003 The Museum of Modern Art, New York

The Museum of Modern Art, New York, Web site: www.moma.org/visit_moma/index.html. Design by Allegra Burnette, programming by Tanya Beeharilall and George Hunka, May 2002, © 2003 The Museum of Modern Art, New York

The Museum of Modern Art, New York, Web site: www.moma.org/about_moma/building/index.html. Design by Allegra Burnette, programming by Tanya Beeharilall and George Hunka, May 2002, © 2003 The Museum of Modern Art, New York

Figure 5.39   FREE PLACEMENT GRIDS (LEFT), LAYOUT (RIGHT)

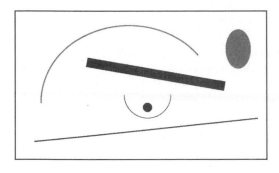

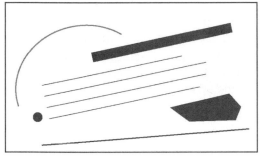

Some sites don't appear to use grids at all. These types of layouts are referred to as *free placement* and are based on the "intuitive" placement of elements inspired by content (Figure 5.39). For example, Figure 5.39, top left shows a free placement grid, or lack of grid, for a hypothetical parachute club home page. Figure 5.39, top right is the actual layout based on that free placement grid. Figure 5.39 bottom left is the grid for an inside page of the same club, and Figure 5.39 bottom right indicates a layout for an inside page. Both pages use a free placement layout inspired by the feeling and freedom of parachuting.

Although most commercial sites rely on internal structure to organize complex information, there are some sites that effectively use minimal or no structure. One such site is the Wolvesburrow Productions site (www.wolvesburrow.com). The home page of this site can be categorized as free placement and it is questionable whether or not its use of graphics and space best communicates its identity or services. In most cases, free placement should be used sparingly and in conjunction with internal structure such as is (www.cabedge.com) or (www.juxtinteractive.com).

5.16 SUMMARY

Page layouts give a Web site its look and feel. You derive the layout based on two major considerations: design concepts and information architecture (IA). The six steps to create IA are: (a) define goals, (b) define audience, (c) create and organize content, (d) formulate visual presentation concepts, (e) develop site map and navigation, and (f) design and produce visual forms.

With a good idea on IA and design themes, Web site designers can create page layouts with various kinds of information located on a site in a two-dimensional arrangement that achieves the desired visual effects.

The fundamental steps in creating layouts begin with thumbnails and result in a comprehensive layout, or "comp" as it is commonly referred to in design circles.

Typography is an important layout element that many find difficult to master. It is important for a Web designer to become familiar with typography basics: anatomy of type, font styles and families, spacing, and so forth. Detailed information helps you select and manipulate type to achieve intended effects. For a Web page, type designation and spacing control are achieved with CSS declarations.

Grid systems help the relative positioning of elements on a page and are central to creating layouts. A well-designed grid can make messages clearer and contents easier to read. Creating grids that are flexible enough to fit on windows of different sizes and resolutions is a particular challenge for Web site design. The grid system in a layout is usually implemented by HTML tables.

EXERCISES

Review Questions

1. Analyze a current site of your choice. Go through the steps in IA and answer the following questions:

   - What do you think the goals of this site are?
   - Who is the target audience?
   - What is the concept for the site?
   - How would you describe the corporate identity?
   - How effective is the navigation for the site?
   - How effective are the visuals for the site?

2. Choose an existing Web site. Analyze the corporate identity of that client. How is its logo used on the site? Is it consistent? Articulate in two sentence or less the image this company is trying to project. Is this image consistent with their other

marketing materials such as billboards, print advertising, or TV commercials? What is the corporate color?

Assignments

1.   Review the steps in Section 5.3. Choose an existing Web site which in your estimation has poor IA. Re-create the Web site's IA. Be sure to follow all the steps indicated in Section 5.3. Be as thorough as possible in your investigation.

2.   Refer to the first review question in this chapter. Use the same company for this question. Now that you've analyzed the IA for this company, see if you can understand the formal aspects of this site. Begin with the grid. Print out several pages of this site. See if you can identify the underlying grid used in these layouts. Notice any consistencies or inconsistencies with the grid. Be sure to draw the actual grid lines on the printed Web site.

3.   Create your own grid structure. Refer to the Williams-Sonoma examples in Figures 5.7, 5.8, 5.9, and 5.10. Rework the existing Williams-Sonoma grid. Change the column width, logo position, horizontal rules, and margins. Create three new layouts based on this new grid; home page, level 1, and level 2 pages of the site. Compare your new layout with the current site. Critique the two grid possibilities. Which one is more aesthetically pleasing? Which one is easier to read? Are they simply variations, and is each equally successful?

4.   Choosing typefaces: Choose a topic for a single page of a site. This can be your personal site or one for your client. Try to find one or two typefaces that may look appropriate for the subject matter. Remember to avoid typefaces that overpower the message. An example of that may be found in Figure 5.23. Let's say that you're designing a Web site for a company that produces rust prevention products, and your job is to select an appropriate headline and subhead font. The first choice can be described as "illustrative" because it literally imitates the idea of rust. Illustrative fonts need to be used sparingly because they can overpower the layout and tire the reader after several lines.

5.   Navigation variations: Choose a Web site for this exercise that has a poorly designed navigation system. Design three variations on the current navigation, improving the placement of links, logo, and text.

6.   Subtle text variations: Take a large block of text that may appear on your personal Web site. Experiment with different leading and fonts. Try to select an appropriate type with both vertical and horizontal spacing that you think looks aesthetically pleasing. Increase leading by 1 point to see how it affects readability. Find suitably sized headlines and subheads that look pleasing with existing text.

CHAPTER 6

Controlling Page Style: Cascading Style Sheets

A Web page has two important aspects: document structure and presentation style. The *cascading style sheet* (CSS) is a language to specify the presentation style. Material covered in Chapters 4 and 5 helps us design the visual presentation of our site. CSS provides the means to implement that well-designed style.

In the past, HTML alone must specify both the structure and the presentation of a page. As the Web evolves and advances, the trend is to separate document presentation from document structure. In this way, different styles can be attached to the same structures and therefore provide greater flexibility for processing and presenting documents.

XHTML has deprecated many presentation-related elements and attributes. The focus of HTML shifts to structuring documents so they can be processed by programs automatically. The Document Object Model (DOM; Section 10.5) recommended by W3C will then provide a standard programming interface for accessing and editing documents under program control (Chapter 10).

CSS, or simply style sheets, will then supply the capability of specifying presentation styles and associating them with HTML elements in multiple ways. CSS brings unprecedented power and control over presentation styles. With CSS, you can suggest display styles to browsers, print formats to printers, and device-dependent styles for other media such as page readers for the vision impaired. This chapter focuses on display styles for visual browsers.

Hence, a Web page consists of two basic parts: XHTML code and CSS code. The latter may be placed in one or more separate files, called *style sheets*. By providing a set of *style rules*, a style sheet indicates the presentation style for various elements in a Web page. By associating a style sheet with an XHTML page, you control the styling of that page. Without such a style guide, a browser can only use its default styles and any user preferences for displaying the HTML elements. CSS is not an advanced technique that one may choose to

Figure 6.1   XHTML + CSS = WEB PAGE

ignore for simple applications. On the contrary, XHTML and CSS must be applied together to create any real Web page (Figure 6.1).

Concepts, rules, usage, and examples of style sheets are presented to give you a comprehensive view of CSS and how it is used in practice. The coverage allows you to apply XHTML and style sheets to implement the design and layout ideas discussed in earlier chapters.

6.1   WHAT IS CSS?

CSS is a language, recommended by W3C and supported by major browsers, for specifying presentation styles for XHTML, HTML, and other documents. CSS consists of the following components:

- *Style declarations*—A style declaration is given in the form

  `property : value`

  There are many properties (more than 50) for the various presentational aspects of HTML elements, including *font properties*, *color and background properties*, *text properties*, *box properties*, and *classification properties*. Listings of CSS properties are available on the Web (see the WDP Web site). Most properties can be associated with all HTML elements when appropriate. Obviously, putting a font property on an `img` element does nothing. Some, such as `text-align`, apply only to block elements. Others, such as `vertical-align`, apply only to inline elements. A few styles apply only to specific elements. For example, `list-style-type` is only for list items. CSS documents the applicability of each style property. Browsers provide default presentation styles to all HTML elements. By associating your own style declarations you can control the presentation style of an entire page and how any element in it is displayed.

- *Selectors*—CSS defines selectors to give you multiple ways to indicate which style properties are assigned to which HTML elements. Assigning style properties by selectors is in addition to defining the `style` attributes for XHTML elements.

- *Inheritance and cascading rules*—CSS defines how values for properties assigned to an HTML element are inherited by its child elements. For example, because of inheritance, font and background settings for body can affect the entire HTML document. In addition, because of no inheritance, margin, padding, and border declarations do not affect child elements. CSS documents the inheritance status of each style property. When conflicting style declarations occur on a single HTML element, cascading rules govern which declaration will apply.

You can find CSS documentation at W3C. The WDP Web site also provides many links to CSS documentation.

With CSS, you define style rules and attach them to HTML elements, thus controlling their presentation style. Hence, each Web page may have an HTML file and a set of style rules. A style rule consists of a selector and one or more style declarations separated by semicolons. Therefore, the general syntax for a style rule is:

```
selector
{       property₁ : value₁ ;
        property₂ : value₂ ;
            . . .
        propertyₙ : valueₙ
}
```

A simple selector can be just the name or names of the HTML elements that take the style. Figure 6.2 shows the anatomy of a style rule.

Getting to know the different style properties, their possible values, and the effect they have on page presentation is part of learning CSS. But we already know quite a few things about CSS: length units (Section 2.11), color values (Section 2.12), font properties (Section 2.13), width and height (Section 3.8), horizontal alignment (Section 2.10), vertical alignment (Section 2.18) of inline elements, and more. We will reinforce and build on this knowledge in this chapter. You'll get a comprehensive view of CSS and learn how to apply them in practice.

Style Sheets

A *style sheet* is a file (usually with the .css suffix) that contains one or more style rules. In a style sheet, comments may be given between /* and */.

Figure 6.2   STRUCTURE OF A STYLE RULE

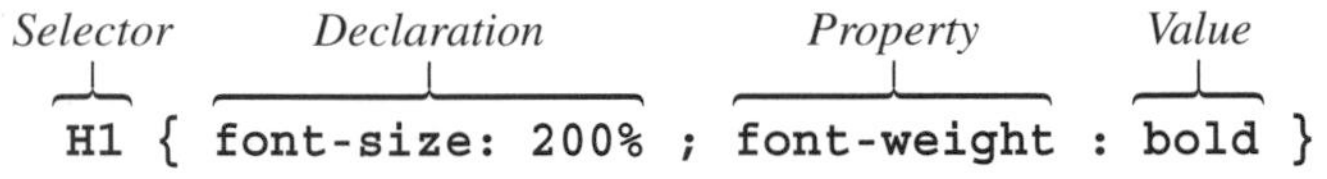

```
        Selector      Declaration          Property      Value
                                                ┊          ┊
        H1 { font-size: 200% ; font-weight : bold }
```

You have multiple ways to associate style rules with HTML elements, making it easy and flexible to specify styles. For example, the rule

```
h1 { font-size: large }
```

specifies the font size for all first-level headers to be `large`, a CSS predefined size. And the two rules

```
h2 { font-size: medium }
h3 { font-size: small }
```

give the font size for second- and third-level headers. These rules only affect the font size; the headers will still be bold because that is their default `font-weight`.

To make these three headers dark blue, the rules can become

```
h1 { font-size: large; color: #009 }
h2 { font-size: medium; color: #009 }
h3 { font-size: small; color: #009 }
```

As mentioned in Chapter 5, a well-designed site should use a consistent set of font family, size, and line height settings for all its pages. CSS rules can help the implementation of this immensely.

Attaching a Style Sheet

To attach the three rules to a Web page, you can place them in a file, such as `myfile.css`, and put the following `link` element inside the `head` element of the XHTML code:

```
<link rel="stylesheet" type="text/css" href="myfile.css" />
```

This external-file approach allows you to easily attach the same style sheet to multiple pages of your Web site. You can even use style sheets at other sites by giving a full URL for the `href`. Figure 6.3 shows the relation between a Web page and its style sheet.

Figure 6.3   **ATTACHING A STYLE SHEET**

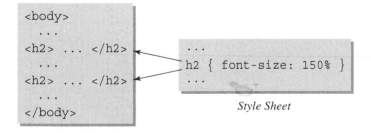

Style Sheet

A `.html` file may have one or more `link rel="stylesheet"` elements. At the beginning of a style sheet file (before all style rules), you can include other style files with the statement:

```
@import url("target-sheet-url");
```

Instead of a separate file, you can include rules directly in a Web page via the `style` element

```
<style type="text/css">
body { font-size: small }
h1 { font-size: large; color: #009 }
h2 { font-size: medium; color: #009 }
h3 { color: #009 }
</style>
```

which is also placed inside the `head` element. This is the `style`-element approach. The external-file approach has advantages. It makes changing the style that affects multiple pages easy. And a browser needs to download the style sheet only once for all the pages that use it, making your site faster to load.

A Brief History of CSS

Realizing the need to separate document structure from document presentation, Robert Raisch produced the *WWW HTML Style Guide Recommendations* in June 1993. The work laid the foundation for the development of style sheets. Later, in 1994, Håkon Lie published *Cascading HTML Style Sheets—A Proposal*, which suggested the sequencing of style sheets applicable to a Web page.

W3C worked to make CSS an industry standard. In 1996, W3C made its first official recommendation, *Cascading Style Sheets, Level 1* (CSS1), which allows you to separate style from content and gives much more control over styling than before. W3C continued to evolve CSS as browser support slowly evolved. In May 1998, the next version of style sheets became *Cascading Style Sheets, Level 2* (CSS2).

CSS2 is a superset of CSS1 and adds support for media-specific style sheets so that authors may tailor the presentation of their documents to visual browsers, aural devices, and so on. This specification also supports content positioning, downloadable fonts, table layout, features for internationalization, and more. These specifications can be found on the Web at

www.w3.org/TR/REC-CSS1/
www.w3.org/TR/REC-CSS2/

Support for CSS by browsers had been sparse. Now, major browsers are committed to style sheets and provide increasingly better support for CSS, especially CSS1. Our coverage in this chapter is based primarily on CSS1.

As CSS became popular and sophisticated, W3C decided, in 2001, to divide CSS into *specification modules* to make it more manageable. This means different aspects of style such as color, font, positioning, selector, table, box model vertical, box model horizontal, and so on will be specified by separate specifications maintained by different working groups. The modularization work will eventually lead to the CSS3 standard.

It is recommended that you use CSS for styling Web pages. Style-related HTML elements (e.g., <font> and <center>) and attributes (e.g., bgcolor and alink) are being deprecated and won't work in the future. NN7, Mozilla, IE6, Opera 6, and later versions of browsers provide good support for all but the most esoteric features of CSS1 and CSS2.

6.2   OVERALL STYLING OF A PAGE

Making the pages of a site look unified and consistent is the most basic requirement for Web design. Decide on the page margins, font, foreground and background colors, and heading and link styles. Then apply them to every page in your site. If a page deviates from the overall style, it should be by design and with good reasons.

CSS makes overall styling easy to enforce. Most style properties set for the body element apply to the entire page through inheritance.

As mentioned, the font type, style, and leading (line separation) can affect the readability as well as the look and feel of the entire site (Section 5.11). It is advisable to use standard CSS font sizes (Section 2.13) rather than pixel or point settings. In this way, your font will work well under different screen sizes and resolutions. In addition, use more line separation to increase readability. For example, the WDP Web site uses the following:

```
body
{   font: small Verdana, Geneva, Arial, helvetica, sans-serif;
    color: black;                  /* foreground */
    background-color: white;       /* (1) */
    margin: 0px  0px  30px  0px;   /* top right bottom left*/
    border: none;                  /* (2) */
}
```

The running text is set to small (one notch below medium) for the entire page. The font style property allows you to specify all font-related properties in one place in the general form:

font: *style variant weight size / line-height family*

Only the *size* and *family* are required. (See Section 2.13 for font properties and values.)

Normally, `line-height` is 120% of `font-size`. To improve readability of textual materials on screen, we recommend

```
h1, h2, h3, p, li { line-height: 150% }
```

to set line spacing to 1.5 × `font-size` for the indicated elements. These `line-height` settings are used on the WDP site.

The `background-color` of an element can be set to a specified color (line 1) or `transparent`, which is the initial value. It is also possible to specify an image for the background. We will see how to use background images later in Sections 6.15 and 6.18. Page margins are set to 0 except for the bottom, which is 30 pixels. We also make sure no border is used for the page (line 2).

We have discussed how to specify colors (Section 2.12) and fonts (Sections 5.7 and 5.8). The WDP site uses the following set of section header styles:

```
h2                          /* in-page heading   */
{  font-weight: bold;
   text-transform: capitalize;
   color: #666;
   font-size: medium;       /* predefined size   */
}

h2.red {  color: #933; }    /* Page top heading */

strong.heading              /* subhead           */
{  font-weight: bold; display: block; }
```

The body, heading, line height, and hyperlink styles (Section 6.5) form a good basic set for the overall styling of a page.

6.3 CENTERING AND INDENTING

To center text or other inline elements such as images, use the

```
text-align: center
```

declaration. The `text-align` property applies to block-level elements and controls the horizontal alignment of their child inline elements. The possible values are `left`, `right`, `center`, and `justify`, as discussed in Section 2.10.

For example, you can use an HTML element

```
<h2 class="center">Topic of The Day</h2>
```

for any text you wish centered and provide a style rule such as

```
h2.center { text-align: center; color: #006600 }
```

to specify the display style. In this way, not every h2 element but only those with the class="center" attribute will be centered. To associate the same rule with all six different headings, you can code it as follows:

```
h1.center, h2.center, h3.center, h4.center, h5.center, h6.center
{ text-align: center; color: #006600 }
```

As mentioned in Section 2.6, the core attribute class is used by style rule selectors to associate styles.

By omitting the element name in front of the class name, a selector addresses any HTML element with the given class attribute. For example, the rule

```
.center { text-align: center; color: #006600 }
```

applies to all these elements

```
<h1 class="center">Topic of The Day</h1>
<h3 class="center">Lunch Menu</h3>
<p class="center">Some text</p>
```

Figure 6.4 shows the class selector.

To center a block element such as a table, use something like

```
<table class="center" ...>
...
</table>
```

and the style rule

```
table.center { margin-left: auto; margin-right: auto }
```

With this style, a browser automatically computes equally sized left and right margins to center a block element. If a table has a caption, you may need to center it with automargins as well. Older browsers such as IE 6 do not support automargins, and you may have to resort to the deprecated center element. Ex: **CenterStyle** demonstrates the centering of different elements.

To indent the first line of a paragraph, use

```
p {  text-indent: 3em }
```

To indent entire paragraphs, you can increase the left and/or right margins as desired. For example,

```
p.abstract {  margin-left:  5em; margin-right: 5em }
```

Figure 6.4   THE CLASS SELECTOR

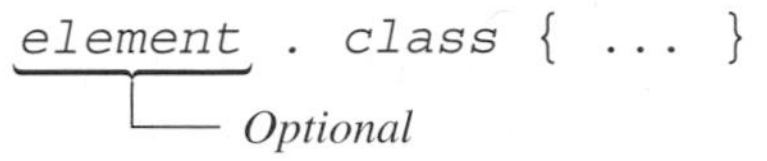

```
element . class { ... }
          └─── Optional
```

centers a paragraph with the left and right margins each increased by 5em (Section 2.11).

6.4 SELECTORS

A style sheet is inherently separate from the HTML page it controls. This supplies important advantages. However, the price to pay for keeping styling separate from structure is having to tell which style rule applies to what HTML element. This is exactly what a *selector* does. It associates a rule to a set of HTML elements. Different forms of selectors give you the ability to easily associate rules to elements of your choice:

- *Element selector*—The simplest selector is the tag name of an HTML element. It associates the rule with the named element and applies to every instance of that element in the HTML file. For example, the rule

  ```
  h3 {  line-height: 150%  }
  ```

  is used on the WDP Web site.

- *Universal selector*—The symbol * used as a selector selects every HTML element. It makes it simple to apply certain styles universally.

- *Class selector*—The `tagName.className` selector associates a rule only with elements having `tagName` and the `class=className` attribute. For example,

  ```
  h2.cap {  text-transform: uppercase }
  ```

  makes all h2 in the cap class ALL CAPS.

  The WDP Web site uses the style rule

  ```
  img.anchor {  border: none }
  ```

  to eliminate borders for graphical link anchors, such as

  ```
  <a href="handson.html"><img class="anchor"
      src="img/handson.jpg" alt="Handson Experiments"  /></a>
  ```

  If the `tagName` part is omitted, then the selector is shorthand for `*.className`, and the rule applies to any HTML element with the `class=className` attribute. For example,

  ```
  .emphasis { font-style: italic; font-weight: bold }
  ```

  makes the attribute `class="emphasis"` meaningful for many elements.

- *Attribute selector*—The selector `tag[attr]` selects the element `tag` with the attribute `attr` set (to any value). The selector `tag[attr="str"]` selects `tag` with `attr` set to `str`. The selector `tag[attr=~"str"]` selects `tag` where the value of `attr` contains the space-separated word `str`. For example, the class selector `tagName.someName` is the same as the attribute selector `tagName[class="someName"]`.

- *Id selector*—The `#idName` selector associates the rule with the HTML element with the unique `id` attribute `idName`. Hence, the rule applies to at most one HTML element instance. For example,

```
#mileageChart { font-family: Courier, monospace; color: red }
```

applies to `<table id="mileageChart"> ... </table>` only. The same selector may also be given as `table#mileageChart`.

- *Contextual selector*—A sequence of selectors separated by spaces, in the form `s1 s2 s3 ...`, selects the last selector contained (a descendant) in the previous selector and so on. For example,

```
a img { border-style: none }
```

eliminates borders for all link anchoring images (`img` in the context of a). If you use > instead of SPACE to separate selectors, then it means the next selector is a child of the previous selector. If + is used, it makes the next selector an immediate sibling of (next to) the previous selector.[1]

- *Pseudoclass selectors*—The *pseudoclass* is a way to permit selection based on information not contained in the document. The four most widely used pseudoclasses are the selector suffixes `:link`, `:active`, `:visited`, and `:hover`. They are usually applied to the a element to control hyperlink styles (Section 6.5).

- *Pseudoelement selectors*—These are fictitious elements for the purpose of assigning styles to well-defined parts of the document content. CSS1 provides two pseudoelements, `:first-line` and `:first-letter`, allowing you to specify styles for the first line and first letter of an element. For example, `p:first-line` means the first line of a paragraph, and `p:first-letter` means the first character of a paragraph. CSS3 introduces additional pseudoelements.

Selectors sharing the same properties can be grouped together in one rule to avoid repeating the same rule for different selectors. To group selectors, list them separated by commas. For example,

```
h1, h2, h3, h4, h5, h6 { color: blue }
```

is shorthand for six separate rules, one for each heading. Be sure to use the commas. Otherwise, the selector turns into a contextual selector. Table 6.1 lists selector examples for easy reference. Complete specifications of CSS selectors can be found at W3C. The W3C CSS3 recommends selectors with improved

---

[1]Browser support for > and + in selectors is not uniform.

Table 6.1   CSS SELECTOR EXAMPLES

Selector	Selector Type
`body { background-color: white }`	Element
`*.fine or .fine { font-size: x-small }`	Universal + Class
`h2.red { color: #933 }`	Class
`table.navpanel img { display: block }`	Contextual

`a.box:hover`
`{ border: \#c91 1px solid;`
`  text-decoration: none; }`
	Pseudoclass in Class

`p, ul, nl { line-height: 150%; }`	Element Shorthand

syntax, based on element attributes and finer code contexts. Selector specifications are advancing, but browser support is lagging behind. We can look forward to even more flexibility and power in style control.

6.5 HYPERLINK STYLES

Hyperlink style is an integral part of the overall look and feel of a Web site. You do not style hyperlinks through the `a` tag directly because `<a>` is used for both linking and anchoring.

Four pseudoclass selectors allow you to specify visual styles to indicate whether a hyperlink is not visited yet, visited already, ready to be clicked (the mouse is over the link), or during a click. For example,

```
a:link { color: #00c;  }       /* shaded blue for unvisited links */

a:visited { color: #300; }     /* dark red for visited links */

a:active                       /* when link is clicked */
{   background-image: none;
    color: #00c;               /* keeps the same color */
    font-weight: bold;         /* but turns font bold */
}

a:hover                        /* when mouse is over link */
{   background-color: #def;    /* turns background gray-blue */
    background-image: none;
}
```

Figure 6.5 LINK STYLES

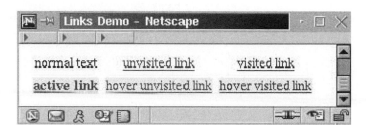

In case you are wondering, these four selectors do inherit any style properties from the a element and can selectively override them. Figure 6.5 shows these different link styles.

Sometimes it is useful to have different classes of links (e.g., external and internal links). In that case, you can use selectors in the form

```
a.external:link
a.external:hover
```

Hyperlinks are usually underlined; to avoid the underline, you can add the rule

```
a { text-decoration: none }
```

Be advised that Web surfers are used to seeing the underline for hyperlinks. Unless you have a very good reason, don't remove the underline.

6.6 CONFLICTING RULES

With the variety of selectors, multiple style rules could apply to a given HTML element. For example, the two rules

```
p { font-size: normal }
li p { font-size: small }
```

both apply to a <p> element within an <li> element. Intuitively, we know which one applies. Because CSS intrinsically rely on such conflicts, there are very detailed and explicit ways to decide which among all applicable rules applies in any given situation (see Section 6.23). Generally, a rule with a more specific selector wins over a rule with a less specific selector. Selectors in order of decreasing specificity are Id selector, class selector, attribute selector, contextual selector, element selector. If an element has a style attribute in HTML (an in-element style attribute), it is the most specific.

This arrangement allows you to specify global styles for elements and modify those styles with contextual rules. Special cases can be handled with class selectors. One-of-a-kind situations can be handled with Id selectors or in-element style attributes.

6.7 STYLE PROPERTIES

With a good understanding of selectors, we are now ready to tackle the rich set of available style properties and their possible values. You will see that there are many properties to give you fine control over the presentation style, including properties for font, color, text, and the box around an element. Many properties apply generally. Others are for inline or block elements only. Unrecognized properties are ignored.

When displaying a page, the browser presents each HTML element according to its style properties. If a property is not specified for an element, then that property is often *inherited* from its *parent element*. This is why properties set for the body element affect all elements in it. Because of inheritance, it is important to make sure that all elements are properly nested and end with closing tags.

When a property has a percentage value, the value is computed relative to some well-defined property. For example, margin-left: 10% sets the left margin to 10% of the available display width. Each property that admits a percentage value defines the exact meaning of the percentage.

With a good understanding of CSS syntax, we are now ready to put that knowledge to use and see how CSS is applied in practice.

6.8 A NAVIGATION BAR

Easy and convenient navigation is critical to the success of any Web site. The two main questions from a user's viewpoint are: Where am I in the site? How to get where I need to go? A good navigation system must clearly identify each page and provide consistent visual clues and feedback for hyperlinks.

A navigation bar (navbar) or panel collects important links in a central place. Visitors expect to find navigation constructs on the top and left sides of pages. Frequently, auxiliary navigation links are also placed on the right and bottom sides. Hyperlinks can appear "charged" or "armed" when the mouse cursor is positioned over them. This is the so-called *rollover* effect. A logical and consistent design of rollovers can help the user feel in control when visiting a site.

Let's put what we've learned about style sheets to work and construct a navigation bar with rollovers (Ex: **Navbar**) just by defining style rules. Such a navbar is easy, fast loading, and simple to maintain.

Figure 6.6 shows the navbar that we will build. Its HTML code is as follows:

```
<head><title>Navbar</title>
<link rel="stylesheet" href="navbar.css"
      type="text/css"  title="navbar" />
</head>
<body style="margin-top: 30px">
<!-- enter div below on one line -->
<div class="navbar">
    <span class="self">Overview</span>|              (1)
    <a href="syl.html">Syllabus</a>|
    <a href="sch.html">Schedule</a>|
    <a href="proj.html">Projects</a>|
    <a href="home.html">Homework</a>|
    <a href="map.html">Site Map</a>|           (2)
    <a href="res.html">Resources</a>|
    <a href="qa.html">Q &amp; A</a>        (3)
</div>
</body>
```

Here, the navbar code is given on multiple lines for easy reading. In a file, it is on one line with no extra spaces. We have also used nonbreaking spaces (lines 2 and 3) to ensure the navbar stays together on one line. Such a navbar is not unlike the ones used for college course Web sites. It can be placed in any appropriate page to provide in-site navigation. The navbar has these features:

- It is a block element enclosed in `div`.
- The link to the current page is inactive and is displayed in a golden color with a boldface font. This helps identify the current page clearly.
- Links are displayed without the usual underline, which makes the navbar clean looking.
- Vertical bars visually separate the links and give the navbar a customary distinctive look.
- A matching gold color background lights up when the mouse is over a link on the navbar. This rollover behavior is widely used on the Web for responsive navigation.

Figure 6.6   STYLE SHEET DEFINED NAVIGATION BAR

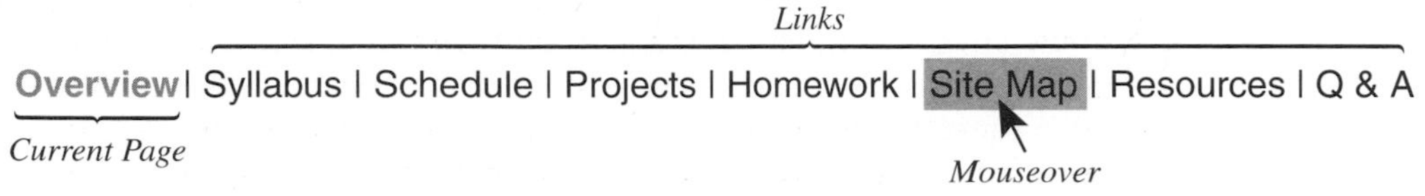

Links

Overview| Syllabus | Schedule | Projects | Homework | Site Map | Resources | Q & A

Current Page   *Mouseover*

To make this work, the file navbar.css specifies styles for the navbar and its child elements:

```
div.navbar                    /* div class navbar              */
{  font-family: Arial, Helvetica, sans-serif;
   white-space: nowrap      /* keeps navbar on one line */
}

div.navbar > span.self     /* span.self in navbar    (4)*/
{  font-weight: bold;        /* bold face font               */
   color: #c80;             /* golden foreground color   */
   padding: 3px             /* breathing room              */
}

div.navbar > a:link        /* hyperlink inside navbar   */
{  padding: 3px;            /* padding not inherited      */
   color: #300;            /* dark red for hyperlink    */
   text-decoration: none   /* no underline              */
}

div.navbar > a:hover       /* mouse over link in navbar */
{  background-color: #eb0; /* golden background         */
   color: #200;            /* darker red for visibility */
   padding: 3px;
   text-decoration: none
}
```

When a link on the navbar happens to link to the page being viewed (the current page), this link must be modified to become inactive and look distinct. This brings two important advantages:

1. The user won't get confused by clicking a link that leads to the same page.

2. The distinct-looking link name helps identify the current page.

The class self (lines 1 and 4) fills this need by specifying a different style for such a current-page link. But this also means the navbar code must be modified slightly when it is placed on a page whose link appears on the navbar.

When you enter the listed code into files, you should be able to experiment with this navbar right away. For ready-to-run files, see the exc6 folder in the example package.

6.9   PAGE FORMATTING MODEL

To use the style properties effectively, some understanding of the CSS page formatting model will help. In this model, the formatted elements form a hierarchy of *rectangular boxes*. Block-level elements produce *block boxes*. Text and inline elements produce *inline boxes*.

For example, `<p>`, `<h2>`, `<ul>`, `<li>`, `<table>`, and `<div>` each generates a block box. And `<em>`, `<strong>`, `<a>`, `<span>`, `<img>`, and plain running text form inline boxes.

The *initial containing box* (root box) corresponds to the root of the document tree (`body` or `frame` for this discussion). In this box, a vertical stack of block boxes of the same width as the root box is formatted.

A box is displayed at a position determined by the formatting of its containing element. The box for each element has a core area to display the content of the element and *padding*, *border*, and *margin* areas surrounding the content. Figure 6.7 shows the block formatting box. An inline box is the same, but its height is always set only by the `line-height` property.

Two distinct formatting modes are used:

- *Block mode*—If a parent block element contains only block elements, then the child elements are formatted in *block mode*. Each block box is by default as wide as the available width (the content width of its parent box) Thus, the available width becomes the width of the child box:

$$\text{available width} = \text{left(margin} + \text{border} + \text{padding)}$$
$$+ \text{ content} + \text{right(padding} + \text{border} + \text{margin)}$$

  Each block box is just high enough for its contents. The vertical separation between block boxes is controlled by the top and bottom margin properties of adjacent boxes. In normal flow, vertically adjoining margins are collapsed and become one margin whose height is the maximum of the two adjoining margins.

- *Inline mode*—If a parent block element contains all inline elements and text, then the child elements are formatted in *inline mode*. An inline box flows horizontally to fill the available line width and breaks automatically to form several lines when necessary. Horizontal margin, border, and padding will be respected.

Figure 6.7   CSS BLOCK BOX MODEL

Margin (transparent)

Border (top, right, bottom, left)

Padding (top, right, bottom, left)

Within a line, inline boxes (Figure 6.8) may be aligned vertically according to their `vertical-align` properties. The rectangular area that contains the inline boxes on a single line is called a *line box*. The line box is just tall enough to contain the inline boxes plus one half *leading* (leading = `line-height` − `font-size`) on top and bottom. Thus, the height of a text inline box is exactly `line-height`, and the height of an `img` inline box is the height of the image plus the leading. Top and bottom margins, borders, and paddings do not contribute to the line box height. A browser may render these outside the line box or clip them.

To see how all this works, let's revisit an example in Section 2.18.

```
<h3 style="color: blue">Alignments with respect          (A)
to the whole line:</h3>
<p><span style=                                           (B)
"color:blue">vertical-align: top</span>
<img alt="preface" src="u_preface.gif"
     style="vertical-align: top" /> in a line with
another <img alt="loon.gif" src="loon.gif"
style="vertical-align: baseline" /> image.</p>
```

Figure 6.9 shows the box hierarchy for this example. Two block boxes of different heights are formatted inside the containing box. The first block box corresponds to h3 (line A) and contains one line box that encloses one inline box for the header text. The second block box corresponds to p (line B). It contains one line box that encloses five inline boxes vertically aligned as indicated. Their bounds are outlined by dotted lines.

If a block element contains both block and inline elements, block boxes will be generated to contain the inline boxes, resulting in block mode formatting. Thus, the code

```
<div>Mixed inline and <p>block elements</p></div>
```

is treated as if it were

```
<div><div>Mixed inline and </div><p>block elements</p></div>
```

Two implications of the inline mode are:

Figure 6.8　CSS INLINE BOX MODEL

Figure 6.9   VISUAL FORMATTING MODEL

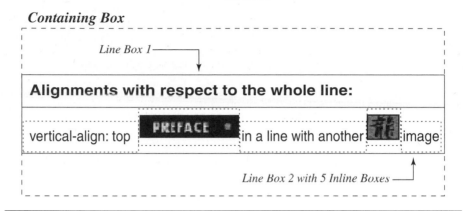

- Unless there is sufficient line box height, any padding or border around inline elements may overlap adjacent lines. Even inline box content may bleed to adjacent lines.
- A line box adds extra top and bottom spacing equal to one half leading to the vertical extent of its inline boxes. This may result in extra white space above and below inline images, for example.

This discussion pertains to the normal flow of CSS visual formatting. Perhaps it is enough for most Web development tasks, but much more information is available (see links on the WDP site).

6.10   SETTING MARGIN, BORDER, AND PADDING

The size of the margin is set with the properties:

```
margin-top: length        margin-right: length
margin-bottom: length     margin-left: length
```

Padding and border are set similarly, and shorthand notations are available. For example,

```
padding: 2px
```

sets the padding on all four sides to 2 pixels. And

```
margin: 50px 10% 50px 10%            /* top right bottom left */
```

sets the four margins. With such shorthand, there can be from one to four values:

1. One value: for all sides
2. Two values: the first value for top and bottom; the second value for right and left
3. Three values: for top, left-right, and bottom
4. Four values: for top, right, bottom, and left, respectively

These may seem confusing, but there is a uniform rule: The values go in order for top, right, bottom, left. If fewer than four values are given, the missing values are taken from the opposite/available side. If a margin is negative, it causes the box to invade the margin of an adjoining box.

The padding area uses the same background as the element itself. The border color and style are set with specific border properties. The margin is always transparent, so the parent element will shine through. The vertical margin between two displayed elements (e.g., a paragraph and a table) is the maximum of the bottom margin of the element above and the top margin of the element below. Sometimes this behavior is termed *margin collapsing*.

The horizontal width of a box is the element width (i.e., formatted text or image) plus the widths of the padding, border, and margin areas. The vertical height of a box is determined by the font size (or height of image) and the line height setting.

6.11 NAVBAR USING BORDERS

Let's take the navigation bar example (Ex: **Navbar**) from Section 6.8 and build a different, and perhaps improved, version (Ex: **NavBorder**) (Figure 6.10):

- Items on the navbar are separated by borders rather than the VERTICAL-BAR character.
- On mouseover, the selected link is highlighted with a colored box and a thin black border, looking like a button.

The HTML code for the new navbar is the same as before with two differences:

1. The VERTICAL-BAR characters are gone.
2. An empty span is added at the end.

Figure 6.10   NAVBAR WITH BORDER SEPARATORS

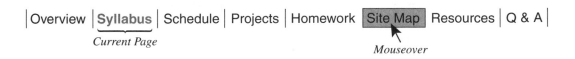

Here is the HTML code:

```
<head> <title>Navborder</title>
<link rel="stylesheet" href="navborder.css"
      type="text/css"  title="navborder" />
</head>
<body>
<div class="navbar">
   <a href="index.html">Overview</a>
   <span class="self">Syllabus</span>
   <a href="sch.html">Schedule</a>
   <a href="proj.html">Projects</a>
   <a href="home.html">Homework</a>
   <a href="map.html">Site Map</a>
   <a href="res.html">Resources</a>
   <a href="qa.html">Q &amp; A</a>
   <span class="self"> </span>                        (7)
</div></body>
```

Again, remember to keep the navbar on one line. The white-space span added (line 7) provides the vertical line at the end of the navbar.

The style sheet navborder.css adds the declaration

```
border-left: thin #000 solid;
```

to each element on the navbar. These left borders replace the *vertical-bar*s and actually do a better job. When the mouse is over a link, the top and bottom borders appear in addition to turning the background color golden. This gives a neat button look (Figure 6.10). Elements on the navbar also have finer control over the padding on the four sides: 1 pixel for top and bottom, and 2 pixels for the left and right.

Here is the style sheet code:

```
div.navbar                      /* div with class navbar  */
{  font-family: Arial, Helvetica, sans-serif;
   white-space: nowrap          /* keeps navbar one line  */
}

div.navbar > span.self          /* span.self in navbar    */
{  font-weight: bold;           /* bold face font         */
   color: #c80;                 /* golden foreground      */
   border-left: thin #000 solid;
   padding: 1px 2px;            /* padding not inherited  */
}

div.navbar > a:visited,
div.navbar > a:active,
```

```
div.navbar > a:link,             /* link inside navbar      */
{  padding: 1px 2px;             /* padding not inherited   */
   color: #300;                  /* dark red for link       */
   border-left: thin #000 solid;
   text-decoration: none         /* no underline            */
}

div.navbar > a:hover             /* mouse over link         */
{  background-color: #eb0;       /* golden background       */
   color: #200;                  /* dark red more visible   */
   padding: 1px 2px;             /* padding not inherited   */
   border-top: thin #000 solid;
   border-bottom: thin #000 solid;
   text-decoration: none
}
```

6.12 BORDER PROPERTIES

From the previous example, we can see that borders can form a box or can be used in other creative ways. You can set the width, color, and style of all four borders.

Values for the border-style property can be dotted, dashed, solid, double (two lines), groove (3-D groove), ridge (3-D ridge), inset (3-D inset), or outset (3-D outset). The three-dimensional varieties use the border color to create a three-dimensional look (see Section 6.13). The border-style property can take one to four values for the four sides: top, right, bottom, left. A missing value is taken from the opposite/available side.

Values for the border-width can be thin, medium, thick, or a length. The value for border-color can be any color. Both properties can take one to four values, as usual.

You can also set border-top-width, border-right-width, border-bottom-width, and border-left-width independently.

The properties border-top, border-right, border-bottom, and border-left each can take a length, a border style, and a color. You may specify one, two, or all three for the particular side of the border. We used

```
border-left: thin #000 solid;
```

in our navbar example. The property border takes the same three values and applies them to all four sides.

6.13   STYLED BUTTONS

Let's put together a click button with style sheet rules (Ex: `Button`). Figure 6.11
shows such a button. The HTML code

```
<a class="button" href="home.html"> Enter Site </a>
```

is simple and innocent looking. The button depends on the style sheet:

```
a.button                      /* hyperlink as button           */
{  font-family: Arial, Helvetica, sans-serif;
   font-weight: bold;
   text-decoration: none;
   background-color: #eb0;    /* golden background             */
   color: #200;
   padding: 2px;              /* breathing room                */
   border-width: 3px;         /* enough width for 3D effect (1) */
   border: outset;            /* un-depressed button look   (2) */
   border-color: #eb0;        /* base color for 3D effect    (3) */
}

a.button:active               /* when button is clicked        */
{  border: inset;  }          /* depressed button look      (4) */
```

A `button` class hyperlink displays a three-pixel border (line 1) in the `outset`
style (line 2). The browser automatically creates a three-dimensional border
derived from the given border color (line 3) that is lighter and brighter for
the top and left borders and deeper and darker for the bottom and right
borders. The selector `a:active.button` is for an active (being clicked) link in
the `button` class. In general, an active link (`a:active`) inherits all the styles
of the `<a>` element. In this case, `a.button:active` inherits from `a.button`. The
`a.button:active` style changes the border style from `outset` to `inset` (line 4),
creating the depressed button look.

   A button like this is not very useful by itself. If you put several of them
in a paragraph, you can run into display problems with the buttons invading

Figure 6.11   A STYLE SHEET BUTTON

the lines above and below. The three-dimensional button is a component to construct navigation bars, as we'll see next.

A Three-Dimensional Navigation Bar

Arranging several three-dimensional buttons in a row or column, we can easily build a handsome and responsive navigation bar. Let's build a vertical navigation bar (Ex: **ButtonBar**) as shown in Figure 6.12.

We need to make all three-dimensional buttons the same width and stack them vertically surrounded by some breathing room. The button labels also need centering. All these are done with style code. The HTML source for the three-dimensional navigation bar is as follows:

```
<head> <title>3D button</title>
<link rel="stylesheet" href="3dbutton.css" type="text/css"
      title="3dbutton" />
</head>
<body>
<div class="dbar">                                              (a)
<a class="button" href="entry.html">Store Front</a>
<a class="button" href="promotion.html">Products on Sale</a>
<a class="button" href="customer.html">Customer Service</a>
<a class="button" href="shipping.html">Free Shipping</a>
</div>
</body></html>
```

It is easy to add more buttons on the navigation bar.

Figure 6.12   THREE-DIMENSIONAL NAVIGATION BAR

Mouseover   *Mousedown*

The three-dimensional buttons are arranged inside a styled div (line a), which provides the width, the background, and the text-centering properties for the navigation bar as follows:

```
div.dbar
{   width: 170px;                   /* width of navbar        */
    background-color: #a70;         /* darker gold background */
    border: 1px #630 solid;         /* dark gold thin border  */
    padding: 3px;                   /* around button column   */
    text-align: center;             /* centers each button    */
}
```

The width and the colors of the navbar can be easily customized. The declaration for a.button is the same as before with the addition of three declarations (lines b-d)

```
a.button                           /* same as Ex Button      */
{       ...

    display: block;                 /* 3 more declarations (b) */
    width: 94%;                     /*                     (c) */
    margin: 3px auto 3px auto       /*                     (d) */
}
```

which ask the browser to format the button as a block element rather than an inline element (line b). This means the buttons are in block boxes with the same 94% width (line c) as based on the parent div and stacked with the indicated vertical separation (line d) and centered horizontally (line d).

The on-mouseover and on-click behavior of the buttons are defined as follows:

```
a.button:hover                     /* mouse over */
{   color: white;   border-color: #eb0;   }

a.button:active                    /* clicked    */
{   border: inset;   }
```

The full example can be found at the WDP Web site.

6.14 FORMATTING TEXT

We have seen the text-align property which, when applied to block-level elements, controls the horizontal alignment of child inline elements.

For text formatting, you have further control over letter and word spacing (Section 5.10), line height, horizontal and vertical alignment, first-line indentation, decoration, and transformation.

- `word-spacing` and `letter-spacing`: Control tracking (spacing between words) and kerning (spacing between characters). Values are `normal` or a length to add or subtract from the normal spacing.
- `line-height`: Controls spacing between lines of text. It sets the height between adjacent baselines. Values can be a length, a percentage, or a number. The percentage is relative to the current font size. The number is a multiple of any font size in use for the element or a child element.
- `vertical-align`: Controls vertical alignment of inline elements such as a word or an image. Values include `sub` and `super` in addition to settings mentioned in Section 2.18.
- `text-align`: Controls the horizontal alignment of text within an element (Section 2.11).
- `text-indent`: Controls first-line indentation within a block element. Value is a + or −, length, or percentage (Section 6.3).
- `text-decoration`: Specifies added decoration for text. Values are `none`, `underline`, `overline`, `line-through`, and `blink`.
- `text-transform`: Calls for certain transformations on the text in the element. Values are `capitalize` (first letter), `uppercase`, `lowercase`, and `none`.

The pseudoelement `:first-letter` is used to specify special styling for the first letter in an element, usually a paragraph. Here is an example (Ex: **DropRaise**) that gives the *drop cap* and *raised cap* effects that we saw in Figure 5.29. The HTML code is

```
<p class="initial">
How does it begin, the child asks anxiously...</p>
<p>Once upon a time, there was a family
of rabbits ... </p>
```

To produce the drop cap effect, the style rules are:

```
p.drop:first-letter
{   font-size: 280%;
    font-weight: bold;    float: left;
    margin-right: 3px;    margin-bottom: -6px
}
```

The rule affects only the first letter of any p element with class `drop`.

The first letter is almost three times the normal font size, bold face, and floated to the left (like an image). The letter also has an increased right margin to give some breathing room to the text following it and a reduced bottom margin to allow the third line to come under the letter.

The raised cap effect is a bit simpler:

```
p.raise:first-letter
{   font-size: 220%;  font-weight: bold;
    letter-spacing: 2px;  /* not margin */
}
```

Since we are not floating the character, we used `letter-spacing` instead for the breathing room.

The pseudoelement `first-line` is used to specify styling for the first line in an element, usually a paragraph. For example,

```
p.initial:first-line {  text-transform: uppercase  }
```

sets the first line of an initial paragraph to ALL CAPS.

6.15   ELASTIC BANNERS

Let's apply style sheets to the `table` element to construct an *elastic banner*, which can stretch and shrink horizontally to fit different screen sizes and resolutions (Ex: **Elastic**). These banners are useful in fluid pages (Sections 5.12 and 6.22) that adjust well to different screen and window sizes. Figure 6.13 shows the same banner stretching and shrinking. The left and right ends, the leading part, and the spacing between the letters all stretch or shrink to fit on the screen while preserving the overall look of the banner.

The HTML code for the elastic banner is simple:

```
<head> <title>Elastic Banner</title>
  <link rel="stylesheet" href="elastic.css"
        type="text/css"  title="elastic" />
</head>
<body>
<table class="banner" width="100%" cellpadding="0" cellspacing="0">
 <tr>
   <td class="left"> </td> <td class="spacer"> </td>
   <td class="char">E</td> <td class="char">L</td>
```

Figure 6.13   ELASTIC BANNERS

```
     <td class="char">A</td> <td class="char">S</td>
     <td class="char">T</td> <td class="char">I</td>
     <td class="char">C</td> <td class="right"> </td>
   </tr>
 </table>
 </body> </html>
```

We have a class banner table and table cells of different classes: left, right, spacer, and char. Note that a nonbreaking space gives something to display. Otherwise, an empty table cell would disappear without even displaying the background. The nonbreaking space font size is set very small to increase shrinkability.

The styles are in elastic.css.

```
table.banner td { height: 40px; } /* cell height */

table.banner td.left              /* stretchable left end */
{ background-color: red;
  background-image: none;
  width: 20%;
  border-right: solid white 2px; /* (1) */
  font-size: xx-small
}

table.banner td.right             /* stretchable right end */
{ background-color: blue;
  background-image: none;
  width: 20%;
  border-left: solid white 2px;  /* (2) */
  font-size: xx-small
}

table.banner td.spacer            /* stretchable middle spacer */
{ background-color: green;
  background-image: none;
  width: 15%;
  font-size: xx-small
}

table.banner td.char              /* banner letters */
{ background-color: green;
  background-image: none;
  color: white;
  font-family: Courier;           /* monospace font */
  font-size: 150%;
```

```
    font-weight: bold
}


body
{   background-color: white;
    margin: 0px;                        /* (3) */
}
```

The left and right parts each have a 2-pixel white border as the white separators (lines 1 and 2). The left, right, and spacer have percentage widths. The characters have minimum widths dictated by the font used. When formatting the table, a browser will try to allocate enough horizontal space for the characters. Together, they may take up to 45% of the available width. The rest of the width is allocated to the left, spacer, and right parts in a 20:15:20 proportion. To ensure that the top banner starts at pixel (0,0), we set the margin width to 0 in body (line 3).

6.16 ROLLOVER NAVIGATION BARS

The pseudoclass selectors a:link, a:visited, a:hover, and a:active combine to make hyperlinks interactive and responsive. The *rollover effect*, when a hyperlink changes appearance as soon as the mouse is positioned over it, is popular and widely used on the Web. There are several ways to perform rollovers. Commonly, it involves writing JavaScript to change the image of the hyperlink upon the mouseover event. This will be described in Chapter 9.

As you saw in Section 6.8, rollovers can also be achieved with style sheets. Style-sheet-defined rollovers are faster loading, more responsive, and easier to maintain than those based on JavaScript. We have seen how text-based navigation bars with rollovers can be constructed. Now let's look at an example in which the hyperlinks are anchored on images. Many Web designers prefer image as anchors because they look so much sharper than browser-based fonts.

To achieve the rollover effect (Ex: **RollImgBar**), we can make a border appear on mouseover as shown in Figure 6.14. The images on the left navbar are 140 by 16 black-on-gray GIFs packed without gaps in a table of one column. The table is placed inside a div whose background is set to match exactly the gray background of the images. The width of the div is set 6 pixels wider (146 pixels), and the table is centered horizontally in the div. This provides a comfortable margin around the images for the rollover borders. The HTML code here shows the rollover bar is a div containing a table. The table code is abbreviated by giving only one typical link represented by a table row (lines a-b).

```
<div class="leftbar">
<table width="140" cellspacing="0" cellpadding="0">
```

Figure 6.14   BORDER AROUND IMAGES

```
<!-- typical row -->
<tr valign="middle" align="center">                    (a)
<td><a href="main.html"><img src="nav/overview1.gif"
     alt="overview" /></a></td>
</tr>                                                   (b)

    <!-- more such rows -->

</table></div>
```

Figure 6.15 shows the adding of borders to an image. The images used on this navbar are 140 by 16 GIFs. The style sheet provides a gray vertical panel to layout the images and allow room for the rollover border. The task involves using contextual selectors and making a number of things work together.

```
/* parent and background for entire navbar */
div.leftbar                                            (c)
{  width: 146px;
   background-image: url('nav/navbkg.gif');            (d)
}
```

Figure 6.15   BORDERS AROUND AN IMAGE

140×16	142×18	142×18
Overview	Overview	Overview
GIF Image	*Add border*	*Rollover*

```
div.leftbar > table  /* centered table in div */
{   margin-left: auto;
    margin-right: auto;
}

div.leftbar > table td  /* cell in table */
{   width: 144px;                                               (e)
    height: 26px;                                               (f)
}

div.leftbar > table a
{   display: block;                                             (g)
    border:  #dde3ee 1px solid;                                 (h)
}

div.leftbar > table a:hover
{   border: #0f6 1px solid; }                                   (i)

div.leftbar > table img
{   border-style: none; }
```

The div (line c) provides enough width and matching background (line d) for the images, which are centered horizontally and vertically (line a) in table cells with the width for the images and its borders and sufficient height for vertical separation of the images (lines e-f).

Making a a block element (line g) is critical because it gives the a element a block box, rather than an inline box, suitable for displaying borders around the anchor image. The gray border (line h) around the a element is not visible against the table background, which has the same color. But this invisible border becomes visible on mouseover (line i), completing the rollover effect.

The full example is in the example package, and you can also experiment with it and see the source code on the WDP Web site.

6.17   PIECING IMAGES TOGETHER

Web developers often use tables to lay out all or part of a page. Frequently, images must be aligned and pieced together exactly without intervening gaps. A navigation bar composed of images is an example. Understanding the page formatting model helps in these applications.

Here is the XHTML code that piece together four hyperlink images (Figure 6.16):

```
<head><title>Image Composition</title></title>
<link rel="stylesheet" href="composeimage.css"
    type="text/css"  title="Compose Image" />
```

Figure 6.16   IMAGE PIECES

```
</head>
<body style="border: none; margin: 0px">                              (1)
<table class="images" cellpadding="0"
                      cellspacing="0" border="0">                    (2)
<tr>
<td><a href="a.html"><img src="1-1.jpg" width="200"
      height="80" alt="image 1" /></a></td>
<td><a href="b.html"><img src="1-2.jpg" width="114"
      height="80" alt="image 2" /></a></td>
</tr><tr>
<td><a href="c.html"><img src="2-1.jpg" width="200"
      height="80" alt="image 3" /></a></td>
<td><a href="d.html"><img src="2-2.jpg" width="114"
      height="80" alt="image 4" /></a></td>
</tr>
</table></body>
```

The composed picture is shown in Figure 6.17. The body style (line 1) places the combined image at the upper left corner of the page without any margins. To eliminate gaps, the style file composeimage.css is the key:

```
table.images img
{   border: none;                                   /* (3) */
    display: block;                                 /* (4) */
}

table.images a { display: block; }                  /* (5) */
```

The following actions help remove any intervening gaps:

• Delete unnecessary white-space characters in the table source code.

• Set table cell padding, spacing, and border to zero (line 2).

Figure 6.17   COMPOSED IMAGE

- Remove the image border (line 3) and change the image display box from inline to block (line 4). This avoids any unspecified vertical separation.
- Set the hyperlink `display` also to `block` to be doubly sure.

Independent of table cells, you can use `div` to compose a horizontal strip of images and a vertical stack of such strips with consecutive `div` elements. These constructs can also be placed within table cells.

We can compose the same dragonfly with `div` as follows:

```
<div class="images" style="height: 80"><a href="a.html"><img
    src="1-1.jpg" width="200" height="80" alt="image 1" /></a><a
    href="b.html"><img src="1-2.jpg" width="114" height="80"
    alt="image 2" /></a></div>
<div class="images" style="height: 80"><a href="c.html"><img
    src="2-1.jpg" width="200" height="80" alt="image 3" /></a><a
    href="d.html"><img src="2-2.jpg" width="114" height="80"
    alt="image 4" /></a></div>
```

The style rules are:

```
div.images
{  line-height: 0px; white-space: nowrap;  }     /* (6) */

div.images img {  border: none; }
```

Be sure to eliminate the vertical separation of the inline box and disable line wrapping (line 6) so the images will always stay together.

6.18 BACKGROUND IMAGES

In practice, a banner often contains custom-designed graphics. If you make the banner graphics into a series of segments and put them in a row of table cells, you can use the ideas in Section 6.15 to make the banner elastic. Such banners are useful in fluid layouts (Section 5.12) that shrink and stretch depending on screen size and resolution. The elasticity is designed in the banner so it can preserve its appearance as much as possible. Make small color images for the background of stretchable spacers so they match seamlessly with other parts of the banner. To set the background to that defined by an image, use the background-image style property. For example, to make myblue.gif the background image of a td element in a banner, you may use

```
table.banner td.right
{    background-image: url(myblue.gif)   }
```

If necessary, the given image is automatically repeated horizontally and vertically to fill the entire background. To gain control over the repetition, you can set background-repeat to repeat (horizontally and vertically, the default), repeat-x (only horizontally), repeat-y (only vertically), or no-repeat.

Pictures and sketches as backgrounds for table cells can also help create fluidity in layout grids. The table cell automatically crops the background image depending on the space available to it (Section 5.13).

Setting background image for the body element is another convenient way to customize the look of a site. You can use a well-designed tile pattern (Figure 6.18) to make a margin, a watermark, or a special paper effect for your pages. Patterns 1 and 2 (Figure 6.18), when repeated, make vertical and horizontal stripes, respectively. The other patterns work in both directions. Repeat pattern 6 to give a page an antique paper look. Be careful using such background tiles for entire pages. They often tend to distract attention and annoy visitors.

The background-position property lets you specify the starting position of a background image: top left, top center, top right, center left, center center, center right, bottom left, bottom center, or bottom right. You can put the starting position anywhere on the page with

```
background-position: x y
```

Figure 6.18   TILE BACKGROUND PATTERNS

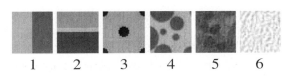

1   2   3   4   5   6

where *x* and *y* can be a length, (e.g., 50px) or a percentage (0% 0% is top left and 100% 100% is bottom right).

Combining starting position with repetition gives you many ways to create backgrounds. For example (Ex: `Bgimg`),

```
body
{    background-image: url(tile4.gif);
     background-repeat: repeat-x;
     background-position: bottom left;
}
```

makes a tiled bottom margin at the end of your page.

A background image also has an *attachment* property, background-attachment, with either a `scroll` (default) or `fixed` value. With a fixed attachment, a background image remains in place as the page content scrolls (Ex: `Attach`). Thus, you can place a background watermark or logo, for example, at a fixed position on the screen. Thus, the code

```
body
{    background-image: url(tile4.gif);
     background-repeat: repeat-y;
     background-position: top right;
     background-attachment: fixed;
}
```

gives you a tiled right margin that stays in place while you scroll the page.

6.19   LIST AND OTHER STYLE PROPERTIES

You can associate properties with `ol` and `ul` to control list-item marker type (`list-style-type`), marker image (`list-style-image: url(...)`), and whether the marker is placed inside or outside the list (`list-style-position: inside` or `outside`). We have discussed these in Section 2.15.

The following `list-style` is shorthand notation to specify the type, image, and position of a list style:

```
ul.compact
{  list-style: circle inside  }
```

Other handy style properties include:

- `display: block`—Useful to display inline elements, such as an image, as a block element (Ex: `RollImgBar` in Section 6.16).
- `display: inline`—Useful to display block elements inline. For example you can make a header run-in with the paragraph following it.
- `float`—To make an element float to the left or right with other content flowing around it.

- `clear`—To make an element clear floating blocks on the left, right, or both. See Sections 2.17 and 3.7 for examples of `float` and `clear`.
- `white-space: pre`—To preserve white space in preformatted text. The style declaration is useful for preformatted inline text such as

```
<p>Here is <span style=
   "white-space: pre">a       hint    :-)</span></p>
```

For preformatted text with multiple lines, the `<pre>` element is the right choice.

- `white-space: nowrap`—To disallow line breaks unless explicitly called for by `<br />` (Ex: **Nest** in Section 3.10 and Ex: **CSSlayout** in Section 6.22).

6.20 POSITIONING

CSS uses three *positioning schemes* to place block and inline boxes for page layout:

- *Normal flow*—This is the normal way inline and block boxes are flowed in the page layout.
- *Floating*—A floating element is first laid out according to the normal flow and then shifted to the left or right as far as possible within its containing block. Content may flow along the side of a floating element.
- *Absolute positioning*—Under absolute positioning, an element is removed from the normal flow entirely (as if it were not there) and assigned a position with respect to a containing block.

You may set the `position` property of an element to specify how it is positioned in the page layout:

- `position: static`—The element follows the normal flow. This is the default positioning scheme of elements.
- `position: relative`—The element is laid out normally and then moved up, down, left, and/or right from its normal position. Elements around it stay in their normal position, ignoring the displacement of the element. Hence, you must be careful not to run into surrounding elements, unless that is the intended effect. Relative positioning can supply fine position adjustments. For example (Ex: **Position**),

```
p.spacing { position:relative; left: 1em } /* move right 1em */
p.morespacing { position:relative; left: 3em }
```

gives more room after the bullet in the list (Figure 6.19):

Figure 6.19   RELATIVE POSITIONING

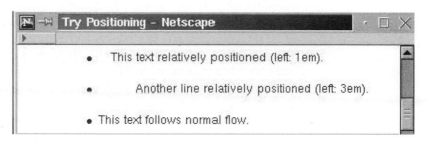

```
<ul><li> <p class="spacing">This text relatively positioned
    (left: 1em).</p></li>
<li><p class="morespacing">Another line relatively positioned
    (left: 3em).</p> </li>
<li> <p>This item follows normal flow.</p></li></ul>
```

Relative positioning is also useful in refining vertical alignments of adjoining elements.

- position: absolute—This property applies only to block elements. The element is taken out of normal flow entirely and treated as an independent block box. Its position is given by the left, right, top, and bottom properties relative to the element's containing (parent) block. The bottom (right) setting gives the distance between the bottom edge (right edge) of the block box to the bottom (right edge) of the containing box. In this case, ensure there is a well-defined bottom or right edge. This means, for example, giving the height or width of the element being positioned.

    For example (Ex: **AbsoluteNav**), add these positioning declarations to dbar (Section 6.13)

```
div.dbar
{   ...
    position: absolute;
    top: 30px;                      /* 30 pixels from top */
    left: 20px;                     /* 20 pixels from left */
}
```

to position a navigation bar in the body element. Then increase the left margin of the contents with something like

```
<div id="content">
...
</div>
```

together with CSS rules for #content to specify enough left margin for the contents (Figure 6.20).

- position: fixed—This property applies only to block elements. An element with fixed positioning is placed relative to a display medium rather than a point in the page. The medium is usually the screen viewport or a printed page. The familiar browser window is the on-screen viewport that can usually be resized and scrolled. A fixed element will be at the same position in the browser window and will not scroll with the page. A block fixed with respect to a printed page will show up at the same position on every page.

By adding the following statement (Ex: **FixedNav**)

```
@media screen                       /* for viewport on screen */
{  div.dbar { position: fixed; }  /* note syntax            */
}
```

to the end of the preceding dbar style sheet, we override absolute to fixed. Now, dbar will stay and not scroll with the textual content (Figure 6.21). To ensure the navbar won't be repeated on each printed page, consider also including the statement:

```
@media print                        /* for printed pages    */
{  div.dbar { position: absolute; }  /* note syntax         */
}
```

It is a good idea to take printing into account when using fixed positioning primarily for the screen.

If no explicit positions are given (via left, top, etc.), a fixed-position element will first be placed according to normal flow and then fixed to the display medium.

Figure 6.20   NAVBAR WITH ABSOLUTE POSITIONING

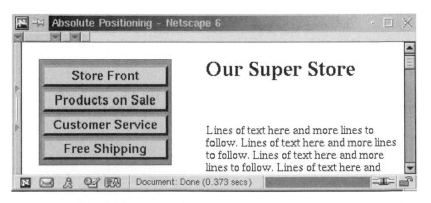

Figure 6.21 **FIXED POSITIONING**

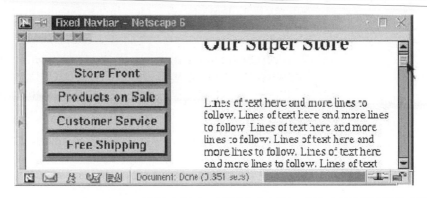

Fixed Positioning: An Example

With fixed positioning, you can easily position page elements such as top banners and navigation bars at fixed positions so they will always be visible and usable no matter how the page is scrolled (Ex: **Fixed**). Let's see how this is done by studying an example (Ex: **ICMPage**). The index page for research on the ICM site at Kent State University (Figure 6.22) has

- a top banner with a page-id-logo graphic that is placed on the right half of the page

Figure 6.22 **ICM RESEARCH PAGE**

- a left navigation bar
- textual content placed under the top banner and to the right of the navbar, with comfortable margins

The top banner and left navbar have fixed positioning so they stay in place as the contents scroll up and down (Figure 6.23). Any content that moves up past the bottom edge of the top banner becomes invisible, hidden by the top banner. This effect is achieved by putting the top banner in a layer that is closer to the screen than the content layer.

The top banner is a table with fixed positioning (line 1):

```
<table id="topbanner" width="100%" border="0"          (1)
      cellpadding="0" cellspacing="0">
   <tr><td style="width:50%"> </td>                (2)
      <td><img src="titresearch.jpg" width="416"
            alt="ICM Research" height="80" />           (3)
   </td></tr>
</table>
```

The code on line 2 puts the JPEG image (line 3) on the right half of the page.

The top banner code is followed by a table containing the left navbar and the content.

```
<table width="100%" border="0" cellpadding="0"
      cellspacing="0">
<tr><td colspan="5" style="height:150px"> </td></tr>  (4)
<tr>
 <td style="width: 25px"> </td>
 <td align="center" valign="top" style="width:20px">
   <div class="rollover"><img src="../mnu/c5.gif" ... />   (5)
      <br /><img src="../mnu/cb.gif" ... /></div></td>
 <td align="center" valign="top" style="width: 110px">
   <div class="navbar">
    <a href="../index.html" ... >                          (6)
       <img src="../mnu/mnhome.gif" ... ></a>
    ...
   </div></td>
   <td style="width:30px"> </td>
   <td valign="top">
      <!-- content begin -->
      ...
      <!-- content end -->
   </td>
</tr>
</table>
```

Enough vertical spacing is given (line 4) to place the navbar and content well below the top banner, which is taken out of the normal flow due to its fixed positioning. If the code on line 4 is taken out, the content would begin at the top of the page and be obscured by the top banner. Code for the left navbar is a vertical arrangement of rollovers (line 5) and hyperlinked images (line 6). The details can be found on the WDP site.

The style sheet for fixed positioning of the top banner, rollover images, and navbar is as follows:

```
#topbanner   /* id selector */
{   position: absolute;                      /* A */
    left: 0px; top: 0px;                     /* B */
    padding-top: 0.6em;                      /* C */
    padding-bottom: 20px;                    /* D */
    background-image: url(../mnu/bg.jpg);    /* E */
}


@media screen   /* overriding positions */
{   #topbanner  /* id selector */
    {   position: fixed;                     /* F */
        z-index: 1;                          /* G */
    }

    div.navbar    /* id selector */
    {   position: fixed; z-index: 1;         /* H */
        line-height: 0px; width: 110px;      /* I */
    }
}
```

Figure 6.23   FIXED BANNER AND NAVBAR

© Paul Wang

```
        div.rollover
        {    position: fixed; z-index: 1
             line-height: 0px;
        }
}

div.navbar a { display: block; }              /* J */
a img { border-style: none }                  /* K */
```

The top banner starts at the upper left corner of the viewport (lines A-B). It contains an image 80 pixels high (line 3), a top padding (line C), and a bottom padding (line D). The top banner also uses the same background image (line E) as the body element, so everything matches. The screen settings override the preceding positions and make the top banner and the left navbar fixed with respect to the screen viewport (lines F and H). The declarations on lines I-K control the display of an image-based navbar as we have seen. The z-index declarations (lines G and H) have to do with stack levels and are discussed next.

Fixed Positioning, Stack Levels, and Visibility

With positioning, elements may overlap. The top banner in the ICM example overlaps the top part of the table (line 4). To manage overlapping elements, each element also has a z-index property that designates its *stack level* on the z-axis. The *x* and *y* directions are in the viewport plane, and the *z* direction is the depth perpendicular to the viewport plane. An element with a larger stack level is in front of one with a smaller stack level. The element in front will obscure any elements behind it. Because the initial value for background-color is transparent, the element behind may show through the background areas of the element in front. But if background-color is set to anything else, nothing will show through.

Figure 6.24 shows an example (Ex: **Caption**) in which the overlapping effect is used to place a caption (line A) on a photograph (line B).

```
<head><title>CSS Caption</title>
<link rel="stylesheet" type="text/css" href="caption.css" />
</head><body>
<div id="text1" class="caption">Neptis Butterfly</div>          (A)
<p><img id="image" class="photo" src="neptis.jpg"              (B)
        alt="A butterfly image" /></p>
</body>
```

The style file caption.css places the photograph and the text caption at the same starting position (lines C and D). The caption is in front (z-index: 1) of

Figure 6.24   **CSS-BASED CAPTION**

the photograph (z-index: 0 by default) and right aligned in a width just 2 pixels short of the image width (line F).

```
img.photo
{  position: absolute; left:10px; top:10px;        /* (C) */
   width: 179px; height: 144px
}

div.caption
{  position: absolute; left:10px; top:10px;        /* (D) */
   z-index: 1;                                      /* (E) */
   width: 177px;                                    /* (F) */
   color: black; text-align: right
}
body {  background-color: grey  }
```

The CSS property visibility can be set to visible (the default) or hidden. A hidden element is not rendered even though the space it occupies is in the page layout. Thus, you may regard hidden elements as fully transparent.

Unless specified, the z-index of an element is the same as that of its containing element. The root containing element (body) has z-index 0.

By setting the stack level for the top banner and the left navbar to 1 (lines E and F), they come in front of the other elements, all with stack level 0.

Any element with an explicitly set z-index also starts its own *local stacking context* with it being the local root element and having a local stack level 0.

Under JavaScript control, positioning, stack levels, visibility, and other style properties can combine to produce interesting dynamic effects (Chapters 9 and 10).

CSS fixed positioning is a choice to consider when you are thinking about using frames (Section 3.18). Banners and navigation bars can use `fixed` positioning and are always present on the page (just like frames). The approach avoids the drawbacks of frames and achieves similar layout effects and page loading economy, as we see next.

6.21   PRINTER-FRIENDLY PAGES

A persistent problem on the Web is the difficulty of producing pages on the printer. Problems include pages being too wide, images too big and time-consuming, background colors and background images making text unreadable or simply wasting color ink, hyperlinks (without underlines) disappearing, text in color becoming too faint to read, and so on. Many users have black-and-white-only printers. Even if they do have color printers, some browsers allow the user to disable printing the backgrounds and/or to select a black-and-white printing mode. These are factors Web designers must face when making pages printer friendly.

To make a page *printer-friendly* means to eliminate such problems so it prints clearly and economically on desktop printers. To achieve this, you have two choices: (a) design the page for both the screen and the printer (not easy) or (b) provide a separate version for printing. The printer-friendly version can be prepared manually or generated by tools on demand.

With CSS, you have another option that can often be better. As indicated in Section 6.20, you can control the screen presentation (`@media screen`) and printer style (`@media print`) separately and make the same page suitable for both screen and printer.

In a style sheet file, place general style rules first, followed by screen-only rules inside `@media screen { ... }`, and then by printer-specific rules inside `@media print { ... }`.

For the WDP site, screen-only styles are as follows:

```
@media screen
{   div.pagecontent { width:  445px; }       /* A */

    a {  color: #00c; }

    a.box:link, a.box:visited
    {   border: white 1px solid; }

    a.box:active, a.box:hover                 /* B */
    {   border: #c91 1px solid;
        text-decoration: none;
    }
```

```
a.imglink:link, a.imglink:visited, a.imglink:active
{   border: white 1px solid;
    display: block;
}
a.imglink:hover                              /* C */
{   border: #c91 1px solid;
    display: block;
}
}
```

On-screen content width is set to 445px (line A). Box-style text links (line B) and image links (line C) have a thin golden-yellow border on mouseover.

The WDP site uses the following to make pages printer friendly:

```
@media print
{ div.pagecontent
  {   width: 557px;                              /* 1 */
      font-size: medium; line-height: 100%;    /* 2 */
  }
  h1, h2, h3, p, li { line-height: 120%; }            /* 3 */
  a, h2, h2.red { color: black; }          /* 4 */
  body { border-top: black 1px solid; }      /* 5 */
}
```

A somewhat wider content width (557 instead of 445px), a larger font size, and normal leading (line 2-3) are used for printing. The link and headers will be printed in black (line 4), and a thin borderline defines the top margin in the absence of the browser window (line 5).

6.22 CSS AND PAGE LAYOUT

CSS alone or together with HTML `tables` can implement layout grids (Section 5.12) for Web pages. We saw in Section 3.11 how tables can be used to enforce a page layout. In this section, let's see how CSS can also help. Later, in Chapter 11, we'll also see how tools can help generate HTML templates with associated style sheets for site production.

The layout shown in Figure 6.25 has a combined top banner and navbar, a left navbar, and a bottom banner that can potentially contain navigation links as well. The content is framed in the center. As the content scrolls, the banners and navbars stay in place on the screen. But this is not implemented with frames. Instead, CSS `fixed` positioning is used (Ex: **CSSLayout**).

Although the page involves many different files, the layout involves only two files: `main.html` and `main.css`.

Figure 6.25   LAYOUT WITH CSS POSITIONING

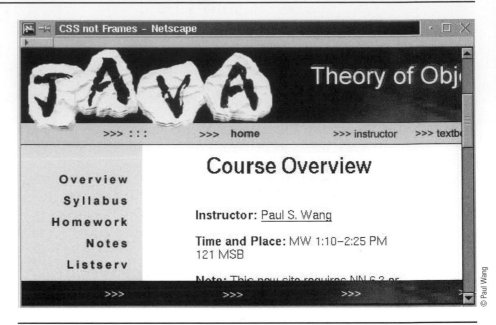

© Paul Wang

The overall structure of the body of `main.html` is:

```
<!-- a: body with CSS defined margins -->

<!-- b: top banner and navbar with CSS fixed positioning -->

<!-- c: left navbar with CSS fixed positioning -->

<!-- d: page content -->

<!-- e: bottom navbar with CSS fixed positioning -->
```

Let's go through these five parts.

The body style (part a) is:

```
body
{   color: black;
    background-color: white;
    font-family: Arial, Helvetica, sans-serif;
    margin-left: 150px; margin-top: 150px;        /* 1 */
    margin-bottom: 60px;                          /* 2 */
    background-image: url(nav/navbkg.gif);        /* 3 */
    background-repeat: repeat-y;
```

```
        background-position: top left;
        background-attachment: fixed;                    /* 4 */
}
```

The margins (lines 1 and 2) define the area for page content (part d), which is the only child element of body that is in the normal flow. All other parts (a, b, c, and e) use fixed positioning and are taken out of the normal layout flow. An image provides the light-gray background (Section 6.18) for the left navbar (lines 3 to 4).

    The positioning of parts b, c, and e are first set as absolute and then fixed with respect to the screen viewport (line 6) as follows:

```
div.topbanner
{   position: absolute; top: 0px; left: 0px;
    background-image: url(topbarBG1.gif);
    white-space: nowrap;         /* on one line */
    height: 93px;  width: 100%;
}

div.topbar
{   position: absolute; top: 93px; left: 0px;
    background-image: url(topbarbg.gif);
    white-space: nowrap;         /* on one line */
    height: 27px;  width: 100%;
}

div.topbar img {   border: none  }

div.leftbar
{   position: absolute; left:0px; top:150px; }

div.bottom                                    /* 5 */
{   height:30px; position: absolute;
    left:0px; bottom: 0px;
}

@media screen   /* overriding positions */       /* 6 */
{   div.topbanner
    {   position: fixed  }
    div.topbar
    {   position: fixed  }
    div.leftbar
    {   position: fixed  }
    div.bottom
    {   position: fixed  }
}
```

For the bottom banner (line 5), the height is needed because we are positioning with respect to bottom.

The content (part d) has comfortable left and right margins:

```
div.content
{    font-size: 100%; margin-right: 15%; margin-left: 8%; }
```

Now let's see the <body> code in main.html:

```
<body>
<!-- top banner and navbar begin -->
<div class-"topbanner">
<map id="home"> ... </map>
<map id="notes"> ... </map>
<img src="topbar01.gif" width="900" height="93" alt="topbar" /><img
src="topbar05.gif" width="100" height="93"  alt="topbar" /></div>
<div class="topbar">
<img src="topbar02.gif" width="214" height="27" alt="topbar" /><img
src="topbar03.gif" width="158" height="27"
        usemap="#home" alt="overview" /><img
src="topbar04.gif" width="528" height="27"
        usemap="#notes" alt="notes" />
</div>
<!-- top banner and navbar end -->

<!-- left navbar begin -->
<div class="leftbar">
<table class=navbar width="146" cellspacing="0" cellpadding="0">
<tr align="center" valign="middle">
  <td><a href="main.html"><img src="nav/overview1.gif"
                                alt="overview" /></a></td></tr>
<!-- more left navbar links -->
</table></div>
<!-- left navbar end -->

<!-- content begin -->
<div class="content">
<h2 class="title">Course Overview</h2>

<!-- more and more content -->

</div>
<!-- content end -->
<!-- bottom bar begin -->
<div class="bottom">
<table cellspacing="0" cellpadding="0" width="100%">
```

```
<tr><td style="background-image: url(btbarBG.gif);">
<img src="btbar.gif" width="900" height="30" alt="bottom bar"/><img
    src="btbar2.gif" width="100" height="30" alt="bottom bar" />
</td></tr></table>
</div>
<!-- bottom bar end -->
</body>
```

You need a browser that supports fixed positioning correctly for this layout to work. The resulting layout has fixed top, left, and bottom parts framing the content without using HTML frames. The complete example is included in the example package and can also be tested at the WDP Web site.

6.23   THE CASCADE

A Web page may have several style sheets coming from different origins: the page author, the user (via preferences), and the browser. The user may specify rules such as underline hyperlinks via browser options, and a browser always has its default styles for HTML elements.

A style sheet may also @import other style sheets. The @media may specify different styles for elements depending on the presentation medium. All of this creates a situation in which multiple style declarations applying to the same element may conflict with one another. In this case, the *cascading order* determines which one applies.

The CSS-defined cascade is quite complicated and detailed. But remembering these rules will be adequate for most occasions:

- User style rules override default rules of the browser.

- A declaration from the page author overrides another by the user unless one declaration is designated important (by putting !important at the end of a declaration), in which case the important declaration takes precedence.

- Conflicting rules in author style sheets are selected based on selector specificity (Section 6.6).

- Everything being equal, a rule later in a style sheet overrides one that is earlier. Imported rules are earlier than all rules in the importing sheet.

CSS Validation

Style sheets can get complicated and may contain hard-to-detect errors. This is because unrecognized rules or rules with typos are ignored by browsers.

To check your style sheets, you can use CSS validation services at W3C or the Web Design Group (www.htmlhelp.com/tools/csscheck).

6.24 FOR MORE INFORMATION

A practical collection of information on CSS has been presented here. Application of CSS in dynamic HTML can be found in Chapter 10.

Browsers are still making progress to fully support CSS, CSS2, and CSS3. See the CSS2 specification and CSS3 recommendations for other properties and complete information on style sheets.

See the WDP site for links to lists of CSS properties, W3C specifications, validation services, CSS positioning examples, and more.

6.25 SUMMARY

A Web page consists of HTML code for document structure and CSS code for document presentation. CSS brings unprecedented power of style definition to the Web developer.

Style sheets can be attached to multiple Web pages, and a page can easily switch style by using different style sheets. The arrangement gives great flexibility to page styling and site maintenance.

A CSS consists of style rules; each has a selector and a set of declarations. A style declaration specifies a value for a property. There are also special rules such as @import and @media.

A CSS provides flexibility in rule specification. You can specify style properties for HTML elements (element tag as selector), any element in a class (*.class selector), any particular element in a class (tag.class selector), an element inside another element (contextual selector), or a single element with a specific id (id selector). The pseudo-class selectors (:link, :active, :visited, :hover) are handy for styling hyperlinks. And pseudo-element selectors (:first-line and :first-character) help style text materials.

The CSS page formatting model uses block and inline boxes to flow contents onto the displayed page. The top and bottom margins that give the vertical separation for inline boxes are controlled by the line-height only, whereas the vertical separation of block boxes is affected by margin, padding, and border settings.

CSS positioning (normal, relative, absolute, fixed) can be used to flexibly place page elements and to fix them with respect to different display media.

Innovative use of CSS can bring three-dimensional buttons, rollover effects on image links, stay-in-place navigation bars (fixed positioning), and framelike page layouts.

EXERCISES

Review Questions

1. Why is it good to separate document structure and document style?

2. What is a style rule? A style declaration? A selector? A style property? What is the syntax of a style rule?

3. How is a style sheet attached to a Web page? Give code for the two ways.

4. How do you call for the SMALL-CAPS style?

5. Discover the white space property and explain how it's used.

6. List the different CSS selectors and give examples.

7. How many ways can you think of to eliminate the border around an image that serves as a link anchor?

8. How does a style sheet include another? What is style inheritance?

9. What is style conflict and how is it resolved?

10. Explain the CSS page formatting model.

11. Explain background image positioning and attachment.

12. Consider CSS positioning. What are the values and meanings for the position property?

13. Is the layout in Section 6.22 a fixed-width layout or a fluid layout (Section 5.12)? Experiment and explain how the effects are achieved.

14. Explain the cascading aspect of CSS.

Assignments

1. Construct a left navigation bar with image-based buttons. Use style rules to specify no image border for any image inside the navigation bar.

2. Put the three-dimensional navigation bar (Section 6.13) technique to use in your Web pages. Note how the text labels on the buttons do not look as sharp as those provided through graphical images.

3. Take an h2 headline and put it in a table cell. Take a picture, such as the monarch butterfly, and put it in the next cell on the same table row. Use style rules to align the bottom of the headline with the bottom edge of the picture.

4. Consider the cellpadding and cellspacing attributes for table. They affect all cells in a table. What if you just want to add some room between the first and second rows or the second and third columns? Apply your knowledge of style rules and create a table with these features.

5. Demonstrate as many ways as you can find to put a sequence of images on a single line with no gaps in between. Make sure the images will not wrap into multiple lines due to browser window resizing.

6. Put two images in adjacent table cells in a table row. Make sure there is no gap between the images no matter how the browser window is resized.

7. Put two images in adjacent table cells in a table column. Be sure there is no gap between the images. Make sure your code follows the full XHTML Strict template as given in Section 2.1.

8. Apply the rollover navigation button ideas given in Section 6.16 in a Web page of your own.

9. Take the layout example in Section 6.22 and check it on three of the most popular browsers (e.g., NN, IE, and Opera).

10. Take the layout example in Section 6.22 and use `absolute` positioning instead. What can be achieved?

11. Some browsers may use a nonzero default top-, left-, and right-margin setting for `body`. Which browsers have this behavior? For layout purposes, you may want to use `margin: 0px` for `body` to be sure.

12. Is it possible to set a background color or background image for a `div` element? Experiment.

13. Use an HTML table to layout a page in which

   - The top banner is full width and fluid as well as fixed to the browser viewport. This banner starts at the very top of the page, is always visible, and does not scroll with the page.
   - A left navbar is also fixed and always visible.
   - The page content is below the top banner and to the right of the navbar with comfortable margins on all four sides.

CHAPTER 7

Color and Graphics

Increasingly, people access the Web with high-quality color monitors. Therefore, colors and color graphics are important dimensions of Web site design. Understanding colors and how they can be used to enhance visual communication is the first step in the effective use of color in site designs.

Color, like many other design factors, appears deceptively simple to use. Color options appear in numerous software packages on the market. Color can be selected, spilled, painted, airbrushed, or filtered in virtually every shade. Conservative color, wild color, pattern and textured color are everywhere, and most of us have been exposed to it since we were children. From chalk art, to crayons, to the craft project in junior high, to painting a room in our house, most of us have worked with color in one way or another.

When people declare that they are not artists, they often say, "I can't even draw a stick figure." No one ever says, "I don't really know anything about color." This assumed knowledge can often lead to poor color choices by most novices. Designers, this odd breed of professionals who are often thrown into the general mix with other "artists," such as sculptors or painters, are usually not born with an innate sense of color. Instead, most designers are formally trained to understand color and its meaning in communication. Aesthetics, combined with communication, is at the root of choosing color. Applying color for purely aesthetic reasons is a luxury awarded to actual artists, who do not necessarily have to answer to the public, much less a paying client. Designers, on the other hand, have to do just that—articulate and defend their color choices and their merits.

This chapter introduces basic color theories and relates them to digital images and Web design. The understanding is basic to creating and manipulating graphical images for your site. As you read through the sections, keep in mind that color is a highly subjective area for most clients, who have specific color preferences and find it difficult to compromise on this aspect of a project. You will have to give this matter careful consideration if you run into this problem. Be prepared to negotiate tactfully.

7.1   A HISTORICAL NOTE ON COLOR THEORY

Over the years, scientists and artists have studied why human beings respond to some color combinations more favorably than to others. Often, color preferences can be very subjective and personal. This adds a dimension of difficulty for formulating theories about color. Early work and experimentation began with the development of the color wheel (Section 7.2). These theories continued to evolve over decades to explain particular patterns and behaviors. Distinguished colorists include Newton, Goethe, Holze, and Albers, who explained both measurable color attributes (colorimetry) and subjective color choices.

Fundamental to any color theory is the ability to distinguish colors and give them precise names. Let's say you selected a yellow. Is it a brown-mustard yellow or a bright-sunshine yellow? Even those are imprecise descriptions subject to interpretation by individuals. How would you actually pinpoint any particular color without ambiguity?

In the 1990s, Albert Henry Munsell, an art professor in Boston, developed one of the most influential color-modeling systems and a notation for precisely naming colors. Munsell's system identified three independent components of color:

- *Hue*—According to Munsell, hue is "the quality by which we distinguish one color from another." Light with different hues has different wavelengths. The terms *hue* and *color* are often used interchangeably in common language. But we will try to avoid that here.
- *Value*—"The quality by which we distinguish a light color from a dark one." It measures how *bright* or *dark* a color is. At full value (brightness), a color of any hue appears white. At zero value (no brightness), any color appears black.
- *Chroma*—The richness of hue. It differentiates deep blue from pale blue, for example. Chroma is also known as the color's *saturation*. Adding white paint to red reduces its saturation, or chroma, making it paler. A color at full saturation is a pure hue. A color at zero saturation is a shade of gray.

Munsell also developed a system to quantify hue, value, and chroma, making it possible to precisely specify colors. His system has been adapted by PANTONE in their color matching system as well as by TRUEMATCH or CIE systems and others.

Johannes Itten was the first to realize the harmony in color pairs according to their spatial relationships. He defined and identified strategies for successful color combinations.

7.2   THE COLOR WHEEL

As most of us remember from early childhood, there are three *primary hues*—red, yellow, and blue (Figure 7.1)—that can combine to obtain all other color hues. For example, green = yellow + blue, orange = yellow + red, and purple = blue + red. These are the *secondary hues* (Figure 7.1). *Tertiary colors* are yellow-orange, red-orange, red-purple, blue-purple, blue-green, and yellow-green. These colors are created by mixing secondary colors (Figure 7.1).

In 1666, Sir Isaac Newton developed the first circular color diagram, and since that time, the traditional color wheel has evolved many variations (Figure 7.2). Generally, a color wheel is a diagram that represents color hues and their interrelationships in a circular pattern. Most color wheels begin with the primary and secondary hues and then show a chromatic relationship between analogous colors.

The color wheel groups *active* and *passive* colors. Often, warm, high-saturation, bright colors appear to come forward and are said to be active. Cool, low-saturation, dark colors appear to visually recede and are said to be passive. Some colors appear to be neutral.

Figure 7.1   PRIMARY, SECONDARY, AND TERTIARY COLORS

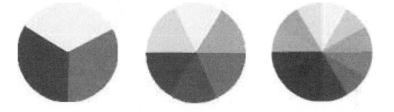

Figure 7.2   COLOR WHEEL

7.3 COLOR HARMONY

In general, people have strong likes and dislikes when it comes to color. Whatever their preferences, most people respond positively to the harmonious use of color. Harmony may be defined as a pleasing arrangement of parts, such as in music. Harmonious color creates an inner sense of order, a visual balance, which engages the viewer. Color harmony implies that a color scene is neither boring nor chaotic. As indicated by the principle of unity and variety (Section 4.5), it is important to know how much and what colors to include in a design. If you don't include enough color, you run the risk of boring the viewer. On the other hand, if you overwhelm the viewer with too much color, the visuals may not make any sense. The idea that more color is better isn't a good one because color, like any other element in design, has to be used for a reason, and it has to make sense in the overall composition. The human brain tends to reject what it doesn't understand. Like much of design, harmonious color is subjective, and in the final analysis, color choices sometimes come down to what the client likes or dislikes. Despite its subjectivity, there are some general principles for using color or achieving color harmony. These have to do with understanding color contrast, complement, analogy, and context.

7.4 COLOR CONTRAST

As with the contrast of forms (Section 4.7), the figure-ground relationship is important for contrast in color. The color difference between a subject (or figure) and its surrounding field (ground) creates contrast—the more contrast between a figure and the ground, the more visible it becomes.

Contrast of color comes in two basic varieties: *value contrast* (light vs. dark color) and *hue contrast* (difference in color hue). But there is more to color contrasts.

Figure 7.3   HUE CONTRAST AND VALUE CONTRAST

Itten's Color Contrasts

In his two well-known books, *The Art of Color* and *The Elements of Color*, Johannes Itten writes about the effectiveness of color relationships with respect to seven distinct color contrasts:

1. *Contrast of hue*—The difference between hues such as yellow, blue, and red (Figure 7.3). The contrast is formed by the juxtaposition of different hues. The greater the distance between hues on the color wheel, the greater the contrast. Figure 7.4 shows low, moderate, and high hue contrasts.

2. *Light-dark contrast*—Examples include black and white, night and day, dark gray and light gray. The contrast is formed by the juxtaposition of light and dark values. This contrast is also effective in a monochromatic composition. Figure 7.5 shows different value contrasts.

3. *Cool-warm contrast*—Red, orange yellow (warm) contrasted with blue, green, and brown (cool) (Figure 7.6).

4. *Complementary contrast*—Opposing colors on the color wheel that create maximum contrast: yellow, violet, blue, orange, red, green (Figure 7.7).

Figure 7.4   LOW, MODERATE, AND HIGH HUE CONTRASTS

Figure 7.5   LIGHT, MEDIUM, AND DARK VALUES

Figure 7.6 CONTRAST: WARMTH, SATURATION, AND EXTENSION

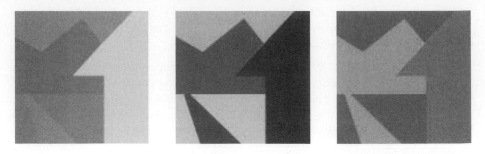

5. *Simultaneous contrast*—Contrast when the boundaries between colors perceptually vibrate, sometimes creating interesting illusions (Figure 7.7). This is an effect that occurs when two adjacent colors enhance or reduce their optic saturation:

   • White looks whiter when surrounded by a darker value.

   • Gray appears more intense when surrounded by a lighter value.

   • Colors can appear lighter or darker depending on their surrounding value and hue.

6. *Contrast of saturation*—Contrast between pure, intense colors and more neutral, pale colors.

7. *Contrast of extension*—Involves assigning numeric properties to color and then using them in weighing proportional amounts next to one another (Figure 7.6).

Figure 7.7 CONTRAST: SIMULTANEOUS AND COMPLEMENTARY

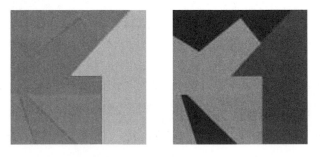

Analogous Colors

Analogous colors are any three colors that are side by side on a 12-part color wheel such as green, yellow-green, and yellow. This type of color is often found in nature, and it tends to be pleasing (Figure 7.8).

Complementary Colors

Complementary colors are two colors that are directly opposite each other on the color wheel, such as red and green or orange and blue (see Figure 7.8). Complementary colors generally look very good together in a design. These opposing colors create maximum contrast, which can be a powerful tool in a composition. However, be careful when using complementary colors. Green and red tend to vibrate when used next to each other. It is also not advisable to use them in many cases, especially for text. An important point to keep in mind about complementary colors is that they do not necessarily give you contrast of value (Figure 7.9). Take red and green, for example. Just because this combination provides maximum hue contrast doesn't mean that the same combination creates the same value contrast. This is a very important point to keep in mind when designing pages that will be printed on a black-and-white printer.

Figure 7.8   ANALOGOUS AND COMPLEMENTARY COLORS

Figure 7.9   VALUE VS. HUE CONTRAST

The use of complementary colors is significant in print. Painters especially work extensively with complementary colors. Figure 7.10, *Child Reading* by Pierre Auguste Renoir, illustrates this technique beautifully. On the other hand, if you mix red and green paints together in unequal parts, this will create a dull red or a grayish green depending on the prominence of the color you added. Then tone down both colors with white and mix them together. This combination will yield a superior range of neutralized grays. The next time you're at a museum and you see a classic painting by Degas or Monet, notice how the shadows were created. The richness of tone may have been created using this technique. According to José M. Parramon, the author of *Color Theory*, this combination creates a range of neutralized complementary colors, and it is where you'll find harmony.

A final word on complementary colors is this: Strive to create contrast of brightness as well as contrast of hue. If both are not possible, brightness is a more critical factor when you're designing Web pages.

Color Context

Color context refers to the environment in which colors are seen. Color context has to do with surrounding colors and how they impact the use of color. In Figure 7.11, we can see that the yellow square looks more brilliant against a black background and very pale and dull against the white background. The yellow square also looks bigger against the black background than against the other three backgrounds. In addition, the yellow square begins to vibrate against the light green, almost producing a blurring effect on the yellow.

Figure 7.10   COMPLEMENTARY COLORS

Figure 7.11 **COLOR CONTEXT**

Warm and Cool Colors

Warm colors are associated with sunlight and fire, whereas cool colors are associated with moonlight and water. Warm colors are said to appear in closer proximity, and cool colors tend to create a sensation of distance. As you develop your own layouts, this is a good rule to keep in mind when you begin choosing your background and foreground colors. Examples of warm colors are red, orange, and related hues. Green, violet, and ultramarine are cool colors. Except for orange-red, all hues can be made warmer by mixing in a little yellow or red. For example, if you add a little red to purple, it will become red-violet. The same can be done to make colors cooler. If you add blue, blue-green, or white to a color, you will cool it down. Green can be cool or warm depending on whether yellow or cyan is the dominant color in the mix. Yellow can also be cool or warm. All colors, warm and cool, may appear warmer or cooler depending on their placement. In the case of Figure 7.12, we see that the grapes on the left look warm, and those on the right look cool.

Saturation

Saturation is a term used to describe the degree of color purity. In painting, this term remains theoretical, and it means something a little different on computers. On the computer, if color isn't saturated enough, the image may appear lifeless. On the other hand, if color is oversaturated, the image may appear unrealistic or too intense (see Figure 7.13). This will be discussed later in the chapter. For now, we need to say that pure colors mixed with black, gray,

Figure 7.12 **WARM AND COOL COLORS**

© PhotoDisc Collection/
Getty Images

Figure 7.13   EXAMPLES OF SATURATION

or white diminish in color or hue. They become pale or dull, and the color always appears less bright than the original color. When mixed with other hues, pure colors become transformed into either reddish, bluish, or greenish tones. Colors created with these mixtures are called *unsaturated* colors. In fact, if you mix equal parts of two complementary colors, you will get the lowest level of saturation.

7.5   COLOR FOR THE WEB

Knowing why some color combinations work better than others will improve your ability to make color choices. With the color concepts and theories discussed so far, let's see how actual Web sites put them to use.

The Herman Miller site (hermanmiller.com) uses a very effective soft palette of colors (Figure 7.14). Numerous colors throughout the site identify different sections. As an example, we've included just eight color sections to show why they work well together. The eight-color sample uses complementary colors from the secondary and tertiary palette (Figure 7.14). Purple and green are complementary because they appear opposite each other on the color wheel, creating dynamic hue contrast. Orange and blue-green also work well for the same reason. Light and dark lavender, derivative of dark purple, provide a necessary value shift, creating contrast of value. Warm orange and soft yellow-green contrast effectively with the cool dark green, blue-green, purple, lavender, and cool gray. Dark gray appears as an accent color for typography and for rules, providing good value for readability, while black rollovers indicate activity on the buttons. Black, in this case, is neutral and does not interfere with the overall diverse color palette. Many sites limit their colors to four or

Figure 7.14   HERMAN MILLER WEB SITE COLORS: SAMPLE 1

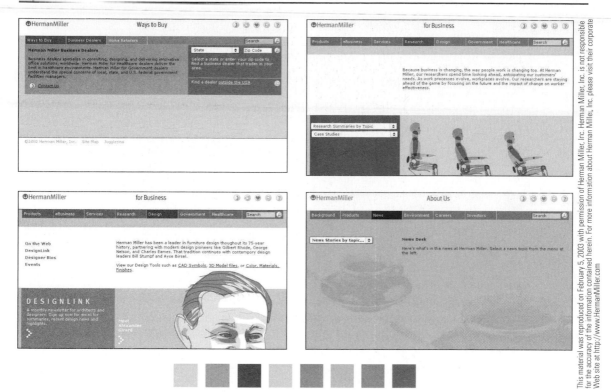

six choices. This can be both effective and smart in terms of unifying the site. Remember, more color isn't necessarily better. In the case of Herman Miller, the site contains diverse information, so the multicolor palette makes sense. Color choices support the message and support aesthetics in the overall design.

The American Institute of Graphic Arts' (AIGA) *Journal of Interaction Design* (loop.aiga.org) uses a limited color palette on their site. The site is relatively small, and the nature of their information is not as complex as on the Herman Miller site. Loop does a good job of stretching one hue, such as brown or blue, with various values of the same hue. For example, the bands of colors at the top all contain the same hue but with different values. This effect is sometimes used because it provides variety and depth without complicating the design with another color. The word *loop* appears in the lightest value on the top of the vertical bands in both the blue and brown pages. Another feature of this palette is the sensitivity used in arranging typography. The levels of information such as headlines, subheads, body copy, and links copy are organized with meaning and employ the same kind of value discretion found in the graphics. Notice that Figure 7.15 has a full-color photograph at the bottom right corner that

Figure 7.15   LOOP PARTIAL SITE PALETTE: SAMPLES

stands out dramatically against the simple colors used in the rest of the layout. This is another good reason to use a simple color palette: It allows the reader to focus on the photographs and not be confused by color on every part of the page. Finally, we need to point out the color inside the photograph. Sensitivity to color includes choosing colors in photographs used on the site. In this case, the yellow is a complement to blue, providing a single, dynamic accent on the page. These simple yet often overlooked choices play a vital role in the overall success of a design.

The amount of information on the site does not correlate with the number of colors used. There are large sites that use very limited color palettes, whereas others use extensive palettes. Color is not a random choice. As stated previously in this chapter, color is just one part of design, and it has to work in tandem with type, layout, space, and concept. The Discovery Channel site (discovery.com) is quite large. It has many distinctly different sections, all with varying subsections that have to work together in one site. The major sections must have their own identity but remain true to the parent site. The following six examples illustrate many of the main sections and show both the simplicity and diversity of color.

The home page for discovery.com (Figure 7.16) uses a simple navy blue background contrasted with white and a warm tan color. This conservative layout and choice of color allow for the many featured logos on the page such as the Discovery Channel, Animal Planet, Travel Channel, and so forth, all in different shapes, sizes, and colors. All of the samples shown have consistently placed elements that add to the unity of the site:

- Logo appears in the upper left corner.
- Channel name, all in lowercase, appears with no breaks.
- Banner ads appear immediately to the right of the logo.
- Global navigation bar is at the bottom of the banner ad.
- Local navigation is always on the left.
- Featured topic, with a large photo, is prominently placed in the center.
- Large headline is placed to the right of the photo.
- Sneak previews are located to the right of the featured topic.

Figure 7.16   DISCOVERY CHANNEL SAMPLES: 1

Layouts follow a specific template with little variation, yet each channel has its own unique color. Discovery Health (Figure 7.16), for example, uses bright, vibrant orange, which contrasts with the complementary blue used in the banner ad. The .com copy for the most part appears in the lighter value of the same color, allowing it to be visible, but recedes so the focus remains on the main title. This effect is used in Figures 7.16 and 7.17.

The bright purple and yellow used for Discovery Kids (Figure 7.16) are appropriate for the topic. Purple and yellow are located opposite each other on the color wheel, which create maximum hue contrast. Again, we see the use of complementary color to create this strong visual impact.

Animal Planet (Figure 7.17) is all about animals and nature, so it makes good sense to use analogous colors such as dark green, light green, yellow-green, and yellow. Analogous colors, as you recall, are any three colors that appear next to one another on the color wheel. They are pleasing visually and often appear in nature. The soft yellow-green used behind the Daily Animal News seems appropriate and adds to the natural jungle theme.

TLC.com (Figure 7.17) projects a dramatic, actionlike urgency with its strong red and black. Contrasted with all white type, this approach is striking. The bright yellow banner ad stands out well on this saturated red background.

Figure 7.17   DISCOVERY CHANNEL SAMPLES: 2

The Discovery Channel (Figure 7.17) uses a deep-water royal blue, reminiscent of divers and deep-sea adventures. The bright yellow banner ad, again, contrasts effectively with the deep saturated blue both in value and hue.

7.6   THE MEANING OF COLOR

Unlike any other language, color is immediate communication. It truly is the only language, other than music, that doesn't require any words. Is it any wonder that color is used in symbols and signs all over the world? You may not have to know how to read to see the red stop sign or recognize a yellow caution sign in the United States. We can discuss light in many different aspects; it has its physics and mathematics manifestations. We can discuss color in terms of light and energy. By far our most meaningful discussion of color is about the perception of color.

The Web is a global medium and, thus, it requires us to consider the meaning of color in a much broader context. Color, like style, aesthetics, or even food preference, is largely influenced by our culture. In the United States, for example, red means danger; in China, it means joy and festivities; in Japan, it means anger; in the Middle East, it means evil. Know your primary audience. Know how colors are perceived in each country and culture. Do your homework and research that region of the world. This exercise will go a long way to ensure that your site truly caters to a global audience. Figure 7.18 presents some other examples of color and meaning in different parts of the world.

Our color preferences are also rooted in the time period we live in. If you lived in ancient Egypt, you would associate black with seeds sprouting from the earth. Statues of Osiris were painted black for that reason. In that same time period, green herbs were used to heal common ailments such as colds. Wooden statues painted in red were used as spiritual aids and buried with the mummified bodies in the Inca's culture. Regardless of color's power to communicate nonverbally, a person's language plays a significant role in color perception. Not all ideas can be expressed in some languages. According to Benjamin Whorf's linguistic relativity hypothesis, a language limitation can affect a person's color perception. An example is the Shona language in Zimbabwe and the Boas language in Liberia, both of which have no words to distinguish red from orange. For them, red and orange are only one color, and they can't perceive a difference between them. According to psychologist E. R. Jaensch, climate can also influence our color preferences. If you visit warmer climates, you will see that people there prefer to wear warm, bright colors. People living in less sunny climates prefer darker, cooler, more subdued colors.

Regardless of the culture, the time period, or the product that you're selling, color choices remain subjective. Color schemes are ultimately decided by designers and their clients, and sometimes the clients' spouses. When defending your design choices, it is wise to know which battles you can win and

Figure 7.18 THE MEANING OF COLORS IN DIFFERENT GEOGRAPHIC LOCATIONS

COLOR	W. EUROPE & U.S.	CHINA	JAPAN	MIDDLE EAST
RED	danger, anger, stop	joy, festivity	anger, danger	danger, evil
YELLOW	caution, cowardice	honor, loyalty	grace, nobility childish gaiety	happiness, prosperity
GREEN	sex, safety, sour, go	youth, growth	future, youth energy	fertility, strength
WHITE	purity, virtue	mourning, humility	death, mourning	purity, mourning
BLUE	masculinity, calm authority	strength, power	villainy	
BLACK	death, evil	evil	evil	mystery, evil

which you can lose. Most people have very definite color dislikes and likes, and regardless of the color theory, market research, or color's global meaning, the final deciding factors are often personal. As collaborators in the design process, it is a designer's job to advise clients on the most appropriate color choices based on what we know about color and meaning in the overall context of the design.

7.7 COLOR AND READABILITY

Much of what we have already discussed about color can be applied to readability. For example, we know that contrast is critical to readability, so choose your color combinations wisely to provide a clear path to your message. Figure 7.19 is a good example of effective use of color. The type "Cross Australia" links the red map image on the circle nicely. Equally, the east and west arrows appear in red, which further punctuates the point of the poster. *Type & Contrast* by Alton Cook and Robert Fleury is a good book to read if you would like more information about color and creative color combinations used for print, many of which may be applied to Web design. Allan Haley in his essay on

Figure 7.19   **COLOR WITH A PURPOSE**

"Effective Typography," found in the *Type & Contrast*, is quoted as saying this about color and readability: "Good typography is not pretty design. Pretty design calls attention to the window, not the view. Pretty design is the designer's fingerprints left on the window of communication. Good typographic communication is not pretty—it is smart. It helps the reader assimilate and understand the message." Haley goes on to say that type needs to be readable, and while competing for the viewer's attention, a designer needs to create easy-to-use, inviting text. According to Haley, this ease of use will be the most valuable aspect of design to your viewers.

So, what else can we say about color and readability? Perhaps the most useful way of selecting color may be summarized by Alan Peckolick in his essay "Designing with Type and Color" (in *Type & Contrast*). According to Peckolick, we should select color according to three key factors:

1. *Intuition*—Apply personal sensitivity to color selection. Trust that "gut" feeling, but don't rely on it solely without considering other factors.

2. *Knowledge*—Color should be seen as another element in your design. It should not be used to "enhance" black-and-white forms. It should add something meaningful to your message such as setting the mood, introducing cultural meaning, or connecting through spontaneous associations with your viewers.

3. *Experimentation*—Experience can be the best teacher for knowing how to use color. In this case, you can benefit greatly from someone else's experience by studying effective color applications that already exist on the Web.

7.8 COLOR ON COMPUTERS

When preparing a document for printing, designers typically work with *CMYK* colors (cyan, magenta, yellow, and black), which combine to create a four-color printing process (Figure 7.20). CMYK colors are *subtractive*. Each absorbs colors from incoming light (which is normally white) and lets only cyan, magenta, yellow, or nothing through.

Unlike CYMK printing, computers use the *RGB* (red, green, and blue) color model that works on the principle of *additive color*. Computers create colors through light emissions with a set of primary colors: red, green, and blue. And the primary colors combine to produce all different colors. Figure 7.21 shows how the primary colors add to form other colors.

The Web as a color display medium presents some unique problems. An obvious problem is the inability to control or predict the color characteristics of a viewer's computer platform or monitor. This is mostly due to the fact that

Figure 7.20 **CMYK COLOR MODEL**

Figure 7.21 **RGB COLOR MODEL**

different monitors have different *gamma values* (Section 7.9). Thus, when you design a light blue background on your computer, this same color may slip into dark violet or slimy green on different displays. It's something to think about when you're designing backgrounds.

Fortunately, we can look forward to a few solutions to this problem in the near future. One answer lies in embedding color and gamma information directly into images. Apple's ColorSync system (www.apple.com/colorsync/) is designed to place a filter inside GIF or JPEG images, storing information directly inside the format. The next step is for browsers to interpret this information and display it with adjusted RGB and gamma values on their own platforms as closely as possible to the original image. Present-day versions of browsers do not do this, but they will soon.

Another viable option is the new image format PNG, as explained in the next section.

7.9 WHAT IS GAMMA?

As we just mentioned, images prepared on one computer often look different on another. Monitors use different technologies and come from different manufacturers. They have different electronic and screen properties because of the color characteristics of the display and the nonlinear relation between perceived brightness and the voltage/energy applied to generate light. The brightness is usually proportional to the applied voltage raised to a power. This power is known as *gamma* (www.cgsd.com/papers/gamma.html).

$$\text{light output} = \text{voltage}^\gamma$$

The energy, or *voltage*, in this formula is derived from the pixel values in an image file (GIF, JPEG, PNG, etc.). If the value of the power γ (gamma) is 1.0, then there is no color distortion.

Typical computer display gamma values are close but vary slightly. Strictly speaking, the red, green, and blue components can have slightly different gamma values. Because of the difference in the gamma value, an image that is just right on a Mac will look too dark and more reddish on a personal computer. It is advisable to check all your images on different platforms and make color and brightness adjustments when necessary.

Gamma Correction

The idea of gamma correction is simple: To counter the effects of the gamma value of a target display, we can transform the image first so the transformed image will produce the correct display of the original image. The transformation applies a $1/\gamma$ power to the image to cancel the gamma on a target platform, reducing it effectively to 1.0. Figure 7.22 shows the same JPG image with gamma 1.0 (left) and gamma 2.5 (right). You can experiment with

Figure 7.22   GAMMA CORRECTION

gamma correction by applying different gamma values to an image on the WDP Web site.

An image file can contain the gamma and other color parameters of the platform where the image has been generated. This can allow automatic gamma and color correction on platforms where these parameters are different. GIF and JPEG, the two standard image formats for the Web, do not contain such information. But the Portable Network Graphics (PNG) (www.libpng.org/pub/png/) format, endorsed by the W3 consortium and regarded as a replacement for GIF, does. Furthermore, PNG uses a lossless compression scheme. But browsers supporting PNG are still not widely available. See www.cgsd.com/papers/gamma.html, the gamma correction page, for more details.

7.10   COLOR MODELS AND COLOR ENCODING

Color models are different ways to quantify and represent colors. The RGB and CMYK models are the most basic and best known. Red, green, and blue (RGB) are the primary stimuli for human color perception and are the *primary additive colors*. With RGB, the red, green, and blue optical components are added together to form other colors. RGB is widely used for TV, computer monitors, and the Web. With CMYK, transparent materials (ink mostly) are used to absorb the cyan, magenta, and yellow components (the primary subtractive colors) from white light, and the remaining unabsorbed optical components are reflected from the substrate. Because combining all of CMY won't produce pure black, black (K) has to be introduced in the CMYK model. CMYK is used primarily in printers and the printing process.

The whole range of human color perception is quite large. The set of possible colors (the GAMUT) that can be produced by the RGB or CMYK model is actually a proper subset of the human-perceivable color space.

Colors are produced on a display screen by creating color pixels. Each pixel on the screen consists of three closely positioned dots: a red, a green, and a

Figure 7.23   COLOR HUES

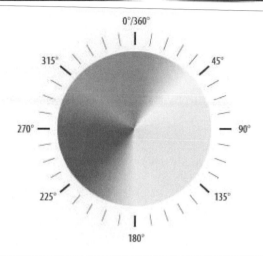

blue. By varying the strengths of the RGB components, you get different color pixels. The RGB model is used widely on computers and the Web/Internet. CSS uses color names and RGB codes to specify color. Section 2.12 lists ways to specify colors in style sheets. The RGB hex encoding is due to the binary nature of computers where numbers grow by powers of 2. With 8 bits, an RGB component can be represented in 256 different strengths (0 through 255). A total of 24 bits is enough for all distinguishable colors in the RGB GAMUT.

HSB (or HLS) is another color model. In HSB, colors are represented by hue, saturation, and brightness (or lightness/luminance).

- *Hue*—The basic property that distinguishes one color from another (e.g., blue from red). Hue is measured as the degree of an angle between 0 and 360° (0 red, 120 green, 240 blue; Figure 7.23).

- *Brightness*—The strength of the hue measured as a percentage of the full strength. For example, a red with R=200 is at a brightness of 78 percent (200/255). A color with zero brightness is black.

- *Saturation*—The purity of a color, at a given hue and brightness, measured as a percentage. For example, the green color rgb(20, 80, 20) has a saturation of 75 percent ((80 − 20)/80). Reducing the saturation to 0 percent gives rgb(20, 20, 20), a gray-scale color. The hue of a color with zero saturation is undefined.

Figure 7.24 shows the brightness and saturation of the color red (hue = 0).

Photo-processing tools often allow multiple color models. For example, the color picker in Photoshop uses HSB, RGB, CMYK, and CIELAB color models and converts between them automatically.

Figure 7.24   RED BRIGHTNESS AND SATURATION

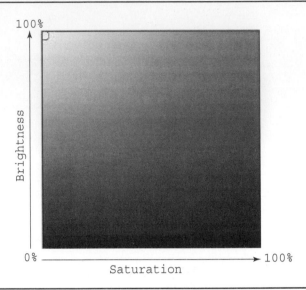

To illuminate the HSB model further, let's consider conversion from RGB to HSB (Ex: **RGB2HSB**). Let floating-point double quantities max and min be

```
max = maximum(R, G, B);
min = minimum(R, G, B);
```

where R, G, and B are integers in the range [0, 255]. The Brightness and Saturation, as percentages, are:

```
Brightness = (int) (100*(max / 255));
Saturation = (int) (100*(max - min) / max);
```

The Hue is a bit more complicated to compute. The following JavaScript (Chapter 9) function shows the logic for computing the HSB values from given RGB values:

```
function rgb2hsb(R, G, B)
{  var Brightness, Saturation=0, Hue=0;
   var max, min, d, factor, ans;
   R = check(R); G = check(G); B = check(B);
   max = Math.max(Math.max(R, G), B);
   min = Math.min(Math.min(R, G), B);
 // compute brightness
   Brightness = Math.round(max*100 / 255);
```

```
// if not black, compute Saturation and Hue
   if ( max > 0 )
   {  d = max - min;
// compute Saturation
      Saturation = Math.round(d*100 / max);

// compute Hue
      if (d > 0)
      { if (max == R)
          factor = (G - B)/d;
        else if (max == G)
          factor = 2 + (B - R)/d;
        else
          factor = 4 + (R - G) / d;

        if (factor < 0)
          Hue = Math.round((6 + factor)*60);
        else
          Hue = Math.round(factor*60);
      }
   }
   ans = [ Hue, Saturation, Brightness ];
   return ans;
}
```

The HSB model covers a total of $360 \times 101 \times 101 = 3,672,360$ definable colors, much less than the 16,777,216 defined in the RGB space. The number of truly different HSB colors is even smaller. For example, all colors with `Brightness==0` are black, and all colors with `Saturation==0` have no defined hue. Therefore, multiple RGB values may convert to the same HSB value.

CIELAB

LAB is a standard color model established by CIE (Commission Internationale de l-Eclairages), an international body of color scientists. The LAB standards make it possible to communicate color information accurately. L describes relative lightness; A represents relative redness-greenness, and B represents relative yellowness-blueness.

Photoshop uses LAB as its *native color space* because LAB can be converted to other color spaces accurately. The LAB color space may become the preferred mode for communicating color information from one computing device to another in the graphic arts because of its ability to store data and convert them without loss.

7.11 COLOR PALETTES

A computer color monitor can display all $256^3 = 16,777,216$ colors. But it takes more than just the monitor to achieve 24-bit true color. You also need a video memory of 24 bits per pixel on the screen and a video adapter capable of processing 24-bit data. To reduce cost, some computers support only 16-bit per pixel or on older models 8-bit per pixel. With 16- or 8-bit color, an operating system color table, called the *system palette*, is used to map color codes to actual colors to be displayed. The system palette can associate the 4,096 sixteen-bit colors (256 eight-bit colors) to any chosen set of 4,096 (256) colors. By loading a different color palette, an application program can use a different set of colors.

Reloading the system palette is possible but time-consuming and will make other applications that use the default system palette appear in strange colors. Because of this, Web browsers tend to rely on the operating system default palette.

When a Web page requests a color outside the color palette, a browser may take one of two approaches: It can use the closest supported color instead, or it can *dither* the color. Dithering is a technique of using an overlapping lattice of pixels in two colors to simulate the unsupported color. Dithered color regions and images can look strange and unattractive. It is advisable to stay within the supported colors and avoid dithering.

In the 256-color days, Web designers were advised to stay within the 216 so-called *Web-safe colors*—that is, colors with RGB values limited to `00`, `33`, `66`, `99`, `CC`, and `FF`. These used to be the only colors supported consistently across major browsers and operating systems.

The majority of modern computers support 16-bit or full 24-bit color, and current browsers render colors with a high level of consistency. It is no longer necessary to limit your design to the Web-safe colors any more. Checking your design on different browsers and computers is still a good idea.

Color palettes are also used in graphical images to provide *indexed color*. The palette is simply a table that associates color codes with colors. The number of colors could be 2 (black and white), 16, or 256 (GIF). A palette in the image file can specify which 2, 16, or 256 of the possible colors to use. Raster image manipulation programs, such as Photoshop, allow the user to create, edit, manipulate, and save palettes for images. For example, in reducing an image to 16 colors, the program can compute a *best fit* set of 16 colors for the image at hand, or you may pick a standard 16-color palette such as the Windows color palette.

What Is Duotone?

A gray-scale image may have 256 shades. But normally, a single color can only accommodate 50 shade levels. By adding colors, the number of different shades increases by 50 per color. A duotone involves any two colors, a tritone involves three and a quadtone involves four colors. The latter two are less frequently used. Convert a gray scale to a duotone to add richness. Color images must first be converted to gray scale before turning them into duotones.

7.12   IMAGE ENCODING FORMATS

Graphical images can be stored in many different digital formats that have different characteristics. In *raster graphics*, images are digitized by recording their colors at a grid of *sampling points* (Figure 7.25). The finer the grid, the larger the number of sampling points and the better the resolution. Each sampling point results in a *color pixel* (picture element) stored in a *raster image file*. A raster image usually does not need to record each and every pixel individually. Compression methods can significantly reduce the image file size. Display software reproduces the pixels to render a raster image on a computer screen or printer.

In *vector graphics*, images include geometric objects such as points, lines, and curves. Geometric information can be combined with raster information to represent a complete image. Vector image encoding provides accurate information on geometric objects in the image and avoids representing every pixel. Hence, vector images are usually smaller and easier to scale. Display software must understand the geometric information to render vector graphics files.

Currently, the only widely used vector graphics system is Macromedia Flash. The W3C is recommending the Scalable Vector Graphics (SVG) standard for the Web. Although support for vector graphics is still lagging behind, we expect major browsers to provide native support for SVG in the near future.

Figure 7.25   RASTER IMAGE

GIF, JPEG, and PNG

Currently, the only image compression formats generally accepted on the Web are:

- Graphics Interchange Format (GIF)—A raster format suitable for icons, logos, cartoons, and line drawings. GIF images can have up to 256 colors (8-bit).

- Joint Photographic Experts Group (JPEG) format—A raster format usable for color and black-and-white pictures with continuous changing color tones for display. JPEG images can store up to 16.8M colors (24-bit). Images created using a scanner or digital camera are usually stored in TIFF (Tagged Image File Format), JPEG, or GIF.

- Portable Network Graphics (PNG) format—A format designed to replace GIF. PNG really has three main advantages over GIF: alpha channels (variable transparency), gamma correction (cross-platform control of image brightness; Section 7.9), and two-dimensional interlacing (a method of progressive display). Browser support for PNG is increasing steadily, and ideally, PNG will soon replace GIF.

Aliasing and Anti-aliasing

As you may expect, sampling a continuous image at discrete points may run into problems. Raster images often contain jagged edges (e.g., staircase effect on slanted lines), lost or distorted details (fine features missed or hit by sampling points), or disintegrating texture patterns (Figure 7.26). These errors are known as *aliasing artifacts*.

Anti-aliasing methods have been developed to reduce the effects of aliasing. One popular anti-aliasing technique involves sampling at a resolution several times (e.g., three times) higher than the target image file resolution. Then compute the value of each image pixel as the weighted average of the values from a number of neighboring sample points (e.g., nine points). There are many fine anti-aliasing algorithms. No matter what the method, anti-aliasing seeks to soften the jagged edges by setting pixel values so that there is a more

Figure 7.26   ALIASING IN RASTER IMAGES

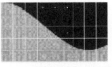

Original   *Rendered*

gradual transition between one color to a very different color. Figure 11.10 shows the effect of anti-aliasing.

Anti-aliasing makes lines and edges in a picture look much smoother by using pixels whose color is a blend of the object color and the background color. A graphical object or text font anti-aliased with one background color won't look right on a different background.

Colors in Raster Images

In a raster image, each pixel is a color dot. The size of a raster image file depends on how many colors it uses. You have these choices:

- Monochrome—black and white
- Gray Scale—different levels of gray (up to 256 shades)
- Indexed—Each pixel color is indicated by an index into a color palette. The palette may contain a set of up to 256 colors. The smaller the palette, the fewer bits are needed for each index.
- High Color—thousands of colors, 15 to 16 bits per pixel
- True Color—16.8 million colors, 24 bits per pixel

Dithering

Dithering is the attempt by a computer program to approximate a color from a mixture of other colors when the required color is not available. Dithering can occur when reducing the number of colors of an image or displaying a color that a browser on an operating system doesn't support. In such cases, the requested color is simulated with an approximation composed of two or more other colors that can produce it. The result may or may not be acceptable to the graphic designer. The image may also appear somewhat grainy because the colored area in question consists of different pixel intensities that average to the intended color.

There are several methods or algorithms for color dithering:

- *Pattern dithering* uses a fixed pixel pattern.
- *Diffusion dithering* propagates the error made in replacing a color pixel by a supported color to neighboring pixels.

Pattern dithering is most useful in filling a larger area with a desired color. Diffusion dithering works well for continuous tone pictures.

7.13   WEB SAMPLES COLOR CRITIQUE

The Web has always been a democratic medium where people could quickly learn from one another. Whether learning new code or learning new tips about software, this medium has increased the development of many new ideas, including the ones about how to improve site design. Although there seems to be a plethora of poorly designed sites on the Web, we can learn a great deal from some of the good ones that exist today.

Design students often ask: Which color should I use? How much color should I include? Is one color enough? What is the best way to use two colors? How can I work within a corporate identity palette and still use other colors? Let's look at how existing developers have answered these questions.

The Adobe Corporation (adobe.com) has responded with the always popular "less is more" solution. By using red, black, and white in their navigation bar, they have simplified a major part of their interface design. In Figure 7.27, we see that full color is only applied to the featured products and other significant images. This kind of treatment allows the viewer to focus on the most important things on the page, leaving interface design to quietly stay in the background supporting corporate identity and providing directions for where to go in the site.

Lufthansa Airlines (lufthansa.com) chose a similar solution (Figure 7.28). By using yellow and blue, two complements for their corporate color, they also used full color in images only. Gray and black are used as supporting colors in rectangles, and other areas provide contrast, create hierarchy, and direct attention to the text.

MetaDesign (metadesign.com) used a similar treatment of black and red, but they decided to saturate the eye with a red background, one of their corporate colors chosen for its powerful, gripping effect (Figure 7.29). The pure red background is at times overwhelming and at other times strong and confident. Depending on which way you prefer to see this combination, the MetaDesign site designers did a good job of controlling text readability, an often difficult task, by using solid, dark backgrounds. The designers also used good

Figure 7.27   ADOBE CORPORATION

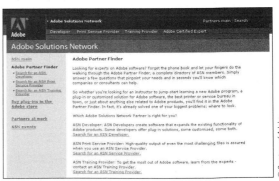

Figure 7.28   LUFTHANSA

Figure 7.29   METADESIGN WEB SITE

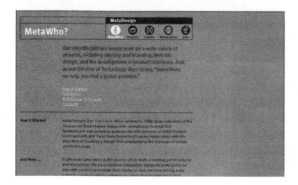
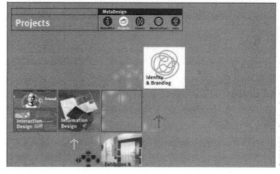

judgment by choosing navigation symbols to streamline directions to different locations of the site. Full-color, square-cut photos add geometric strength to a classic grid-oriented, Swiss design.

If you're a computer illustrator and want to have a presence on the Web, which colors would you choose for your Web site? Ron Chan (ronchan.com) decided to go with nostalgic, classic, light blue as a background and simple black-and-white text, allowing his flat, colored illustrations to do all of the work in promoting his portfolio (Figures 7.30 and 7.31). In this case, the illustrations are featured on a white background, allowing maximum contrast between background and foreground. Open black navigation squares, effectively placed out of the way, point to the main feature of the site. Secondary navigation appears discreetly to the right of the illustrations, allowing viewers to quickly select another illustration.

The creative director at Digiknow (digiknow.com), a mid-size web development/marketing firm in Cleveland, Ohio, decided to revamp their old image

Figure 7.30   RON CHAN WEB SITE

Figure 7.31   RON CHAN WEB SITE

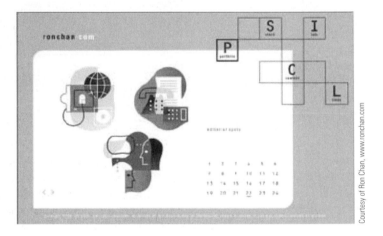

and go with the simpler, cleaner design on their new site (Figure 7.32). The new interface consists of two basic colors, gray and sage green. Lighter and darker values of each color were used to create variety and depth. A dark rust-orange color was used as the primary highlight on rollovers and links, creating a look that holds together tightly throughout the site. With this interface treatment, it is easy to see how additional color, no matter how subtle, stands out on the page (Figure 7.32, left).

Formally strong, geometric layout created by Miranda Hall-Carrier for the School of Visual Communication Design at Kent State University, uses

COLOR PLATES

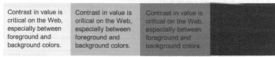

Figure 2.7   **COLOR NAMES**

Figure 7.1   **PRIMARY, SECONDARY, AND TERTIARY COLORS**

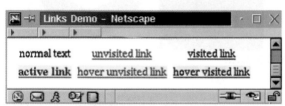

Figure 5.27   **DARK GRAY TYPE ON COLOR BACKGROUNDS**

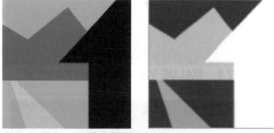

Figure 7.2   **COLOR WHEEL**

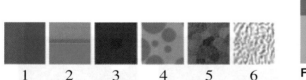

Figure 6.5   **LINK STYLES**

Figure 7.3   **HUE CONTRAST AND VALUE CONTRAST**

Figure 6.18   **TILE BACKGROUND PATTERNS**

Figure 7.4   **LOW, MODERATE, AND HIGH HUE CONTRASTS**

Figure 6.24   **CSS-BASED CAPTION**

Figure 7.5   **LIGHT, MEDIUM, AND DARK VALUES**

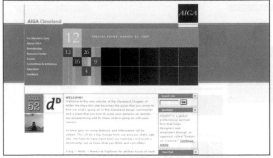

Figure 7.36   AIGA CLEVELAND SITE: LEVELS 1 AND 2

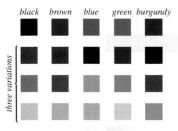

black   brown   blue   green   burgundy

three variations

Figure 7.37   CONSERVATIVE COLOR PALETTE

Figure 7.38   HYPOTHETICAL TRAVEL SITE

Company
ABC Company
Super ABC Company
    Super ABC Company
        Super ABC Comp
            Super ABC
                Supe

Figure 10.14   COLOR FADE IN

Figure 11.3 ORIGINAL SCAN OF CHILDREN

Figure 11.4 ADJUSTED PHOTO USING LEVELS COMMAND

Live Demo
L i v e   D e m o
i v e   D e m

Figure 10.15   IN-PLACE FADE-IN

Figure 11.14   COLOR REPLACEMENT

Figure 11.15   REDDISH SCAN AND COLOR ADJUSTMENT

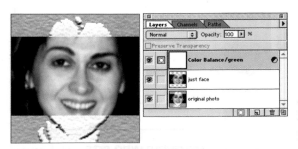

Figure 11.24   GREEN FACE: COLOR ADJUSTMENT IN PHOTOSHOP

Figure 7.32   CURRENT DIGIKNOW SITE

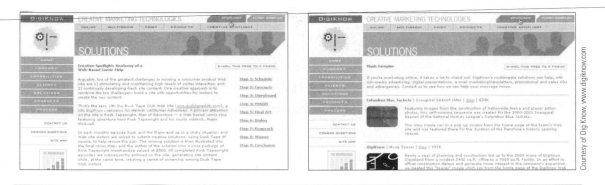

Courtesy of Dig Know, www.digiknow.com

the school's yellow and gray identity colors (Figure 7.33). Navy blue, used as accent color in the navigation bar, works well with bright yellow in this elegantly designed space.

Rugged, earthy, irreverent Harley Davidson (harley-davidson.com) has consistently maintained their corporate image in promotion and advertising. Their Web site is no exception (Figure 7.34). A strong palette of earthy colors is used throughout the site. Primary brown and orange are used as accents in text and bars. Rusty reds and yellow ochers appear in carefully chosen, well-placed photographs. The black navigation and background lend support to their already strong image.

The Motivo (motivo.com) marketing/design firm took the quiet, understated approach with light periwinkle blue, light lemon, green, and soothing grays as their primary colors (Figure 7.35). Color in this case reflects the "light"

Figure 7.33   SCHOOL OF VISUAL COMMUNICATION DESIGN: HOME PAGE AND LEVEL 1

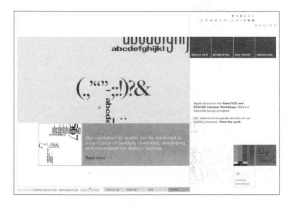
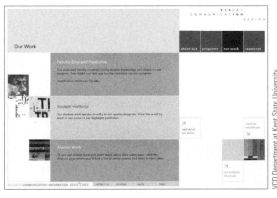

VCD Department at Kent State University, created by Miranda Hall-Carrier

Figure 7.34 HARLEY DAVIDSON

Figure 7.35 MOTIVO'S WEB SITE

graphics created with thicks and thins, stressing depth on the page. Working in conjunction with logo colors, their site is unified with square-cut photos, clean, readable typography, and lots of white space. Full color and black-and-white images are used to create drama on the page, leading the viewer to important points in the content.

Leading the way with smart use of the Web media, *AIGA Cleveland* (aigacleveland.org) has taken a colorful approach to their Web design (Figure 7.36). Bright, tangerine fields along with constructive use of spot color make this site informative and fun. Like many organization sites on the Web, AIGA Cleveland is in the business of providing vital information on various topics to its members. Since the emergence of the Web, they have made several revisions to their site, delivered more speed, improved efficiency, and at the same time added more content. AIGA Cleveland is a good example of how one

Figure 7.36   AIGA CLEVELAND SITE: LEVELS 1 AND 2

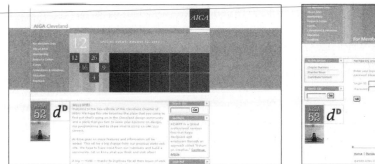

AIGA Cleveland Chapter

Web savvy organization continues to make effective use of the media through evolving design.

7.14   COLOR APPLICATION

By now, you have learned some basics about color, but would you know how to choose appropriate colors for your next Web site project? Would you know how to program those colors? Here are a few more suggestions on color application and coding.

Let's say that you were commissioned to design a Web site for a gardening center. If you're like most people, you would probably choose greens, yellows, or other springtime colors. If asked to design a site for a traditional, full-service travel agency, you may consider using blue to represent the oceans, green for golf courses, or yellows and oranges found in sunsets. We instantly recall images of familiar subjects, and it may be tempting to use those comfortable solutions on our own projects. Unfortunately, that familiarity may also make your design appear trite. Luckily, design does not need to reinvent the color wheel to be engaging and effective. On the contrary, many successful design solutions are based on familiar clichés that have been reinterpreted to communicate a new message. That is exactly what makes them interesting.

If gardening centers bring to mind the color green, what colors do the less visual insurance or legal firms bring to mind? These companies don't necessarily conjure up immediate colors, making them more difficult to define. One of the obvious and perhaps overused colors in the insurance industry, law firms, or medical centers may be blue, green, or gray, which may be associated with stability, reliability, and strength. Be sure to listen carefully to your client when discussing identity and perception. If a client wants to be perceived as ultraconservative, these colors may be fine, but there is still ample room for variation within that palette. Your client may want to be perceived as stable, traditional, but also as catering to a wide audience and "standing out" from the competition. You need to adapt and go beyond cliché choices. Colors themselves are neither conservative nor radical; rather, it is our perception that makes them so. When it comes to colors, a good rule is to choose a palette of colors that works well together and helps support your concept.

Figure 7.37 takes five colors often considered conservative (black, brown, blue, green, and burgundy) and shows you variations on this old theme. The first row at the top shows five original colors. The following three rows show variations. Varying even one color in the palette gives you a different feel for the overall Web site.

Now, let's go back to the travel agency example. One way designers find engaging solutions is to think beyond the clichés. Suppose I were to give you an assignment to create a home page for a travel agency that takes a different approach in its color treatment. Instead of the usual sunsets and blue waters, what would you use? The answer lies with the problem itself. What destinations does the travel agency specialize in? Are they exotic planners or are cruises their specialty? Do they specialize in Europe, Asia, or the continental United States? Your color choices will be greatly influenced by the answers to these questions.

The travel site in Figure 7.38 made a particular point of not using blue. Instead, the color palette is light and neutral, with small splashes of color—in this case, red, green, brown, gray, pink, and yellow, which you would not necessarily expect. Examine the example carefully and then notice how the HTML scripting is used to re-create this page in the browser.

Figure 7.37 CONSERVATIVE COLOR PALETTE

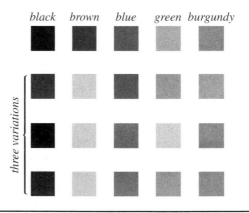

Figure 7.38   HYPOTHETICAL TRAVEL SITE

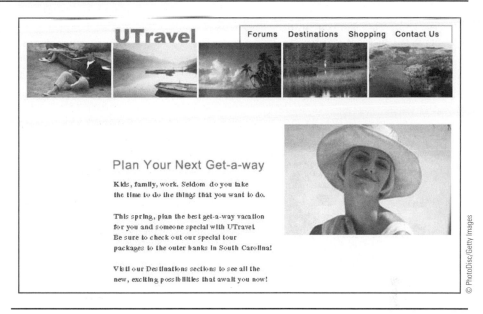

7.15 SUMMARY

The Web, with its combination of computer screens, color encoding standards, and color specifications in Web pages, constitutes a distinct medium for the presentation and manipulation of color. Mastery of color on the Web requires a combination of artistic and programming abilities.

As you develop your own Web sites, keep in mind that color is subjective, and color choices will probably be made in collaboration with your clients. Contrast in value, as well as color, plays an important role in design. Trust your intuition as well as theoretic knowledge when applying color, and remember that color is just one of the factors in your design. It should not be used simply to "enhance" black-and-white forms. It should add something meaningful to your message such as setting the mood, introducing cultural meaning, or connecting through spontaneous associations with your viewers.

Finally, experiment with color. Use digital image tools such as Photoshop and try to apply different colors to your images. Don't necessarily settle on your first choice. Study Web sites that use color effectively and take note of the color combinations. Being aware of color and its use will give you the confidence to create effective, aesthetically pleasing Web sites.

EXERCISES

Review Questions

1. What is a color wheel and what is its purpose?

2. What are primary colors?

3. What are secondary colors and how are they created?

4. What are tertiary colors and how are they created?

5. What is the difference between complementary and analogous colors? Where do you find each one on the color wheel?

6. What are color contrasts and why are they important?

7. Describe color dominance in design.

8. What is the difference between hue contrast and value contrast? Which one is more critical in the design of Web sites?

9. You can produce color contrasts but not necessarily value contrasts. Explain how this works and give examples.

10. What is color context and why is it important?

11. What is simultaneous contrast and how would you use it in Web design?

12. Describe the difference between warm and cool colors. Give examples of each.

13. What does saturation mean? How can it be achieved in a tool such as Photoshop?

14. How do type and readability relate to color? What is the most critical aspect of choosing type color?

15. According to Peckolick, what are the three key factors in color selection? Discuss each one.

16. What is gamma? What is gamma correction?

17. What are color models? What is the difference between print and computer screen color models?

18. Discuss hue, brightness, and saturation. What is the difference between them?

19. What is a duotone? How would you make one in a tool such as Photoshop?

20. What are GIFs and JPGs? What is the difference between them? When would you use each one and why?

Assignments

1. Study Itten's contrasts. Choose or create a simple image using geometric shapes and design a composition that you can manipulate. See if you can demonstrate your understanding of his contrasts by duplicating your illustration using contrast of hue, light-dark contrast, cool-warm contrast, and so on.

2. Create three simple images. You can use a photograph or a spot illustration for this exercise. Create one using three primary colors, the other using only three secondary colors, and the last using three tertiary colors of your choice. Compare the illustrations. What differences do you see among the three? Which one is the most attractive? Does each one communicate differently? How?

3. Select a Web site that you think uses color well. Identify the color scheme used on the site. Are they primary, secondary, analogous colors, or complementary colors? Identify the palette.

4. Select one page of the site that you think is designed well. Create two variations on the original color scheme. Make one color dominant and the other value dominant. Use maximum contrast in both color and value designs. Compare the two compositions. Analyze which one looks more aesthetically pleasing.

5. Go to your favorite museum and choose a painting that you really like. Write down or draw in color pencil or marker the colors used. As an exercise in a tool such as Photoshop, create a simple Web page with any design you wish using those same colors. Try to find interesting color combinations that you may not have thought of before.

6. In a tool such as Photoshop, select or create one image with two variations. Create one using warm colors and the other using cool colors. Compare and contrast the two images.

7. Create three simple geometric shapes in a tool such as Photoshop. Color one using CMYK color and the other using RGB color. Examine each image on a 216 monitor, in thousands of colors, and in millions of colors. Then convert the RGB values to Web-safe colors? Discuss the differences.

8. Consider the RGB to HSB conversion function in Section 7.10. In your own words, explain how this function works and explain each line of the code.

9. Make the rgb2hsb program (Section 7.10) into a complete JavaScript program. Run it and check the conversion values against those displayed by a tool such as Photoshop.

10. Using a programming language you know, write a program to convert HSB to RGB.

CHAPTER 8

Forms and Form Processing

When users surf the Web, information flows from servers to browsers. But the Web is not a one-way street. Information can also be collected from users by browsers and sent to servers, or client-side scripts (Chapter 9), for processing. The Web would be much less useful without the ability to request and process user input. In fact, e-business and e-commerce are dependent on the interactive exchange of information between users and servers.

To make the cycle of user input collection, server-side processing, and response work, client-side (browser) support, HTTP support, and server-side support are needed. The HTML form enables browsers to collect information from users and to send the data obtained to a designated server via an HTTP POST or GET query. The receiving server invokes specified programming, commonly a CGI program, to process the data and to provide a response (Figure 8.1).

This chapter gives you a clear understanding of HTML form processing, enables you to design forms, and introduces server-side programming to support HTTP queries from HTML forms and from URLs. Examples illustrate how forms work in practice. This introduction gives you an overview and a good foundation for further materials on Perl and CGI programming in Chapter 13.

Figure 8.1   FORM PROCESSING

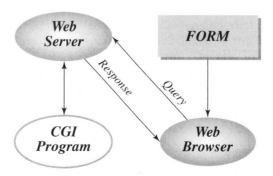

8.1   WHAT IS A FORM?

The form element of HTML is designed to collect input from Web surfers for processing on the server side. You place different types of *input-control*[1] elements inside a form to receive user input for server-side processing. The form element may contain any kind of block elements so you can include instructions, explanations, and illustrations together with input controls.

For example (Ex: **SimpleForm**), the following sample form

```
<form method="post"                            (1)
      action="/cgi-bin/member.cgi">            (2)
<pre>
Full Name: <input name="fname" size="35" />    (3)

Email:     <input name="email" size="35" />    (4)

           <input type="submit" value="Send" /> (5)
</pre>
</form>
```

requests the full name (line 3) and email address (line 4) from the user and sends the collected information via an HTTP POST query (line 1) to the program member.cgi (line 2) on the server side. XHTML requires method to be either post or get in lowercase. This form involves three input controls (lines 3, 4, and 5). The form data are sent when the user clicks the submit button (line 5). Figure 8.2 shows the display of such a form.

Figure 8.2   A SIMPLE FORM

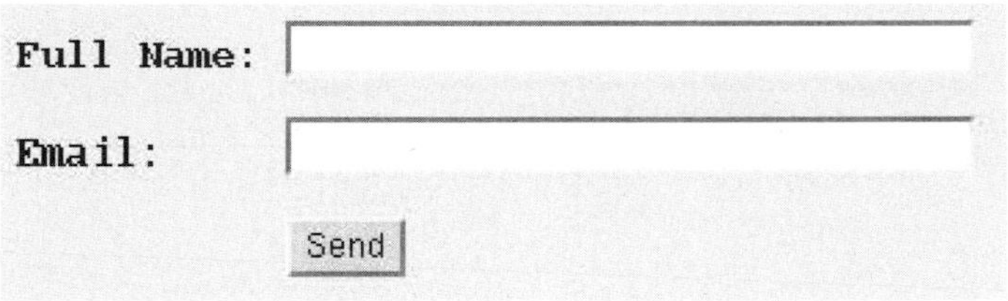

---

[1] Input controls used to be limited to within forms and were known as *form controls*. We will use the term *input control*.

8.2 A HISTORICAL NOTE

The form concept was completely missing from HTML 2.0 (1995), the first standard for HTML. At that time, the Web was mostly a one-way street for information dissemination: URLs led to pages, and hyperlinks in those pages led to more pages.

To remedy the situation and to collect user input, the ISINDEX tag was introduced, which was a kind of *primitive form mechanism*. ISINDEX displays a user prompt and collects any string typed. That input string is attached to the end of the host page's URL and sent via an HTTP GET query.

The HTML 3.2 standard (1977) includes both the ISINDEX element and the fill-out form (FORM) element. Also introduced are various user input collection elements designed to work within a FORM. A FORM can be submitted to any URL-designated server-side program via either the GET or the POST query. The method (application/x-www-form-urlencoded) to encode user input for transmission within an HTTP query is also defined. Furthermore, HTML 3.2 introduced a method for users to upload files based on the FORM.

ISINDEX has been superseded, and XHTML has deprecated isindex in favor of the form element.

8.3 FORM BASICS

The HTML fill-out form involves three phases: collecting user input, sending HTTP queries, and server-side processing. Let's first take a closer look at collecting user input with the HTML form element and the various input controls available.

A typical form element consists of these essential parts:

1. Instructions for the user on what information is sought and how to fill out the form.
2. Blanks, produced by input collection elements, to be completed by the user.
3. Text or label for each input control to clearly indicate the exact information to be entered.
4. A button, displayed by an input element of type submit, for the user to submit the completed form. The value attribute of a submit button gives the label on the button.
5. An HTTP query method, given by the method attribute of form, for sending the form data to the server. It is advisable always to use the post method even though get is the default.

6. The URL of a server-side program to receive and process the collected form data given by the *required* action attribute[2] of the form element.

Thus, a form is generally coded as follows:

```
<form method="post or get" action="program-URL">
    any number of block elements that
        may contain input-control elements
</form>
```

Input-control elements include input, select, textarea, and button. Input controls are inline elements. When a form is submitted, all values collected by input-control elements within the form will be sent to the server-side program.

In the past, input controls could only be placed inside form elements or the input controls would be ignored by browsers. Now input-control elements may be placed outside the form for other purposes such as interactions with client-side JavaScript (Chapter 9). Under XHTML, a form may only contain block elements (of any kind). Thus, be sure to enclose input controls in block elements before placing them inside a form. A form may not contain another form, so no form nesting is allowed.

Different kinds of input-control elements are available to make collecting user input easy: short input, long input, multiple choices, selection menus, and file uploading. Let's look at input-control elements.

8.4 TEXT INPUT

The simplest and most frequently used input control is the text input element that receives a text string. For example,

```
<input name="lastname" type="text" size="20" maxlength="30" />
```

displays a one-line input window of size 20 (20 characters wide) with a maximum user input of 30 characters. The name attribute specifies the *key* for the input element (or any other input-control element). User input becomes the *value* of the input control. The received input is submitted as a key-value pair—for example,

```
lastname=Katila
```

to the server-side program. The value attribute can be used to specify an initial value to be displayed in the input window—for example,

```
value="your last name"
```

---

[2]If not given, some browsers assume the URL is the same as the URL of the page containing the form.

Figure 8.3   A textarea

Multiline text input can be collected with the inline element textarea. For example (Ex: **Area**),

```
<p>Please let us have your comments:<br />
<textarea name="feedback" rows="4" cols="60">
 Tell us what you really
 think, please.
</textarea></p>
```

can be used to collect user feedback in a 4-row by 60-column input window. Content inside the textarea element (plain text with entities) gives the initial display in the input window (Figure 8.3). The user may type more than four lines, in which case a vertical scroll bar appears. (A horizontal scroll bar appears if any line has more than 60 characters.)

Because of the automatic scrolling feature, textarea is sometimes useful to present longer information inside an area of limited size. For such purposes, the readonly="readonly" attribute can be added to make an input window uneditable. Notice how the readonly attribute is specified. Unlike before, XHTML does not allow such Boolean (true/false) attributes to be abbreviated (given without values).

8.5 USER SELECTIONS

Radio Buttons

A group of *radio buttons* allows the user to choose exactly one from a number of choices. Clicking one choice selects it and deselects all others in the group. Each button is an input element of type radio, and all buttons in the group have the same name.

Figure 8.4 shows the display of the following radio button group (Ex: **RadioButton**):

```
<!-- inside or outside a form -->

<p style="font-size: larger; font-weight: bold;">
```

Figure 8.4   RADIO BUTTONS

Choose a color: ⊙ Red ○ Green ○ Blue

```
 Choose a color:
<input id="r" type="radio" name="color"
                       value="red" checked="checked" />    (a)
   <label for="r" style="color: red">Red</label>           (b)
<input id="g" type="radio" name="color" value="green" />
   <label for="g" style="color: green">Green</label>
<input id="b" type="radio" name="color" value="blue" />
   <label for="b" style="color: blue">Blue</label>
</p>
```

Here we have three radio buttons named color. The button with the value red is checked (line a) as the initial selection (Caution: no attribute abbreviation). Selecting a button pops the previous choice, like pushing buttons on a radio. The data sent to the server-side program are the name-value pair of the selected radio button.

The label element associates any enclosed inline element as the label for an input control whose id is given by the for attribute. In this example, the label Red (line b) is for the input field on line a. By identifying the label, a browser usually allows the user to also click the label to make a selection.

Check Boxes

You can use *check boxes* to allow users to choose several items from a list of choices. A check box is an input element of type checkbox. Clicking a check box selects or deselects it without affecting other check boxes. Thus, a user may select all, none, or any number of check boxes.

Figure 8.5 displays the following form (Ex: **CheckBoxes**):

```
<!-- inside or outside a form -->
<p style="font-size: larger; font-weight: bold;">
```

Figure 8.5   CHECK BOXES

Your favorite sports: ☑ Tennis ☑ Baseball ☐ Wind Surfing

```
Your favorite sports:
<input id="t" type="checkbox" name="tennis" />
    <label for-"t">Tennis</label>
<input id="b" type="checkbox" name="baseball" />
    <label for="b">Baseball</label>
<input id="w" type="checkbox" name="windsurf" />
    <label for="w">Wind Surfing</label>
</p>
```

For check boxes,

- Any number of items can be initially checked.
- A user may pick any number of choices, including none.
- Each selected item is sent to the server-side program as *name=on*.

Pull-down Menus

When there are many choices, a pull-down menu can save space and make the form cleaner and clearer. The `select` element is an input control for this purpose. You include any number of `option` elements inside a `select` element as the choices.

The code for a user to select a state in their address (Ex: **PullDown**) is outlined as follows:

```
<!-- inside or outside a form -->
<p style="font-size: larger; font-weight: bold;">State:
<select id="statename" name="statename" size="1">
  <option value="0"> Pick One </option>
  <option value="Alabama"> Alabama </option>
  <option value="Alaska"> Alaska </option>
  ...
</select></p>
```

Figure 8.6 shows the menu before and after it is pulled down. The `size` attribute specifies how many options are displayed on the menu at one time. If `size` is 1,

Figure 8.6   A PULL-DOWN MENU

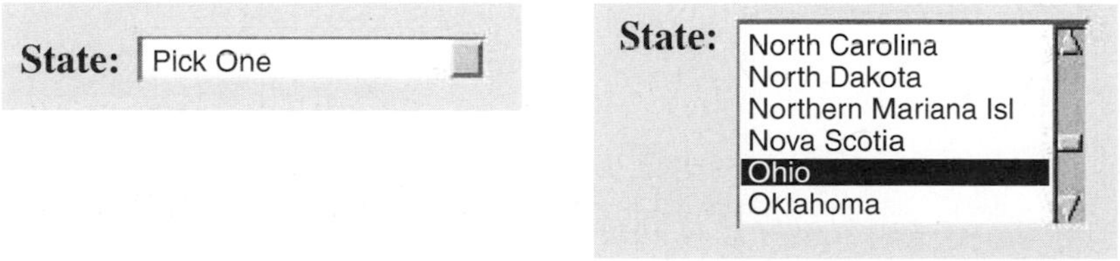

then the menu initially displays the first option with a pull-down button beside it. Typically, size is 1 and the first option is an instruction on how or what to pick. To allow multiple choices, the Boolean attribute multiple="multiple" must be given. Otherwise, only one choice is allowed. Data sent to the server-side program include one name-value pair of each option chosen.

Sometimes options can be divided into different groups to make the selections better organized and easier for the user. optgroup can separate options into groups. For example (Ex: **OptGroup**), the form

```
<form method="post" action="/cgi-bin/wb/reflect.pl">                (1)
<p style="font-size: larger; font-weight: bold;">Menu:
<select id="menu" name="menu" size="1" multiple="multiple">
   <option value="0"> Your Menu </option>
 <optgroup label="Soup">
   <option value="hot and sour">Hot and Sour Soup</option>
   <option value="egg drop">Egg Drop Soup</option>
   <option value="chicken noodle">Chicken Noodle Soup</option>
 </optgroup><optgroup label="Salad">
   <option value="garden">Garden Salad</option>
   <option value="spinach">Spinach Salad</option>
   <option value="fruit">Fruit Salad</option>
 </optgroup>
</select></p>
<p><input type="submit" value=" Order Meal "></p>                  (2)
</form>
```

results in the display shown in Figure 8.7. The CGI program reflect.pl (line 1) displays form data and environment variables received and can be a good checker for your HTML forms (Section 8.19).

If the multiple="multiple" attribute is added to select, the user picks the first item with a simple mouse click (left mouse button) and picks each additional item with CTRL-click. It is a good idea to set a sufficient size for

Figure 8.7   MENU OPTION GROUPING

menus allowing multiple picks. Most Web surfers may not be aware of this mouse usage, and therefore, the checkbox may be a better choice for users to pick multiple items. Let's look at the submit button (line 2) next.

8.6   SUBMIT BUTTONS

The basic Submit button for a form is

```
<input type="submit" value="button-label" />
```

Use a meaningful *button-label* such as Continue, Go, Register, or something similar that relates to the purpose of the form.

A form may have multiple Submit buttons with different values. For example, a membership application form may have a Join button and a Trial button for a regular or trial membership. Data sent to the server-side program include the submit="value" for the clicked Submit button.

You may customize the look of a Submit button by using an *image input element* (Ex: **ImageInput**):

```
<input type="image" src="url" name="key" alt="..." />
```

Data sent to the server-side program are in the form

```
key.x=x0
key.y=y0
```

where (x0, y0) is the position of the mouse cursor in the image when clicked.

As an alternative to the input-based Submit button, you can also use the button element to create Submit buttons. For example (Ex: **Button**),

```
<button name="submit" value="join">Join the Club</button>
```

displays a Submit button with the label Join the Club and sends submit="join" to the server-side program. By placing an img element inside button, you obtain a graphical button of your own design.

It is possible to invoke programmed actions on the client side before submitting a form to the server-side program (Chapter 9). A button-type input element or a button-type button element is useful for this purpose.

8.7   FILE UPLOADING

So far, user input is collected from the keyboard or the mouse. But it is also possible to receive file uploads from the user's computer. This is done with the file-type input element (Ex: **FileUpload**).

```
<form method="post" action="/cgi-bin/receive.cgi"
      enctype="multipart/form-data">
```

Figure 8.8   FILE UPLOADING

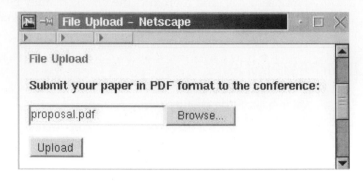

```
<p style="font-size: larger; font-weight: bold;">
Submit your paper to the conference:</p>
<p><input type="file" name="paper" accept="application/pdf" /></p>
<p><input type="submit" value="Upload" /></p>
</form>
```

Figure 8.8 displays the file uploading form where the Browse button allows the user to pick a file from the local file system.

Several points worth noting about file uploading are:

- The query method must be post.
- The enctype="multipart/form-data" is needed to specify a data encoding format different from the default application/x-www-form-urlencoded.
- The accept attribute specifies the MIME type for the uploaded file. If accept is not specified, then there is no restriction on the file type.
- Very old browsers may not support form-based file uploading.
- Server-side processing must deal with the multipart/form-data data encoding.

See Section 13.20 for server-side processing of form uploading.

8.8   OTHER input ELEMENTS

A hidden input element is not displayed with the form. But its *key=value* pair is sent along with other form data to the server-side program. A hidden input field can supply values to customize general-purpose programs on the server side or to provide *session control* where multiple forms are involved in a sequence of user interactions.

For example, a feedback form may use the following hidden input

```
<input type="hidden" name="receiver" value="pwang@cs.kent.edu" />
```

to inform the server-side program where to send the feedback.

Figure 8.9 shows a shopping cart with a Change Qty button and a Remove button. These are actually submit buttons in two separate forms with hidden form fields. For example, the form for the Remove button looks like

```
<form action="/cgi-bin/wb/reflect.pl" method="post">
  <div>
  <input type="hidden" name="ps_session" value="45d2b15ff4dbb8d" />
  <input type="hidden" name="func" value="cartDelete" />
  <input type="hidden" name="product_id" value="11" />
  <input type="Submit" name="delete" value="Remove" />
  <input type="submit" value=" Remove "></div>
</form>
```

The only input element displayed is the Remove button.

A reset input element

```
<input type="reset" value="Clear form" />
```

or a reset button

```
<button type="reset">Clear All Form Entries</button>
```

displays a button that resets the values of all input fields in a form.

A password input element is just like a text input element, but the browser will not display the text entered. It is not secure because the password is sent to the server side in plain text with no encryption. Don't get confused. The familiar user id and password dialog you see on the Web is not a result of the password input in a form. It is usually caused by an authentication request from the Web server.

Figure 8.9   SHOPPING CART WITH BUTTONS

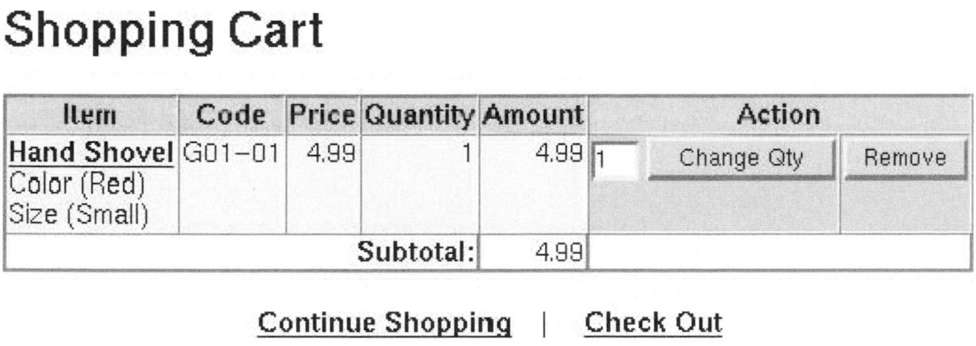

Shopping Cart

Item	Code	Price	Quantity	Amount	Action		
Hand Shovel Color (Red) Size (Small)	G01–01	4.99	1	4.99	1	Change Qty	Remove
		Subtotal:		4.99			

Continue Shopping | **Check Out**

8.9   TABBING ORDER

When filling out a form, a Web surfer can use the TAB key to go to the next entry in the form. If for some reason a form wishes to deviate from this *tabbing order*, input controls may be given explicit tabbing positions (integers between 0 and 32,767) using the `tabindex="number"` attribute. An input control with `tabindex="0"` or no `tabindex` attribute will be visited after any elements with a positive `tabindex`. A smaller positive `tabindex` is visited first.

A form control may also specify an `accesskey="char"` attribute. It means the user can go to that form entry directly by typing the character `alt-char` (Ex: **AccessKey**).

8.10   FORM LAYOUT

Forms are critical components of Web sites. Forms without a good design can be confusing and unpleasant. It is important to design the visual layout of a form that is clear, simple, attractive, and easy to follow. The page containing the form must also be visually integrated with the site.

Here are some rules to follow:

- A form usually uses a single-column format. Related items, such as first name and last name, can be grouped on the same line.
- Entries are labeled consistently, and the `label` tag is used to bind labels to input controls in the HTML code.
- Text to explain the form is placed before and outside the form.
- Instructions for individual entries can be placed before, after, or beneath each entry, but they must be consistently placed for all the forms in a site.
- Required and optional entries are clearly indicated.
- Avoid long forms. Group related entries together to divide a long form into smaller, more manageable parts.
- Avoid repeatedly asking for the same information.

The `fieldset` element brackets a set of related input controls and gives it a *legend* (title). For example (Ex: **FieldSet**),

```
<fieldset>
  <legend>Shipping Information</legend>
  ...
</fieldset>
<fieldset>
  <legend>Billing Information</legend>
```

Figure 8.10   GROUPING FORM ENTRIES

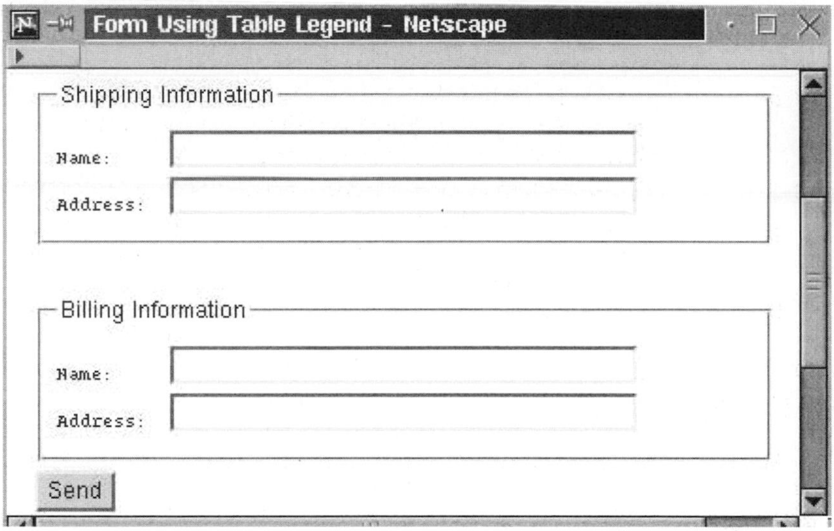

```
                  . . .
</fieldset>
```

groups the input controls and displays the legends, as shown in Figure 8.10.

Form Layout with Tables

In practice, forms are often displayed using a table layout. The `table` element is placed inside the `form` element to organize and align the input controls and labels. A style sheet for forms can be established to apply to all forms of a particular site.

The source code for the form displayed in Figure 8.11 is (Ex: **FormTable**):

```
<form action="/cgi-bin/wb/reflect.pl" method="post">
<table width="400">
```

Figure 8.11   TABLE-FORMATTED FORM

```
<tr><td class="fla"><label for="state">State:</label></td>
  <td> <select id="state" name="state">
        <option>(US State Codes)</option>
        <option>AL</option>
        ...
        <option>WY</option>
      </select></td></tr>
<tr><td class="fla"><label for="zip">Postal Code:</label></td>
  <td><input id="zip" name="zip"
            size="20" maxlength="20" /></td></tr>
<tr><td class="fla">Credit Card Type:</td>
  <td><input type="radio" id="va" name="card"
            value="Va" checked="checked" />
      <label for="va">Visa    </label>
      <input id="mc" type="radio" name="card" value="MC" />
      <label for="mc">MasterCard    </label>
      <input type="radio" id="ds" name="card" value="dc" />
      <label for="ds">Discover</label></td></tr>
</table></form>
```

And the style sheet included with

```
<link rel="stylesheet" href="form.css" type="text/css"
  title="form" />
```

contains style declarations for the form label cell background color (line 1), form label font (line 2), input field background color (line 3), and so on.

```
td.fla { background-color: #d2dbff }                    /* 1 */

form label, form option
{  font-family: Arial, Helvetica, sans-serif }          /* 2 */

form input, form select { background-color: #eef }   /* 3 */
```

8.11 HTTP BASICS

To understand form data submission by a browser and form processing on the server side, it is necessary to have some basic ideas about the HTTP protocol. On the Web, servers and clients (browsers) follow the Hypertext Transfer Protocol (HTTP) for communication. Hence, Web servers are sometimes called HTTP servers, and browsers are known as HTTP clients, as mentioned in Chapter 1 (Figure 1.5).

The HTTP protocol governs how the Web server and client exchange information. HTTP employs the connection-oriented TCP/IP to support a reliable bidirectional communication channel connecting the client and server. We described HTTP briefly in Section 1.14. Let's now take a closer look.

When a browser requests a page (e.g., the user clicks a hyperlink) or sends form data (e.g., the user clicks the Submit button) it starts the following sequence of events:

1. *Connection*—The client opens an HTTP connection to a server specified by the URL.
2. *Query*—The client sends an *HTTP request* to access a resource controlled by the server.
3. *Processing*—The server receives and processes the request.
4. *Response*—The server sends an *HTTP response*, representing the requested page or the results of form processing, back to the client.
5. *Transaction finished*—The transaction is finished, and the connection between the client and server may be kept open for a follow-up request, or it may be closed.

The form `action` attribute specifies the URL of the server-side program to receive and process the form data. The program is usually a CGI program (Section 1.13), but it can be an active page (Section 1.13) or a servlet (a special Java program for capable servers). Figure 8.1 shows the form processing data flow.

8.12   HTTP MESSAGE FORMAT

An HTTP message can be a request (query) or a response that consists of a sequence of ASCII characters conforming to the required format:

```
initial line              (different for query and response)
HeaderKey1: value1        (zero or more header fields)
HeaderKey2: value2
HeaderKey3: value3
                          (an empty line separating header and body)
Optional message body contains query or response data.
The amount and type of data in the body are specified
in the headers.
```

The header part consists of one or more *message headers*. Each message header is a key-value pair. HTTP defines what header keys can be used. Each message header ends in RETURN and NEWLINE, but in deference to UNIX systems, it may also end in just NEWLINE.

The Query Line

The initial line identifies the message as a query or a response.

- A query line has three parts separated by spaces: a *query method* name, a server-side path (Universal Resource Identifier, or URI) of the requested resource, and an HTTP version number.

```
GET    /path/to/file/index.html   HTTP/1.1
POST   /cgi-bin/script.cgi        HTTP/1.1
HEAD   /path/to/file/index.html   HTTP/1.1
```

- The GET method requests the specified resource and does not allow a message body.
- The HEAD query requests only the header part of the response for the requested resource.
- The POST method allows a message body consisting of form data for server-side processing.

The Response Line

A response (or status) line of an HTTP message also has three parts separated by spaces: a version number, a status code, and a textual description of the status. Typical status lines are

```
HTTP/1.1   200   OK
```

for a successful query, or

```
HTTP/1.1   404   Not Found
```

when the requested resource cannot be found.

The POST Query

HTML forms usually specify the post request method resulting in a browser-generated POST query. The query sends the form data to the program designated by the action URL.

A POST query contains a Content-Type header, a Content-Length header, and a message body consisting of *URL-encoded* form data. The content-type header is usually:

```
Content-Type: application/x-www-form-urlencoded
```

The receiving Web server processes the incoming data by calling the URI-specified form-processing program (typically, a CGI program). The program receives the message body containing the encoded form data, processes it, and generates a response.

Here is a sample POST query:

```
POST /cgi-bin/register-user HTTP/1.1
HOST: www.SymbolicNet.org
From: jDoe@great.enterprise.com
User-Agent: NetScape 6.2
Content-Type: application/x-www-form-urlencoded
Content-Length: 132

name=John+Doe&address=678+Main+Street&...
```

Form Data Encoding

The body in a POST query is a string *form-urlencoded* by the following procedure:

1. The string is in the form of a series of entries separated by &. Each entry is a *name=value* pair.

2. Each SPACE within an entry is replaced by a +.

3. Unsafe characters (Section 2.16) in the name and value parts are then encoded. Each unsafe character is replaced by %*hh* where *hh* is its ASCII code in hexadecimal. For example,

=	%3D or %3d	+	%2B or %2b
&	%26	%	%65

4. Non-ASCII characters are UTF-8 encoded (Section 3.1) into bytes and then any unsafe byte is %*hh* encoded.

A server-side form-processing program must decode the form data before processing it.

Data Posting via GET Queries

As an alternative to the POST query, form data can be sent via a GET query by appending the form-urlencoded data at the end of the URL locating the server-side program. In this case, the data sent are known as a *query string* and are joined to the URL by a ? character:

url_of_server_side_program?*query_string*

The query string is passed to the target program for processing.

Many long URLs you see on the Web are caused by attached query strings.

GET Versus POST

A GET request does not require a form; it can be just a URL with a hard-coded query string. Thus, any hyperlink can potentially generate a GET request.

Either the get or the post method may be used for a form. Is there a difference? In most cases, there is little difference. Some say if a form does not send user data to be recorded at the server side, the GET method is the right choice. Otherwise, the POST method is the right choice. For example, a form for making payments or membership registration should use the POST method.

Software implementations may put a length limitation on URIs. Thus, a very long query string may not work. File uploading must also use the POST request to send a body using the encryption type multipart/form-data.

8.13   CGI OVERVIEW

User data sent by a Web client require customized processing on the server side. Whether via a POST or a GET request, the query goes to a Web server, which relays the data to a *target program* (e.g., specified by the action attribute), receives its output, and sends that output back to the client as an HTTP response. The *Web server* here refers to the piece of software, such as Apache, that takes care of HTTP requests on a particular host. The target program may be a software module loaded into the server, a Java servlet, an active-page interpreter (ASP, PHP), or a stand-alone CGI program. We will focus on CGI programs in this text.

A CGI program is a stand-alone executable that is invoked by the Web server each time a request for the CGI is received. The server process and CGI process perform *interprocess communication* and cooperate following the Common Gateway Interface.

The Common Gateway Interface governs the way a Web server interacts with these external programs. Those conforming to the CGI are known as CGI programs. A popular scripting language for CGI programming is *Perl*. But CGI programs can be written in any language. For security reasons, CGI programs must usually be placed in special directories where programs accessible through Web servers are placed. These CGI directories can use any name but are usually given the name cgi-bin. A URL containing a cgi-bin leads the Web server to an executable program which will be invoked and connected through the standard Common Gateway Interface.

Here are some details on the Common Gateway Interface (Figure 8.12):

- For a POST query, a CGI program receives the form-urlencoded query body through standard input.
- For a GET query, a CGI program receives the form-urlencoded query string through the environment variable QUERY_STRING.
- The Web server transmits environment variables to the CGI program. Query headers, the query string, and other incoming data are sent to the CGI program through a set of predefined environment variables.

Figure 8.12   CGI INTERFACE DATA FLOW

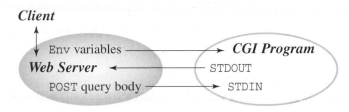

- A CGI program's standard output goes to the Web server, which relays the output back to the Web client in a well-formed HTTP response.

Complete information on the CGI specification can be found on the Web:

hoohoo.ncsa.uiuc.edu/cgi/interface.html

The rest of the chapter introduces CGI programming. Examples are given in Perl (Chapter 13).

8.14 OUTLINE OF A CGI PROGRAM

A CGI program (or *script*) is invoked by the Web server that provides input to the CGI program and receives its output. Typically, a CGI program follows this outline:

1. *Determines request method and receives input data*: The request method is given by the REQUEST_METHOD environment variable. For a POST query, the data are read from standard input, and the length of the data is indicated by the CONTENT_LENGTH environment variable. For a GET query, the input data are the value of the QUERY_STRING environment variable.

2. *Decodes and checks input data*: The form-urlencoded input data are decoded, and the key-value pairs are recovered. The correctness of the input data is checked. Incomplete or incorrect input results in a request to the user for the correct information.

3. *Performs tasks*: The input data are complete and correct. The program now processes the information and performs required actions.

4. *Produces output*: A generated response is sent to standard output. The response is usually in HTML format.

Receiving and Decoding Input

The value of the environment variable REQUEST_METHOD is either GET or POST. And the CGI program gets the raw input data in the format

```
name1=value1&name2=value2&name3=value3
```

where the names and values are URL-encoded. To decode each name and value:

1. Convert each + character to a SPACE.
2. Convert each %*xx* sequence to a single character whose ASCII code is *xx* in hexadecimal.

Then check the decoded input for correctness and completeness.

Formatting Output

Most likely, a CGI program, after processing the input, sends back an HTML document to provide a response to the user. Data sent to standard output by the CGI program are captured by the Web server and included in an HTTP response message. For HTML, the CGI output follows this format:

```
Content-Type: text/html       (HTTP header)
empty line
the HTML page                  (HTTP body)
```

If the CGI program knows the exact length (in bytes) of the body, it should send an additional header, for example,

```
Content-Length: 256
```

Note that all headers must be sent before the empty line that marks the end of headers.

The Content-Type header indicates the MIME type of the message body. For example, to send a GIF image by itself, the output can be:

```
Content-Type: img/gif
Content-Length: 1258
empty line
the image in GIF format
```

If a CGI program wishes to send a response specified by a URL, it sends a single-line output

```
Location: url
```

which instructs the server to return the specified document if the *url* is local or the client to retrieve the *url* if it is not local. For example, a user registration program can send the user to one URL for successful registration and to another otherwise. This technique is useful in many similar situations.

8.15   GETTING STARTED WITH CGI PROGRAMMING

Let's begin with a toy CGI program (Ex: **Hello**) that collects the name and email address of a person and responds with a "Hello" message. The HTML form (Figure 8.13) that collects the user information has the following code:

```
<p style="font-weight: bold; font-size: larger">
Complete this form:</p>
<form method="post" action="/cgi-bin/hello.cgi">
 <table width="400">
  <tr>
    <td class="fla"><label for="name">Full Name:</label></td>
    <td><input id="name" name="name" size="35" /></td>
  </tr><tr>
    <td class="fla"><label for="email">Email:</label></td>
    <td><input id="email" name="email" size="35" /></td>
  </tr><tr>
  <td></td><td><input type="submit" value="Send" /></td>
  </tr></table>
</form>
```

The server-side program that receives the information, as indicated by the action attribute, is hello.cgi, which has the following Perl code:

```
#!/usr/bin/perl
## hello.cgi--a toy CGI program                              ## (1)

use CGI qw(:standard);  ## cgi perl module                   ## (2)

var $name = param('name');                                   ## (3)
```

Figure 8.13   FORM FOR Hello **EXAMPLE**

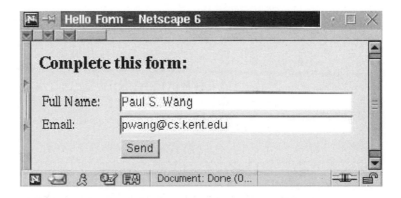

```
var $email = param('email');                              ## (4)

## Send response to standard output
print "Content-type: text/html\r\n\r\n";                  ## (5)
print <<END;                                              ## (6)
<?xml version="1.0" encoding="UTF-8" ?>
<!DOCTYPE html PUBLIC "-//W3C//DTD XHTML 1.0 Strict//EN"
    "http://www.w3.org/TR/xhtml1/DTD/xhtml1-strict.dtd">
<html xmlns="http://www.w3.org/1999/xhtml"
      xml:lang="en" lang="en">
<head><title>Hello</title></head>
<body style="background-color: #def">
<h3>Hello $name,</h3>
<p>The email address you sent is</p>
<p>$email</p></body></html>
END
```

After sending the form, the user sees a response page similar to the one shown in Figure 8.14.

Now let's look at the CGI program. The very first line of this CGI program

```
#!/usr/bin/perl
```

identifies Perl as the *interpreter* of the code to follow. The first two characters of the file must be #! followed by the location of the **perl** command. This location can be different on different computers.

The next line is a *comment*. In a **perl** program, anything from a # character to the end of the line is a comment that is ignored by the interpreter.

The program then declares to use the Perl module *CGI* (line 2), a collection of code for easy CGI programming. In Section 13.19, we'll find out more about Perl modules and the CGI Perl module (CGI.pm).

Figure 8.14   Hello RESPONSE PAGE

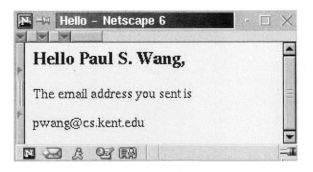

Two variables $name and $email are defined (lines 3-4). These are *scalar variables* in Perl, and they use the $ prefix. Also, Perl statements and declarations terminate with the semicolon (;). The CGI.pm supplied function param is handy to retrieve and decode incoming form data (sent via either GET or POST). The notation 'name' is a *single-quoted string*. Everything inside the single quotes (except a single quote, of course) is taken literally as a character.

After receiving the form data, this toy program sends back a "hello" message. This is done by sending a valid HTML page to *standard output*. The content type line is sent first by calling print (line 5). The argument to print is a *double-quoted string*, which can contain variables and special characters such as \n (NEWLINE) and \r (RETURN). To stand for themselves in a double-quoted string, special characters such as $, ", @, %, and \ can be escaped. Place a \ in front of the character to escape it. For example,

```
$red_h2 = "<h2 class=\"red\">";
```

Note the two consecutive end-of-line markers (\r\n RETURN-NEWLINE). They are needed to mark the end of the header and the beginning of the body of an HTTP message. The simpler version

```
print "Content-type: text/html\n\n";
```

is also acceptable. The HTML code for the response page is sent next as the message body. The output statement (line 6)

```
print <<END;
```

sends all subsequent lines to standard output until it sees a line consisting only of the specified identifier END. Variable substitution is performed before the lines are sent. This output notation is adopted from *Csh* (the UNIX C shell).

A Perl program ends when it runs out of statements or when the function exit is called.

8.16   DEPLOYING CGI PROGRAMS

A CGI program is deployed by placing it in the cgi-bin directory designated by the Web server. The cgi-bin directory should allow Web access:

chmod o+rx cgi-bin

And any CGI program placed in this directory must also allow Web access:

chmod o+rx *program.cgi*

When deploying a Perl program, make sure the first line of the program

```
#!/usr/bin/perl
```

indicates the location of the **perl** command on that particular host. If you *copy and paste* a Perl script, make sure you delete and retype the first line using a text editor on the host computer. Hidden characters on the first line have caused many a headache for the unwary.

Make sure your Perl program works by testing it from the command line. The shell-level command

```
./program.cgi
```

invokes the program and displays the output. Then, test your Perl program as a CGI from the Web.

More likely than not, a Perl CGI program will use the CGI.pm Perl module with the line

```
use CGI qw(:standard);
```

For this to work, you need to ensure that Perl on your computer has that module installed in a location included on the Perl variable @INC, which is a list of directories where Perl headers and modules are found. If you are installing a Perl script on a host meant to serve the Web, all this is most likely already set.

Once deployed, the URL to reach the CGI program is in the general form:

```
http://host/cgi-bin/program.cgi
```

Use this URL as the value of the action attribute in a form, for example.

8.17 CGI EXAMPLE: CLUB MEMBERSHIP

The Ex: **Hello** program is very simple. Let's look at a more realistic example (Ex: **JoinClub**) that has users join a club of some sort by filling out a form. The form (Figure 8.15) collects the user's full name and email address and sends the form data to a server-side program join.cgi.

```
<form method="post"
      action="http://www.club.com/cgi-bin/join.cgi">
...

</form>
```

The program join.cgi, written in Perl, performs these tasks:

1. obtains and checks the incoming form data
2. sends an error message to the user if any input is missing
3. sends email to the club manager with the information
4. outputs a page to acknowledge joining the club

```
#!/usr/bin/perl
## join.cgi--Perl script for
##           sending email to the manager
```

Figure 8.15   JOINING club.com

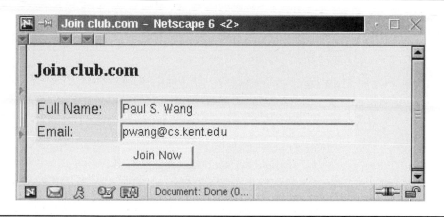

```
use CGI qw(:standard);          ## cgi perl module

var $err_msg = "", $club="club.com";                    ## (1)
var $subject = "-s 'New Member club.com'";
var $cmd="/bin/mail $subject manager\@$club";
var $xhtml_front =
'<?xml version="1.0" encoding="UTF-8" ?>
<!DOCTYPE html PUBLIC "-//W3C//DTD XHTML 1.0 Strict//EN"
    "http://www.w3.org/TR/xhtml1/DTD/xhtml1-strict.dtd">
<html xmlns="http://www.w3.org/1999/xhtml"
     xml:lang="en" lang="en">';
var $name = param('name');    ## form data
var $email = param('email');  ## form data               ## (2)

if ( ! $name )  ## $name is empty                        ## (3)
{  $err_msg .= "<p>Name must be specified.</p>";
}

if ( ! $email ) ## $email is empty                       ## (4)
{  $err_msg .= "<p>Email must be specified.</p>";
}

if ( $err_msg )                                          ## (5)
{  error();          ## function call                    ## (6)
   exit(1);          ## abnormal termination             ## (7)
}

## mail notice to manager
```

```
open(MAIL, "| $cmd");                                    ## (8)
print MAIL "Name: $name\n";
print MAIL "Email: $email\n";
print MAIL "to join $club";
close(MAIL);                                             ## (9)

## Send response to standard output
print "Content-type: text/html\r\n\r\n";                 ## (10)
print <<END;                                             ## (11)
$xhtml_front
<head><title>Thanks for Joining</title></head>
<body style="background-color: white">
<h3>Thank you $name.</h3>
<p>Welcome to $club.  Your membership will
be processed shortly.</p>
<p>We will email you at <code>$email</code> about
your new membership at $club.</p>
</body></html>
END
```

After the standard opening lines, the program proceeds to define seven variables: $err_msg, $club, $subject, $cmd, $xhtml_front, $name, and $email (lines 1-2). Again, the param function from the CGI.pm module helps retrieve the incoming form data. The $xhtml_front is a constant string representing the initial lines of an XHTML page.

The $name and $email strings are checked (lines 3-4). Both must have values. If the user failed to fill in a form field, the corresponding value retrieved would be an empty string. If $name is an empty string, then the expression ! $name (not $name) becomes true. In case any of these is empty, an appropriate string is appended to the $err_msg variable, which will be used later for error reporting.

In Perl, the period operator (.) concatenates two strings. The expression

```
$str1 .= $str2
```

is the C-like shorthand for

```
$str1 = $str1 . $str2
```

If there is any error (line 5), the error() function is called (line 6) and the program ends (line 7). In Perl, a function call takes the usual form

```
function_name(arg1, arg2,...)
```

It is possible to omit the parentheses around the arguments. Normal termination is exit(0), and abnormal termination, as on line 7, is exit(1).

If there is no error, the program continues and sends email to the club manager about the new member. The program opens a mailing process to receive the data to be mailed (line 8). The channel to send to the mailing process is given the arbitrary name MAIL. The content of the email is sent to

Figure 8.16   MEMBERSHIP RESPONSE PAGE

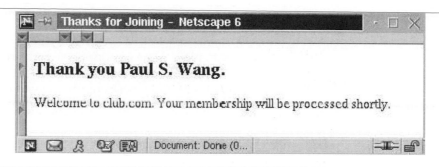

MAIL via the Perl print function. Closing the output channel (line 9) finishes sending the mail. The remaining task is to send an acknowledgment page (Figure 8.16) to the user using the same output technique (line 11) as before.

The error function is defined at the end of this Perl program. It uses a sequence of print calls to send a page containing the $err_msg:

```
sub error()
{    print "Content-type: text/html\r\n\r\n";
     print "$xhtml_front\r\n";
     print '<head><title>Error</title></head>';
     print '<body style="background-color: white">';
     print '<h3>Data Missing</h3>';
     print "<p>$err_msg Please go BACK, make corrections, ";
     print 'and submit the form again.</p> </body></html>';
}
```

This program checks only the presence of the email address. But the email address given may also be invalid. A check can make this program more complete. It is also common practice to check form input on the client side as the user fills out the form (Section 9.15). Client-side checks are good, but no substitute for server-side checking because CGI programs can always be invoked without using the HTML forms that have the checks.

Multistep Forms

Forms are used for many purposes on the Web. Many e-commerce and e-business applications involve filling out a series of forms. To process such *translation sessions* correctly, a server-side program, CGI or otherwise, must keep track of which subsequent form submission goes with which prior form input. We will explain how session control is done with *HTTP cookies* in Section 13.22.

8.18   CGI ENVIRONMENT VARIABLES

Under CGI, an important way to communicate information from the Web server to the CGI program is via environment variables. An *environment variable* is one that's already in place when a program starts to run. So, a program can simply access its value to obtain the data.

A server will always provide these environment variables:

- SERVER_NAME: domain name of the host computer
- SERVER_ADDR: IP of the host computer
- PATH: command search path
- GATEWAY_INTERFACE: version of CGI, (e.g., CGI/1.1)
- SERVER_ADMIN: email address of the server administrator
- SERVER_SIGNATURE: name/version, domain, and port of the server program
- DOCUMENT_ROOT: full path of the top document directory
- SERVER_SOFTWARE: *name/version*... of the Web server such as

```
Apache/1.3.12 (Unix) ApacheJServ/1.1 PHP/4.0 mod_ssl/2.6.6
    OpenSSL/0.9
```

The preceding quantities are fixed for a Web server running on a particular host computer and are independent of the incoming HTTP request.

The server also transmits the following environment values that are dependent on each request:

- SERVER_PORT: port used by the server (e.g., 80)
- SERVER_PROTOCOL: protocol used (e.g., HTTP/1.1)
- TZ: local time zone (e.g., U.S./Eastern)
- REQUEST_URI: the URI of this request
- REQUEST_METHOD: the HTTP request method (GET, POST, HEAD, . . .)
- CONTENT_LENGTH: length of POST request body in bytes
- CONTENT_TYPE: the MIME content type designation of body
- QUERY_STRING: string after first ? of the URI given
- AUTH_TYPE: user authentication type used, if any (e.g., basic or digest)
- SCRIPT_NAME: URI of the CGI program
- SCRIPT_FILENAME: full path of the CGI program
- PATH_INFO: the part of the URI after the CGI name and before any query string
- PATH_TRANSLATED: full path for PATH_INFO
- REMOTE_ADDR: IP of client
- REMOTE_PORT: port of client

Other environment values relate to the HTTP headers of a particular request:

- HTTP_ACCEPT: MIME types client prefers or accepts
- HTTP_ACCEPT_LANGUAGE: language accepted (e.g., en-us)
- HTTP_ACCEPT_CHARSET: character set preferred or accepted (e.g., ISO-8859-1, utf-8)
- HTTP_REFERER: URL of the page containing the form submitting the request
- HTTP_COOKIE: cookie information
- HTTP_ACCEPT_ENCODING: data encoding preferred or accepted
- HTTP_HOST: host name part of the request URL
- HTTP_USER_AGENT: for example, Mozilla/5.0 (X11; U; Linux i686; en-US; rv:0.9) Gecko/20019 Netscape6/6.2

In a Perl program, you can easily access the value of an environment variable with the notation

$ENV{*var_name*}

For example,

```
$str = $ENV{'QUERY_STRING'};
$agent = $ENV{'HTTP_USER_AGENT'};
```

A rather complete list of environment variables is given here. The meaning of some are already clear. Others will be explained as they are used.

8.19   DATA RECEIVED ON THE SERVER SIDE

Let's look at a CGI program that displays the form input that it receives. This program can be handy for checking what your form is sending to the server side.

The program performs these steps:

1. Sets the $xhtml_front variable to a constant string (line A) and calls the htmlBegin function (line B) to begin output of the response page.
2. The HTTP request method is obtained from the environment variable REQUEST_METHOD (line C).
3. The form input is obtained either from the request content (line D) or the environment variable QUERY_STRING (line E). The Perl operator eq (ne) compares strings for equality (nonequality). The operator || is logical OR.
4. The form input is displayed with HTML code (line F).

```perl
#!/usr/bin/perl

$xhtml_front = '<?xml version="1.0" encoding="UTF-8" ?>        ## (A)
  <!DOCTYPE html PUBLIC "-//W3C//DTD XHTML 1.0 Strict//EN"
      "http://www.w3.org/TR/xhtml1/DTD/xhtml1-strict.dtd">
  <html xmlns="http://www.w3.org/1999/xhtml"
      xml:lang="en" lang="en">';

htmlBegin("Reflect CGI", "white", $xhtml_front);                ## (B)

### displaying post query string from form

$input="";
$method = $ENV{'REQUEST_METHOD'};                               ## (C)

if ( $method eq "POST" || $method eq "post" )                   ## (D)
{   read(STDIN, $input, $ENV{'CONTENT_LENGTH'});
}
elsif ( $method eq "GET" || $method eq "get" )                  ## (E)
{    $input=$ENV{'QUERY_STRING'};
}

if ( $input ne "" )                                             ## (F)
{   print "<h2>Submitted String from $method Query:</h2>";
    print "<p style=\"font-size: larger; color: #c33\">";
    print "<code>$input </code></p>";
}
print "</body></html>";
exit(0);

################ subroutines ####################

sub htmlBegin
{   my $title=$_[0];      ### page title                        ## (G)
    my $bg =$_[1];        ### background for body
    my $front = $_[2];    ### XHTML code                        ## (H)

    print "Content-type: text/html\n\n
        $front
        <head><title>$title</title></head>\n
        <body style=\"background-color: $bg\; margin: 20px\">\n";
}
```

The notations $\$\_[0]$, $\$\_[1]$, and $\$\_[2]$ (lines G–H) refer to arguments one, two, and three passed to the function (line B). The keyword my declares the variables local to the function.

A more elaborate version of this CGI program has been placed on the WDP Web site:

www.sofpower.com/cgi-bin/wb/reflect.pl

When testing a new form, this CGI program can be used to reflect back to you the form input for easy checking.

8.20 CONTENT LENGTH

When the server is using the new HTTP/1.1 protocol, the connection between the server and the client is kept alive after the server sends the response[3]. The server closes the connection only when the client so requests via the

```
Connection: close
```

header or after a time-out interval. The keep-alive feature makes the Web much more efficient.

To avoid having to close the connection, the server can include a Content-length header so the client knows when the response body has been fully received. A Web server can supply the length of a static file very easily. But when it comes to the content length of a dynamically generated page, this is trickier. Most servers do not generate the content length for dynamic pages and are forced to shut down the connection.

But this shutdown can be avoided if a CGI program provides the content length header itself. It is a good idea for a dynamically generated page always to supply the content length header under HTTP/1.1. A CGI program can check the SERVER_PROTOCOL environment variable to see if HTTP/1.1 is being used. When sending the content with length information, make sure the byte count matches the length of the content exactly.

As a simple example, let's look at a CGI program in Perl (Ex: **ImageGet**) that receives the name of a GIF file and sends that along with length information.

```
#!/usr/bin/perl
#### getimage.pl
use CGI qw(:standard);

$file = param('gif');                                       ## (1)
open(IMG, "img/$file") or error_reply("can't open $file"); ## (2)
$size = -s IMG;                                             ## (3)
```

_____

[3]Under HTTP/1.0, the server-client connection is closed after each response.

```
read(IMG, $bytes, $size);                              ## (4)

binmode(STDOUT);                                       ## (5)
print "Content-type: image/gif\r\n";                   ## (6)
print "Content-length: $size\r\n\r\n";                 ## (7)
print $bytes;                                          ## (8)
exit;
```

The program receives the GIF file name (line 1), opens it for reading (line 2), obtains the size of the file (line 3), and then reads the whole file into the variable $bytes (line 4).

Now the program is ready to produce output. Standard output is set to binary mode (line 5) to allow GIF data. The content type (line 6) and content length (line 7) headers are sent, followed by an empty line and the GIF file (line 8).

The error_reply subroutine sends an error message in HTML:

```
sub error_reply()
{   my $msg=$_[0], $page="", $len;    ## local variables
    $page .= "$xhtml_front <head><title>Error</title>" .
            "</head><body><h3>$msg</h3></body></html>";    ## (9)
    $len = length($page);                                  ## (10)
    print "Content-type: text/html\r\n";
    print "Content-length: $len\r\n\r\n";                  ## (11)
    print $page;
}
```

Note how the HTML page is constructed in a string $page (line 9) so we can measure its length (line 10) for the Content-length header (line 11).

8.21 SUMMARY

HTML provides many ways to collect user input:

```
<input type="text" ... />            (single-line text)
<textarea> ... </textarea>           (multiline text)
<input type="radio" ... />           (radio buttons)
<input type="checkbox" ... />        (check boxes)
<select><option ... /> ... </select> (menus)
<input type="image" ... />           (mouse position)
<input type="submit" ... />          (submit button)
<input type="button" ... />          (click button)
<input type="reset" ... />           (reset button)
<input type="hidden" ... />          (hidden data)
<input type="file" ... />            (files)
```

Hidden input elements can send data built into a form.

Input controls are inline elements and must be enclosed in block elements before being placed inside a form. It is important to design forms that are simple, clear, and integrated with the site.

Collected form data are url-encoded and sent, via an HTTP POST or GET request (specified by the method attribute) to a prescribed server-side program (specified by the required action attribute) for processing. A GET request has no message body and can only send a URI to the server. A POST request can send a URI and a message body. XHTML allows input controls to be placed outside forms and in any block or inline elements. A form sends only data from input controls inside the form. When possible, a CGI program should use the HTTP Content-length header to preserve the HTTP connection between the server and the client.

Form data are often processed by CGI programs. A CGI program is an independent program invoked by the Web server to handle incoming data. Such data may come from an HTML form or from a URL with an attached query string. CGI programs communicate with Web servers following the Common Gateway Interface. The Perl scripting language uses a C-like syntax and is a popular, free language for writing CGI programs.

A server-side program processes incoming requests by determining the request method, obtaining the form data or query string, checking the completeness and correctness of the form data, performing required tasks on the data, and sending a response page back to the user. If something is wrong with the input form data, an error page is sent back. The reflect.pl CGI program, placed at the WDP Web site, demonstrates receiving form data and can be used for checking new forms.

Designers and programmers should work together to create fill-out forms. It is important to format forms for clarity and ease of use. Reply pages from a server-side program must preserve the look and feel of the site to avoid confusion.

More coverage of CGI programming with Perl can be found in Chapter 13.

EXERCISES

Review Questions

1. What HTML elements can be placed inside the form element?

2. What happens if an input control is placed outside the form element?

3. What is the difference between radio buttons and check boxes?

4. In a Web page, when and why should you use the GET and the POST request methods?

5. Which Perl module supplies the `param` function? What does the `param` function do?

6. What is form-urlencoding?

7. Describe the sequence of actions needed for a server-side program to decode form data.

8. What is a hidden input control? How is it used?

9. How should the first line of a Perl program be coded? What prefix does a Perl scalar variable use?

10. What operator in Perl concatenates strings?

11. What is a cgi-bin?

12. What techniques help reply pages produced by server-side programs maintain the look and feel of the Web site?

13. Why is the content length information needed for the HTTP 1.1 keep-alive feature to work?

Assignments

1. Design a form to use as many `input` controls as you know. Make sure the form is formatted well and easy to follow.

2. Experiment with the background color of `input` controls. Can you set them to reasonable colors to enhance the appearance of a form? Show your code.

3. Deploy Ex: **Hello** (Section 8.15) on your computer and experiment with it. Try sending the form with some input missing.

4. Take the Ex: **Hello** (Section 8.15) example and format the form with a table, making it look as clear as you can.

5. Take Ex: **Hello** and modify it to use the GET method. Test to make sure it works.

6. Modify the Ex: **Hello** form to use the `reflect.pl` CGI program at the WDP site instead (Section 8.19). Study the url-encoded string for the form data.

7. Start your browser and type in the `location` box the URL of the CGI program used by Ex: **Hello**. Type a ? at the end of that URL and then continue with the url-encoded string you found in Assignment 6. Enter this URL and see what response page you get. Explain this way of invoking a CGI program.

8.   Design a form with several text input fields. Write a CGI program that displays all the incoming text strings as a single string.

9.   Write a short CGI program that when called will display the values of a set of environment variables.

10. Write a CGI program that when called with no form data will send an HTML form to the user for collecting information to be processed again by the same CGI program.

## CHAPTER 9

Client-Side Scripting: JavaScript

For a Web page, HTML supplies document content and structure, and CSS provides presentation styling. In addition, *client-side scripts* can control browser actions associated with a Web page. *Scripts* are programs written in a simple and easy-to-use language to specify control of other programs. Client-side scripts are almost always written in the *JavaScript* language to control browser actions.

Tasks performed with client-side scripts include:

- asking the browser to display information
- making the Web page different depending on the browser and browser features
- monitoring user events and specifying reactions
- generating HTML code for parts of the page
- modifying a page in response to events
- checking correctness of user input
- replacing and updating parts of a page
- changing the style and position of displayed elements dynamically

Client-side scripting can make Web pages more dynamic and more responsive. We will see how JavaScript is used in combination with other Web constructs for user interface purposes. The emphasis is in applying JavaScript in practice rather than studying it as a programming language.

What Is JavaScript?

JavaScript is a widely used scripting language originally developed by Netscape for both client-side and server-side scripting. The language is becoming an international standard, approved by the European standards body ECMA, the European Computer Manufacturers Association (ECMA-262), in 1997 and later by the ISO in 1998. Client-side JavaScript is used widely and supported well by major browsers including Netscape Navigator (NN), Internet Explorer (IE), AOL, Mozilla, and Opera. We shall present client-side JavaScript for adding dynamism and interactivity to Web pages and refer to it simply as *JavaScript*.

Contrary to what the name might suggest, JavaScript programs are not written in Java, which is another programming language. JavaScript programs are embedded in Web pages and executed by browsers that provide the *host environment* or execution context. JavaScript code can generate HTML code to be included in the page and perform tasks in reaction to certain events. The host environment supplies document objects, browser objects, and JavaScript built-in objects for script manipulation. These objects can represent the entire document and well-defined parts in it such as windows, buttons, menus, pop-ups, dialog boxes, text areas, anchors, frames, history, cookies, and input/output. Objects provide useful *methods*, functions contained in the objects, for various purposes.

The host environment also provides a means to connect scripting code with events such as focus and mouse actions, page and image loading, form input and submission, error, and abort. Scripting code can also perform computation as the page is loading. Thus, the displayed page is the result of a combination of HTML, CSS, and JavaScript actions.

9.1   GETTING STARTED

JavaScript is an object-oriented language, and many constructs are similar to those in C++ or Java. Let's look at our first JavaScript program (Ex: **Date**), which generates some simple HTML code for a page:

```
<head><title>Javascript Demo</title>
<link rel="stylesheet" href="date.css" type="text/css" />
</head><body>
<p>Go <em>Web Design and Programming</em> teams!</p>
<p>You are using <span class="blue">
<script type="text/javascript">                          // (1)
  var d = new Date();                                    // (2)
  var time = d.getHours() +":"+ d.getMinutes()+".";      // (3)
  var agent = navigator.userAgent;                       // (4)
  document.write(agent + " and the time is "
              +  time + "</p>");                          // (5)
</script></span></p>
<p>Do you know where your project is?</p>
</body></html>
```

The <script> element (line 1) contains the JavaScript code, and the type attribute is required. Text lines enclosed in the <script> element are treated as program code of the given type and not to be displayed.

Figure 9.1   JAVASCRIPT-GENERATED PAGE

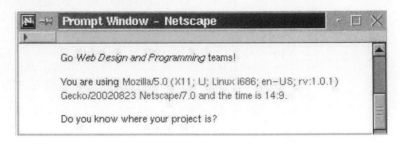

The variable d is set to a Date object (line 2) created by the operator new followed by the constructor call Date(). A constructor is a function you call to obtain new objects. The getHours and getMinutes methods of Date are used to construct the time string (line 3). Simple JavaScript statements are terminated by a semicolon (;). Comments are either from // to end of line or enclosed by /* and */.

In JavaScript, a *string literal* is given inside double quotation marks (lines 3 and 5). The operator + concatenates strings and objects, such as numbers, to strings. The variable agent is set to the name of the user agent (browser) executing this program, and the name is obtained from the userAgent attribute of the built-in navigator object (line 4).

The write method of the document object inserts the given string into the HTML code of the document where the <script> element is located (line 5). The JavaScript-generated content is displayed in blue (Figure 9.1).

This simple example gives an idea of JavaScript programming. Learning JavaScript involves understanding its syntax, semantics, objects and methods, the host environment provided by the browser, events and event handling, and effective applications in practice. Let's first look at how JavaScript code is deployed in a Web page.

9.2   EMBEDDING JAVASCRIPT IN A WEB PAGE

A JavaScript program usually consists of various code parts that cooperate to do the job. Where and how to place code in a Web page depend on the purpose of the code. But generally, the code can appear either in <script> elements or as values of event-handling attributes of HTML tags. Any number of script elements can be placed in head, body, block, and inline elements. Place a script in the head element unless it generates document content, as in Ex: **Date**.

- Code for defining functions or creating data structures are placed in <script> elements inside the page's <head> element.

- Code for generating HTML to be displayed as part of the page are placed in `<script>` elements inside the `<body>` where the generated HTML code will be inserted.

- Code for actions triggered by events are given as values of *event attributes* of HTML tags. The code is usually a function call or a few short statements. `onfocus`, `onblur`, `onclick`, `onmouseover`, and `onmouseout` are examples of event attributes.

A JavaScript program often works for a set of pages, not one. In that case, it is better to place the code in a separate file. The file can then be attached to a Web page as follows:

```
<script type="text/javascript" src="file.js"></script>
```

The `src` attribute of `<script>` gives the URL of the program file. Note that we used the conventional `.js` file name suffix.

With file inclusion, any corrections or improvements in the `.js` file will be reflected in multiple pages automatically. Furthermore, a browser will download the program only once, reducing download time for these pages. Older browsers that do not support client-side scripting will ignore the `<script>` tag, and the program file will not be included. If the code is placed in the `<script>` tag, then the following construct is often used to avoid the code being mistaken as page content by older browsers:

```
<script type="text/javascript">
<!--
  var d = new Date;

  ...

// -->
</script>
```

Few modern browsers do not support JavaScript. To make code easier to read, examples in this text do not employ this code hiding technique.

The `<noscript>...</noscript>` element can be given after the `<script>` element to supply alternative content for nonscripting browsers, but it is seldom useful.

9.3   A BRIEF HISTORY OF JAVASCRIPT

In 1995, Netscape initiated an effort to create a language to make the Java support in its browsers more accessible to nonprogrammers. The easy-to-use scripting language developed by Brendan Eich and his group at Netscape was first named LiveScript and then changed to JavaScript as it was released in December 1995. The name was a source of confusion for many years to come.

JavaScript got popular and widely used by Web designers mainly to add interactivity to pages through image swapping (rollovers). Microsoft responded to JavaScript in part by releasing its own VBScript language. Microsoft also released an ill-fated *Windows port* of JavaScript called JScript in July 1996.

As the popularity of JavaScript grew, the problem of cross-platform compatibility became a big issue. In November 1996, Netscape and Sun began to standardize the language with the help of ECMA. ECMAScript standardized the core JavaScript language and leaves its host environment to provide browser and document objects.

Now the only thing that stands in the way of a powerful, easy-to-use, and platform-independent client-side scripting language is incompatible object models in host environments. Browser vendors and others, working with the W3C, are converging to the W3C DOM (Document Object Model) as the standard for implementing objects to represent documents in applications (Section 10.5).

With standardized core language features and host environments, JavaScript promises to be the language of choice, in combination with XHTML, CSS, and DOM (Chapter 10), to deliver dynamism and interactivity to the Web.

9.4 ROLLOVERS

One of the most frequent applications of JavaScript is to switch images on mouseover events. It provides good responsiveness to Web pages, and users like the effect. A basic rollover is simple. Take two images (Figure 9.2): `dragon1.jpg` on the left and `dragon2.jpg` on the right. We want to display the first image, the *base image*, in a page, switch it to the second image, the *mouseover image*, when the mouse is over the image, and then switch back to the base image when the mouse leaves the image.

Most often, rollovers are used to enliven a hyperlink. To achieve the effect, we define actions connected to the `onmouseover` and `onmouseout` events of a hyperlink element `<a>` anchored on an image or text to be rolled over. Here is an example (Ex: **Rollover**):

```
<a href="index.html"
  onmouseover="document.getElementById('icon').src='dragon2.jpg'" (A)
```

Figure 9.2   IMAGE ROLLOVER

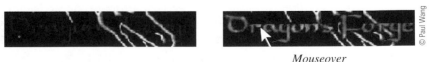

Mouseover

© Paul Wang

```
      onmouseout="document.getElementById('icon').src='dragon1.jpg'"    (B)
    ><img src="dragon1.jpg" id="icon"                                   (C)
          style="border: none" width="225" height="42"
          alt="Entry Icon" />
    </a>
```

The action for onmouseover (line A) is a JavaScript expression that sets the source attribute for the icon element in the document object to dragon2.jpg, the second image. The getElementById method of the document object is handy to obtain any element by giving its id. The name icon is the id (line C) we have given to the image element.[1] The onmouseout action switches the images again. Clicking the image leads to the target page.

In general, you can give one or more JavaScript statements (separated by ;) inside double quotation marks to define the action in response to an event:

```
onSomeEvent="st1; st2;..."
```

To avoid long JavaScript code in an element tag, it is good practice to define an *event-handling function* and simply call that function.

To achieve the rollover on an image that may or may not be a link, put the onmouseover and onmouseout attributes in the img tag instead[2] (Ex: **ImgRoll**):

```
<img onmouseover="this.src='dragon2.jpg'"              (D)
     onmouseout="this.src='dragon1.jpg'"              (E)
     src="dragon1.jpg" id="icon"
     style="border: none" width="225" height="42"
     alt="Dragon Icon" />
```

Note the use of the symbol this to refer to the img element itself (lines D and E).

The rollover effect is not limited to a single element. You can easily re-place/restore an image when the mouse is over/out some other element. In general, a mouseover, a mouseout, or any other event from any element can trigger any well-defined JavaScript actions on the page. The dynamic effects are only limited by your design and imagination.

9.5   PRELOADING IMAGES

The responsiveness of a rollover depends on the speed at which the images are swapped. The loading of the second image is triggered by the mouseover event and can cause a significant delay when it happens for the first time. To avoid this annoying sluggishness, we should keep rollover image files small and preload them right after the page is loaded.

---

[1]XHTML has no name attribute for img, which old browsers may still use for naming an image.
[2]Older browsers do not support event-handling attributes for the img tag.

Loading an image is simple with JavaScript. Create a new Image object and set its src attribute to the image URL. This causes the image to download across the Internet. Once loaded, an image displays immediately upon request. When called, loadImage loads the image given by the url:

```
<script type="text/javascript">
function loadImage(url)
{   if (document.images)    // if browser supports images
    {  img = new Image();   // obtains a new image object
       img.src = url;       // downloads the image
       return img;
    }
}
</script>
```

The script is placed inside the <head> element.

The loadImage function is triggered by the onload event on body, which occurs immediately after page loading completes.

```
<body onload="loadImage('dragon2.jpg')">            (F)
```

The call (line F) downloads the mouseover image for the rollover (Ex: **Preload**). Because the mouseout image dragon1.jpg has already been loaded as part of page loading, it does not need to be loaded again. With image preloading, the HTML code in Section 9.4 remains working, only faster. The effect of preloading is increased when more than one mouseover images are involved.

9.6   ACTIVE NAVIGATION BARS

A well-designed navigation system is essential for any Web site with more than just a few pages. Designing a handsome and functional main navigation bar for major pages can help the site's usability, visual appeal, and unity.

Such a navigation bar often involves image-based links. Making these rollovers provides much appreciated interactivity. But we need to do more than put the same navigation bar on selected pages. If there is a link on the bar pointing to the current page, that link must be deactivated and appear distinctive. Users can become confused or annoyed if clicking a link leads to the same page, as if something is wrong. The distinct looking link also serves as an identifier for the current page, clearly marking the page being displayed. We shall refer to this as the *page-id* image. Thus, a rollover navigation link normally involves a set of three images: base, mouseover, and page-id.

With JavaScript rollovers, we present a solution that is simple and effective. Figure 9.3 shows how the olive background marks the current page, how it follows the mouse cursor in the navbar, and how it disappears when the cursor reaches Main page, a self-link purposely rendered inactive.

Figure 9.3   Main Page **NAVBAR ACTIONS**

Mouseout	*Mouseover*	*Mouseover*

The implementation of this navbar (Ex: **StdNavbar**) makes it easily customizable and reusable for your Web projects:

- Each page linked on the navbar is given a *pageId* and is placed in a file *pageId*.html.
- Each entry on the navbar is an anchored image whose id attribute is set to its *pageId*. The image rolls over with a mouseover and a mouseout image whose names are directly derived from the *pageId*, such as *pageId*over.gif and *pageId*out.gif.

The navbar itself is a one-column table, where each row entry has the same structure and represents an image-anchored link. The entry for the main.html page is:

```
<tr><td align="left" valign="top">
     <a href="javascript:toPage('main');"            (1)
        onmouseover="over('main')"                    (2)
        onmouseout="out('main')">                     (3)
        <img id="main" alt="main"                     (4)
             src="images/mainout.gif" width="130"
             height="25" style="border: none" />
     </a>
</td></tr>
```

We see the *pageId* main (line 1) is passed to the mouseover event handler over (line 2), and the mouseout event handler out (line 3) is defined in the file stdnavbar.js, which also contains the function toPage called by the hyperlink (line 1)

```
function toPage(pageid)
{   if ( pageid != myid )
    {   window.location = pageid + ".html"; }
}
```

where the variable myid has been set to the *pageId* of the current page. Thus, this function loads the destination page only if it is not the page itself. The browser built-in window object represents the current Web page and contains its URL location as well as other elements (Section 9.12). In general, the code

```
window.location = url;
```

loads a new page given by the *url*. The toPage function assumes that these pages are in the same directory. It is a simple matter to generalize this program to accept pages located in different directories.

The row navbar entry for the service.html page is the same as the preceding entry with the character sequence main replaced by service everywhere. The row entries for other pages on the navbar table are made in the same way.

File stdnavbar.js

Code in the file stdnavbar.js enables the desired rollover actions to work. It is included in each page with

```
<script type="text/javascript" src="stdnavbar.js"></script>
```

inside the <head> element.

The stdnavbar.js is our first substantial JavaScript program. We go through this example carefully to explain the JavaScript code and how the program makes the navbar work.

The JavaScript file begins with customizable constants and functions:

```
///////     stdnavbar.js    ///////

// Customize imgDir, pageIds, imgSuffix,
//    and image file names

// imgDir: relative URL of image dir  constant
const imgDir="images/";  // may need to use var for IE

// imgSuffix: image file suffix constant
const imgSuffix = ".gif";

// pageIds: a constant array of page ids
const pageIds= [ "home", "main", "service", "contact" ];

// Image file names
// overImg returns a mouseover image URL
function overImg(pageid)
{  return imgDir + pageid + "over." + imgSuffix;
}
```

```
// outImg returns a mouseout image URL
function outImg(pageid)
{   return imgDir + pageid + "out." + imgSuffix;
}
//////// No customization necessary beyond this line ////////
```

Edit the values of these variables and the definition of the `overImg` and `outImg` functions to suit your Web project.

Arrays

The `pageIds` is an array. JavaScript arrays can be created in the following ways:

```
var a = new Array(arrayLength);
var b = new Array(element0, element1,..., elementN);
var c = [element0, element1,..., elementN];
```

where `c` is a read-only array. The length of an array is recorded in its `length` attribute (e.g., `c.length`). Array elements can be set and retrieved with

```
a[0] = "first";
a[1] = "second";
var value = b[6];
```

The index runs from 0 to `length` − 1. Accessing an undefined array entry gives the value `undefined`. Assigning to an element beyond the end of the array increases its length. Array methods include:

`pop()`	removes and returns last element
`shift()`	removes and returns first element, ex: `e=a.shift()`
`unshift(e1,e2,...)`	inserts elements in front and returns new length
`push(e1,e2,...)`	inserts elements at end and returns new length
`concat(arr2,...)`	joins the given arrays to the array and returns a new array
`reverse()`	changes the array itself to go backward

Document Images

The `document` object represents a Web page, and it contains elements. The `document.images` is an array of `Image` objects, each representing an image introduced by an `img` element in the document source code. If the browser is one of the very few that does not support images, then `document.images` is undefined. The `src` attribute of an `Image` object records the URL of the image file for this image. An image will be loaded when its src is set to a URL. This is how the loadImage function works.

```
function loadImage(url)
{  if ( document.images )          // (5)
   {    img = new Image();         // (6)
        img.src = url;             // (7)
        return img;
   }
}
```

The function causes image downloading by creating a new image object (line 6) and setting its src attribute (line 7). The function also returns the image object. But it does all this only if the browser supports images (line 5). If document.images is null (or undefined) and the Web page is known to contain images, then the browser does not support images. JavaScript considers null or undefined to be false in logical tests.

The next function calls loadImage on each mouseover image (line 9) to preload it so the navbar is ready to rollover. The for loop (line 8) works in the usual C++ and Java fashion.

```
var imgLoaded = false;    // flag

function preloadImages()
{  if (document.images)  // if defined
   {    for (var i=0; i < pageIds.length; i++)      // (8)
        {  loadImage(overImg(pageIds[i]));          // (9)
        }
        imgLoaded = true;
   }
   if (document.images[myid])
   {    document.images[myid].src = overImg(myid);  // (10)
   }
}
```

The function also sets the imgLoaded flag and makes the current page link stand out with its mouseover image (line 10). Note how an image is accessed with its name attribute as the images array index (line 10). Image preloading is triggered by the onload event of the <body> element, just after page loading:

```
<body onload="preloadImages()"  ... >
```

The over and out functions for the rollover effect are provided by:

```
function over(pageid)
{  if (document.images && imgLoaded == true)       // (11)
   {    if ( pageid != myid )                       // (12)
        {  document.images[pageid].src =
                   overImg(pageid);                 // (13)
```

```
      }
        document.images[myid].src = outImg(myid);   // (14)
    }
}

function out(pageid)
{  if (document.images && imgLoaded == true)
   {  if ( pageid !- myid )
      {  document.images[pageid].src =
                   outImg(pageid);
      }
      document.images[myid].src = overImg(myid);   // (15)
   }
}
```

The over function changes the image for the pageid link to the mouseover image (line 13), provided that pageid is not the same as myid. For the current page link, the mouseout image is used for page identification (line 14). The out function does the opposite.

Note that, instead of using three images for each rollover, we used only two. The mouseover image (line 10) doubles as the page-id image (line 15). And the page-id image performs a *reverse rollover* (line 14) to indicate that it is not an active link.

The WDP site puts the stdnavbar.js to use for the page-top navbar (Figure 9.4) with the following customizations:

```
///////    wdprollover.js    ///////

var imgDir="img/";        // image directory URL
var imgSuffix = ".gif";   // image file suffix

// pageIds: an array of page ids
var pageIds= ["authors", "chapters", "examples", "faq",
              "feedback", "handson", "main", "ordering",
              "updates", "resources", "projects", "preface",
              "toc", "sitemap"];
```

Figure 9.4 WDP SITE NAVBAR

```
function overImg(pageid) // image for mouseover
{   return imgDir + "o_" + pageid + imgSuffix; }

function outImg(pageid) // image for mouseout
{   return imgDir + "u_" + pageid + imgSuffix; }

// mouseover image double as page identification
function selfImg(pageid)
{   return imgDir + "o_" + pageid + imgSuffix; }
```

9.7 MAKING COMPARISONS

JavaScript uses the usual set of comparison operators

```
==   !=   >   >=   <   <=
```

for *comparing strings, numbers,* and *objects,* returning a `true` or `false` Boolean value (lines 11 and 12). The comparison is straightforward if the two operands compared are of the same type. When they are not, the following rules apply:

- When comparing a number to a string, the string is automatically converted to a number.
- When only one of the operands is a Boolean, it is converted to 1 (for true) or 0 (for false).
- When comparing an object to a string or number, the object is converted to a string (via its `toString` method) or number (via its `valueOf` method). Failure to convert generates a run-time error.

The *strict equality operators* `===` and `!==` can be used if the operands must be of the same type.

You can also use the built-in value `undefined`

```
if ( var == undefined )
```

to see if a variable has been assigned a value.

9.8 BUILT-IN FUNCTIONS

In JavaScript, you can use strings and numbers interchangeably in most situations. You can also explicitly convert a string to a number, and vice versa. The JavaScript built-in functions `Number( arg )` and `String( arg )` convert their arguments to a number and a string, respectively.

The functions `parseInt( str )` and `parseFloat( str )` return the integer and floating-point values of the argument *str,* respectively.

The function encodeURI(*url*) (decodeURI(*url*)) takes a complete URL and performs the URL encoding (decoding). The function eval(*str*) executes *str* as a piece of JavaScript code.

In JavaScript, strings are objects and have many useful fields and methods, including:

- *str*.length—the length of the string
- *str*.charAt(*i*)—char at position *i*; 0 is the first character
- *str*.substr(*i*, *length*)—substring starting at index *i* until the end of string or with the optional length
- *str*.indexOf(*substr*)—first index of *substr* in *str* or -1 if not found
- *str*.lastIndexOf(*substr*)—last index of *substr* in *str* or -1 if not found

String methods related to pattern matching are described in the next section.

9.9 MATCHING PATTERNS

The myid variable is critical in the entire setup of our rollover navbar. It is computed from the URL of a page by the myPageId function:

```
function myPageId()
{   var str = document.URL;          // (13)
    var re = /([^\/]+)\.html$/;      // (14)
    var found = str.match(re);       // (15)
    if ( found ) return found[1];    // (16)
    else return null;
}

var myid = myPageId();
```

The URL of the current page is obtained from the document.URL attribute (line 13). A *regular expression pattern* (Section 9.10) is constructed (line 14) to pick the *name* part in the *name*.html suffix of the URL. The match method of the String object is used to apply the pattern to the string and obtain parts in the string that match the pattern (line 15). The matching results are stored in an array and assigned to the variable found. If no part of the string matches the pattern, found is null. Generally, JavaScript converts an empty string, zero, undefined, or null to false and all other values to true in a test. If the match is successful, the returned array is organized as follows:

```
found[0]    // the matched string ($0)
found[1]    // the first substring remembered ($1)
found[2]    // the next substring remembered ($2)
. . .
```

Without assigning a name to the array, the same results can be accessed using the built-in variables $0, ..., $9 as indicated. You request remembering of substrings in a pattern match with parentheses in the regular expression. In the example,

```
var re0 = /[^\/]+\.html$/;
```

matches a sequence of one or more (+) characters, each not a SLASH ([^\/]), followed by .html at the end of the string ($). And it will match the end of strings such as

```
var str ="http://wonderful.com/services/index.html";
```

Thus, the following tests return true:

```
str.search(re0)      // returns index, or -1 for no match
re0.test(str_obj)    // returns true, or false for no match
```

The pattern

```
var re = /([^\/]+)\.html$/;
```

adds parentheses to remember the substring preceding .html when the pattern matches. For the preceding example, the string remembered is index. Thus, either one of the following two statements

```
var found = url.match(re);
var found = re.exec(url);
```

returns an array where

```
found[0]      // is index.html
found[1]      // is index
```

9.10 PATTERNS

A *pattern* refers to a characterization of a string. Strings that fit the characterization are said to match the pattern. For example, "containing ABC" is a pattern. Any string that contains the three-character sequence ABC matches it. "Ending with .html" is another pattern. When you define a pattern, you divide all strings into two disjoint sets: strings that match the pattern and those that don't.

A pattern is expressed using *regular expressions* in the form

/regex/

where *regex* can be a fixed string such as /xyz/ to match only the three characters or an expression involving special pattern matching characters.

The character ^ ($) when used as the first (last) character of a regular expression matches the beginning (end) of a string or line. The regular expression

\d matches any digit (0–9). Additional single-character expressions include \n (NEWLINE), \f (FORM FEED), \t (TAB), \r (RETURN), \v (VERTICAL TAB), \s (a white-space character, same as [\f\n\r\t\v]), \b (word boundary, a white space at the end of a word), \B (nonword boundary), and \cx (control-*x*).

You compose patterns with additional notations. Table 9.1 shows some of these special characters. Here are some examples:

/\d*/	matches zero or more digits
/[A-Z]+/	matches a sequence of one or more uppercase letters
/i\d?/	matches i followed by zero or one digit
/[^\/]+/	matches one or more characters not /
/\/|\\/	matches / or \
/ing\b/	matches ing at the end of a word
/(exp)/	matches a given *exp* and remembers the match

To illustrate usage of patterns, Table 9.2 lists more examples. As you can see, many characters (e.g., ^ and +) have special meaning in a pattern. To match such characters themselves, you must escape them to avoid their special meaning. This is done by preceding such a character with the \ character.

Let re be a pattern. Then either of the following

```
re.test(str)
str.search(re)
```

performs a quick matching and returns true or false. These are faster than str.match(re) because we are not looking for the matched strings.

Table 9.1   JAVASCRIPT PATTERN SPECIAL CHARACTERS

Character	Matches
.	Any character except NEWLINE
*	Preceding item zero or more times
+	Preceding item one or more times
?	Preceding item zero or one time
{n}	Preceding item *n* times
{m,n}	Preceding item *m* to *n* times
(x)	Item *x*, captures matching string
x|y	Item *x* or item *y*
[abc]	Any one of listed characters
[^abc]	Any character not listed

Table 9.2 PATTERN EXAMPLES

Pattern	Matching Strings
/l.ve/	love, live, lxve, l+ve
/^http/	http at the beginning of a string
/edu$/	edu at the end of a string
/L+/	L, LL, LLL, LLLL, . . .
/BK*/	B, BK, BKK, . . .
/D+HD/	DHD, DDHD, DDDHD, . . .
/.*G/	Any string ending in G
/G?G/	G or GG
/^$/	Empty string
/[a-z]9/	a9, b9, . . ., or z9

Adding the character i to the end of a pattern makes the pattern *case insensitive*. For example,

/#ddeeff/i   matches #ddeeff, #DDEEFF, #dDeEfF,...

You can also use patterns to replace substrings within another string. The replace method of String is used this way:

```
str.replace(re, newStr)
```

For example, we can compute the over image from the out image with

```
outimg = "images/mainout.gif";
overimg = outimg.replace(/out/, "over");
```

Replacement is made for the first occurrence of a match. To replace all occurrences, add the flag g to the end of the pattern. For example,

```
line.replace(/ +/g, " ")
```

replaces all sequence of one or more spaces with a single space.

Often the replacement string is computed from the matched substring. You can use $0, $1, ..., $9 in the replacement string. And you can use a function call to compute the replacement string.

The split method takes a fixed or patterned delimiter and breaks up a string into an array of several substrings at the delimited positions. The following example breaks up a string where a SPACE is found

```
str = "<p> Chapter Introduction </p>";
arr = str.split(" ");   // delimiter is space
// arr[0] is "<p>",  arr[1] is "Chapter", and so on
```

But there are extra spaces between the words; hence, this simple split results in many empty substrings in the result array. In such a case, you can use a pattern for splitting:

```
arr = str.split(/ +/);
```

For a full reference to regular expressions and patterns, see JavaScript documentation on the Web at

developer.netscape.com/docs/manuals/javascript.html

9.11   JAVASCRIPT OBJECTS

JavaScript provides access to language objects (`Array`, `Boolean`, `Date`, `Function`, `Math`, `Number`, `RegExp`, `String`) for programming and *browser objects* (`navigator`, `window`, `document`, `location`, `history`, `frame`, `Image`, `Form`, etc.) for access and manipulation of the browser and the displayed document. Complete reference information for these objects can be found on the WDP site.

The language objects make writing programs easy. We have used a `Date` object in our first JavaScript program (Section 9.1). The `pageIds` used in the rollover navbar example (Section 9.6) is an `Array` object. `String` objects are common, and the `search` and `match` methods have been discussed.

In Section 9.1, we also used the `navigator` object to obtain the name of the browser (`navigator.appName`, e.g., Netscape or Microsoft Internet Explorer). Additional `navigator` attributes include `appVersion` (browser version), `appName` (browser name), `language` (language used, e.g., `en` or `en-US`), `mimeTypes` (array of all MIME types supported), `platform` (computer on which the browser is running), `plugins` (array of plug-ins installed), and `userAgent` (the HTTP user-agent header to use).

For example, you may use code such as

```
if ( /^en/i.test(navigator.language) )
   window.location = "english/index.html";
if ( /^fr/i.test(navigator.language) )
   window.location = "french/index.html";
...
```

to direct browsers to the correct language entries on your site, using the `test` method of the regular expression object. It is also a good idea to check for the availability of plug-ins when a page contains audio, video, or other multimedia content (Chapter 12 and Section 12.17 in particular).

The links listed at the WDP site will lead you to official documentation for JavaScript built-in objects.

9.12   WINDOWS

The window is the top-level object for each Web page loaded. It contains all other objects related to the page and many attributes (data values) including:

- document—the object that represents the structure and content of the Web page (HTML code)
- location—the current URL
- history—a sequence of URLs visited previously
- frames—an array of frames in the window

The window history can be used to go back and forth on the list of visited pages. For example,

```
history.back();          // reloads the previous page
history.forward();       // reloads the next page
history.go(-3);          // goes back three pages
```

Note that history is shorthand for window.history. Because JavaScript code works in the context of the current window, you can use method and attribute names in the current window directly.

For a page with a frameset element, each frame is also represented by its own window object. These objects are kept on the frames array. Thus,

```
frames["top"]
frames["left"]
frames["right"]
```

give you the window objects for the frames using their name or id attributes.

Dialog Windows

The window object's alert, confirm (Ex: **Confirm**), and prompt methods pop up a dialog window. The user usually must respond to the dialog before proceeding.

The alert method of window displays a warning message. For example (Ex: **Alert**), a function that checks the validity of credit card numbers can easily display a warning (Figure 9.5):

```
function checkCC(number)
{   if ( credit card number invalid )
    {   window.alert("The credit card number is invalid.");
        return false;
    }
    else return true;
}
```

Use a prompt box to collect user input interactively. The call

```
window.prompt(message, default-string)
```

Figure 9.5   ALERT WINDOW

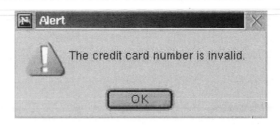

displays a prompt dialog with the given message and the optional default input string in an input box. For example (Ex: **Prompt**),

```
var email = window.prompt('Please enter your email address:');
window.confirm("Email is:  " + email);
```

obtains an email address (Figure 9.6) and displays a confirmation dialog (Figure 9.7). The prompt method returns either the input or null if the user cancels the dialog. The confirm method returns true or false.

Figure 9.6   PROMPT WINDOW

Figure 9.7   CONFIRMATION WINDOW

Opening New Windows

To open a new window, use

```
window.open("URL", "window-name", "options")
```

If `window-name` is an existing window, it will be used to display the page identified by the given URL. Otherwise, a new window to display the given page will be made. If the URL is an empty string, a blank window is displayed. For example,

```
window.open("http://www.abc.org","Abc")         // (1)
window.open("http://www.abc.org","Abc",          // (2)
        "scrollbars=yes,toolbar=no")
```

opens a new full-size full-featured browser window (line 1) or one without any toolbars (line 2) (Figure 9.8).

If you use pop-up windows for offsite links, then users can close that window to return to your site. To make it less likely for users to wander off to the other site, and to make it clear that it is a side trip, you may decide to omit the toolbars for the new window. Thus, offsite links may be given as follows (Ex: **PopupWindow**):

```
<a href="javascript:window.open('http://www.abc.org')">
```

Alternatively, the function

```
function popWindow(URL, w, h)
{  window.open(URL, "", "toolbar=no" +
                        ",dependent=yes" +
                        ",innerwidth="+ w +
                        ",innerheight="+ h);
}
```

Figure 9.8   A POP-UP PICTURE

© PhotoDisc/Getty Images

opens a new window for the given URL, without any toolbars, and with a content area specified by w and h. Such windows are also useful to display a pop-up picture (Figure 9.8), some product data, or other auxiliary information. The WDP site uses pop-up windows for examples, figures, and resource links. Use width and height instead if you wish to set the outer dimensions of the pop-up window.

The options screenX and screenY position the upper-left window corner relative to the screen. Some yes-no options for window.open are:

- dependent—Makes the new window a child of the current window so it will close automatically if the current window closes.
- location—Displays the location entry or not.
- menubar—Adds the menu bar or not.
- resizable—Allows resizing or not.
- scrollbars—Enables scroll bars or not.
- status—Adds bottom status bar or not.
- toolbar—Includes the toolbar or not.

Opening a new window with no options sets all yes/no options to yes. But if you supply some options, then most unspecified yes/no options are set to no. Some features of window.open() are still not standardized across all browsers.

Descriptions here apply to traditional window objects in JavaScript. DOM-inspired window objects are discussed in Section 10.19.

9.13 CREATING USER INTERACTIONS

By connecting JavaScript code to user-generated events, a variety of interactions can be added to a Web page. Many elements support the onmouseover, onmouseout, onclick, onfocus, and onblur (lost focus) events.

A Slide Show

We can use link-generated events to make a slide show (Figure 9.9). Pictures of mouth-watering food are displayed one by one. Users control the display with a Next and a Previous button (Ex: **Slides**).

The HTML for the page can be coded as follows:

```
<head><title>Slide Demo</title>
<script type="text/javascript" src="slide.js">
</script></head>
<body style="background-color: #000"
    onload="changeSlide()">                              (a)
<p style="text-align: center">
<img src="" id="myimg" alt="slide" /><br /><br />        (b)
```

Figure 9.9 JAVASCRIPT SLIDE SHOW

© Steve Cohen/FoodPix

```
<a href="javascript:prevSlide()"><img src="prev.gif"        (c)
style="border: none"
alt="previous slide" /></a>    
         <a href=
    "javascript:nextSlide()"><img src="next.gif"             (d)
style="border: none" alt="next slide" /></a></p>
</body>
```

The centered image with id="myimg" is the display area where the image src is left empty (line b). Its image source is set with the onload event handler of the body element (line a). Clicking the Next (Previous) button calls the nextSlide() (prevSlide()) function (lines c and d). Modern browsers support the onclick event for images, and you may use that event to change the slides instead.

The slide.js file contains the code for loading and changing the images. The pic array contains the pictures to be displayed and is the only quantity you need to customize for your own slide show. Make sure all images are the same size.

```
const pic = [ "pancake.jpg", "dessert.jpg",
            "meat.jpg", "cake.jpg", "pasta.jpg" ];

var slide = new Array();
var index = 0;             // current slide index

function loadImage(url)
```

```
{  if (document.images)
   {    rslt = new Image();
        rslt.src = url;
        return rslt;
   }
}

if ( document.images )   // preloading all images
{  for (var n=0; n < pic.length; n++)
   {    slide[n] = loadImage(pic[n]); }
}
```

The images are preloaded into the slide array indexed by index, the global variable that controls which image is showing through a call to changeSlide().

```
function changeSlide()
{
    document.getElementById('myimg').src = slide[index].src;
}
```

Going forward and backward on the slides is just a matter of incrementing and decrementing index in a circular fashion.

```
function prevSlide()
{   if(--index < 0)
    { index = pic.length-1;
    }
    changeSlide();
}

function nextSlide()
{   if( ++index >= pic.length)
    { index = 0
    }
    changeSlide();
}
```

9.14   A CONVERSION CALCULATOR

HTML input controls also provide many opportunities for user interaction. Let's see how input elements can be used outside a form to construct an inch-centimeter conversion calculator supported by client-side JavaScript (Figure 9.10).

The HTML code for the conversion calculator example (Ex: **Convert**) is:

```
<head><title>Inch Centimeter Converter</title>
<script type="text/javascript" src="convert.js">
```

Figure 9.10   A JAVASCRIPT-BASED CONVERSION CALCULATOR

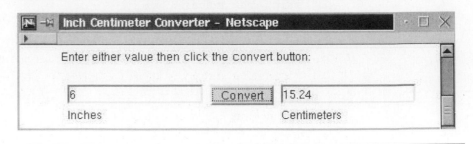

```
</script></head><body onload="init()">                    (1)
<p>Enter either value then click the convert button:</p>
<table cellspacing="6">
<tr valign="top">
  <td><input id="inch" size="20" onfocus="reset()" />    (2)
      <br />Inches</td>
  <td><input type="button" value="Convert"               (3)
          onclick="convert()" /></td>
  <td><input id="cm" size="20" onfocus="reset()" />       (4)
      <br />Centimeters</td>
</tr></table></body>
```

Events from the three input elements are connected to event-handling functions. The inch (line 2) and cm (line 4) text input fields will reset themselves when focus is gained. A button click triggers the actual conversion (line 3).

JavaScript is initialized onload (line 1) by calling the function init()

```
var inf, cmf;

function init()
{   inf = document.getElementById('inch');
    cmf = document.getElementById('cm');
}
```

which sets up two global variables inf (the inch input element) and cmf (the cm input element). These make the convert and reset operations easy to program:

```
function reset()
{   inf.value = "";   cmf.value = "";   }       // (5)

function convert()
{   var i = inf.value.replace(/ /,"");          // (6)
    if ( i )                                     // (7)
    {  cmf.value = i * 2.54; return; }           // (8)
```

```
var c = cmf.value.replace(/ /,"");
if ( c )
{  inf.value = c / 2.54; }                        // (9)
}
```

Both elements are set to contain no input when either one gains focus (line 5).

After entering a number in either field, the user clicks the Convert button (line 3), which calls the convert function to display the conversion results.

The input string from the inch field is obtained (line 6), and any unintentional spaces are removed. If this input is not empty (line 7), the centimeter conversion is computed and displayed (line 8), and the function returns. Here again, you can see how strings and numbers are used interchangeably in JavaScript. If the inch field has no input, then the cm field is processed exactly the same way.

JavaScript allows you to use strings in arithmetic computations (lines 8 and 9). Note, unlike in Java or C++, the JavaScript / operator always performs a floating-point division and returns a floating-point result.

9.15   FORM CHECKING

When using forms to collect information, it is important to check the correctness of the data entered by Web users. The programs considered in Chapter 8 demonstrate how to check the input data as the first step in server-side form processing. But if such checks are made on the client side, users can make immediate corrections as they fill out the forms. Client-side form input validation is fast and responsive and can make filling out forms more pleasant and less confusing for users.

By connecting event handlers to form elements, we can write JavaScript programs to check form input on the client side. This does not mean that we can move form input checking from the server side to the client side because savvy users and Web developers can submit input to the server-side through other means without going through the form with the client-side checks. Hence, client-side checks are primarily to enhance the user interface and to avoid invalid data being sent to the server side. It is a good idea to use client-side checks, but they are not replacements for server-side checks.

Let us consider an example (Ex: **EmailCheck**) in which we check the validity of an email address entered on a form (Figure 9.11). The HTML code for the form is typical but with added event handlers so that form submission is through JavaScript.

```
<head><title>Email Validation</title>
<script type="text/javascript" src="emailcheck.js"> </script>
</head><body>
<form method="post" id="myform"
      action="/cgi-bin/wb/joinclub.cgi">
```

Figure 9.11 CLIENT-SIDE FORM VALIDATION

```
<table cellspacing="3" style="margin: auto">
<tr>
  <td><p style="text-align: right; font-weight: bold">
      Your Name:</p>
  </td>
  <td><input id="name" name="name" size="30" />
  </td>
</tr><tr>
  <td><p style="text-align: right; font-weight: bold">
      Your email:</p>
  </td>
  <td><input id="email" name="email" size="30"
          onchange="checkEmail(this)" />                    // (1)
  </td>
</tr><tr><td></td>
  <td><input type="button" value="Submit"
          onclick="checkForm()" />                          // (2)
  </td>
</tr>
</table></form></body>
```

The onclick handler for a button is set to checkForm (line 2), which checks all
input data in the form and proceeds to submit only if all input data are correct.
Otherwise, the form will not be submitted, and the user gets a chance to make
corrections right away without leaving the form page.

To make filling out forms even more user friendly, onchange handlers
(line 1) can be attached to individual input fields so the particular input can be
checked as soon as it is entered. Here the notation this represents the object
for the input element with id="email".

The checkForm function is as follows:

```
function checkForm()
{  if ( checkEmail(document.getElementById('email'))  // valid email
```

```
            && checkName(document.getElementById('name')) // and name
      )                                                    // given
  {   document.getElementById('myform').submit();          // submit form
  }
}

function checkName(nm)
{   if ( nm.value )
        return true;
    else
        return formErr(nm, " empty string ");
}
```

The `checkEmail` function is called from `checkForm` as well as triggered by the change event (line 1). The `formErr` function is used to alert users of incorrect data.

```
function formErr(entry, msg)
{   alert(entry.id + ": " + msg + " is invalid.");   // (3)
    entry.focus();                                   // (4)
    entry.select();                                  // (5)
    return false;
}
```

An alert window is used to display the form entry id and the given message `msg` (line 3). Then it gives the form entry input focus (line 4) and selects the text for editing (line 5).

The `checkEmail` function is called with the email input entry (em). The actual checking of `em.value` as an email address involves many technical details. The following check will catch malformed email addresses most of the time.

Basically, we check to see if the email is in the form *user@host* and then check the *user* and *host* separately for validity. Here is an outline of the steps:

1. Check the *user@host* form. Only one @ is allowed. Any trailing period (.) as well as leading and trailing spaces are removed. The `twoPart` pattern (line 6) performs this check and matches the *user* and *host* parts (lines 7 and 8). The email address with possible leading and trailing characters removed is stored (line 9).

2. Each of *user* and *host* is a dot (.) separated list of atoms (the pattern `dotPat` on line 11) that does not contain disallowed characters (\s ( ) < > @ , " \ : / ; . [ ]). The string `atom` helps define a pattern for a sequence of allowed characters—an atom (line 10). If *user* does not match `dotPt` (line 12), then it must be a quoted name (line 13) in a form such as `"Mary Jane"`. Otherwise, the *user* part cannot be accepted (line 14).

3. After checking *user*, *host* is checked. It may be an IP address in the form [123.45.94.33]. The brackets are necessary, and each part is a number less than 256 (lines 15 and 16).

4. Otherwise, *host* must be a domain name with atoms separated by dots (line 17). There should be two or more atoms (lines 18 and 19), and the last atom is a *top-level domain*, which has two or more characters (line 20).

```
function checkEmail(em)
{ var str = em.value;
  var twoPart=/^ *([^ @][^@]*)@([^@]+[^@\. ]+)\.* *$/; // (6)
  var part=str.match(twoPart);                          // (7)
  if ( part==null ) return formErr(em, "'"+str+"'");
  var user=part[1];
  var host=part[2];                                     // (8)
  em.value = user+"@"+host;                             // (9)

  var atom ="[^\\s \\( \\) < > @ , \" \\\\" +           // (10)
            "\\/ : ; \\. \\[ \\] ]+";
  var dotPt=new RegExp("^" + "(" + atom +               // (11)
                    ")(\\." + atom + ")*$");

// See if "user" is valid
  if ( user.match(dotPt)==null )                        // (12)
  {   if (! user.match(/^"[^"]+"$/))                    // (13)
      return formErr(em, "The username '" + user+"'"); // (14)
  }

  var ipPt= /^\[(\d+)\.(\d+)\.(\d+)\.(\d+)\]$/;         // (15)

  var ipArr=host.match(ipPt);
  if ( ipArr!=null )
  { for (var i=1;i<=4;i++)
    { if (ipArr[i]>255)                                 // (16)
        return formErr(em, "The IP '"+ host +"'");
    }
    return true
  }

// Host is domain name
  if ( host.match(dotPt)==null )                        // (17)
      return formErr(em, "The domain '" + host +"'");
  var atomPt=new RegExp(atom,"g");
  var dArr=host.match(atomPt);                          // (18)
  var len=dArr.length;
```

```
if (len<2)                                              // (19)
    return formErr(em, "The domain '" + host +"'"),
var tld =dArr[len-1];
if (tld.length<2)                                       // (20)
    return formErr(em, "The ending '" + tld+"'");
return true;
}
```

9.16 MENU ACTIONS

By connecting JavaScript functions to a pull-down menu (select), we can define actions in response to user selections. For example, a pull-down menu can present different services or products of a company on a navigation bar. Selecting a product can lead directly to a page for that product. This technique can simplify complicated navigation bars with many target pages. The ability to tie any JavaScript actions to any set of user selections presents limitless other possibilities. Figure 9.12 shows a navigation bar with a pull-down menu for sporting goods (Ex: **MenuAction**). The HTML code shows the pull-down menu defined by a select element (line A).

```
<head><title>Pulldown Menu of Links</title>
<link rel="stylesheet" href="menuaction.css"
     type="text/css"  title="menu action" />
<script type="text/javascript" src="menuaction.js"></script>
<table class="menubar" cellspacing="5">
<tr valign="middle" align="center">
<td><a href="home.html">Homepage</a></td>
<td><select name="selurl" id="selurl" size="1"              (A)
       onchange="menuAction(this)">
 <option value="-1">Sporting Goods :</option>
 <option value="-1"></option>
 <option value="baseball/index.html">Baseball:</option>
 <option value="baseball/gloves.html"> - Gloves</option>
 <option value="baseball/bats.html"> - Bats and Balls</option>
 <option value="-1"></option>
```

Figure 9.12   PULL-DOWN NAVIGATION MENU

```
<option value="surfing/index.html">Surfing:</option>
<option value="surfing/boards.html"> - Boards</option>
<option value="surfing/suits.html"> - Wet Suits</option>
<option value="-1"></option>
<option value="tennis/index.html">Tennis:</option>
<option value="tennis/racquets.html"> - Racquets</option>
<option value="tennis/shoes.html"> - Shoes</option>
<option value="tennis/misc.html"> - Strings and Grips</option>
</select></td>
<td><a href="contact.html">Contact Us</a></td>
</tr></table>
```

The option value is a target URL or -1 for spacers. The onchange event handler is called when an option is selected. The pull-down menu can be seen in Figure 9.13.

    The presentation is defined by the following style code:

```
table.menubar
{  border-top: solid #0f6 20px;
   background-color: #dde3e8;
   font-weight: bold;
}

table.menubar select
{  background-color: #dde3e8;
   font-weight: bold;
   display: block
}

table.menubar a
{  text-decoration: none;
   color: black;
}
```

Figure 9.13   THE PULL-DOWN MENU

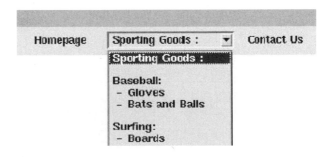

```
display: block
}
```

```
table.menubar td { width:150px }
```

The font and background of the `select` element are matched with those of the menu bar. Inline elements on the menu bar use block display boxes to eliminate any extra line separation beneath them.

The JavaScript function `menuAction` receives a `select` object `sel` (line a), obtains the index of the selected entry (line b), and gets the value of the selected option (line c). The selected index is reset to 0 (line d) so that the menu bar is not disturbed after the selection. If the `url` value is `-1`, nothing is done. Otherwise, the target URL is loaded (line e).

```
function menuAction(sel)                      // (a)
{   var index = sel.selectedIndex;            // (b)
    var url = sel.options[index].value;       // (c)
    sel.selectedIndex = 0;                    // (d)
    if ( url != -1)
    {   window.location=url;  }               // (e)
}
```

This example shows how HTML, CSS, and JavaScript combine to achieve form and function for Web sites.

9.17 EVENTS AND EVENT OBJECTS

The preceding sections illustrate the application of JavaScript in many useful ways and at the same time provide examples of JavaScript programming. The basic technique is simple: You define event-handling functions and attach them to events associated with HTML elements. A general description of event handling and the available objects can help you create other effects for Web users with JavaScript.

Following HTML 4.0 and the DOM[3] Level 2 Event Model, XHTML specifies *event attributes* for elements that are used to connect events to handlers.

- Window events—`onload` (page loaded) and `onunload` (page unloaded) attributes are available in `body` and `frameset` elements.

- Mouse events—`onclick` (left mouse button clicked), `ondblclick` (left mouse button double-clicked), `onmousedown` (left mouse button pressed), `onmouseup` (left mouse button released), `onmousemove` (mouse moved), `onmouseover` (mouse over element), and `onmouseout` (mouse left element) attributes are common to most HTML 4.0 elements. But

---

[3]See Chapter 10.

some versions of JavaScript may only support these in form elements and links.

- Input control events—onfocus (the element gained focus), onblur (the element lost focus), onchange (content of element changed), onsubmit (form submitted), onreset (form reset), and onselect (element content is selected) attributes are for all input-related elements.
- Keyboard events—onkeydown (a keyboard key is being pressed), onkeypress (a key is pressed), and onkeyup (a key is released) are common to most HTML 4.0 elements. But some versions of JavaScript may only support these in images, links, and text areas.

HTML elements are represented by objects (Chapter 10) that can be accessed and manipulated by JavaScript. Setting the onevent attribute records an event-handler function for that event in the object for that HTML element.

Using Event Objects

When an event takes place, an *event object* is created to represent information related to the particular event. This event object event is available for event handlers to extract event-related information such as which key is pressed, which mouse button is clicked, what are the x and y coordinates of the mouse event, and so on.

Consider the slide show example, (Ex: **Slides**) in Section 9.13. It would be convenient to be able to use the LEFT- and RIGHT-ARROW keys on the keyboard to go back and forth on the slides. This can easily be done with key events.

Add the key event handler (Ex: **KeyEvent**) to the body element:

```
onkeydown="keyGo(event)"
```

Note that we transmit the event object to the handler function keyGo.

```
function keyGo(e)
{   if ( e.keyCode == 39 )
        nextSlide();
    else if ( e.keyCode == 37 )
        prevSlide();
}
```

The keyCode property of an event object gives the JavaScript value of the key involved. The value 39 (RIGHT-ARROW) goes to the next slide, and the value 37 (LEFT-ARROW) returns to the previous slide. See the WDP site for hands-on experiments to find values of JavaScript keyCodes.

The W3C-recommended DOM Level 2 Event Model begins to standardize event names, event objects, their properties, and methods (see the WDP site).

9.18   SCROLLING TEXT

For each Web page, there is a window object that contains all other objects for the page (Section 9.12). If the page has frames, each frame has a frame object and its own window object too. We have seen many methods for window in Section 9.12. Additional window methods include:

- scrollTo—Scrolls a window to a given position.
- setTimeout("*expression*", *delay*)—Schedules a one-time evaluation of the quoted expression, which can be a function call, after the specified *delay* in milliseconds. If you use any variables or function arguments in *expression*, make sure they are global.
- setInterval("*expression*", *interval*)—Repeatedly evaluates an expression or calls a function each time the given time interval, in milliseconds, passes.

As an example (Ex: **Scroll**), let's look at how a text-scrolling window is achieved. The text window in Figure 9.14 scrolls continually after the page is loaded. It can also stop and resume the scrolling when the user clicks the window.

The HTML code is as follows:

```
<head><title>Text Scrolling</title>
<link rel="stylesheet" href="scroll.css"
      type="text/css"  title="scroll" />
<script type="text/javascript" src="scroll.js">
</script></head>
<body onload="scrollInit(document.getElementById('region'))">   (1)

<p><input id="region" class="scroll" size="50" value=""
        onfocus="pause(this)" /> </p>                            (2)
</body>
```

After the page is loaded, the scrollInit function is called (line 1) with the object representing the form input element with id="region". The method getElementById is very convenient and will be used extensively in Chapter 10. The init function sets up the scrolling message and other control parameters

Figure 9.14   SCROLLING WINDOW

ments and so on. This message scrolls continually. Use

and starts the scrolling. Clicking the scrolling window generates `focus` events that, through the function `pause`, stop and resume the scrolling.

The style sheet

```
body { background-color: cyan; }

input.scroll
{    color: rgb(100%,84%,12%);
     background-color: rgb(6%,45%,5%);
     font-weight:bold;
     font-size: larger;
}
```

gives the dark green background and the amber boldface font for the scrolling window.

The JavaScript function `scrollInit` sets up the scrolling:

```
// customization begin
var myMessage=
    "   This message scrolls continually. " +
    "Use this JavaScript program for Ads, news, " +
    "announcements and so on.";
var speed=150;
// customization end

function scrollInit(field)
{    message=myMessage;
     inputField=field;
     if ( message.length == 0 ) return;
     while ( message.length <
             myMessage.length+3*field.size )          // (a)
         message += myMessage;
     start = 0; pauseFlag=false;
     end = myMessage.length;
     scroll();                                        // (b)
}
```

To perform scrolling, the steps are simple:

1. Make a *scrolled string* that is long enough by repeating the given message.

2. At predetermined intervals, display a substring of the scrolled string starting at the next character position.

3. When the starting point reaches the end of the given message, go back to the beginning again.

The scrolled string `message` is built to be at least as long as the original message (`myMessage`) plus three times the size of the scrolling field. Because we do not know exactly how many characters an input field of a given *size* can display, we assume it will not be long enough to hold 3 × *size* characters.

The scroll function actually performs the scrolling display.

```
function scroll()
{    if ( pauseFlag ) return;
     inputField.value=message.substring(start);
     if ( ++start == end ) start=0;
     setTimeout("scroll()",speed);                // (c)
}
```

If pauseFlag is not true, a substring of message starting at index start is displayed. The start is incremented and set back to 0 if it reaches end. The setTimeout method of window is called to trigger the next call to scroll (line c).

By setting pauseFlag to true, the scrolling stops. To resume the scrolling, set the flag to false and call scroll() (line d). The pause function always calls the blur() method of the scrolling field so it loses focus and is able to receive another focus event. Thus, the same event alternatively stops and resumes scrolling.

```
function pause(field)
{    if ( pauseFlag )
     {    pauseFlag=false;
          scroll();               // (d)
     }
     else pauseFlag = true;
     field.blur();                // (e)

}
```

9.19   TESTING AND DEBUGGING

Much time can be spent on testing and debugging programs. JavaScript programs are no exception. After writing a JavaScript program, always test it in the HTML page where it needs to work. If something is wrong, the problem may involve:

- Syntax errors—typos, spelling mistakes, missing quotation marks, strings across multiple lines, missing or unmatched brackets, or incorrect object names or ids. JavaScript is case sensitive: myObject is not the same as myobject. Incorrect syntax is the most common problem.

- Run-time errors—problems that only occur when the script is executing. Accessing a nonexisting object attribute and using a null or undefined without first checking the quantity are examples.

• Logical errors—mistakes in the solution logic that make the script do the wrong thing or display the wrong information.

It pays to use a good editor that can display the code structure and automatically show balancing brackets and so forth. Tools such as the Borland IntraBuilder and NetObjects ScriptBuilder for developing JavaScript are also available.

When you load a page containing JavaScript, any syntax or run-time errors are displayed in the Javascript Console (Figure 9.15), a window you can display by selecting the Tools/Javascript Console option on the Tasks menu (Netscape 6.x) or by entering `javascript:` in the Location box (earlier Netscape). Errors are listed with source code line numbers so you can find them easily. By enabling the display of JavaScript errors, Internet Explorer will display any errors in an alert dialog window.

To isolate problems in your code, you can put `alert` calls in various key points in your script to trace its progress through the code and display values of variables and function arguments.

You can build your own error reporting window

```
function errorWindow()
{   errWindow = window.open("", "Javascript Errors",
            "toolbar=0,scrollbar=1,width=400,
            height=300");
}
```

and display your own error messages in it:

```
errWindow.document.writeln( "value of email is " + email );
```

For hard-to-find bugs, you may need to use the Netscape JavaScript debugger called Venkman. It works well with Netscape Version 7.0 and later and supports break points, backtracing, stepping, and so on. Venkman offers a visual environment and works on Windows, Mac, and UNIX platforms

Figure 9.15   JAVASCRIPT CONSOLE

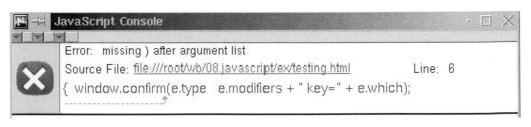

Figure 9.16   VENKMAN JAVASCRIPT DEBUGGER

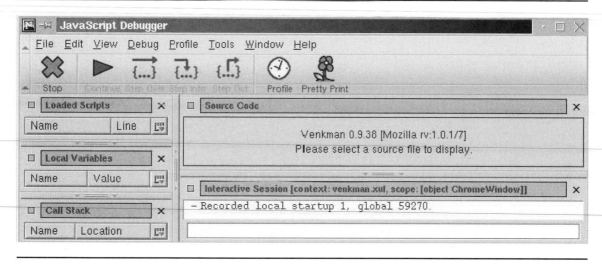

and, after installation, can be started from the Tools>Web Development menu (Figure 9.16). You can download the debugger from the Web:

developer.netscape.com/software/jsdebug.html

9.20 FOR MORE INFORMATION

An introduction to JavaScript and its application has been provided. For more information on the syntax and semantics of JavaScript, its standardization, events, object model, and tools, see related Web sites and the resource pages on the WDP site.

Our coverage continues in Chapter 10, where the JavaScript interface to the Document Object Model and application in DHTML are presented.

9.21 SUMMARY

JavaScript is a standard scripting language to manipulate browser, window, and document objects. JavaScript programs are responsive because they are executed by the browser on the client side.

JavaScript programs can be placed in their own file and introduced into any Web page with the code

```
<script type="text/javascript" src="filename.js"> </script>
```

Or they may be placed directly in an HTML file with

```
<script type="text/javascript">
...</script>
```

JavaScript syntax is similar to Java and C++. It is actually easier because you may use strings and numbers interchangeably and concatenate strings with numbers and other objects by the + operator. Built-in objects, such as `Date` and `Math`, and functions, such as `eval`, `encodeURI`, and `decodeURI`, make programming easier.

There are two ways to create arrays:

```
var b - new Array(element0, clcmcnt1, ..., elementN);
var c = [element0, element1, ..., elementN];
```

You use zero-based indexing, `b[0]`, to access array cells. Because JavaScript deals mostly with textual materials, a strong pattern matching ability is built-in. You may use either of these notations for string matching:

```
str.search(re)
re0.test(str)
```

JavaScript can make a page more interactive and dynamic by responding to events generated by the user. Applications range from rollovers to creating new windows to scrolling texts.

When creating rollovers for a navigation bar, it is not enough to change a base image to a mouseover image. We must also ensure that the link becomes inactive and appears distinctive when it is on its own page. This is the page-id image. Thus, each navigation rollover usually involves three images: base, mouseover, and page-id. Sometimes it is practical to make the mouseover image double as the page-id image. In that case, we recommend that the page-id image do a reverse rollover on mouseover.

Further, you can coordinate the names for the rollover images and the `.html` files so exactly the same HTML and JavaScript code for the navigation bar work in any target page.

Another important application is checking the validity of form input so users may correct mistakes immediately.

EXERCISES

Review Questions

1. What are the ways to create arrays in JavaScript? How are array cells indexed? How are they assigned?

2. What is the difference between the `window.url` and the `document.URL` quantities?

3. In JavaScript, how is a pattern specified and matched?

4. What is a regular expression? What is the regular expression that matches the string `Netscape` at the beginning of a string? At the end of a string? As a separate word?

5. When specifying patterns, what does *escaping a special character* mean?

6. What is a dialog window? How do you use dialog windows in JavaScript?

7. How are new windows created in JavaScript? What options control the features of the window to be created?

8. How do you concatenate strings in JavaScript? In Perl?

9. Describe in your own words conditions for a valid email address. Are there TLDs with more than three characters?

10. How do you go about debugging JavaScript programs?

11. Start NN and launch the JavaScript Console. Test JavaScript code in the evaluation input field.

Assignments

1. Write a simple Web page that displays the `userAgent`, `appName`, and `appVersion`.

2. Follow Section 9.4 and create a text rollover by changing the `color` and/or `background-color` styles of the text.

3. Modify the code for Ex: **StdNavbar** (Section 9.6) and move the mouse event handling from the links to the `img` elements.

4. Make the Ex: **StdNavbar** (Section 9.6) more general by employing a set of three equally sized images for each rollover: a mouseout image, a mouseover image, and a page-id image. The page-id image is used to indicate the current page, which becomes an inactive link on the navbar. Make sure to test the visual effect of your rollover design. The user should have a feel of control following the mouse.

5. Further improve the Ex: **StdNavbar** (Section 9.6) by adding a `mousedown` event handler. Usually, this handler can perform the same actions as the `mouseover` handler.

6. Further automate the Ex: **StdNavbar** (Section 9.6) by generating its code with `document.write`. This can be done by implementing a JavaScript function

genNavbar(), which takes as arguments a list of page-ids and the id of the current page.

7. Write a JavaScript pattern that picks the parts before and after the decimal point of a number. Write another pattern that will only match any valid CSS color notation that begins with #.

8. The Ex: **StdNavbar** uses a fixed document file suffix (.html). Make this customizable with a configuration variable:

```
var pageSuffix = "htm";      // page suffix
```

Note also that Section 9.9 (line 14) fails to pick up the page-id if the document.url has an htm ending or an in-page anchor ending stocks.html#ibm, for example. Fix this problem as well.

9. Consider the slide show in Section 9.13. Remove the hyperlinks on the previous and next images and use the onclick event to change slides.

10. Follow the inch-centimeter conversion program (Section 9.14) and write a Fahrenheit-Celsius conversion calculator.

11. Follow the inch-centimeter conversion program (Section 9.14) and the RGB to HSB conversion function (Section 7.10) and write a two-way RGB-HSB conversion calculator.

12. Take the menu-based navigation program in Section 9.16 and modify it to use onclick events on the option elements.

13. It has been reported that IE:

- Encounters an error when window.open is given a window title that contains white space.
- Does not recognize the standard JavaScript const declaration.

Find out if your version of IE still has these problems.

## CHAPTER 10

Document Object Model and Dynamic HTML

The term *Dynamic HTML*, often abbreviated DHTML, refers to the technique of making Web pages dynamic by client-side scripting to manipulate the document content and presentation. Web pages can be made more lively, dynamic, or interactive by DHTML techniques.

With DHTML, you can prescribe actions triggered by browser events to make the page more lively and responsive. Such actions may alter the content and appearance of any parts of the page. The changes are fast and efficient because they are made by the browser without having to network with any servers. Typically, the client-side scripting is written in JavaScript, which is being standardized. Chapter 9 introduced JavaScript and basic techniques for making Web pages dynamic.

Contrary to what the name may suggest, DHTML is not a markup language or a software tool. It is a technique to make Web pages dynamic through client-side programming. In the past, DHTML relied on browser- and vendor- specific features. Making such pages work for all browsers requires much effort, testing, and unnecessarily long programs.

Standardization efforts at W3C and elsewhere are making it possible to write *standard-based DHTML* that works for all compliant browsers. Standard-based DHTML involves three aspects:

1. JavaScript—for cross-browser scripting (Chapter 9)
2. Cascading Style Sheets (CSS)—for style and presentation control (Chapter 6)
3. Document Object Model (DOM)—for a uniform programming interface to access and manipulate the Web page as a document

When these three aspects are combined, you get the ability to program changes in Web pages in reaction to user- or browser-generated events. Therefore, you can make HTML pages more dynamic.

Popular with Web developers, supported by all major browsers, and standardized, JavaScript provides the ability to program browser actions in response to events. To have true cross-platform DHTML, we still need a uniform way for JavaScript to access and manipulate Web documents. This brings us to the DOM.

10.1   WHAT IS DOM?

With cooperation from major browser vendors, the W3C is establishing the *Document Object Model* (DOM) as a standard *application programming interface* (API) for scripts to access and manipulate HTML and XML documents. Compliant clients, including browsers and other user agents, provide the DOM specified API to access and modify the document being processed (Figure 10.1). The DOM API gives a logical view of the document where objects represent different parts such as windows, documents, elements, attributes, texts, events, style sheets, style rules, and so on. These *DOM objects* are organized into a tree structure (the DOM tree) to reflect the natural organization of a document. HTML elements are represented by *tree nodes* and organized into a hierarchy. Each Web page has a document node at the root of the tree. The head and body nodes become *child nodes* of the html node (Figure 10.2).

From a node on the DOM tree, you can go down to any child node or go up to the parent node. With DOM, a script can add, modify, or delete elements and content by navigating the document structure, modifying or deleting existing nodes, and inserting dynamically built new nodes. Also attached to the document are its style sheets. Each element node on the DOM tree also contains a *style object* representing the display style for that element. Thus, through the DOM tree, style sheets and individual element styles can also be accessed and manipulated. Therefore, any parts of a page can be accessed, changed, deleted, or added, and the script will work for any DOM-compliant client.

Figure 10.1   DOM-COMPLIANT BROWSER

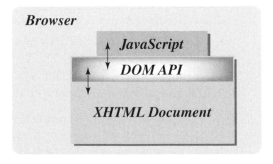

Figure 10.2   DOM TREE STRUCTURE

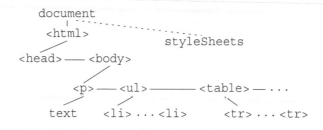

DOM also specifies events available for page elements. As a result, most events that had been reserved for links now work for all types of elements, giving the designer many more ways to make pages dynamic and responsive.

10.2   A DEMONSTRATION

Let's look at a simple example (Ex: **DomHello**) to illustrate DHTML. Figure 10.3 shows a page with the phrase Hello World Wide Web. Figure 10.4 shows that phrase becoming blue (see color insert) in a larger font on mouseover. The phrase goes back to normal again on mouseout. This is not an image rollover.

The HTML source for the page is:

```
<head><title>Hello WWW with DOM</title>
<script type="text/javascript" src="hwww.js">
</script></head><body>
<p>Move the mouse over the phrase:</p>
<p><span id="hello" onmouseover="over()"
        onmouseout="out()">Hello World Wide Web</span>
---and see what happens.</p>
</body></html>
```

Figure 10.3   HELLO WWW

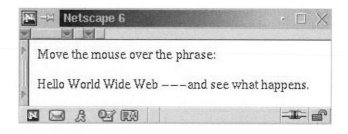

Figure 10.4   MOUSE OVER PHRASE

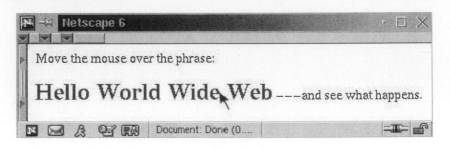

Note we have attached the onmouseover and onmouseout event handlers to part of a paragraph identified by the span with id="hello".

The JavaScript-defined event-handling functions are in the file hwww.js:

```
function over()
{   el = document.getElementById("hello");    // (1)
    el.style.color = "blue";                   // (2)
    el.style.fontSize = "18pt";                // (3)
    el.style.fontWeight = "bold";              // (4)
}

function out()
{   el = document.getElementById("hello");
    el.style.color = "";         // sets to default value
    el.style.fontSize = "";
    el.style.fontWeight = "";
}
```

The over function obtains a reference to the target <span> by using the getElementById method of the document element (line 1). The document is the root node of the DOM tree and offers many useful fields and methods. The convenient call

```
document.getElementById(str)
```

gives you the element with *str* as id. It returns a reference to the node on the DOM tree that represents the desired element or null if not found.

Once you have the node for a particular element, you can go to work on that node, accessing information from it or making changes to it. Here the over function sets style properties for the element (lines 2-4) causing the <span> to display in blue with 18-point boldface font (Figure 10.4). The out function sets these style properties to the empty string to go back to the default display (Figure 10.3).

10.3 DOM HISTORY AND ARCHITECTURE

Early browsers such as Netscape Navigator (NN) 3.0 and Internet Explorer (IE) 3.0 have their own object models for representing documents. Starting as early as 1997, the W3C began to organize the DOM working group for establishing a cross-platform and language-neutral standard for access, traversal, and manipulation of document objects. The first W3C recommendation was DOM Level 1, which was completed in October 1998. DOM Level 1 specifies a *standard object-oriented interface* to HTML and XML documents. The Level 1 Core specifies the most central interfaces for the DOM tree. The DOM Level 1 HTML and XML specifications inherit from the Core and specialize in HTML and XML documents, respectively. The DOM specification for HTML/XHTML is the most important for Web Site development. The very first DOM specification, informally referred to as DOM Level 0, was built on existing conventions and practices supported by NN 3.0 and IE 3.0. A second edition of DOM Level 1 is being finalized.

In November 2000, DOM Level 2 was completed, and it extended Level 1 by adding support for XML 1.0 namespaces, CSS, events and event handling for user interfaces and for tree manipulation and tree traversal. The DOM Level 2 HTML specification became a W3C recommendation in early 2003. DOM Level 3, still being developed, will add more sophisticated XML support, the ability to load and save documents, and so forth.

As DOM evolves through levels of enhancements, its basic architecture remains stable. The DOM architecture consists of *modules* covering different domains of the document object model:

- DOM Core—Specifies the DOM tree, tree nodes, its access, traversal, and manipulation. The DOM Range and DOM Traversal modules provide higher level methods for manipulating the DOM tree defined by the Core.
- DOM HTML—Inherits from the Core and provides specialized and convenient ways to access and manipulate HTML/XHTML documents.
- DOM XML—Inherits from the Core and provides support for XML-specific needs.
- DOM Events—Specifies events and event handling for user interfaces and the DOM tree. With DOM Events, drag and drop programs, for example, can be standardized.
- DOM CSS—Defines easy-to-use ways to manipulate cascading style sheets for the formatting and presentation of documents.

There are other modules, and they can be found at the W3C site: www.w3.org/DOM/.

When using JavaScript to write DOM-related code, it is important to realize that not everything has been standardized. In particular, the window object is very browser dependent. In addition, certain fields such as `element.innerHTML` and `document.location` are not part of the DOM specification.

10.4   BROWSER SUPPORT OF DOM

Major vendors realize the importance of DOM and have begun to make their Web browsers DOM compliant. NN 7 and IE 6 already have good DOM support. In particular, NN led the way in supporting DOM Level 1 and Level 2. Most examples in this chapter work under both NN 7, IE 6, and later versions.

To detect the extent of DOM support that a user agent (browser) provides, the following type of JavaScript code can be used:

```
var imp = document.implementation;
if ( typeof imp != "undefined" &&
    imp.hasFeature("HTML", "1.0") &&
    imp.hasFeature("Events", "2.0") &&
    imp.hasFeature("CSS", "2.0")
  )
{
    . . .
}
```

A browser is DOM compliant if it supports the interfaces specified by DOM. But it can also add interfaces not specified or add fields and methods to the required interfaces. For example, NN and IE both add `innerHTML` to the `HTMLElement` interface. It is easy to test if a field or method is available in a browser. For example,

```
if ( document.getElementById )
    . . .
```

tests if the `getElementById` method is available in the `document` object.

DOM compliance test suites are available from www.w3.org/DOM/Test/.

10.5   DOM API OVERVIEW

According to W3C, DOM is a "platform and language neutral interface that allows programs and scripts to dynamically access and update the content, structure and style of documents. The document can be further processed and the results of that processing can be incorporated back into the presented page."

The DOM specifies an API (application programming interface) and provides a structural view of the document. DOM lists required interface objects and the *methods* (functions in the object) and *fields* (data entries in the object) each object must support. It is up to compliant browsers (agents) to supply concrete implementation, in a particular programming language and environment, for these objects, fields, and methods. NN, IE, and other browsers support DOM through standard JavaScript (Figure 10.5).

As an interface, each DOM object exposes a set of fields and methods for JavaScript to access and manipulate the underlying data structure that actually implements the document structure. The situation resembles a radio interface exposing a set of knobs and dials to the user. If the radio interface were standardized, then a robot would be able to operate any standard compliant radio.

The DOM tree represents the logical structure of a document. Each tree node is a Node object. There are different types of nodes that all *inherit* the basic Node interface. Inheritance is an important object-oriented programming (OOP) concept. In OOP, interfaces are organized into a hierarchy where *extended interfaces* inherit methods and fields required by base interfaces. The situation is quite like defining various upgraded car models by inheriting and adding to the features of a base model. In DOM, the Node object is at the top of the interface hierarchy, and many types of DOM tree nodes are directly or indirectly derived from Node. This means all DOM tree node types must support the properties and methods required by Node.

On the DOM tree, some types of nodes are *internal nodes* that may have *child nodes* of various types. *Leaf nodes*, on the other hand, have no child nodes. While DOM has many uses, our discussion focuses on *DOM HTML*, which applies to HTML documents.

For any Web page, the root of the DOM tree is an HTMLDocument node, and it is usually available directly from JavaScript as document or window.document. The document object implements the HTMLDocument interface, which gives you access to all the quantities associated with a Web page such as URL, stylesheets, title, characterSet, and many others (Section 10.14). The field document.documentElement gives you the child node of type HTMLElement

Figure 10.5   THE DOM API

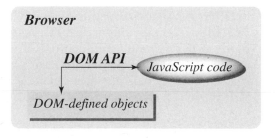

that typically represents the <html> element (Figure 10.2). HTMLElement (Section 10.9) is the base interface for derived interfaces representing the many different HTML elements.

DOM Tree Nodes

The DOM tree for a Web page consists of different types of nodes (subtypes of Node), including:

HTMLDocument—Root of the DOM tree providing access to pagewide quantities, style sheets, markup elements, and in most cases, the <html> element as a child node.

HTMLElement—Internal and certain leaf nodes on the DOM tree representing an HTML markup element. The HTMLElement interface provides access to element attributes and child nodes that may represent text and other HTML elements. Because we focus on the use of DOM in DHTML, we will use the terms element and HTML element interchangeably. The document.getElementById(*id*) call gives you any element with the given *id*.

Attr—An attribute in an HTMLElement object providing the ability to access and set an attribute. The name field (a string) of an Attr object is read-only, and the value field can be set to a desired string. The attributes field of an HTMLElement object gives you a NamedNodeMap of Attr objects. Use the length property and the item(*index*) method of the named node map to visit each attribute. All DOM indexes are zero-based.

Text—A leaf node containing the text inside a markup element. If there is no markup inside an element's content, the text is contained in a single Text object that is the only child of the element. The wholeText (or data) field returns the entire text as a string. Set the data string or call the replaceWholeText(*str*) method to make *str* the new text.

10.6 GETTING STARTED WITH DOM

Let's create a simple calculator (Ex: **DomCalc**) to demonstrate DOM and DHTML. The user enters an arithmetic expression and clicks a button to perform the required computations. The answer is displayed in the regular running text of the page (Figure 10.6).

The HTML source shows the code for the input control (line A), the GO button (line B), and the <span> for displaying the computed result (line C).

```
<head><title>DOM Calculator</title>
<link rel="stylesheet" href="domcalc.css"
```

Figure 10.6   A DHTML CALCULATOR

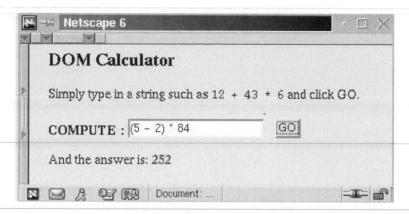

```
          type="text/css"  title="Dom Calculator" />
<script type="text/javascript" src="domcalc.js"></script>
</head>
<body onload="init()">  /* initialization onload */
<h3>DOM Calculator</h3>
<p>Simply type in a string such as
   <code>12 + 43 * 6</code> and click GO.</p>
<p><strong>COMPUTE : </strong>
  <input id="uin"
         value="(5 - 2) * 8" maxlength="30" />      (A)
    <input value="GO" type="button"
                     onclick="comp('uin')" />        (B)
</p><p id="par">And the answer is:
<span id="ans">00</span></p>                         (C)
</body>
```

The calculator is initialized immediately after page loading. The init and the comp (line B) event handlers are in the JavaScript file domcalc.js:

```
var answer;

function init()
{   answer = document.getElementById("ans")
                    .firstChild;            // (D)
    comp("uin");
}

function comp(id)
```

Figure 10.7   PARTIAL DOM TREE FOR CALCULATOR EXAMPLE

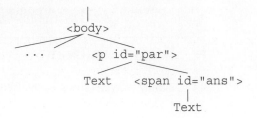

```
{  var el = document.getElementById(id);    // (E)
   var res = eval(el.value);                 // (F)
   answer.data = res;                        // (G)
}
```

The global variable answer is initialized by the init function that is called via the onload event, an event that takes place immediately after page loading is complete. The variable answer holds the Text node, a lone child node in this case, of the ans <span> (line D).

The comp function is called with the id of the user input element. The function obtains the input text as the value field of the input element el (line E), evaluates the input expression (line F), and sets the text of the ans <span> to the result obtained by setting the data field of the Text node answer (line G).

Without DOM, JavaScript-computed results are usually placed in <input> or <textarea> elements (Ex: **Convert** in Section 9.14). Using the DOM interface, script-computed results can be placed anywhere on a displayed page by modifying the DOM tree. Figure 10.7 shows the part of the DOM tree that is used to display the results for the calculator.

HTMLDocument and HTMLElement interfaces are important and provide many methods and properties useful in practice. They inherit from the basic Node interface, which is presented next.

10.7   THE DOM Node INTERFACE

In object-oriented programming, an interface specifies data values (called *fields*[1]) and functions (called *methods*) that are made available to application programs. The Node interface is the base of all other node types on the DOM tree and specifies useful fields and methods for them.

---

[1]In the official DOM specification, fields are called *attributes*. To distinguish them from HTML attributes, we use the commonly accepted term *fields* here.

Node Fields

Fields provided by a Node are read-only and include:

- nodeType—A small integer representing the *derived type* of the node. Figure 10.8 shows common derived node types. The Node interface provides symbolic constants, such as ELEMENT_NODE and TEXT_NODE, for values of nodeType (see the WDP site for a list). The function whichType demonstrates how to determine node type (Ex: **WhichType**):

```
function whichType(nd)                              // (a)
{  if ( nd.nodeType == Node.ELEMENT_NODE )          // (b)
       window.alert("Element Node");
    else if ( nd.nodeType == Node.ATTRIBUTE_NODE )
       window.alert("Attribute Node");
    else if ( nd.nodeType == Node.TEXT_NODE )
       window.alert("Text Node");
    ...
}
```

  The parameter nd is any DOM node whose type is to be determined (line a). The nd.nodeType is compared with the type constants defined by the Node interface to determine the node type of nd (line b).

- parentNode, firstChild, lastChild, previousSibling, and nextSibling—Related Nodes of a node (Figure 10.9).

- nodeName and nodeValue—Strings representing the name and value of a Node. The exact meaning of these strings depends on the node type, as shown in Table 10.1. For example, the nodeValue of any Element or HTMLElement node is null.

- childNodes—A NodeList of child nodes of the node. Some nodes have children and others don't. For an HTMLElement node, child nodes represent the HTML elements and text strings contained in that element.

Figure 10.8   TYPES OF NODES

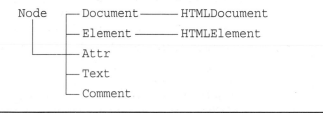

Figure 10.9 NODE RELATIONS

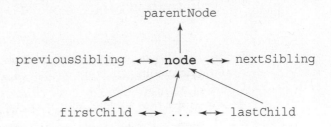

Table 10.1 MEANING OF nodeName AND nodeValue

Node Type	nodeName	nodeValue
Element	Tag name	null
Attribute	Attribute name	Attribute value string
Text	#text	Text string
Entity	Entity name	null
Comment	#comment	Comment string

The length field and the item(i) method of NodeList provide an easy way to visit each node on the node list. For example (Ex: **ChildNodes**), applying the function visitChildren:

```
function visitChildren(id)
{   var nd = document.getElementById(id);
    var ch = nd.childNodes;
    var len = ch.length;          // number of nodes
    for ( i=0; i < len; i++)
    {   nd = ch.item(i);          // node i
        window.alert( nd.nodeName + "  "
                    + nd.nodeValue );
    }
}
```

on the element with id="par"

```
<p id="par">Here is <img ...  /><br /> a picture.</p>
```

displays this sequence

```
#text    Here is
IMG
BR
#text    a picture.
```

- attributes—A NamedNodeMap of Attr nodes representing HTML attributes of the node. Attribute nodes are not child nodes of a node but are attached to the node via the attributes field. DOM defines a NamedNodeMap as a collection of nodes accessible by name. Thus, attributes is a list of Attribute objects representing the HTML attributes for a given node. Let att = nd.attributes be the attribute list of some node nd and you can go through all listed attributes with the code (Ex: **AttrAccess**):

```
var len = att.length;
for ( i=0; i < len; i++ )
{    window.alert(att.item(i).name + " = " +
                 att.item(i).value );
}
```

The length of the attribute list nd.attributes can be browser dependent. NN lists only attributes set explicitly in the HTML code, whereas IE gives all possible attributes. To examine a specific attribute, for example, you can use the code

```
var b = att.getNamedItem("border");
window.alert(b.value);                    // value of border
```

The value returned by getNamedItem is a node with the given name in the NamedNodeMap or null.

The ownerDocument field of a node leads you to the root of the DOM tree. It is worth emphasizing that the fields of Node are read-only. Assignments to them have no effect.

Also, NodeList and NamedNodeMap objects in the DOM are *live*, meaning changes to the underlying document structure are reflected in all relevant NodeList and NamedNodeMap objects. For example, if you get the childNodes of an HTMLElement and subsequently add or remove child nodes, the changes are automatically reflected in the childNodes you got before. This behavior is usually supported by returning a reference to the data structure containing the actual child nodes of the HTMLElement.

Node Methods

In addition to fields, the Node interface provides many methods inherited by all node types. These fields and methods combine to provide the basis for accessing, navigating, and modifying the DOM tree. Specialized interfaces for derived node types offer additional functionality and convenience.

Among Node methods, the following are more frequently used:

- *node*.normalize()—Adjusts the subtree rooted at *node* to remove empty nodes and to combine adjacent text nodes. The resulting *normalized DOM tree* has no empty or adjacent text nodes. Before normalization, a DOM tree may contain empty and/or adjacent text nodes due to spacing and line breaks in the page source code. Such white space is often used to avoid long lines and to make the source code easier to read. For example, the call

```
document.documentElement.normalize();
```

normalizes the entire <html> node.

- *node*.hasChildNodes()—Returns true/false.
- *node*.hasAttributes()—Returns true/false.
- *node*.appendChild(*child*)—Adds *child* as a new child node of *node*.
- *node*.removeChild(*child*)—Removes the indicated *child* node from the *node*.
- *node*.insertBefore(*child*, *target*)—Adds the *child* node just before the specified *target* child of this *node*.
- *node*.replaceChild(*child*, *target*)—Replaces the *target* child node with the given *child*. If *child* is a DocumentFragment, then all its child nodes are inserted in place of *target*.

Note, if *child* is already in the DOM tree, it is first removed before becoming a new child. Section 10.14 shows how to create a new node.

10.8 DOM TREE DEPTH-FIRST TRAVERSAL

Using the DOM for DHTML basically involves accessing nodes and modifying them on the DOM tree. The easiest way to access a target HTML element is to use

```
document.getElementById( id )
```

to obtain the node for the element directly by its *id*.

But it is also possible to reach all parts of the DOM tree by following the parent, child, and sibling relationships. A systematic visit of all parts of the DOM tree, a *traversal*, may be performed *depth-first* or *breadth-first*. In depth-first traversal, you finish visiting the subtree representing the first child before visiting the second child and so on. In breadth-first traversal, you visit all the child nodes before visiting the grandchild nodes and so on. These are well-established concepts in computer science.

Let's look at a JavaScript program that performs a depth-first traversal (Ex: **DomDft**) starting from any given node on the DOM tree. The example demonstrates navigating the DOM tree to access information.

```
var result="";
```

```
function traversal(node)
{   result - "",                                    //   (1)
    node.normalize();                                //   (2)
    dft(node);                                       //   (3)
    alert(result);                                   //   (4)
}

function dft(node)
{   var children;
    if ( node.nodeType == Node.TEXT_NODE )           //   (5)
        result += node.nodeValue;
    else if ( node.nodeType == Node.ELEMENT_NODE )   //   (6)
    {   opcnTag(node);                               //   (7)
        if ( node.hasChildNodes() )                  //   (8)
        {   children = node.childNodes;              //   (9)
            for (var i=0; i < children.length; i++)  //  (10)
                dft( children[i] );
            closeTag(node);                          //  (11)
        }
    }
}
```

Given any node on the DOM tree, the traversal function builds the HTML source code for the node. It initializes the result string (line 1), normalizes the subtree rooted at node (line 2), calls the depth-first algorithm dft (line 3), and displays the result (line 4).

The dft function recursively visits the subtree rooted at the node argument. It first checks if node is a text node (a leaf) and, if true, adds the text to result (line 5). Otherwise, if node is an element node (representing an HTML element), it adds the HTML tag for the node to result by calling openTag (line 7) and, if there are child nodes, recursively visits them (lines 8-10) before adding the close tag (line 11). The subscript notation children[i] is shorthand for children.node(i).

```
function closeTag(node)
{   result += "</" + node.tagName + ">\n";  }

function openTag(node)
{   result += "<" + node.tagName;
    var at;
    if ( node.hasAttributes() )                      //  (12)
        tagAttributes(node.attributes);
    if ( node.hasChildNodes() )
        result += ">\n";                             //  (13)
```

```
    else
        result += " />\n";                              // (14)
}

function tagAttributes(am)
{   var attr, val;
    for (var i=0; i < am.length; i++)                   // (15)
    {   attr = am[i];  val = attr.value;
        if ( val != undefined && val != null            // (16)
            && val != "null" && val != "" )
        {   result +=  " " + attr.name + "=\"" +         // (17)
                    val + "\"";
        }
    }
}
```

The openTag function adds any attributes for the tag (line 12) by calling tagAttributes. The open tag is terminated by either ">" (line 13) for nonempty elements or " />" for empty elements (line 14) conforming to the XHTML convention.

The argument am of tagAttributes is a NamedNodeMap of Attr nodes. The function goes through each attribute (line 15) and adds each defined attribute (line 16) to the result string (line 17). Note the use of the name and value fields of an Attr node.

Figure 10.10 shows the first part of the result of the depth-first traversal when called on the document.documentElement node corresponding to the <html> element of the page. The complete example can be tested on the WDP site.

Figure 10.10   TRAVERSAL OF DOM TREE

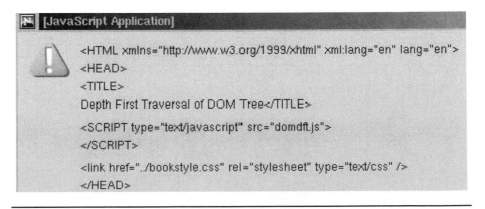

10.9 THE DOM HTMLElement INTERFACE

Derived node types (interfaces extending Node) add fields and methods specialized to a particular node type and may provide alternative ways to access some of the same features provided by Node. HTML markup elements in a page are represented by nodes extending the base HTMLElement, which itself extends Node. For each element in HTML, DOM HTML provides an interface

HTML*FullTagName*Element

that derives from HTMLElement (Figure 10.11). The complete list of all the HTML element interfaces can be found in the DOM HTML specification.

The HTMLElement interface is rather central for DHTML. Before we systematically discuss the fields and methods of HTMLElement, let's see it in action in an example (Ex: **DomNav**) where we combine navigation and modification of the DOM tree to achieve the kind of visual effects attributable to DHTML.

We can illustrate DOM tree navigation visually by visiting a subtree representing a <table> element, for instance. As you traverse the subtree, the part of the table corresponding to the node being visited will be highlighted. A control panel enables you to go up (to the parent node), down (to the first child), left (to the previous sibling), or right (to the next sibling) within the table. The control panel also displays the tag name associated with the current node (Figure 10.12).

Figure 10.11   DOM HTML INTERFACES

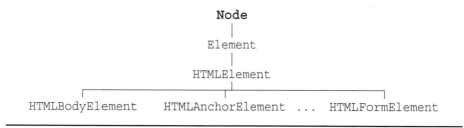

Figure 10.12   DOM TREE VISUAL NAVIGATION

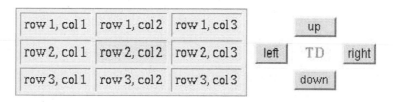

The HTML code for the table that we will be traversing is shown here in easy-to-read form:

```
<table id="tbl" border="1"
       style="background-color: #def"
       cellspacing="4" cellpadding="4" >
 <tr><td>row 1, col 1</td>
     <td>row 1, col 2</td>
     <td>row 1, col 3</td></tr>
 <tr><td>row 2, col 1</td>
     <td id="center">row 2, col 2</td>
     <td>row 2, col 3</td></tr>
 <tr><td>row 3, col 1</td>
     <td>row 3, col 2</td>
     <td>row 3, col 3</td></tr>
</table>
```

In the actual file, we eliminate all line breaks and white spaces between elements to avoid potential extraneous nodes on the DOM tree.

The init() function is executed onload and sets the stage for the visual navigation:

```
var currentNode, tableNode, nameNode, normal, highlight;

function init()
{   tableNode=document.getElementById("tbl");
    tableNode.normalize();
    highlight="#0ff";
    normal=tableNode.style.backgroundColor;                    // (A)
    currentNode=document.getElementById("center");             // (B)
    currentNode.style.backgroundColor  = highlight;            // (C)
    nameNode=document.getElementById("tname").firstChild;
    nameNode.data=currentNode.tagName;                         // (D)
}
```

The JavaScript global variables used are:

- tableNode—the node for <table> that is to be traversed
- currentNode—the node for the current traversal position on the tableNode subtree
- nameNode—the node to display the tagName of currentNode
- normal and highlight—the background colors that indicate visually the part of the table being visited

The init() function assigns initial values to these variables. The normal background color is set to the background of the table (line A). The center cell of the 3 by 3 table is chosen as the starting point of the traversal, and currentNode is set (line B) and highlighted (line C). The text of nameNode, at the center of the control panel, is set using the tagName field of an HTMLElement (line D). The init() function is called onload:

```
<body onload="init()">
```

The control panel (Figure 10.12) for interactive traversal is another table:

```
<table cellspacing="2" cellpadding="2">
<tr align="center">
   <td></td>
   <td><input type="button"
            value="  up  " onclick="up()" /></td>
   <td></td></tr>
<tr align="center">
   <td><input type="button" value=" left "
            onclick="left()" /></td>
   <td id="tname" style="color: #0aa;                    (E)
        font-weight: bold">tag name</td>
   <td><input type="button" value="right"
            onclick="right()" /></td></tr>
<tr align="center">
   <td></td>
   <td><input type="button" value="down"
            onclick="down()" /></td>
   <td></td></tr></table>
```

The data cell id=tname (line E) is used to display the tag name of the current traversal position. The four buttons each trigger a corresponding function that does the obvious. The up() function keeps the traversal from leaving the subtree (line F).

```
function up()
{   if ( currentNode == tableNode ) return;            // (F)
    toNode(currentNode.parentNode);
}

function down()
{   toNode(currentNode.firstChild); }

function left()
{   toNode(currentNode.previousSibling); }

function right()
{   toNode(currentNode.nextSibling); }
```

Each of these four functions calls toNode to visit the new node passed as the argument.

The `toNode` function does the actual work of walking from the current node to the new node given as `nd` (line G). If `nd` is `null` or a leaf node (type `TEXT_NODE`), then nothing is done (line H). If we are leaving an internal node on the subtree, the highlight is removed by calling the `removeAttribute` method of the `HTMLElement` interface (line I). If we are leaving the root `tableNode`, the original background color of the table is restored (line J). The arrival node is then highlighted and set as the current node (lines K and L). Finally, the tag name of the current node is displayed as the text content of `nameNode` (line M):

```
function toNode(nd)                                       // (G)
{  if ( nd == null ||
        nd.nodeType == 3 )  // Node.TEXT_NODE             // (H)
      return false;
   if ( currentNode != tableNode )
      currentNode.style.backgroundColor="";               // (I)
   else
      currentNode.style.backgroundColor = normal;         // (J)
   nd.style.backgroundColor = highlight;                  // (K)
   currentNode=nd;                                        // (L)
   nameNode.data=currentNode.tagName;                     // (M)
   return true;
}
```

The example further illustrates the DOM tree structure, the use of the `style` property of HTML elements, and the `tagName` field. It also shows how DHTML can help the delivery of information, enable in-page user interactions, and enhance understanding.

You can find the complete, ready-to-run version in the example package. You may want to experiment with it and see what it can show about the DOM tree and DHTML.

Assignment 5 suggests adding a display of the table subtree to show the current node position on the subtree as the user performs the traversal.

10.10   `HTMLElement` FIELDS AND METHODS

Every HTML element is represented on the DOM tree by a node of type `HTMLElement`. The `HTMLElement` interface extends the `Element` interface, which in turn extends the basic `Node` interface. We list often-used fields and methods available in any node object of type `HTMLElement`.

- `tagName`—A read-only field representing the HTML tag name as a string.
- `style`—A field to a style object representing the style declarations associated with an element. For example, use *element*`.style.backgroundColor` to access or set the `background-color`

style. Setting a style property to the empty string indicates an inherited or default style. If you change the style of an element by setting its style attribute instead, the new style attribute replaces all existing style properties on that element, and normally, that is not what you want to do. It is advisable to use the style field to set individual style properties you wish to change.

- innerHTML—A read-write field representing the HTML source code contained inside this element as a string. By setting the innerHTML field of an element, you replace the content of an element. This useful field is not part of the DOM specification, but it is supported by all major browsers.

- getAttribute(*attrName*)—Returns the value of the given attribute *attrName*. The returned value is a string, an integer, or a boolean depending on the attribute. Specifically, a CDATA (character data) value is returned as a string, a NUMBER value is returned as an integer, and an on-or-off attribute value is returned as a boolean. A value from an allowable list of values (e.g., left|right|center) is returned as a string. For an attribute that is unspecified and does not have a default value, the return value is an empty string, zero, or false as appropriate.

- setAttribute(*attrName*, *value*)—Sets the given attribute to the specified string *value*.

- removeAttribute(*attrName*)—Removes any specified value for *attrName* causing any default value to take effect.

- hasAttribute(*attrName*)—Returns true if *attrName* is specified for this element and false otherwise.

When setting values, use lowercase strings for attribute names and most attribute values. When checking strings obtained by tagName or getAttribute(), be sure to make case-insensitive comparisons to guard against nonuniformity in case conventions. For example,

```
var nd = node1.firstChild;
var re = /table/i;
if ( re.test(nd.tagName) )
{   ...   }
```

tests a tagName with the case-insensitive pattern /table/i.

HTML input control elements have these additional fields and methods:

- name and value—The name and value strings of an element to be submitted with a form.

- focus()—Causes the input element to get *input focus* so it will receive keyboard input.

- blur()—Causes the input element to lose input focus.

- select()—Selects the current textual content in the input element for user editing or copying.
- click()—Causes a click event on the element.

10.11   A GUIDED FORM

Let's look at a practical example of DHTML in which we use a combination of style, DOM, and JavaScript to implement a *guided form* (Ex: **GuidedForm**). The idea is simple: We want to guide the user visually through the form. This can be done by highlighting the input field that has keyboard focus (Figure 10.13). With a regular form, it is hard to spot which field has input focus. Thus, a guided form can be more user friendly and less confusing.

Here is the HTML code for this example:

```
<head><title>DOM Example: Guided Form</title>
<link rel="stylesheet" href="guidedform.css"
      type="text/css" title="guided form" />
<script type="text/javascript" src="guidedform.js">
</script></head>
<body onload="init()" style="background-color: #def">
<form method="post" action="/cgi-bin/wb/join.cgi">
<p style="font-weight: bold; font-size: larger">
Join club.com</p>
<table width="280">
<tr><td class="fla">Last Name:</td>
    <td><input onfocus="highlight(this)"              (1)
               onblur="normal(this)"                  (2)
               name="lastname" size="18" /></td></tr>
<tr><td class="fla">First Name:</td>
    <td><input onfocus="highlight(this)"
```

Figure 10.13   A GUIDED FORM

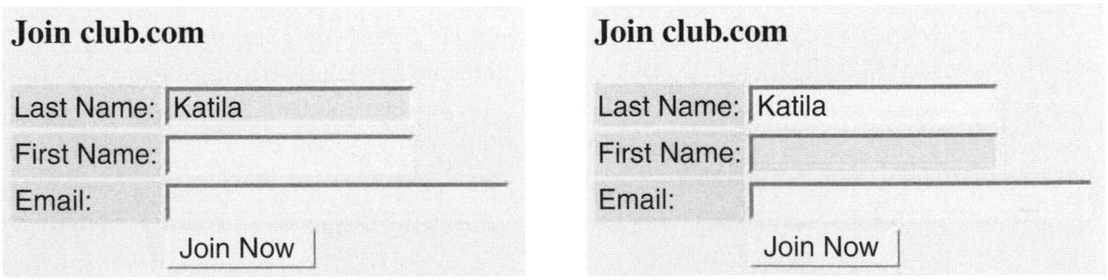

```
                        onblur="normal(this)"
                        name="firstname" size="18" /></td></tr>
<tr><td class="fla">Email:</td>
    <td><input onfocus="highlight(this)"
                        onblur="normal(this)"
                        name="email" size="25" /></td></tr>
<tr><td></td>
    <td><input onfocus="highlight(this)"
                    onblur="normal(this)"
                    type="submit" value="Join Now" /></td></tr>
</table></form></body>
```

The four input controls, last name, first name, email, and submit, call highlight
onfocus (line 1) and normal onblur (line 2). The style of the form is defined in
the guidedform.css file.

```
td.fla
{   background-color: #d2dbff;
    font-family: Arial, Helvetica, sans-serif
}

form input, select, textarea
{   background-color: #eef  }                     /* (3) */
```

The background color of input controls has been softened a bit from pure white
(line 3).

The actual highlighting is done by these JavaScript functions:

```
var base="", high;

function init() {  high = "#9ff"; }            // (4)

function highlight(nd)
{   base = nd.style.backgroundColor;           // (5)
    nd.style.backgroundColor=high;             // (6)
}

function normal(nd)
{   nd.style.backgroundColor=base; }           // (7)
```

The init() function, called onload, defines the highlight color to use. Before
highlighting an input field (line 6), its background color is saved in the global
variable base (line 5) for later restoration. The onblur event handler normal
restores the original background color (line 7).

When experimenting with this example, you can move the input focus
with the mouse or forward with TAB and backward with SHIFT TAB.

10.12   FADE-IN HEADLINES

Another useful DHTML effect provides an easy and efficient way to include page headlines that move into place as they fade in (Ex: **FadeIn**). The effect calls attention to the headline and gives the page a touch of animation.

The HTML code for such a centered headline involves

```
<body id="bd" onload="centerNow('ct', 60, 50, 40, 25)">

<p id="ct" class="headline"
   onclick="centerNow('ct', 60, 50, 40, 25)">Super ABC Company</p>
```

The style of the headline is given by a style rule such as

```
p.headline
{   text-align: center;
    font-family: verdana, arial, helvetica;
    font-size: x-large;
    font-weight: bold;
}
```

The JavaScript function centerNow performs the centering while fading in animation. You specify the target color of the headline and the number of animation steps, and it does the rest. The function call

```
centerNow(id, r, g, b, steps)
```

gives the *id* of the headline element (ct in our example), the red, green, and blue components of the target color rgb(r%, g%, b%), and an integer *steps*, the number of steps for the animation.

To move the text from left to center, we use increasingly smaller right margins for the centered text. Typically, we can begin with a 60% right margin and decrease it to 0% in the given number of steps. The code to set the right margin is

```
element.style.marginRight = setting + "%";
```

To achieve fade-in, we can repeatedly set the color style property

```
element.style.color = rgb(red, green, blue)
```

The animation can begin with the most faded color and gradually change to the least faded color (the target color) in the given number of steps. To fade a color, we increase the rgb components while keeping their ratios. All colors used must keep the ratios among the rgb components as close as possible to the original ratios in the target color. See Figure 10.14 for a sample set of headline fade-in colors.

Here is a procedure to compute the most faded color:

1. Let the target color be rgb($r0$%, $g0$%, $b0$%).

Figure 10.14   COLOR FADE IN

2. Let *high* be the maximum of *r0*, *g0*, and *b0*.

3. Let *m* be a multiplier such that *m * high* = 100.

4. The most faded color is rgb(*m*r0%*, *m*g0%*, *m*b0%*).

The multiplier *m* is $\geq$ 1. The fade-in can then be done by multiplying the target color by a sequence of numbers from *m* to 1 in the given number of steps.

Now, let's see how this is achieved in JavaScript.

```
var steps, mar, m, r, g, b;
var sty=null;

function centerNow(nd, rr, gg, bb, st)
{   mar = 60;                                           // (A)
    steps = st;                                         // (B)
    r =rr;   g =gg;   b=bb;                             // (C)
    if ( sty == null )
        sty = document.getElementById(nd).style; // (D)
    margin_d = mar/steps;                              // (E)
    m = 100/Math.max(Math.max(r, g), b);               // (F)
    color_d = (m-1.0)/steps;                           // (G)
    centering();
}
```

The centerNow function initializes the starting right margin, the total number of animation steps, and the target color values (lines A-C). The sty (line D), the style of the headline element, will be used repeatedly. The percentage setting of the right margin will decrease by margin_d (line E) after each step. The multiplier m begins with the maximum value (line F) and decreases by color_d (line G) after each step.

With these values set, `centering()` is called to perform the actual animation.

```
function centering()
{  if (steps > 1)
   {  sty.marginRight = mar+"%";                // margin
      sty.color="rgb(" +r*m+ "%," +g*m+ "%,"
                  +b*m+ "%)";                    // color
      mar -= margin_d;                           // decrements
      m -= color_d;
      steps--;
      setTimeout("centering()", 18);             // (H)
   }
   else   // final position and color            // (I)
   {  sty.marginRight="0%";
      sty.color="rgb("+r+"%,"+g+"%,"+b+"%)";
   }
}
```

The `centering` function performs one step of the animation. It sets the right margin and color and decrements the quantities that will be used in the next step. The JavaScript built-in function `setTimeout` (Section 9.17) schedules the call to `centering` after 18 milliseconds (line H). A smooth animation requires some 30 frames per second, making the delay between each step about 33 milliseconds. The last step of the animation (line I) ensures we have the correct centered position and the true target color without floating-point errors.

You can easily modify this example for similar visual effects. For example, the in-place fade-in (Figure 10.15) of a centered headline (Ex: **InPlace**) can be done with the same color technique plus changes in the letter spacing. Recall that the style property `letter-spacing` controls the spacing between characters in a piece of text (Section 6.14).

With the variable `sp` set to 1 at first, the JavaScript statements

```
sty.letterSpacing = sp + "px";
sp++;
```

Figure 10.15   IN-PLACE FADE-IN

can be included in a fade-in function that is called for a given number of steps to fade in any target headline. The full example (Ex: **FadeIn**) can be found at the WDP site and in the example package.

10.13   MOUSE TRACKING

DOM also specifies an Event interface to provide standards for an event system, event names, event registration, and event objects. For example, a MouseEvent object has the clientX and clientY fields giving, respectively, the x and y coordinates of the mouse event position in the document display area. Using these coordinates associated with the mousemove event, we can drag an element by moving the mouse.

The following HTML code displays a crystal ball image that when clicked will follow the mouse until the mouse is clicked again (Ex: **DragDrop**):

```
<head><title>Drag and Drop</title>
<script type="text/javascript"  src="dragdrop.js"></script>
</head> <body onload="init()">
<div id="ball"  onclick="drag()"                         (1)
     style="position: absolute;
             top: 20px; left: 20px; z-index: 1">
<img src="crystalball_stand.gif" width="110" height="142"
     alt="Crystal ball on a stand">
</div></body>
```

The technique is straightforward. A mouse click calls the JavaScript function drag() (line 1) that sets up the trackMouse event handler for the mousemove event (line 3). Mouse tracking changes the absolute position of the crystal ball. The left and top style properties are set to the event coordinates plus any scrolling that may have taken place for the browser window (lines 5 and 6).

```
// file: dragdrop.js
var ball, ballstyle;

function init()
{  ball = document.getElementById('ball');
   ballstyle = ball.style;
}

function drag()
{  if ( document.onmousemove )
      document.onmousemove = null;                     // (2)
   else
      document.onmousemove = trackMouse;               // (3)
}
```

```
function trackMouse(e)                                    // (4)
{  var x = e.clientX + window.scrollX;                    // (5)
   var y = e.clientY + window.scrollY;                    // (6)
   ballstyle.left = x + "px"; // left style property
   ballstyle.top = y + "px";  // top style property
}
```

A second mouse click calls drag() and cancels the mouse tracking (line 2).

10.14   THE DOM HTMLDocument INTERFACE

Browsers display Web pages in windows. Each window has a unique document object that represents the entire Web page displayed in the window. The document object contains all other elements in the page.

The document object, implementing the DOM HTMLDocument interface that inherits from the Document interface, offers fields and methods useful for pagewide operations.

HTMLDocument Fields

A select set of fields available from the document object is listed here:

- documentElement—the <html> element of the page
- body—the <body> element of the page
- URL—a read-only string for the complete URL of the page
- title—the title string specified by <title>
- referrer—the read-only URL of the page leading to this page (empty string if no referrer)
- domain—the read-only domain name of the Web server that supplied the page
- cookie—a SEMICOLON-separated string of *name=value* pairs (the cookies) associated with the page
- anchors, applets, forms, images, links—read-only lists of different elements in the page: <a> elements as named anchors, <applet> elements, <form> elements, <img> elements, and <a> and <area> elements as href links, respectively; such a list has a length field, an item(*n*) method, and a namedItem(*name*) method, which returns an element with *name* as id or, failing that, as name

HTMLDocument Methods

Frequently used methods of the document object include:

- createElement(*tagName*)—Returns a newly created element object for the <*tagName*> element. By setting attributes and adding child nodes to this element, you can build a DOM structure for any desired HTML element.
- createTextNode(*textString*)—Returns a node of type TEXT_NODE containing the given textString.
- getElementById(*id*)—Returns the unique HTML element with the given *id* string. We have seen this method used often.
- getElementsByTagName(*tag*)—Returns a list of all elements with the given *tag* name in the document.

10.15   GENERATING NEW CONTENT

Applying the features discussed in the previous section, let's do more with DHTML by adding new content to a displayed HTML page. The content is computed by JavaScript, built into element nodes, and placed on the DOM tree.

A Session-Recording Calculator

To get started, we can take the interactive calculator example (Ex: **DomCalc**) shown in Figure 10.6 and make it more useful by recording the current answer

Figure 10.16   SESSION-RECORDING CALCULATOR

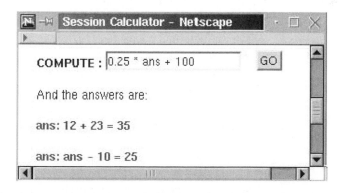

and displaying a history of computation steps. The answer from the previous step can be used in the next step (Figure 10.16).

The HTML code for the session calculator (Ex: **DomSession**) is revised slightly from that for the basic calculator of Ex: **DomCalc**:

```
<body onload="init()">
<h3>DOM Calculator Session</h3>
<p>Simply type in a string such as
   <code>12 + 43 * 6</code> and click GO.</p>
<p><strong>COMPUTE : </strong>
  <input id="uin" name="uin" maxlength="30" />
    
  <input value="GO" type="button"
         onclick="comp('uin')" /></p>
<p>And the answers are:</p>
<div id="session"> </div></body>                    (A)
```

The empty <div> is where the computation session will be displayed (line A).

The init() function (line B) is called onload to obtain the <div> element and store it in the global variable session.

```
var session, ans = 0;   // global variables


function init()
{    session=document.getElementById("session");    // (B)
}


function comp(id)
{    var input = document.getElementById(id);
     var str = input.value;                          // (C)
     ans = eval(str);                                // (D)
     var ansNode = document.createTextNode("ans: "
                         + str + " = " + ans); // (E)
     var parNode = document.createElement("p");      // (F)
     parNode.appendChild(ansNode);                   // (G)
     session.appendChild(parNode);                   // (H)
     input.value="";                                 // (I)
}
```

The comp function, triggered by the GO button, obtains the user input (line C) and evaluates it. The JavaScript function eval (line D) takes any string and executes it as code. The result obtained is stored in the global variable ans (line D), which can be used in the subsequent step. To record the computation step, it creates a new text node (line E), wraps a <p> element around it (lines F and G), and appends the element as a new (last) child of the session <div> (line H). Finally, the input field is cleared (line I), ready for the next step. Users may use ans in the next computation step to perform a session of steps (Figure 10.16).

Further, users may store values for use in subsequent steps by creating their
own variables with input strings such as:

```
taxRate = 0.08
total = subtotal + subtotal * taxRate
```

10.16   A SMART FORM

As another example of dynamically adding and removing page content, let's
add to the guided form discussed in Section 10.11 (Figure 10.13).

A Web site in North America may collect customer address and telephone
information without asking for an *international telephone country code*. But if the
customer selects a country outside North America, it may be a good idea to
require this information as well. In many situations, the information to collect
on a form can depend on data already entered on the form. It would be useful
to have the form dynamically adjust itself as the user fills out the form. This
can be done with DHTML.

As an example, let's design a smart form (Ex: **SmartForm**) that examines
the country setting in the address part of the form and adds or removes (Figures 10.17 and 10.18) an input field for the international telephone code. Our
strategy is straightforward:

1. When the country name is selected, the onchange event triggers a call
   to check the country name.
2. Any country outside North America causes an input field to be added
   to obtain the telephone country code.
3. If the country is within North America, then any telephone country
   code input field is removed.

The HTML code is as follows:

```
<head><title>DOM Example: Smart Form</title>
<link rel="stylesheet" href="guidedform.css"
```

Figure 10.17   SMART FORM I

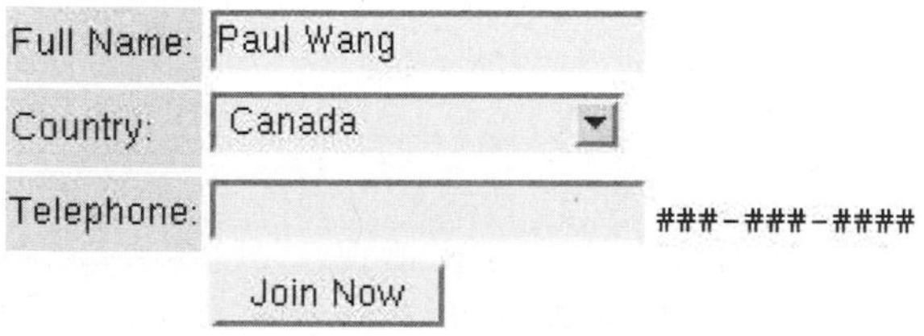

Figure 10.18 SMART FORM II

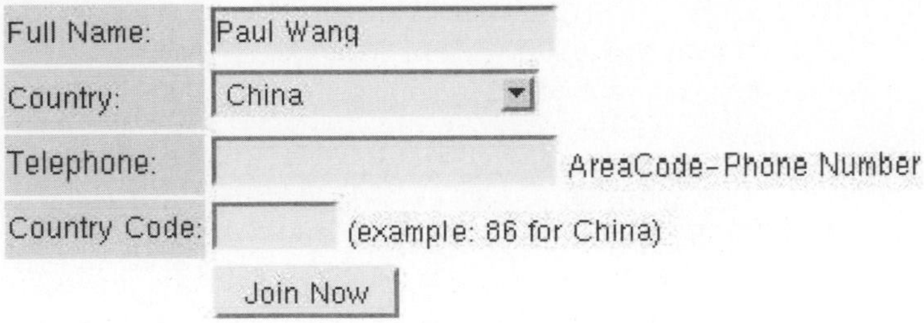

```
        type="text/css" title="dynamic guided form" />
<script type="text/javascript" src="smartdform.js">
</script>
</head>
<body onload="init()" style="background-color: #def">
<form method="post" action="http:/cgi-bin/join.pl">
<p style="font-weight: bold; font-size: larger">
Join club.com</p>
<table><tbody id="tb">                                        (A)
<tr><td class="fla">Full Name:</td>
   <td><input onfocus="highlight(this)"
        onblur="normal(this)"
        name="fullname" size="20" /></td></tr>
<tr><td class="fla">Country:</td>
   <td><select  id="country" name="country"
        size="1"
        onfocus="highlight(this);"
        onchange="countryCode(this);"                      (B)
        onblur="normal(this);" >
     <option value="US">USA</option>
     <option value="CA">Canada</option>
     <option value="MX">Mexico</option>
     <option value="CN">China</option>
     <option value="RU">Russian Federation
     </option>
   </select></td></tr>
<tr><td class="fla" >Telephone:</td>
   <td><input onfocus="highlight(this)"
     onblur="normal(this)"
     name="phone" size="20" /><span id="pinst">          (C)
     ###-###-####</span></td></tr>
<tr id="bt"><td></td>                                       (D)
```

```
<td><input onfocus="highlight(this)"
       onblur="normal(this)"
       type="submit" value="Join Now" /></td>
</tr></tbody></table></form></body>
```

The onchange event of <select> triggers the function countryCode (line B), which can add or remove a form entry for the telephone country code. The new form entry will be a new table row element, a child <tr> of <tbody> (line A) inserted just before the row (line D) for the Submit button.

The init() function, executed onload, sets the telephone instruction node (inode) to the pinst span (lines C and 1). The text child of inode (line 2) can be replaced later by a generic instruction (oph) for other countries (line 3).

```
var oph, iph, inode;


function init()
{   inode = document.getElementById("pinst");    // (1)
    iph = inode.firstChild;                       // (2)
    oph = document.createTextNode(
        " AreaCode-Phone Number");                // (3)
}
```

Two additional global variables (line 4) are used: crow (the table row to be created) and cc (the <input> element for the telephone country code). The isLocal function checks to see if a country is local to North America (line 5).

```
var crow = null, cc=null;                         // (4)

function isLocal(ct)                              // (5)
{   return (ct == "US" || ct == "CA"
                       || ct == "MX" );
}


function countryCode(country)
{   var d1, d2, t1, t2, button;
    var tbody = document.getElementById("tb");
    if ( isLocal(country.value) )                // (6)
    {   if ( crow != null )
        {   tbody.removeChild(crow);             // (7)
            inode.replaceChild(iph, oph);
            cc = crow = null;                    // (8)
        }
        return;
    }
// country outside North America
    if ( crow != null )                          // (9)
    {   cc.value = ""; return;   }               // (10)
```

```
crow = document.createElement("tr");        // (11)
crow.appendChild(makeLabel());              // (12)
crow.appendChild(makeCC());                 // (13)

button = document.getElementById("bt");     // (14)
tbody.insertBefore(crow, button);           // (15)
inode.replaceChild(oph, iph);               // (16)
}
```

A call to countryCode is triggered by the onchange event on the <select> element for the country part of an address. If the given country is in North America, it removes any telephone country code entry from the form, restores the phone instructions, resets the global variables, and then returns (lines 6-8).

The function continues to process country if it is outside North America. If the telephone country code entry is already displayed (line 9), it makes sure any previously entered code is removed and returns (line 10). Otherwise, a new <tr> element is created (line 11), filled with two table cells (lines 12 and 13), and inserted into the table body just before the Submit button (lines 14 and 15). The generic phone instruction is also put in place (line 16).

Each of the following functions makes a <td> element for the table row needed (Figure 10.19). The input element is made to match the style and dynamic behavior of other input controls in the form (lines 17 and 18). A text label is created by makeLabel(), and the actual input element for the telephone country code is created by makeCC(), which also sets the global variable cc.

```
function makeLabel()
{   var t, d;
    d = document.createElement("td");
    d.setAttribute("class", "fla");
    t = document.createTextNode("Country Code:");
    d.appendChild(t);
    return d;
}

function makeCC()
{   var t, d;
```

Figure 10.19 CREATING A FORM ENTRY

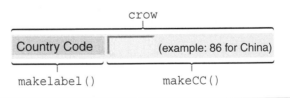

```
        d = document.createElement("td");
        cc = document.createElement("input");                    // (17)
        cc.setAttribute("onfocus", "highlight(this)");
        cc.setAttribute("onblur", "normal(this)");
        cc.setAttribute("name", "cc");
        cc.setAttribute("id", "cc");
        cc.setAttribute("size", "7");                            // (18)
        d.appendChild(cc);
        t = document.createTextNode("(example: 86 for China)");
        d.appendChild(t);
        return d;
}
```

Note that these element creation functions use setAttribute to set up many attributes so the newly created form entry fits in with the style and dynamic behavior on this smart form. Experiment with Ex: **SmartForm** and see for yourself.

One small problem with this form shows up when you click the back button after submitting the form, perhaps because of an error in filling out the form. The form contains the data you entered, but the telephone code entry disappears. It is possible to add code to the init() function called onload to fix this problem, and the solution is left as an exercise (Assignment 8).

10.17   REORDERING ROWS IN TABLES

Applying DHTML, we can make tables more usable by allowing the user to reorder rows based on the contents of cells in any given table column. Thus, tables representing invoices, shopping carts, airfares, addresses, student grades, and so on can be sorted at will by the user. The user may want to list the largest amount first, the least expensive item first, or names alphabetically. With DHTML, the user can do this by clicking the mouse, and the sorting will be performed by client-side JavaScript. Not going back to the server, the redisplay is instantaneous and very dynamic.

For example, the shopping cart in Figure 10.20 is in increasing Amount. The same shopping cart is shown in Figure 10.21 in increasing unit Price.

In this example (Ex: **TableSort**), clicking (double-clicking) a table header cell sorts that column in increasing (decreasing) order.

Sortable Table Organization

The HTML code for the sortable table is organized as follows:

- The first table row is placed within a <thead> element and contains table header (<th>) cells connected to event onclick and ondblclick

Figure 10.20   SHOPPING CART SORTED BY AMOUNT

Your Cart

Item	Code	Price	Quantity	Amount
Shovel	G01	14.99	2	29.98
Power Saw	P12	34.99	1	34.99
Hand Shovel	T01	4.99	10	49.90
Hand Saw	H43	24.99	5	124.95
			Subtotal:	239.82

handlers. These cells have a button look to visually indicate their active nature. Here is a typical <th> cell:

```
<th class="button"
    onclick="sortTable(2, 'num', '1');"
    ondblclick="sortTable(2, 'num', '-1');">Price</th>
```

Figure 10.21   SHOPPING CART SORTED BY PRICE

Your Cart

Item	Code	Price	Quantity	Amount
Hand Shovel	T01	4.99	10	49.90
Shovel	G01	14.99	2	29.98
Hand Saw	H43	24.99	5	124.95
Power Saw	P12	34.99	1	34.99
			Subtotal:	239.82

The arguments to `sortTable` are column position (a zero-based index), numerical or alphabetical ordering (num or str), and increasing or decreasing order (1 or -1). Here is the header for the Item column:

```
<th class="button"
    onclick="sortTable(0, 'str', '1');"
    ondblclick="sortTable(0, 'str', '-1');">Item</th>
```

- The sortable table rows are organized in a <tbody> group with a given id, tb in our example. Each sortable column must contain all numbers or all text strings. Here is a typical row:

```
<tr id="cc" valign="middle" align="right">
    <th>Hand Shovel</th>
    <td align="center">T01</td>
    <td>4.99</td> <td>10</td> <td>49.90</td></tr>
```

The table layout and the button look for clickable table header cells are created with CSS rules (Section 6.12):

```
table.sort tr { background-color:#f0f0f0; }

table.sort th.button
{   background-color: #fc0; border-width: 3px;
    border: outset; border-color: #fc0
}
```

Table Sorting

Now let's look at the JavaScript code for table sorting. As stated in the previous subsection, onclick and ondblclick events on an active table header trigger calls to the sortTable function with appropriate arguments: column position (c), numerical or alphabetical ordering (n), and increasing or decreasing direction (d).

```
var col=null, numerical=false, direction=1;

function sortTable(c, n, d)
{   if ( col==c && Number(d)==direction ) return;      // (a)
    col=c;                                             // (b)
    direction = Number(d);
    numerical = (n == "num");                          // (c)
    var tbody = document.getElementById("tb");         // (d)
    var r = tbody.childNodes;                          // (e)
    n = r.length;
    var arr = new Array(n);
    for ( i=0; i < n; i++ ) arr[i]=r.item(i);          // (f)
```

```
      quicksort(arr, 0, n-1);                                // (g)
      for ( i=0; i < n; i++ ) tbody.appendChild(arr[i]); // (h)
}
```

If c is the same as the recorded column position col and d is the same as the recorded sorting direction (line a), the sorting has already been done, and the sortTable returns immediately. To prepare for sorting, the arguments are stored in the global variables (lines b and c). The child nodes of <tbody> are copied into a new array arr (lines d and f). The copying is needed because tbody.childNodes is a read-only list. The notation (line f)

```
r.item(i)
```

gets you the ith item on the list of child nodes. It is possible that the notation r[i] will also work.

The call to quicksort (line g) sorts the array arr with the quicksort algorithm, one of the most efficient sorting algorithms known. The elements on the sorted arr are then appended in sequence as children of <tbody> (line g).

Inserting existing nodes from the DOM tree into the DOM tree is very different from inserting newly created nodes (Section 10.16). An existing node is first removed from the DOM tree automatically before it is inserted. The removal is necessary to protect the structural integrity of the DOM tree. This is why no explicit removal of child nodes from <tbody> is needed before appending the nodes from the sorted array arr.

If you accept the quicksort function as a magical black box that does the sorting, then we have completed the description of DHTML table sorting. For those interested, the inner workings of quicksort are presented next.

Quicksort

The basic idea of the quicksort algorithm is simple. First, pick any element of the array to be sorted as the *partition element* pe. By exchanging the elements, the array can be arranged so all elements to the right of pe are greater than or equal to pe, and all elements to the left of pe are less than or equal to pe. Now the same method is applied to sort each of the smaller arrays on either side of pe. The recursion is terminated when the length of the array becomes less than two.

```
function quicksort(arr, l, h)
{    if ( l >= h || l < 0 || h < 0 ) return;     // (1)
     if ( h - l == 1 )                            // (2)
     {   if (compare(arr[l], arr[h]) > 0)         // (3)
         {   swap(arr, l, h)    }                 // (4)
         return;
     }
     var k = partition(arr, l, h);                // (5)
     quicksort(arr, l, k-1);                      // (6)
```

```
    quicksort(arr, k+1, h);                    // (7)
}
```

The `quicksort` function is called with the array to be sorted, the low index `l`, and the high index `h`. It sorts all elements between `l` and `h` inclusive. If the sorting range is empty (line 1), `quicksort` returns immediately. If the range has just two elements (line 2), they are compared (line 3), and switched (line 4) if necessary, and `quicksort` returns. For a wider range, `partition` is called to obtain a partition element and the left and right parts of the array. Each of these two parts is sorted by calling `quicksort` (lines 6 and 7).

The call `compare(a, b)` compares the arguments and returns a positive, zero, or negative number depending on whether $a > b$, $a = b$, or $a < b$. The signs are reversed for sorting in decreasing order.

```
function compare(r1, r2)
{   ke1 =  key(r1, col);                       // (8)
    ke2 =  key(r2, col);                       // (9)
    if ( numerical )                           // (10)
    {   ke1 = Number(ke1);
        ke2 = Number(ke2);
        return direction * (ke1 - ke2);
    }
    return (direction * strCompare(ke1, ke2));    // (11)
}
```

For sorting HTML tables, `compare` is called with DOM nodes `r1` and `r2` representing two different table rows. The function `key` obtains the string contents in the designated table cell (lines 8 and 9) and compares them either numerically as numbers (line 10) or alphabetically as text strings (line 11).

The function `key` extracts the textual content (line 12) of the table cell from the given row `r` at the column position `c`.

```
function key(r, c)
{   var cell = r.firstChild;
    while ( c > 0 )
    {   cell = cell.nextSibling;
        c--;
    }
    return cell.firstChild.nodeValue;          // (12)
}
```

The `strCompare` function compares two text strings `a` and `b` by comparing corresponding characters:

```
function strCompare(a, b)
{   var m = a.length;
    var n = b.length;
    var i = 0;
```

```
    if ( m==0 && n==0 ) return 0;
    if ( m==0 ) return -1;
    if ( n==0 ) return 1;
    for ( i=0; i < m && i < n; i++ )
    {  if ( a.charAt(i) < b.charAt(i) ) return -1;
       if ( a.charAt(i) > b.charAt(i) ) return 1;
    }
    return (m - n);
}
```

Swapping two elements on the array is simple:

```
function swap(arr, i, j)
{   var tmp = arr[i];
    arr[i]=arr[j];
    arr[j]=tmp;
}
```

Now we can turn our attention to partition, the workhorse in the quicksort algorithm. The function is called with an array arr and a sorting range, defined by the low index 1 and the high index h, which has at least three elements. The function picks the middle element as the pe (line 13) and partitions the given range into two parts separated by the pe. All elements to the left of pe are less than or equal to pe, and all elements to the right of pe are greater than or equal to pe. The index of the pe is returned (line 18).

```
function partition(arr, l, h)    // h > l+1
{   var i=l, j=h;
    swap(arr, ((i+j)+(i+j)%2)/2, h);                // (13)
    var pe = arr[h];
    while (i < j)
    {  while (i < j && compare(arr[i], pe) < 1)  // (14)
       {  i++; }   // from left side
       while (i < j && compare(arr[j], pe) > -1) // (15)
       {  j--; }   // from right side
       if (i < j) {  swap(arr, i++, j); }        // (16)
    }
    if (i != h) swap(arr, i, h);                 // (17)
    return i;                                    // (18)
}
```

Searching from the left (line 14) and right (line 15) end of the range, it looks for an out-of-order pair of elements and swaps them (line 16). When finished, it moves the pe back into position (line 17) and returns.

The complete quicksort and the table sorting example can be found in the example package.

10.18   A TIC-TAC-TOE GAME

With DHTML, many kinds of interactive games can be implemented. Let's look at tic-tac-toe as an example (Ex: **TicTacToe**). A CSS-controlled <table> can serve as the playing board. Moves are made by clicking the game board squares. Two files, x.gif and o.gif, provide the graphical images for the game tokens (Figure 10.22).

The HTML code for the game board is a three by three <table>:

```
<table class="tic" cellspacing="0" border="0">
<tr><td id="tl" onclick="play('tl')"              (a)
        width="37" height="44"> </td>
    <td id="tc" onclick="play('tc')"              (b)
        width="37" height="44"> </td>
    <td id="tr" onclick="play('tr')"              (c)
        width="37" height="44"> </td>
</tr>

    . . .

</table>
```

The first row is shown here. The other rows are entirely similar. Each table cell (<td>) has an id and a class attribute set to a string such as tl

Figure 10.22   TIC-TAC-TOE GAME

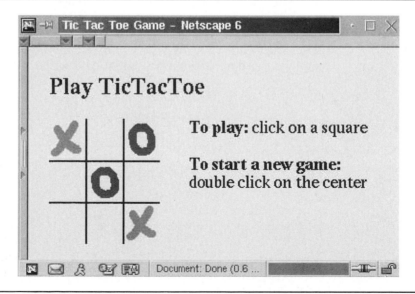

(top left; line a) and `tr` (top right; line c). We thus simply identify the nine game squares. Each `<td>` has a `width` and `height` setting to accommodate the game token image that, when played, will replace the nonbreaking space ` ` placeholder as the content of `<td>`. Onclick, each `<td>` calls `play` with its own id.

The game board is drawn with CSS `border` settings. For example, the style for the top left square is

```
td#tl
{   border-right: thin #000 solid;
    border-bottom: thin #000 solid;
}
```

The style for the center square is

```
td#cc
{   border-top: thin #000 solid;
    border-left: thin #000 solid;
    border-right: thin #000 solid;
    border-bottom: thin #000 solid;
}
```

These table cell styles, when combined with the `cellspacing` and `border` attributes for `<table>`, draw the game board.

In the JavaScript code, nine variables (line 1) are used to indicate whether a game square is open (zero) or taken (nonzero). The function `play` plays a token on the given (`id`) position. It returns immediately if the square is not open (line 2). Otherwise, it proceeds to place a token in the target square. It sets `cell` to the target `<td>` element (line 3), marks the position as taken by player one or player two (line 4), obtains an element object representing the game token (line 5), saves a copy of the content of `<td>` in the global variable `sp` (line 6), and replaces the content of `cell` with the token (lines 7 and 8).

```
var tl=0, tc=0, tr=0, cl=0, cc=0,
    cr=0, bl=0, bc=0, br=0;                      // (1)
var which=false, sp=null;

function play(id)
{   if ( eval(id) > 0 ) return;                  // (2)
    var cell = document.getElementById(id);      // (3)
    eval(id + (which ? "= 1;" : "=2;"));         // (4)
    tnode = token();                             // (5)
    if ( sp == null )
        sp = cell.firstChild.cloneNode(true);    // (6)
    cell.removeChild(cell.firstChild);           // (7)
```

```
        cell.appendChild(tnode);                          // (8)
}
```

The saved sp is used when restoring the game board for another game. Note that the call cloneNode(true) performs a *deep copy* of a node, copying all nodes in the subtree rooted at the node. If the argument false is given, only the children of node will be copied.

The token function creates a new <img> element for x.gif or o.gif depending on the setting of the Boolean variable which (line 9) whose value alternates every time token is called (line 10).

```
function token()
{   var t = document.createElement("img");
    if ( which )                                          // (9)
        t.setAttribute("src", "o.gif");
    else
        t.setAttribute("src", "x.gif");
    which = ! which;                                      // (10)
    t.setAttribute("width", "35");
    t.setAttribute("height", "40");
    t.style.display = "block";                            // (11)
    return t;
}
```

The token image displays as a block element (line 11) so it fits exactly on the board. The center square (id=cc), calls newgame() on double-click, which restores the game board (line 12) and resets the game variables (line 13) for another game.

```
function newgame()
{   blank(tl, "tl"); blank(tc, "tc");                     // (12)
    blank(tr, "tr"); blank(cl, "cl");
    blank(cc, "cc"); blank(cr, "cr");
    blank(bl, "bl"); blank(bc, "bc");
    blank(br, "br");
    tl=tc=tr=cl=cc=cr=bl=bc=br=0;                         // (13)
}

function blank(n, id)
{   if ( n == 0 ) return;   // no token
    var cell = document.getElementById(id);
    cell.removeChild(cell.firstChild);
    if ( sp != null )
        cell.appendChild(sp.cloneNode(true));
}
```

The function `blank` replaces a board position with a token by a copy of the saved blank node `sp`. The function `blank` can be simplified to

```
function blank(n, id)
{   if ( n == 0 ) return;    // no token
    var cell = document.getElementById(id);
    cell.innerHTML = " ";
}
```

for browsers that support the `innerHTML` feature. Under NN and IE, all HTML elements have the `innerHTML` field that gives you the HTML code contained inside the element. You can also set this field to modify the content of any element. It is very convenient for programming.

This simple implementation is functional enough to be used by two players. The Exercises suggest improvements to this program.

10.19   WINDOWS AND FRAMES

Before the introduction of DOM, browsers such as NN and IE already had their own objects for windows, frames, and various HTML elements. DOM makes the document model more complete, systematic, and uniform across all browsers. DOM addresses only the object structure of the document. The window object that represents the on-screen window containing the document is not part of the DOM specification. Many important features of the `window` object do work consistently across major browsers (Section 9.12). In particular `window.document` gives you the root of the DOM tree.

With the introduction of DOM, browser vendors are implementing the window object in the same DOM spirit, leading to a more functional and better defined interface to the `window` object. Since Version 6, NN is leading the way in this regard. Materials in this section show how the `window` object works with frames and the DOM tree in NN 6 and later versions.

The `window` Object

Useful fields of `window` include:

- `window.document`—a reference to the root of the DOM tree conforming to the DOM `Document` interface
- `window.frames`—an array of frames in this window
- `window.innerHeight, window.innerWidth`—the height and width in pixels for content display in the window
- `window.navigator`—a reference to the `navigator` object (Section 9.11)
- `window.parent`—the parent window containing this window or `null`
- `window.top`—the top-level window

- window.screen—an object representing the computer display screen

Many window methods have been described in Section 9.12. We list a few more here.

- window.dump(*str*)—outputs *str* to the JavaScript console
- window.print()—outputs window.document to the printer

Vertical Page Positioning

Sometimes a page layout calls for the positioning of an HTML element at a certain vertical position in the display window. For example, a site entry may be a graphics image or a Flash animation that is vertically centered in the window or starts one third of the way down. Vertical centering is not easy with HTML alone. But it can be done with DHTML. Here is an example (Ex: **VCenter**).

```
<body onload="vcenter()" style="margin: 0">
<table width="100%" cellpadding="0" cellspacing="0">          (1)
<tr><td><img id="padding" src="img/clear.gif"
        alt="padding" width="100" height="150" /></td></tr>   (2)
<tr align="left">
<td style="width:100%; height:300px"><a href="main.html">
   <img src="img/entry.gif" width="1200"
        height="300" style="border-style:none" /></a></td>
</tr></table></body>
```

The entry graphic entry.gif is 300 pixels high. It needs to be centered vertically in the window. We put the graphic in the second row of a table that covers the window width (line 1). The first row is padding provided by a transparent image (line 2) whose height is set dynamically by the JavaScript function vcenter():

```
function vcenter()
{   var ht = window.innerHeight-300;                           // (3)
    ht = (ht - ht%2)/2;                                        // (4)
    var cell = document.getElementById("padding");            // (5)
    cell.setAttribute("height", ht);                          // (6)
}
```

```
window.onresize=vcenter;                                       // (7)
```

To center vertically, vcenter computes the difference of the window inner height and the height of the image to be centered (line 3). Dividing that by 2 gives the height of the desired padding, which is set as the height attribute of the padding image (lines 4-6). The function is called on load and also on window resizing (line 3) so the element stays centered. This idea is easily generalized to perform other dynamically computed vertical positioning.

The WDP Web site provides the complete working version of this example.

10.20   A CODE EXPERIMENTER

For people learning or using HTML, style sheets, and JavaScript, it is often beneficial to experiment with code fragments to see their effects. We can build a page with two frames side by side (Ex: **TryCode**). In one frame, the user can enter and edit code in a text area. With DHTML, the other frame can show the effect of the code (Figure 10.23).

The frameset page has the following code:

```
<head>
<title>Code Experimenter</title></head>
<frameset cols="40%,60%">
   <frame frameborder="1" id="codeframe" src="code.html"
          scrolling="auto" />
   <frame id="resultframe" src="result.html" />
</frameset>
</html>
```

The result.html page is very simple:

```
<head><title>Results</title></head>
<body><p>The result is shown here</p></body>
</html>
```

Figure 10.23   CODE EXPERIMENTER

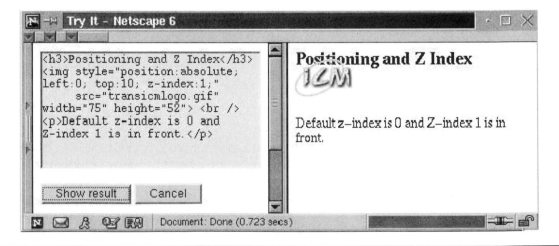

The code.html page contains the textarea for entering and editing experimental code.

```
<textarea style="width:100%; background-color: #def"
          id="code"  cols="65"  rows="16">
Put your HTML code fragment here.                          (1)
Anything that the HTML body
element may contain is fine.                               (2)
</textarea>
<p><input name="result" type="button"
          value="Show result" onclick="show()" />
   <input type="button" value=" Cancel "
          onclick="goBack()" /></p>
<p>You can enter and edit code in this window,
and click on "Show result" to see the result in
the window on the right.  Click "Cancel" to go
back to the hands-on page.</p>
</body></html>
```

The HTML source contained in textarea (lines 1 and 2) can be anything here. The user will enter the code interactively for experimentation. The JavaScript code in code.html supports the desired effects. The Show result button calls show(). It obtains the document object in the window for the frameset (line A). Note that window is the window for the codeframe, and from this frame, window.top (or window.parent) is the window for the frameset. From the resultframe element (line B), we obtain its document object (line C) and the <body> element (line D) in that document to show the code. We applied the HTMLDocument method getElementsByTagName (Section 10.14) to get the body element.

The HTML source in the textarea is assigned as the content innerHTML of the <body> element (lines E and F).

```
<head>
<script type="text/javascript">
function show()
{   var b = window.top.document;                        // (A)
    var f = b.getElementById("resultframe");            // (B)
    var d = f.contentDocument;                          // (C)
    var bb = d.getElementsByTagName("body").item(0); // (D)
    var c= document.getElementById("code");             // (E)
    bb.innerHTML=c.value;                               // (F)
}

function goBack() { window.top.back(); }
</script>
```

This example also shows the use of frame objects and how they can interact under DOM.

10.21 DHTML ACCESS TO WEB SERVICES

DHTML can do many things to make Web pages more responsive and more functional. But up to this point, it is restricted to operating on data already in the page and input by the user from the keyboard. DHTML can be much more powerful and useful if it can manipulate data from other Web pages and perhaps even obtain data from server-side programs. The data thus obtained can be incorporated at appropriate places in a Web page. For example, a stock price can be obtained and inserted in an article on stock trading; a travel page can display weather forecast information of the departure and arrival cities for the travel dates; maps and driving directions can be included for stores and businesses; and so on.

Thus, *Web services* provide well-defined data, and DHTML can fetch such data dynamically and insert them at designated places on the DOM tree. A Web service does not have to return a complete HTML page. It may return just an HTML fragment suitable for inclusion in another Web page. In time, such usage will be common and standardized.

To show how this can work with current DHTML techniques, let's look at a fortune cookie program (Figure 10.24). This program Ex: **Fortune** displays a crystal ball and a "fortune cookie message." Each time the end user clicks

Figure 10.24   FORTUNE COOKIE WEB SERVICE

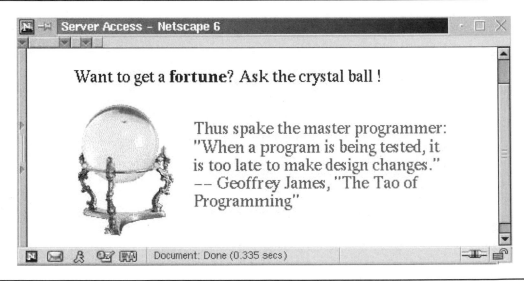

on the crystal ball, a new message from a Web service is displayed. The Web service `fortune.pl` delivers the fortune cookie message in a single `<p>` element.

Let's first look at the HTML code.

```
<?xml version="1.0" encoding="UTF-8" ?>
<!DOCTYPE html PUBLIC "-//W3C//DTD XHTML 1.0 Strict//EN"
    "http://www.w3.org/TR/xhtml1/DTD/xhtml1-strict.dtd">
<html xmlns="http://www.w3.org/1999/xhtml"
      xml:lang="en" lang="en">
<head><title>Web Service Demo: Fortune Cookie</title>
<script type="text/javascript" src="fortune.js">
</script></head><body>
<div style="font-size: larger" >
<h2>Want to get a <b>fortune</b>?</h2>
<p>Ask the crystal ball !</p>
<p>
<img onclick="comp('/cgi-bin/wb/fortune.pl')"          (1)
     margin-right: 1em; margin-bottom: 1em"
     src="crystalball_stand.gif"
     width="110" height="142"
     alt="Crystal ball on a stand">
<p id="ansobj">
<object data="/cgi-bin/wb/fortune.pl" type="text/html"  (2)
        width="400" height="100">
</object></p>
</div>
</body></html>
```

The HTML fragment from `/cgi-bin/wb/fortune.pl` is displayed by the `object` element (line 2). The `comp` function (line 1) is in `fortune.js`.

```
var count=0;

function comp(t)
{  nd = document.getElementById("ansobj")          // (3)
   tx = "<object data=\"" + t + "?" + count++       // (4)
       + "\" type=\"text/html\" "
       + "width=\"400\" height=\"100\"></object>;
   nd.innerHTML = tx;                               // (5)
}
```

The function obtains the parent `nd` of the `object` element (line 3), constructs the HTML code for a new `object` element (line 4), and resets the `innerHTML` of `nd`.

The `fortune.pl` Perl code supplies fortune cookie messages.

```
#!/usr/bin/perl
```

```
$ft = '/usr/games/fortune';                        ## (6)

print("Content-type: text/html\r\n\r\n");
print('<p style="color: blue">' . $ft . "</p>");   ## (7)
exit;
```

The program calls the UNIX utility **fortune** (line 6), which generates a randomly selected message each time it is called. The response consists of a single <p> element (line 7).

10.22 FOR MORE INFORMATION

This chapter gets you started in standard-based DHTML. As DOM, JavaScript, and CSS standards grow and evolve, and as browser compliance becomes more complete and widespread, DHTML will be an increasingly more powerful and effective tool for delivering dynamic Web pages.

For more information on the W3C standards see www.w3c.org. For DOM bindings to the ECMA Script, see

www.w3.org/TR/REC-DOM-Level-1/ecma-script-language-binding.html

For the Netscape implementation of DOM, see the Gecko DOM reference

www.mozilla.org/docs/dom/domref/dom_shortTOC.html

For standard-based DHTML sample codes see, for example,

www.mozilla.org/docs/dom/samples/
dmoz.org/Computers/Programming/Languages/JavaScript/W3C_DOM/
    Sample_Code/
webfx.eae.net

10.23 SUMMARY

DHTML is a technique that combines JavaScript, CSS, and HTML. DOM is a W3C recommended standard API for accessing and modifying HTML and XML documents. DHTML with DOM results in powerful and cross-platform code.

Browsers support the DOM specified API and provide the required objects and methods for JavaScript programming. The window.document object implements the HTMLDocument interface and gives you the root node of a Web page. Each element on this DOM tree corresponds to an HTML element in the source document and implements the HTMLElement interface derived from Element, which extends Node. The document.getElementById method is handy for obtaining the DOM object representing any HTML element with an assigned id. Starting from any node `el` on the DOM tree, you can follow the child (`el.childNodes`, `el.firstChild`), parent (`el.parentNode`), and sibling (`el.nextSibling`, `el.previousSibling`) relations to traverse the entire tree or any parts of it. You can also access and modify element attributes (`el.getAttribute(attr)`, `el.setAttribute(attr, value)`) and styles (`el.style.property`).

The DOM API allows you to systematically access, modify, delete, and augment the DOM tree, resulting in altered page display: `e.removeChild(node)`, `e.appendChild(node)`, `e.replaceChild(new, old)`, `e.insertBefore(new, node)`. New tree nodes can be created in JavaScript with `document.createElement(tagName)`, `document.createTextNode(string)`.

When you combine event handling, including those generated by `window.setTimeout()`, and style manipulations, many interesting and effective dynamic effects can be achieved for your Web pages.

Accessing Web services with DHTML promises to allow developers to add value to Web pages by including information dynamically produced by various services on the Web.

EXERCISES

Review Questions

1. Explain in your own words what DHTML is.

2. What are three important enabling technologies for standard-based DHTML?

3. What is DOM? The DOM tree? The most basic `Node` interface?

4. Name important types of nodes on the DOM tree and describe the DOM tree for a Web page in detail.

5. Write the JavaScript code for obtaining the DOM node for an HTML element with a given `id` and for determining its node type.

6. What is the `nodeName` and `nodeValue` for an `HTMLElement`?

7. Describe the `HTMLElement` interface.

8. Explain the fields and methods in the `HTMLDocument` interface. Which object available by JavaScript supports this interface?

9. How does JavaScript modify the presentation style of an element on the DOM tree?

10.   Compare the window object descriptions in Section 10.19 and Section 9.12.

11.   Explain the concept of Web service and the access of Web services with DHTML.

Assignments

1.   Improve the Ex: **DomHello** in Section 10.2 and make the mouseover action also change the text over the phrase to out of the phrase. Test and see how well it works.

2.   Modify the Ex: **DomCalc** in Section 10.6 and present a display in the form *string = result*.

3.   Test the normalize method of Node (Section 10.7) to see how well it is supported by your browser.

4.   Consider Ex: **DomDft** in Section 10.8. The traversal does not take comments into account. Modify the dft function to remedy this and test the traversal on pages that contain comments. (Hint: Node.COMMENT_NODE is 8.)

5.   Consider the visual navigation of a DOM tree (Section 10.9). Take Ex: **DomNav** and add a tree display of the table. As the user navigates the table, also show the current position on the DOM tree display.

6.   Consider the guided form example in Section 10.11. Add the correctness check of email from Section 9.15 to it.

7.   Follow the in-place fade-in example in Section 10.12 and write the code to achieve fade-out.

8.   Take the disappearing country code problem described at the end of Section 10.16 and fashion a solution.

9.   Add an Unmove button to the tic-tac-toe program in Section 10.18 to take away the last move made.

10.   Improve the tic-tac-toe program in Section 10.18 by adding the ability to play with the computer. (Hint: Add move generation.)

11.   Construct a pocket calculator using DHTML. Layout the LCD window and calculator buttons with a table and simulate the functions of the common calculator with onclick events on the buttons.

12.   Follow the Ex: **VCenter** example in Section 10.19 and use CSS positioning to achieve vertical centering.

## CHAPTER 11

Graphics and Site Production

Site production is concerned with creating all the components that will fit together to form the desired site. Typically, a project team has already made substantial progress and completed the formulation of these items:

- content-only site: structure, navigation system, typical pages, fill-out forms, and textual, graphical and media contents
- look and feel of site: font, spacing, color, and layout
- design of graphical elements: site entry, rollovers, graphics, and images

Based on the graphical designs, image processing tools such as Photoshop that can be used to produce the desired image files ready to drop into the designated spaces in the layout. This is what we call *graphics production*.

Graphics production involves the manufacture of various elements such as navigation bars, hand-drawn images, photographs, charts, illustrations, and so on. These elements are referred to as the "final art." This is normally considered a fairly mechanical procedure, in which you follow specific steps to produce the graphical elements needed.

With graphics production finished, the project team is ready to produce the site. Figure 11.1 shows an overview of the site production process. The three boxes on the third row from the top in this figure constitute the input to the production process. Central to the production effort is an *integrated development environment* (IDE) such as Macromedia Dreamweaver. The IDE provides an effective visual environment to create layout grids, drop in graphics and text, install rollovers, and adjust HTML and styles. The IDE can then generate HTML *page templates*, style sheets (CSS), and JavaScript code. Usually, a set of templates is created for various parts of a site. The generated files often need hand-tuning and editing to become the final files and templates used to obtain the final pages for the draft site.

Hand-tuning can simplify HTML code, make it XHTML compliant, add CSS rules with sophisticated selectors, and customize JavaScript code for the site. Most pages can be produced by dropping contents into an appropriate template. Sometimes other adjustments are needed. The final pages will combine audio/video and CGI files, produced using other appropriate tools,

Figure 11.1   SITE PRODUCTION OVERVIEW

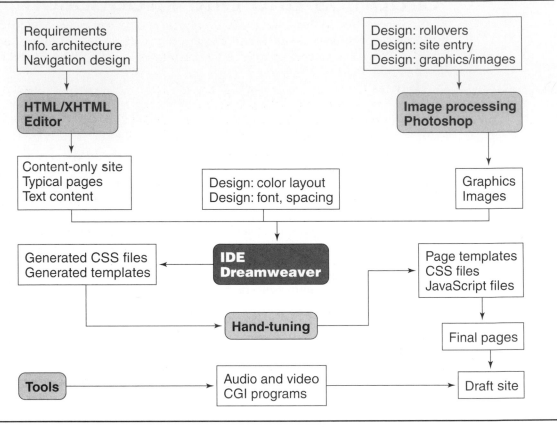

for the complete draft site. Hence, site production achieves the integration of graphics, HTML code, style sheets, and ultimately client-side and server-side programming.

Most Web developers have several production staffs to do this work, but for independent contractors, or freelancers, this is another task to perform themselves. As with any task, the ability to control all aspects of the creative process is highly rewarding. Regardless of who does the production, it is critical that all members of the Web team understand the basics of site production, seeing how their expertise fits into the final product.

11.1   GRAPHICS FOR THE WEB: USING PHOTOSHOP

Once the content-only site and page layouts have been approved and the client has given you permission to proceed, it is time to prepare graphics. This phase of the project is often referred to as "production" phase in print because it is here that you produce the final art. For art production, good software tools are indispensible. In our coverage here, typical tools such as Photoshop and Dreamweaver will be used extensively, and you will learn how to use them as well. Once you learn the concepts and techniques, using other tools will be quite easy.

Perhaps the best way to begin our introduction to creating images is to describe how to perform image processing in Photoshop. Photoshop was originally conceived as a photo retouching tool. Over the years, its capabilities expanded to an image editing and color painting tool. Photoshop is primarily a raster image program used for working with photographs.

Although its capabilities have vastly expanded with every new version, Photoshop's primary functions are to merge and edit color images, to retouch proofs, and to create original or composite artwork, collages, or photo montages for print or on the Web.

There are many good how-to books that explain how to execute particular techniques, including a whole series from Adobe Corporation. This chapter outlines major topics and helps you get started.

The Photoshop Image Editing Model

One way to think about Photoshop is to imagine a big canvas made up of pixels. Each image you open has its own pixels with a different color model. Photoshop allows you to open and combine many different file types, but you will get the most flexibility by working with the native PSD files, or Photoshop documents. A PSD image can be saved in any other format you wish, such as EPS, TIF, GIF, JPG, and so on.

After launching Photoshop, you either open an existing image or create a new image to process. The next thing is selecting a *color mode* in which to work. Available modes include *Bitmap, Grayscale, Duotone, Indexed Color, RGB Color, CMYK Color, Lab Color,* and *Multi Channel.* Each mode automatically provides you with slightly different tool options. For example, If you're working only with a gray scale image for print, you would select the Image>Grayscale option. If you're working on a Web image, you would choose the RGB mode. You can switch modes any time you wish by resaving in a different mode. Let's say that you want to reduce a full color image to a duotone image and then save it as JPG for your site. You would open the image in RGB mode and then switch to Grayscale to strip all colors in the original RGB image, select the Duotone option to create your duotone, and make color adjustments. To save that image as a JPG, however, you need to go back to the RGB mode and then save as JPG. All JPGs must be saved from the RGB mode.

To combine, merge, or join images from several different files is not a problem. You simply open the various files into Photoshop and drag and drop to one another. Files have to be converted to the native Photoshop format before they can be moved (File>Save As). In this way, you can drag and drop all the images into one file and combine them using layers. The image being drag-dropped will assume the size and mode of the receiving host image. So, if you drag and drop a 300K CMYK image into a 100K RGB file, the CMYK image will come into a separate layer and it will become a 100K RGB file. You can continue to work in the RGB image, and when you're finished with your task, you can again save the image as a JPG or any file format you wish.

The process for creating final art usually goes like this:

- Obtain the image: digital photo, scanned photograph, or drawing.
- Adjust the image in Photoshop: color balance, cropping, resizing, photo manipulation.
- Process or edit the image in Photoshop using layers.
- If necessary, divide (slice) the image into smaller parts to fit into the layout grid.
- Save images as JPG or GIF. Photographs look best as JPGs. Most icons, logos, and line drawings look best saved as GIFs.
- Reassemble sliced images (now GIFs or JPGs) in your layout grid (normally HTML tables).

11.2 CROPPING AND SCANNING

Most Web graphics, but certainly not all, begin with an existing image, which can be used in its original form, cropped, cut, manipulated, or combined with other images. However, before we continue to examine the actual process of scanning, we need to reiterate that any scanned or printed graphic, text, or sound is protected under the Constitution whether it has a copyright symbol or not (www.whatiscopyright.org). Taking someone else's printed or digital images is illegal, as stated in the Bern Convention for the Protection of Literary and Artistic Works (Paris Text 1971) Article 2 (www.law.cornell.edu/treaties/berne/2.html). If you still have questions about copyrights, there are many good sites that summarize the laws that can help you understand what you need to know before scanning existing images.

Copyright laws are specific and stringent on this topic, and the authors of this book would like to encourage you to consider this before scanning any images that you do not own or have permission to use. The safest way to stay within the limits of this law is to generate your own imagery, commission others to do it for you, or purchase royalty-free images with unlimited usage. The general rule is this: "If you find it in print or on the Web, it is not yours to use, reuse, change, or re-create." Brad Templeton explains some of the myths about copyrights in his article titled "10 Big Myths about Copyright Explained" at www.templetons.com/brad/copymyths.html.

Figure 11.2   SCANNER INTERFACE

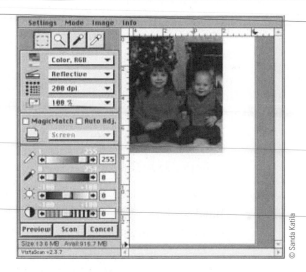

The toddler image in Figure 11.2 was scanned on a Umax Astra 1200, which costs less than $100. Scanners are often sold or bundled with other software, such as Photoshop or Illustrator. If you don't have a scanner, you will find many good choices in today's market.

Scanning for print involves numerous calculations that deal mostly with size, resolution, and output devices. *Output device* refers to the machine that ultimately "rips" your file and prints it at high resolution. This high-resolution file is then used to create a negative that will be used in offset printing. RIP stands for raster image processor, a process for reading digital files and preparing them for high-end printing. For more information on this process, go to http://desktop.about.com/library/weekly/aa062702a.htm.

Resolution on the Web refers to the number of pixels per inch in the image, printer, and computer screen. Preparing images for the Web is much simpler than for print. Size is still a factor, but the final resolution is always 72 dpi. *Dpi* is somewhat of a misnomer in this case because it is a printer's term that refers to dots per inch. This is a measurement of halftone dots per inch in a given image. A more accurate term is *ppi*, which stands for pixels per inch. This makes more sense because scanned images are comprised of pixels, not dots. Nevertheless, you will still see many references to dpi when referring to resolution of scanned images.

The most important aspect of scanning is understanding the relationship between size and resolution. In addition to these two factors, many scanners offer various color choices such as 256 colors, gray scale, halftones, or black and white. A good rule is to capture the most information that you can from the original image during scanning. It is recommended that you scan in either 24-bit color or 256 gray scale and then edit (adjust colors, contrast, and brightness) the image in Photoshop.

Scanning Steps

1. Place the image you wish to scan face down on the scanner.

2. Launch the scanner (Figure 11.2).

3. If scanning a continuous tone (never been printed image) color photograph, it is recommended that you choose the Color, RGB option as opposed to the 256 Colors option. If scanning line art such as logos, it is best to scan the gray scale image and then re-create the logo as a new vector graphic in a program such as CorelDraw, Adobe Illustrator, or Macromedia FreeHand. When scanning a line drawing that will remain as a raster graphic, choose Line Art.

4. Choose the scan size in percentage. It is recommended that you scan larger and then reduce the image in Photoshop.

5. If you have the option, you may choose Automatic Adjustment, but this is often not enough to color correct photos. The photographs in Figures 11.3 and 11.4 were adjusted using the Levels command in Photoshop. The Levels command is recommended for adjusting midtones values.

6. Save the image as Photoshop or any other format you wish (JPG, TIFF, EPS, PNG). Most formats can later be opened in Photoshop and adjusted.

Figure 11.3   ORIGINAL SCAN OF CHILDREN

© Sanda Katila

Figure 11.4   ADJUSTED PHOTO USING LEVELS COMMAND

© Sanda Katila

Scanning Printed Images

Remember that most printed images are protected under copyright law, and you should always seek permission from the owner before using them in your Web sites. If you obtained permission from the owner, you may proceed to scan a printed image, but be aware of the Moiré pattern problem. A *Moiré pattern* is unexpected visual interference created when two or more grids intersect with one another. It is a potential problem whenever you scan a piece of artwork that contains a grid such as the dots (Figure 11.5) forming a printed image. The grid within the original image may interact in unexpected ways with the scanning grid (the array of scanner sampling points) or the computer screen pixel array.

How can you minimize this problem? It is recommended that when scanning printed images, you do the following:

1. Scan the image at twice the resolution as you normally would to capture more information.
2. Use the despeckle filter (Filter>Noise>Despeckle) in Photoshop to minimize the dotted texture.
3. Use the Gaussian blur filter (Filter>Blur>Gaussian Blur). Adjust 0.1–0.9 to "soften" or blur the image and minimize the Moiré pattern.

The result of these three steps is shown in Figure 11.6.

Screen Capture

Often an image comes from the computer screen. The Mac OS makes screen capture easy by supporting it at the system user interface level. To take a picture

Figure 11.5 MOIRÉ PATTERN ON IMAGE

Figure 11.6 REDUCED APPEARANCE OF MOIRÉ PATTERN

of the entire screen, hold down Shift>Command>3. To take a picture of a rectangular section of the screen, hold down Shift>Command>4 (after pressing and releasing the keys, drag across the part of the screen you wish to capture). If you want to take a picture of a window, hold down Shift>Command>4 plus Caps Lock (after pressing and releasing the key combination, click the window you want to take a picture of).

Finally, if you want to copy a section of the screen or a window to the Clipboard instead of saving it as a file, press the Control key as you select the part of the screen or window.

On the PC, you can use a tool such as Paint Shop Pro for screen capture. Choose File>Import>Screen Capture to set up or perform captures. You select the area to capture by mouse operations, and the result goes into a working window on the Paintshop canvas.

On UNIX, the **import** command, part of the ImageMagick toolset (Section 11.4), is handy for screen captures. Give a command in the form

import *filename.gif*

and you'll be able to select a screen area with the mouse to capture and save as a GIF file. The command can handle most graphical formats.

Small Modifications to Existing Graphics

Resizing   It is always preferable to make changes such as size, color, and file size to the original native files created in Photoshop. For that reason, we recommend storing working graphics in a separate place on the server so that you always have access to them. Unfortunately, we sometimes have to work from existing JPGs or GIFs because we are not provided with a native file. Working in Index Color with GIFs will only give you limited options for editing. JPG images also offer limited options in Photoshop. For more editing options, do the following:

- Save your file as a Photoshop document.
- Change GIFs from Index Color to RGB Color (Main Menu>Mode> RGB Color).
- Change the Background Layer to Layer 0 by double clicking it. This will allow you to choose more options.
- To resize your image, choose Edit>Transform>Scale or Edit>Transform>Numeric.

Adding Borders   Follow these steps to add borders to graphics:

- Select All.
- Select>Modify>Border.
- Specify the thickness of the border in pixels.
- Edit>Fill with any color you wish.

Making Transparent-Background GIFs

To create GIFs, you must convert images from RGB Color to Index Color first. If you're going to place that image on a colored or textured background, you need to make sure that your image contains the background color around the edges of the image so that it will blend in. Otherwise, there will be a highly unattractive "halo" effect around your image. To do this, you have to isolate your image on a transparent background. Figure 11.7 shows the type in a separate layer on a checkerboard background indicating that there is no ink there. When you crop the image, be sure that the black color is cropped along with the image as tightly as possible. Merge Layers. Be sure to retain the native Photoshop file for further editing later. Do not collapse layers in that native file. Choose Index Color. If using lots of complex color, choose Web Palette. If using relatively simple color, let's say fewer than 215 colors, choose Exact Palette in the Index Color dialog box. Then Export the image as GIF. This will allow you to select the background color as part of the new GIF image to gracefully transition the edges to your background color. With the Eye Dropper tool, select the background color. That is the part that will be transparent. If you decide to change your background color, you will most likely have to change your GIF as well, unless the new background color is very similar in value to the first GIF. In the case of Figure 11.8, this may mean you can change to a dark blue or dark gray background without creating a new GIF. Yellow or

Figure 11.7 ISOLATE BACKGROUND FROM FOREGROUND

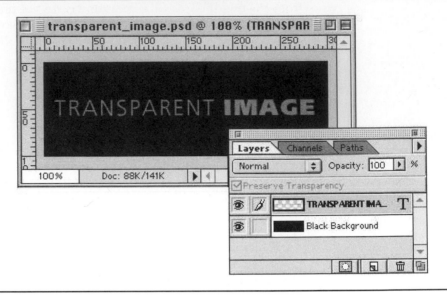

Figure 11.8 CROPPED IMAGE

some other light background would not work because your image edges are black now.

Let's summarize the steps in that process:

- Convert images from RGB Color to Index Color.
- If placing images on a colored background, isolate the image from the background in different layers.
- Crop the image with the background.
- Merge Layers. Be sure to retain the native Photoshop file for editing later.
- Select Index Color. For images with complex color, choose Web Palette, and for simple colors, choose Exact Palette in the Index Color dialog box.

- Export the image as GIF. Notice another dialog box (Figure 11.9).
- With the Eye Dropper tool, select the background color. That background will be transparent.
- Name the file name.gif.

Specifying Bit Depth in Index Color

In addition to specifying the Web or Exact Palette in Index Color, you can also choose Uniform or Adaptive Palette, which allows you to specify the bit depth of an indexed color image. Bit depth, also known as color depth, refers to the number of bits of color information per pixel. It determines the number of colors used to display (or print) an image. For example, if you choose 4 bits per pixel, the image is composed of 16 colors; 6 bits per pixel, 64 colors; 8 bits per pixel, 256 colors. Furthermore, you can specify the exact number of colors to be displayed (up to 256) by choosing Other for Color Depth and entering

Figure 11.9   TRANSPARENCY DIALOG BOX

a value for Colors. The options in the Indexed Color dialog box control only how the indexed color table is created. Adobe Photoshop still treats the image as an 8-bit, 256-color image.

Anti-Aliasing an Image

Anti-aliasing (Section 7.12) gives your images and font types soft edges and smoother transitions to the background (Figure 11.10, right). This is the preferred method of creating, selecting, and copying images. You can set this feature in Photoshop by going to

File>Preferences>General>Anti-alias Postscript

Occasionally, you may not want to use the anti-aliased feature in Photoshop. For an example of this usage on the Web, go to hothothot.com. This entire site was created with aliased images that have the jagged edges characteristic of not blending foreground and background. This was an aesthetic design decision, and it works well in this hot, spicy, hot sauce site. One of the biggest advantages to using aliased images is the file size. Anti-aliased images are significantly bigger than their jagged counterparts. The other time it is preferable to use aliased images is with small type. Text in 9 points or smaller, depending on the type style, tends to look blurry if anti-aliased. For that reason, you may

Figure 11.10   EFFECT OF ANTI-ALIASING (RIGHT)

want to turn that feature off or specify type to be aliased. This feature can be turned off in the type dialog box in most newer versions of Photoshop.

Resizing Images

Photoshop gives you several ways of doing the same function, which may take you a little time to grasp. One way to crop would be to use your cropping tool and resize the image. Be sure that you have Resample Image and Constrain Proportions along with 72 resolution selected. You can also use your Marquee tool to select an area and then choose Image>Crop to achieve the same thing. For best quality, be sure to select the Bicubic option when resizing images. Bilinear and Nearest Neighbor options are faster methods for resizing but do not necessarily give you a better image. Never enlarge 72 ppi images because they will become soft and blurry.

Creating New Graphics for an Existing Web Site

Sometimes designers are asked to create new graphics to match the existing graphics on the site. In other words, designers are not provided with any documentation. So how do we create new graphics to match background color, font style, or some other existing feature? Here are some general guidelines for performing these tasks.

Background Color   Matching the background color in any image is fairly easy. Simply take a screen shot of the existing Web site and open the image in Photoshop. Or download the GIF or JPG images from the Web site to your computer. Open images in Photoshop and convert all Index Colors to RGB. Using the Eye Dropper tool, click on the color you want to match. The matching color will appear in the foreground color inside the Tool Box. Double click the foreground color to open a dialog box, which will give you the Hex and the RGB values of the sample color.

Matching Type Styles   Unfortunately, matching embedded fonts used as graphics to current styles is a challenge, and there is no quick fix to the problem. Designers tend to rely on their type knowledge to guess the name of the font initially and then verify their choices with possible sources. There are literally millions of type foundries on the Internet—from Adobe type fonts to TrueType fonts to any thousand of freeware fonts that could be located anywhere. One way to narrow down your search is to refer back to your five families of type and see if you can narrow down the search by identifying the type as a serif or a sans serif. You can also guess the weight, such as light, medium, or heavy. If it looks similar to something you already recognize, you can examine the

Figure 11.11 ISOLATE BACKGROUND FROM FOREGROUND

letter forms and see if you recognize any feature of the font such as capital Rs or descenders on lowercase gs. This may give you a clue as to what font it is.

Matching Logos Most logos are made up of lines, shapes, and simple colors, which are best created with vector graphic tools. So how do we take an existing logo and place it on a different background or resize it for a different layout? The best solution is to re-create the logo from scratch in a program such as Macromedia FreeHand, Adobe Illustrator, or CorelDraw. In this way, you can reposition the new logo any way you want in your Web site. Begin by downloading the original logo. Import it into a vector graphic program and redraw using shapes and lines. Most of these programs have layers that allow you to place the logo in the bottom layer and redraw the new logo over the old. Save the new logo and import it into Photoshop. Add a new background layer of your choice in Photoshop to match the existing background. See the earlier section on Making Transparent-Background GIFs for placing graphics on a color background. Figure 11.11 shows how to isolate the background from a logo graphic.

11.3 TYPES OF ARTWORK

Original Art or Illustration

Original art or illustration refers to creating, drawing, or assembling your own original images. An illustration can be a drawing, painting, photomontage, or a combination of all three, and it can be produced in a variety of programs such as Adobe Photoshop, Macromedia FreeHand, or CorelDraw.

Figure 11.12 shows a drawing or assemblage of original images. A site that successfully combines photography and illustration (Figure 11.13) can be found at www.hermanmiller.com.

Photography

Photographs for your Web site may be obtained in several ways. You can shoot a photograph yourself with a traditional camera or a digital camera, commission a photographer to shoot an original photograph that will best suit your project, use stock photography, or use royalty-free imagery.

Figure 11.12   SELF-PORTRAIT ILLUSTRATIONS

Figure 11.13   HERMAN MILLER: DESIGN SECTION

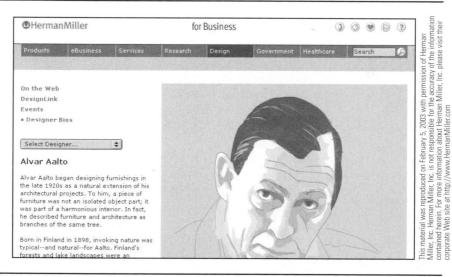

If you choose to commission a professional photographer for your project, be prepared to pay a higher price to obtain the photograph you desire. This option is frequently the most expensive, but it can be well worth the expense. Photographers are generally paid by the hour. Their film expenses and processing fees are added into the overall cost of the job. It is recommended that the fees be negotiated at the onset of the project and articulated in a written contract, which stipulates usage, copyrights, and ownership rights. A professional photographer will shoot the exact image you need. He or she will work with you to customize the end result in a way that no stock photography company can. Photographers are trained to see things in a unique way, and their personal vision, coupled with your art direction, may become a creative force that can change the course of your ideas—something that is often dismissed by the client who may not understand the value of this service. It will require effort to educate the client on this aspect of the project. In the end, your photographer can supply you with a digital photograph on a CD-ROM, a print, or a slide, which you can scan. For Web use, it is recommended that you obtain all the photographs on a CD-ROM with multiple resolutions so that you can use the images at any size you wish.

There are numerous professional photographers who would be happy to help you with your project. One good source for finding photographers in your area is through the American Society of Media Photographers at www.asmp.org.

You may choose to use royalty-free images, which can be obtained online or on a disc. Royalty-free art refers to any art or sound that can be purchased by paying one price and receiving unlimited usage. This means that you can use the image you purchased on brochures, T-shirts, Web sites, and so forth. Unlike stock photography, which requires you to purchase the usage rights, royalty-free images have unlimited usage. These images, which come as both illustrations and photographs, are usually shipped on a CD-ROM or downloaded online. For an extensive list of royalty-free images and a complete list of stock photography companies, go to www.stockphoto.net.

Collages or mixed media are combinations of photographs, drawings, paintings, or other images that you can assemble yourself or commission an artist to create. You can commission a particular artist to create a specific image for you, which can then be scanned and used on your Web site. For example, let's say you were working on a child-care site and your client wanted to post several images that were drawn by preschoolers. You can place the art (let's say that it was created with construction paper and crayons) on the scanner and scan it into your computer. If you did not have a scanner, you can ask your local printer or copy center to provide you with that service.

11.4   TOOLS FOR WEB GRAPHICS: A BRIEF OVERVIEW

This section overviews a number of the most popular programs for creating, editing, and producing Web graphics. The WDP Web site lists additional tools for Web development in the resources section. Popular tools for Mac OS and Windows include:

- Adobe Photoshop
- Macromedia Dreamweaver
- Adobe ImageReady
- Paint Shop Pro
- CorelDraw
- Macromedia Fireworks
- Macromedia FreeHand
- Adobe Illustrator
- Gif Construction Kit
- ImageMagick
- Xfig
- Imaptool
- Adobe GoLive

Adobe Photoshop and Macromedia Dreamweaver

We regard these as the primary tools for Web development. Much has been already discussed about creating graphics and processing images in Photoshop (Section 11.1). The Dreamweaver IDE for integration of layout, HTML code, CSS, and graphics will be presented in Sections 11.8 and 11.11.

Adobe ImageReady

ImageReady is now shipping with Photoshop 7.0. The two applications have always been completely integrated, but with the latest version of Photoshop, they are part of the same package that comes on one CD. ImageReady is a good image-editing tool for optimizing files for the Web, but many users prefer Fireworks's cleaner interface and seamless support for both vector and bitmap objects.

Since Photoshop and ImageReady ship on the same CD, you install both applications simultaneously. Inside Photoshop, you can jump to ImageReady with one click of a button. ImageReady has some of the same tools as Photoshop, but in addition, you will find Animation, Image Map, and Slice palettes at the bottom of ImageReady's screen and a Rollovers palette on the left. Like Fireworks, ImageReady's workspace window allows you to optimize images and preview your document in different file formats and compression rates.

Once you've created your graphics, you can make slices, image maps, rollovers, and simple animations. You can convert images to GIF or Quick-Time animations. Version 7.0 has a new Rollovers palette that displays all the rollovers, image maps, animation sequences, and slices you have added to your document. Unlike Fireworks, which works with both vector and bitmaps, ImageReady is most comfortable with bitmaps. Thus, if you want to create interactive buttons or other graphics, you must use an external program that has polygon or other custom shape tools.

ImageReady is also a little clumsy in the way it handles layers. If you want to add effects to your graphics such as drop shadows, you apply Layer Styles, but because ImageReady objects aren't true vector objects, every time you edit, you create a different layer. Some of the advanced features are a little confusing compared to Fireworks. To perform simple animations, you need to maneuver through layers, slices, frames, states, and objects. Because of this, many users prefer Fireworks's cleaner interface and elegant performance.

Paint Shop Pro

Jasc's Paint Shop Pro is a good-quality, economically priced photo editor. Paint Shop Pro can do many of the things Photoshop can do. It has basic drawing and painting tools, works with layers and layer modes, and accepts a variety of file formats. In addition, you can perform special effects with filters and adjust colors through Color Adjustments and Adjustment Layers. Web graphics tools include JPEG/GIF/PNG Optimizer, image slicing, mapping, and rollover creator. Visual Browser, Multiple-level Undo/Redo, and Batch File Format Conversion allow you to speed up production or graphics in general. For the price, this is a very capable tool with good online support.

Jasc makes a variety of products that can help your Web design and production, such as After Shot, Quick View Plus, Web Draw, and Virtual Painter. For more information, go to www.jasc.com/products/psp.

CorelDraw

CorelDraw 11 is an easy-to-use vector graphic program with a clean interface and easy-to-use tools. Version 11 adds several new illustration tools and better import-export filters. One of the disadvantages to the program is that it has difficulty handling complex files. The strength of the program is the ability to create your own toolbars, menus, and macros as you work and then save that customized workspace for specific tasks. For example, if you build lots of flowcharts, you can design an interface that puts all the most important flowchart tools right at your fingertips.

CorelDraw is not typically used by most professional designers. Most designers use Illustrator or FreeHand to create complex vector illustrations, but CorelDraw has a basic set of tools that work for many tasks. Version 11 introduces a few new tools, including pressure-sensitive smudge and roughen brushes that blur and texturize object outlines, import-export filters that let you open files from other applications such as Photoshop and Illustrator, and symbol support, so you can save artwork to a central library.

Unfortunately, most tools do not respond as well as similar tools in Illustrator or FreeHand. Overall, the work performance is sluggish.

Macromedia Fireworks

Fireworks is both a Windows and Macintosh platform tool for creating, editing, animating, and optimizing Web graphics. Fireworks combines both bitmap and vector editing tools. One of the strengths of the program is being able to automate the workflow to meet the demands of updates and changes.

Since Fireworks is a Macromedia product, it integrates well with both Dreamweaver and Flash. Graphics created in Fireworks export easily with HTML and JavaScript codes. In addition, images and HTML code created in Fireworks automatically update within tables in Dreamweaver.

An important feature in Fireworks is batch processing. This is a convenient way to automatically convert groups of graphic files. In batch processing, you can select from the following options:

- Convert a selection of files to another format.
- Convert a selection of files to the same format with different optimization settings.
- Scale exported files.
- Find and replace text, colors, URLs, fonts, and non-Web216 colors.
- Rename groups of files by adding a prefix or suffix.
- Perform commands on a selection of files.

The latest version of Fireworks, Fireworks MX, has lots of new features that improve its overall production capabilities. The integration between Dreamweaver and Fireworks has been significantly improved. There is now a full range of both bitmap and vector tools to choose from. The bitmap, merge down capability provides more flexibility when creating and managing bitmaps. Some of the other updates include the newly upgraded Property Inspector, which allows easy changes such as stroke, fill, and effect all in one place, and Data-driven Graphics Wizard, which allows you to connect graphics files with XML files to automatically generate graphics. Full XHTML compliance ensures that sites are up-to-date with the latest standards in HTML design by configuring Fireworks MX to generate XHTML code.

Macromedia FreeHand

Macromedia FreeHand, a multiplatform, vector graphic program used by illustrators and Web designers, has evolved into a more Web-friendly production tool in the last few versions. It is an excellent tool for creating line illustrations, storyboards, and layout graphics. You have many options for exporting images for use on the Web. Formats available include BMP, DCS EPS, EPS, HPGL, JPG, PDF, Photoshop, Targa, Text, and TIFF.

For designers and illustrators, FreeHand has added features such as true contour gradients, new pen tools, master pages, smart cursors for automatic joins, and an editable symbol library.

Adobe Illustrator

Adobe Illustrator is a vector graphic program that performs functions similar to Macromedia FreeHand. In fact, many professionals in the design industry use these two programs interchangeably. Although the interface looks and behaves much like its sister product, Adobe Photoshop, the actual tasks that you would perform in creating images are more similar to FreeHand. The latest version of Illustrator, Illustrator 10, has added some new type and drawing tools that increase production and speed up the illustration process. Tools such as enveloping and warping and compound-shape controls to create complex shapes along with the ability to create symbols for repeating graphics to keep the file sizes small attract many professionals in the design industry.

Illustrator 10 also adds a few Web-savvy features such as:

- Vector and raster-based slicing and slice-by-slice optimization
- Enhanced Flash (SWF) support, SVG import, and enhanced export Editable SVG effects
- Scripting support to automate repetitive tasks
- Compound-path compatibility to cut and paste compounds between Adobe Photoshop and Illustrator
- Rollover and animation information preserved in linked Photoshop files

Gif Construction Kit

Gif Construction Kit will help you create animated GIFs and much more. This shareware program is available for download at

www.mindworkshop.com/alchemy/gifcon.html#download

GIF Construction Set Professional is touted as the state-of-the-art animation software which can assemble your original animations through its Animation Wizard, compress files to minimal size, add transparency to existing graphics, and manage your GIF files. Other features of this program include:

- Animated transitions between still images.
- Rotate, crop, color-adjust, and resize all or part of an animation sequence.
- Convert animated GIF files to AVI for use with PowerPoint.

- Create rotating two-dimensional animated graphics.
- Drag and drop between multiple document windows.
- Reverse the order of the images in a GIF file.

ImageMagick

On UNIX systems, ImageMagick is a set of command-line and visual tools for image and graphics processing. With ImageMagick, you can read, write, manipulate, and convert images in almost all major image formats (more than 80 formats), including PNG, GIF, JPEG, PDF, and Photo CD. Here are some things you can do with this freeware program (www.imagemagick.org/):

- Convert images from one format to another (e.g., JPEG to GIF):

  ```
  convert file1.jpg file2.gif
  ```

- Perform screen capture in any supported formats.
- Create a montage of image thumbnails.
- Create transparent images suitable for use on the Web.
- Draw shapes or text on an image as well as decorate an image with a border or frame.
- Produce animated GIFs and create a composite image by combining several separate images.
- Resize images:

  ```
  convert -sample widthxheight+x0+y0 file1.jpg file2.gif
  ```

  The command samples the JPG image starting at ($x0, y0$), resizes to the given dimensions, and produces the resulting image in GIF format. The *display* command provides an X-windows GUI with buttons and menus for the many functions provided by ImageMagick, including rotating, sharpening, blurring, increasing or decreasing contrast, color reducing, and special effects.

The group of commands supplied by ImageMagick include **display**, **animate**, **import**, **montage**, **mogrify**, **convert**, and **combine**.

Also available are interfaces to ImageMagick for popular programming languages such as Perl, C++, and Java. You'll find many Linux systems come with ImageMagick installed.

Xfig

Another useful tool on UNIX is **xfig**. It is an X-windows-based interactive drawing program. The strength of Xfig lies in its treatment of figures as objects such as texts, lines, arrows, circles, ovals, rectangles, polygons, boxes with curved corners, and so on. The drawing mode allows you to enter text and draw figures. In the editing mode, you can modify every aspect of the figures as well as move them to different positions on the canvas.

Each figure has its own depth setting that controls how it overlaps. Thus, each figure object is in its own layer. Xfig saves in its own native .fig format but can export to almost all of the popular graphics formats, including GIF, JPG, and PNG.

You can also import images into an Xfig composition and add text and drawings on top of them, making it simple to add captions or annotations to existing diagrams.

Xfig is usually installed on UNIX systems. You can also download it free from www.xfig.org/.

The `imaptool`

The `imaptool` is a simple UNIX tool to help create client-side image maps (Figure 2.19). When applied on a GIF or JPEG image, `imaptool` allows you to draw a rectangle, circle, or polygon on the image and builds the HTML code for an `area` element. The code can be pasted directly into another application, such as a text editor. You can obtain this free tool from www.sspitzer.org/imaptool.

Visit the WDP Web site for links to graphics and other Web development tools.

11.5   COLOR ADJUSTMENTS

Which tool to use is less important than understanding the graphics processing tasks to perform. Let's begin with color adjustments.

Making photographic tonal value (dark and light) and color (red, green, and blue hue) adjustment for print can be a complicated task, and in many cases, designers hire color correction experts to do this work, especially for high-visibility projects such as annual reports or corporate identity brochures. In the last 10 years, to save time and money, many designers have done this work themselves in Photoshop. For simple black-and-white or two-color projects, which require minimum touch-ups, color corrections in Photoshop are relatively easy and don't require extensive color knowledge. When preparing images for the Web, the color adjustments are easier yet because you don't have to deal with printing or resolution issues. Whatever you see on the screen is generally what you get on the Web. Unfortunately, you still have to deal with other issues such as image size and cross-platform and browser display issues.

Whether we choose to change color for aesthetic reasons or adjust the tone in poorly scanned images, Photoshop provides many options for changing color and tonal adjustments. Photoshop devotes a large portion of their Help files to color and tonal correction, touching on such basics as tonal changes, mixing channels, highlight, midtone, shadow adjustments, and many others. Be sure to read this section for all the details. Numerous how-to books have been written on color correction and tonal correction techniques, as well as dramatic color effects in Photoshop. For that reason, we do not discuss these topics here. However, we do discuss some of the simplest and most effective methods to familiarize you with the basics of color and tonal correcting. Most of the tonal and color correction options are available by going to the menu and selecting the Image>Adjust>Choose option.

Tonal Adjustments

- Image>Adjust>Auto Contrast—Adjusts the highlights and shadows of an image automatically.
- Image>Adjust>Brightness and Contrast—Allows you to manually adjust the brightness and contrast.
- Image>Adjust>Auto Levels—Adjusts the midtones of an image automatically.
- Image>Adjust>Levels—Allows you to manually adjust the midtones.

Color Adjustments

- Hue>Saturation—Adjusts the hue, saturation, and lightness of individual color components in an image which relies on the color wheel. Adjusting the hue, or color, represents a move around the color wheel. Saturation (purity of the color) represents a move across its radius. Use this command to Colorize a gray scale image to simulate a duotone image by reducing color values to one hue.
- Desaturate—Removes all the color from an RGB image and makes it black and white.
- Replace Color—Replaces color in an image by creating a mask based on specific colors in the image. You can adjust the hues, saturation, and lightness values. The mask is temporary, and it is used only in this instance (Figure 11.14).
- Channel Mixer—Modifies a color channel using a mix of the current color channels. This command is used for specialized, creative adjustments and making sepia tone or tinted images.

Tonal Adjustment: Auto Contrast

Auto Contrast allows you to adjust contrast (darks and lights) automatically by remapping the darkest and lightest pixels in the image to black and white, which makes the highlights appear lighter and the shadows appear darker. The remapping is done by removing the white and black pixels by 0.5 percent, which disregards the first 0.5 percent of either extreme when identifying the

Figure 11.14   COLOR REPLACEMENT

lightest and darkest pixels in the image. This clipping of color values ensures that white and black values are representative areas of the image's content rather than extreme pixel values. This feature can be used as an all-purpose color adjustment for most scanned images with moderately good results. To use it, select Image>Adjust>Auto Contrast. For details, see the Photoshop Help file.

Tonal Adjustment: Brightness and Contrast

Brightness and Contrast is another simple feature that allows you to adjust the highlights and shadows in your images for a quick improvement. Slide the triangles to the left or right of the bar and see the difference in your images. Once you have made the appropriate adjustment, click OK and save your image after adding green (complement color) in Color Balance (Figure 11.15).

Figure 11.15   REDDISH SCAN AND COLOR ADJUSTMENT

© Sanda Katila

Tonal Adjustment: Levels and Curves

These two powerful features—Levels and Curves—are primarily used by professional color technicians to set the highlights and shadows in images by assigning their lightest and darkest CMYK ink values to the lightest and darkest areas of detail in the image. In print, designers need to be concerned with specific light and dark values to ensure the quality of the printed photograph. For example, highlighted areas need to have some level of printable dots to define highlights without going to specular white. Specular white has no detail, and so no ink is printed on the paper. A spot of glare is considered specular white, not a printable highlight. In general, Web designers do not have to concern themselves with these issues because images for the Web are not prepared as they are for print. (Type Levels and Curves in Photoshop Help file for more details.)

To modify midtones without setting target values (such as in print), use either the Levels or the Curves feature. In Levels, move the triangles to the left or right; in Curves, stretch the line on the matrix to see immediate results in your image.

Color Adjustment: Color Balance

The Color Balance feature allows you to adjust the RGB or CMYK values in highlights, midtones, and shadows by sliding triangles to the left or right in the Color Balance dialog box (Figure 11.16). In Figure 11.15, the original scan of a photograph has a magenta (reddish) cast over the entire image. To correct this, you can add or subtract colors in the image. In this case, green, a complement

Figure 11.16   COLOR BALANCE DIALOG BOX

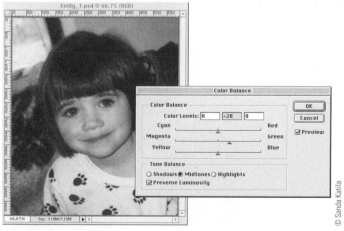

© Sanda Katila

of red, was added to the image to neutralize the magenta in the midtones. This produced a more even effect in the image (right side in Figure 11.15).

11.6 TYPICAL IMAGE PROCESSING TASKS

To provide concrete examples for raster graphics image manipulation, let's look at common tasks and how to perform them in Photoshop.

Isolating Image from Background

Isolating images from their backgrounds to remove the unwanted background or to combine images is a typical task performed in Photoshop, and for that reason, it is described in detail in this section.

To isolate the image from the background, you need to select only the portion that you want or, in this case (Figure 11.17), the portion you don't want. Select the Magic Wand tool and click the gray background. Then choose Select>Inverse to deselect the background, and select the image of the girl. In this case, the task of selecting the background was easily accomplished because the background is an even value of gray, and the Magic Wand tool easily selected the gray pixels. In many cases, selecting unwanted backgrounds and removing them from the photograph may be more difficult (Figure 11.18).

Figures 11.18 and 11.19 illustrate a more complex process of isolating the image from its background. In this example, the background is uneven in value. This means that the background value is patchy and largely consists of similar values as the foreground image of the girl you're trying to select. This mix of values make the selection more difficult because the Magic Wand tool is designed to select similar values. This can be adjusted by choosing the

Figure 11.17   SELECTING AN IMAGE WITH THE PHOTOSHOP MAGIC WAND TOOL

© Sanda Katila

Figure 11.18   SCAN, SELECTION, AND VALUE ADJUSTMENT

Figure 11.19   QUICK MASK MODE, STANDARD MODE, AND FINISHED PHOTO

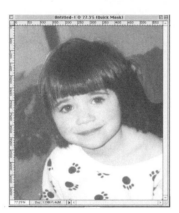  

"tolerance range" on the tool. This tolerance option ranges from 0 to 255 pixels. Zero will target similar pixels, and higher numbers will target a broader range of colors. (See the Photoshop Help file for details.)

To facilitate the selection process, we changed the contrast in the image before selecting any pixels. Figure 11.18 was achieved by adjusting the Brightness and Contrast inside Levels controls. (For a detailed explanation of these levels, see the Photoshop Help file.) Once the contrast was adjusted, we were able to use the Magic Wand tool to select more accurately the pixels in our target image. In addition to the Magic Wand tool, we used the Lasso tool to select as many of the pixels around the girl as we could. After a certain point, it becomes very difficult to accurately select organic shapes, such as hair. For this reason, we toggled from the Standard mode to the Quick Mask mode, and we painted the curvy, difficult to reach places with a paint brush. To locate the Quick Mask mode, see Figure 11.20.

Quick Mask Mode

Figure 11.19 illustrates how the Quick Mask mode works. Quick Mask is found at the bottom right of the toolbar. This mode allows you to "paint in" or "paint out" the areas you want selected or deselected in your image (Figure 11.20). When finished working in this mode, toggle back to the Standard mode to see your selection. Figure 11.19 shows how the painted areas in the Quick Mask mode look in the Standard mode. Finally, to get the white background achieved in Figure 11.19, we "feathered" the selection Menu>Select>Feather 3 pixels to get a soft edge. Then choose Select>Inverse to pick the background and fill it with white ink.

Figure 11.20   TOOL PALETTE IN PHOTOSHOP

Working with Layers

Photoshop gives you the flexibility to edit imported, original, or scanned images in layers quickly and efficiently. Layers are versatile; they allow you to edit each element of your graphic independently so that you can experiment, draw, paste, and reposition elements without affecting other layers. Photoshop lets you create up to 100 layers in an image, each with its own blending mode and opacity for exciting effects (Figure 11.22).

In Figure 11.21, we see the three elements that comprise the square face, where images are positioned in separate layers called "line drawing," "white color," "pink color." Let's examine this image more closely. We need to point out that the square face was originally created in Macromedia FreeHand. Although this image could be created in Photoshop, sometimes it is easier to draw geometric lines in a vector program such as Adobe Illustrator or Macromedia FreeHand. In the square face image, the vector graphic was saved as an EPS in FreeHand and opened in Photoshop at 72 ppi. This automatically rasterized the image and placed it into a layer on a transparent background. Transparent backgrounds in Photoshop mean that layers contain only the pixels that make up the image and nothing more. This transparency is indicated with a checkerboard pattern. (See Figure 11.21, top layer called square face, where the square face layer is positioned on top of the pink layer.) Remember that layers in Photoshop begin with top down, meaning that all the top layers are on the bottom layer. Transparency can also be turned off or on in Photoshop depending on what tasks need to be done.

Figure 11.21   SQUARE FACE IMAGE WITH LAYERS

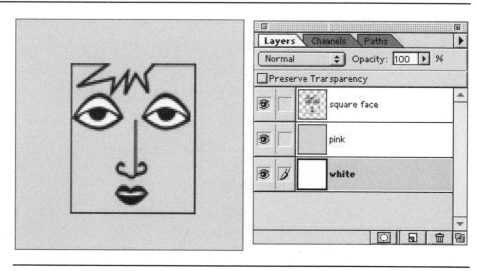

Figure 11.22   BLENDED LAYERS IN PHOTOSHOP

© Senda Katila

Working with Filters

Another common and easy-to-use feature in Photoshop is Filters. Filters allow you to select an area or the entire image and apply any filter located under Filters in the menu bar. Figure 11.23 was created by selecting (with a Rectangle Marquee tool) a portion of the face and applying the Note Paper filter (Filter>Sketch>Note Paper) to the top and bottom. The spiral image was created in FreeHand and brought into Photoshop as an EPS. The spiral was originally black, but it was changed in Photoshop to white. To change the color of the vector graphic, after it appears in the Layer's palette, you follow these steps:

- Open vector graphic in Photoshop.
- Select Preserve Transparency.
- Fill with white ink. To fill with the foreground color, press Alt+Backspace (Windows) or Option+Delete (Mac OS).

Adjustment Layers

One of the easiest ways to make color adjustments to individual layers is with the Adjustment Layers feature. Adjustment Layers allow you to isolate portions of the image and change color balance without permanently altering the original pixels (Figure 11.24). Adjustment Layers are on top of the specified layer like a piece of glass on the original layer, allowing you to make color corrections without damaging the pixels below. Adjustment Layers give you the option to change Levels, Curves, Brightness/Contrast, Color Balance, and Hue/Saturation. To confine the effects of an Adjustment Layer to a single layer below it, you'll need to create a Clipping Group of only those two layers. There is more on Clipping Groups in the next section.

Figure 11.23 **SPIRAL FACE LAYERS**

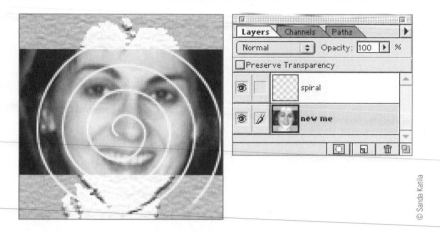

© Sanda Katila

Figure 11.24 **GREEN FACE: COLOR ADJUSTMENT IN PHOTOSHOP**

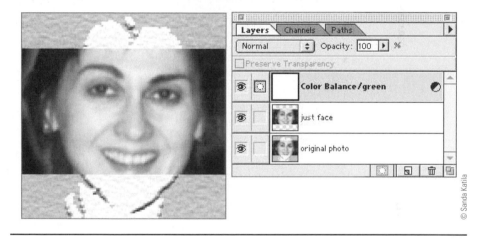

© Sanda Katila

Correcting or changing color is simple with Adjustment Layers (Figure 11.24). To create this green effect, we went through the following steps:

- Select the portion of the face to isolate it on a separate layer. Use the Marquee tool to select, copy, and paste.
- Upon pasting, a new layer will automatically be created with the copied image in place. In Figure 11.24, that layer is called "just face."
- To the right of the Layer's window, click to select New Adjustment Layer. A dialog box will appear with several options under Type.
- Select Color Balance and move the Magenta slider slightly to the Green (left) side until you get the desired effect.

Figure 11.25   GREEN FACE: CLIPPING GROUP

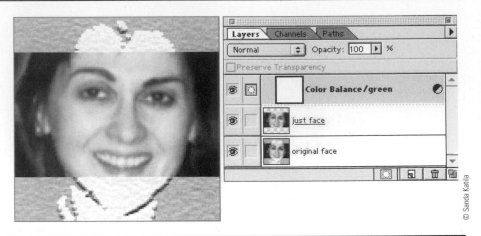

© Sanda Katila

Clipping Groups

Clipping Groups allow you to use the bottommost layer, or base layer, to act as a mask for the entire group. (See the Photoshop Help file for more on Clipping Groups.) For that reason, we were able to isolate the Color Balance layer only to the "just face" layer, allowing the green color to affect only the single layer below. If you look closely, you will see the "just face" layer is underlined in Figure 11.25, designating it as the base layer for the group. The Clipping Group feature has been used to isolate the color balance to the "just face" layer only. Notice that the "original face" layer is not affected by the color balance.

To create a Clipping Group, you do the following:

- Hold down Alt (Windows) or Option (Mac OS), position the pointer over the solid line dividing the Color Balance/green and "just face" layers in the Layers palette (the pointer changes to two overlapping circles), and click.

- Dotted lines appear between the grouped layers. Notice that the base layer name is underlined, and the thumbnails for the overlying layers are indented.

11.7 DESIGNER-PROGRAMMER COOPERATION

The best way to collaborate is to keep all the team members involved at every stage of the site creation process and to communicate constantly about ideas and choices as well as to report progress and project status. An email list server and a draft project site are effective ways to keep the information flowing and available. In addition to reporting ideas, choices, and progress, each team member is responsible for checking email frequently and for monitoring the draft Web site. Prompt reporting of new ideas, suggestions, and concerns is the responsibility of every team member, not just that of the team leaders.

To help streamline the site production process and control the design unity and programming consistency, we suggest the use of *templates* for the entire site. A template is a visual outline of where elements are positioned on a page accompanied by a set of instructions on how to use the template. So, if a banner appears on every page of a particular section, that space is always occupied by a certain graphic. If the logo appears on each page in the left corner, that space is also taken. The rest of the layout, which may contain inline graphics and text, can also be drafted so that each section is consistent. A good template may also contain information about the position of rollovers, forms, and links. Along with the template, it is advisable to have a style sheet for each section so that it can be followed by both designers and programmers. If copywriters are brought in on a project, they will also know where the body text will go, along with suggested subhead, headlines, and section titles. So while designers are working on graphics and templates, programmers can be writing scripts and programming forms. Although each team may proceed according to its personal plan, there are some plans that work better than others. The following procedure is one system that may work for your project.

11.8   FROM LAYOUT DESIGN TO HTML CODE

For the next two sections, we use our own book's Web site as an example to show how HTML code for the layout and graphics design is created and produced using Dreamweaver. Once you create your layout design in Photoshop, you will need to cut the single Photoshop document with layers into smaller JPGs or GIFs and place them into a layout grid defined in Dreamweaver.

When cutting files in Photoshop, it is strongly recommended that you have a good idea of how your table will lay out before cutting any graphics. You should have a basic understanding of how many rows and columns the table or tables will have, whether a graphic is going to be in the foreground or would work better as a repeating background, which cells are going to span multiple rows or columns, and which cells, if any, are going to stretch and how. In this way, you can cut your images and place them directly in Dreamweaver tables.

You can cut your own images in Photoshop and label and place them in Dreamweaver into your own custom-made table. It is recommended that you select Document Relative links rather than Root Relative in Dreamweaver. This will generate links relative to the document in your HTML code, making it easier to move the generated files to a hosting site. (See Section 2.16 for more on relative links.) Dreamweaver allows you to create layers that can be moved inside a layout, allowing you to reposition images wherever you like. Then, you can convert those layers into tables. This is one method for working in Dreamweaver. Again, be sure to check your source code often. Layers often overlap or don't align properly, creating unnecessary rows and columns, complicating source code, and making editing cumbersome.

Another option, which many designers use for cutting images, is *slices*. Slices are parts of the image that can be used as table cells. A slice is a rectangular area of an image that you can use to create links, rollovers, and animations in your Web page. You can create user slices with the Slice tool or from guides and, in ImageReady, a companion software to Photoshop, from a selection. The slices for our book site were created using guides. Simply add guides to an image. Select the Slice tool, and click Slices from Guides in the options bar. When you create slices from guides, any existing slices are deleted. Images created in Photoshop may be cut in Photoshop or in ImageReady, which among many capabilities creates slices. Our book site home page was created using guides, allowing Photoshop to automatically cut the image into cells based on these guides (Figure 11.26).

ImageReady, by default, assigns names to slices with the file name prefix and a sequence number, such as homepage_1, homepage_2. This is impractical if you are going to rely on default settings. The good news about slices, both

Figure 11.26   SLICES IN PHOTOSHOP

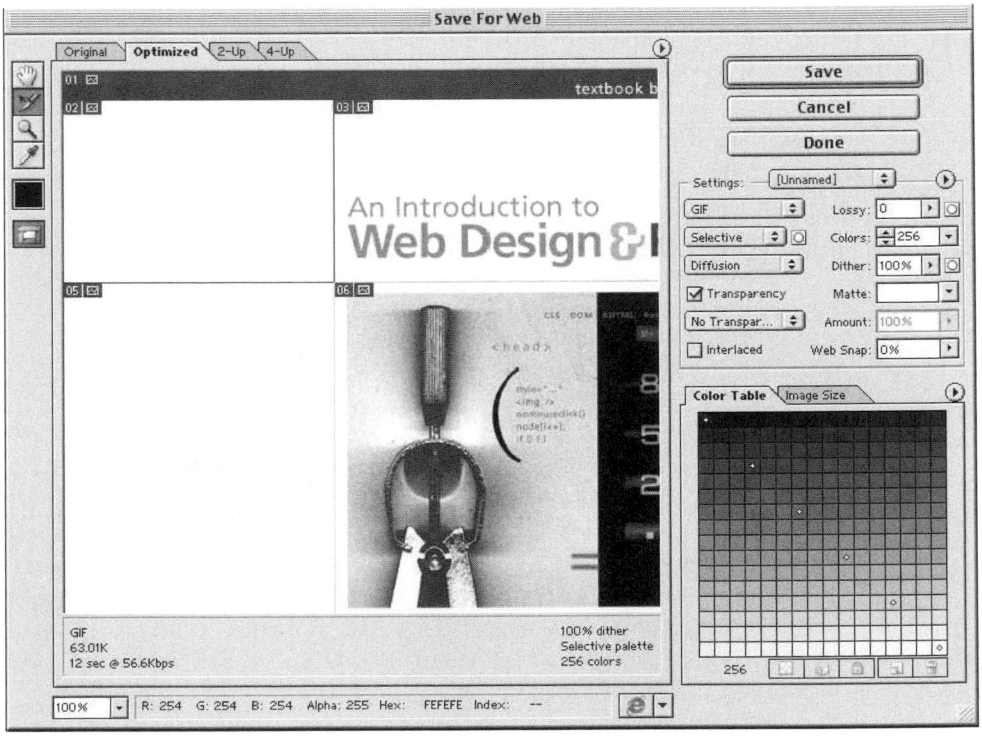

in Photoshop and ImageReady, is that you can edit these names within the application with relative ease. You can also designate which files to save and which slices to ignore while saving. Both ImageReady and Photoshop interpret slices as images, including text and negative spaces, creating large images consisting of nothing. However, you can choose to ignore text and negative space cells and only generate the cells you want.

Depending on your work preference, you can mix and match various Photoshop features with hand-coding. For our book site, we decided to hand-code the black bar. We placed a small black GIF into the background table cell as a repeating graphic, which was the simplest way to solve the problem. The rest of the images were created with slices and placed into the HTML document (Figure 11.27).

Save for Web Feature in Photoshop

Once the image is cut into slices, you can use the Save for Web (File> Save for Web) command to optimize each part of the image. Slices can be made into links, rollovers, and animations in your Web page. Each slice saves its own settings, color palette, links, rollover effects, and animation effects. For example, if one area of an image needs to be optimized in GIF format to support an animation, but the rest of the image is better optimized in JPEG

Figure 11.27   BOOK SITE HOME PAGE

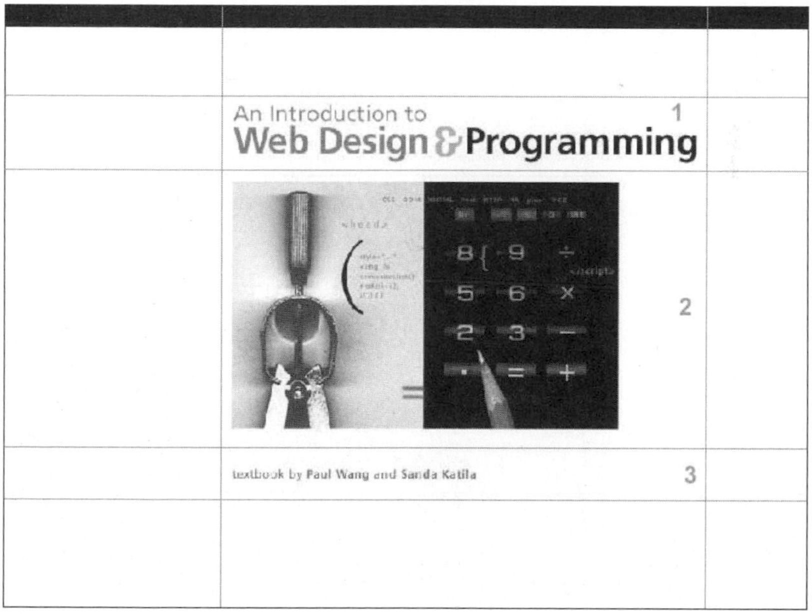

An Introduction to
Web Design & Programming

textbook by Paul Wang and Sanda Katila

© Sanda Katila

format, you can isolate the animation using a slice (Figure 11.26). When you save an optimized image as a Web page, you can specify how HTML files are formatted, how slices are named, how files are named, and how background images are handled. You set these options in the Output Settings dialog box.

For our purposes, we're going to create slices to place into our HTML or drop them into Dreamweaver. Photoshop generates several types of slices that all look different. User slices and layer-based slices are defined by a solid line, and auto slices are defined by a dotted line.

- User slices—Slices created using the Slice tool.
- Layer-based slices—Slices created from a layer.
- Auto slices—Slices created when part of the image is defined neither by layer nor user slices. These are generated every time you add or edit user slices or layer-based slices.
- Subslice—Type of auto slice that is generated when you create overlapping slices.

Dividing, combining, linking, and setting options for auto slices automatically converts them to user slices. This option is preferable because it keeps your slices intact so they will be unaltered if you regenerate the slices.

Figure 11.28   SLICE OPTIONS IN PHOTOSHOP

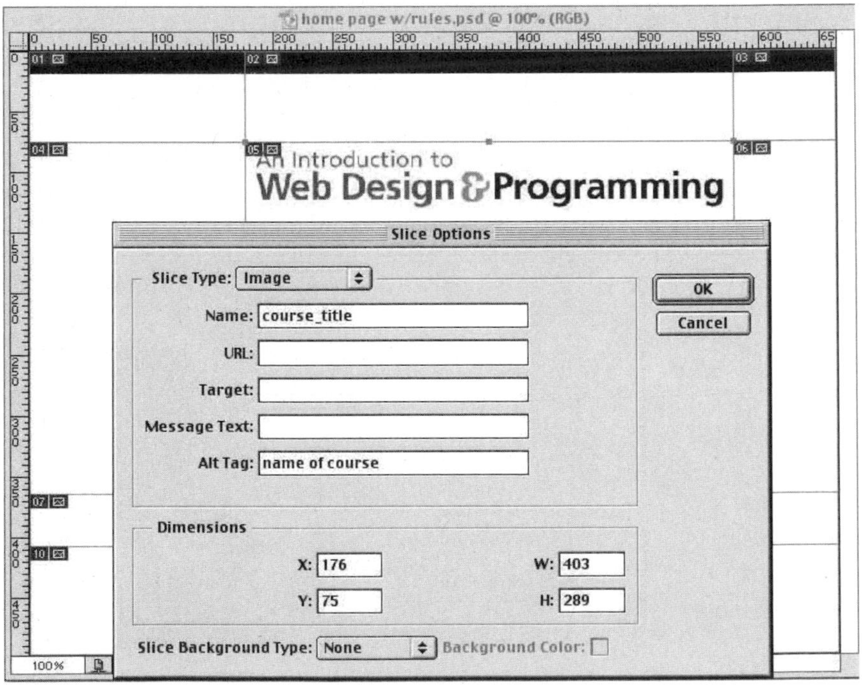

Figure 11.29   INFO PALETTE IN PHOTOSHOP

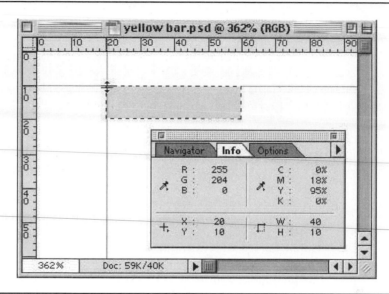

If you wish, Photoshop (or ImageReady) can generate HTML code for aligning slices, using either tables or cascading style sheets. You also have the option to name slices in the Setting output options dialog box.

Photoshop allows you to link slices. Select the slice and put in the URL in the User Slice dialog box (Figure 11.28). Be sure that you understand the difference between slice links and image map links. The main difference between using image maps and using slices to create links is in how the source image is exported as a Web page. Using image maps keeps the exported image intact as a single file, but using slices causes the image to be exported as a separate file. Another difference between image maps and slices is that image maps enable you to link circular, polygonal, or rectangular areas in an image, whereas slices enable you to link only rectangular areas. If you need to link only rectangular areas, using slices may be preferable to using an image map.

Placing Images into Dreamweaver

Once your images are cut and labeled, they can be put in Dreamweaver tables. To ensure that your images are cut to the exact size you wish in Photoshop, you can rely on the Info Palette. Info Palette shows you the width and height of the area selected, the RGB and CMYK colors used, and most important, the x and y coordinates of your image in relation to the canvas (Figure 11.29). This allows you to precisely place and crop your image. Be sure to use your guides to help you align elements (Figure 11.30).

Figure 11.30   USE GUIDES TO ALIGN IMAGES IN PHOTOSHOP

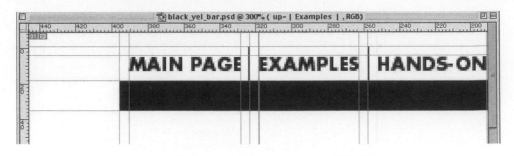

You will need to refer to your approved layout and decide where to best position each image. You may need to expand rows and columns to get the table that best serves your layout. Dreamweaver MX stores all your documents in one root folder on your local directory. It keeps templates and graphics in a separate directory. Your CSS and HTML documents will reside in this one folder during development. Once the site is finished, it can be uploaded to your server.

Text can also be easily manipulated in Dreamweaver using layers (Figure 11.31). Simply create a layer and then type. Text can be imported from other source files from various applications using the Import command and can be assigned attributes such as size, style, and color, which are easily edited.

Figure 11.31   DREAMWEAVER: IMAGES AND TEXT IN LAYERS

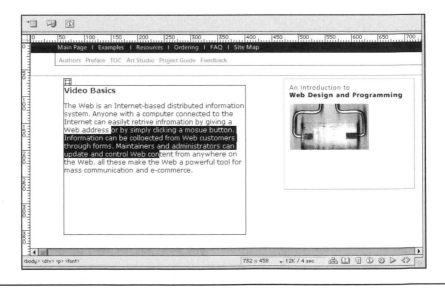

Figure 11.32   LAYERS CONVERTED TO HTML TABLES

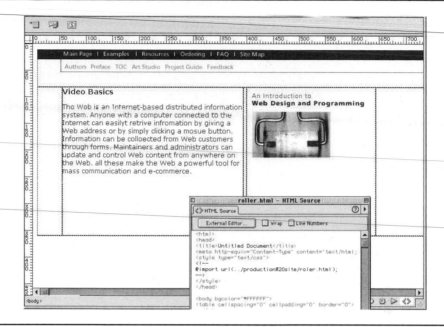

Dreamweaver allows you to alter your own HTML documents as you develop your pages, which can be displayed directly in the application (Figure 11.32).

11.9   GUIDE ON RULES AND LAYOUT TABLE

When placing guide rules in Dreamweaver to implement the layout grid designed for your pages, keep the following points in mind:

- Dreamweaver will generate an HTML table based on the guides placed.
- Each box formed by the guide rules becomes a table cell. Neighboring cells will be displayed next to each other without added spacing. Often the grid calls for cutting a graphic image into several parts for alignment purposes.
- Contents in each table cell are by default left aligned horizontally and middle aligned vertically (Section 3.5) but can use other available cell content alignments (Section 3.3).
- If you are piecing together images in the layout table, see Section 6.17 for information on eliminating gaps and keeping the images together.
- Because table cells may span multiple columns and/or rows, you should eliminate unnecessary box boundaries to minimize the number of table cells created. For example, a row of empty cells should become

one cell that spans the entire row. Similarly, a column of empty cells (e.g., below a navigation bar on the left of the page) can become one cell that spans several rows. If this column takes up a percentage of the available page width, then it can help the fluidity of the page.

- To prevent fluid empty space from collapsing completely, you can place tiny clear or white graphics images in such empty cells and specify the desired minimum width as the image width:

```
<td style="width:10%">
<img src="tiny_clear.gif" width="60" height="1"></td>
```

The same clear GIF can be used as a filler or spacer in all your pages to minimize file downloading. Alternatively, you can use an invisible horizontal rule element (hr) as a filler or spacer

```
<hr style="width:60px; height:1px; color: white;
border-style: none">
```

where you must match the color of hr with its background.

- In making a fluid grid to fit different browser window sizes and screen resolutions, keep in mind that the widths of boxes in the grid are not fixed but represent their relative proportion in the browser window. The generated table cells will have widths set to percentages rather than fixed lengths.

- Fluid grids often use background colors or images to eliminate white space and help the grid expand or shrink with window sizes

Figure 11.33 FINISHED LAYOUT IN PHOTOSHOP

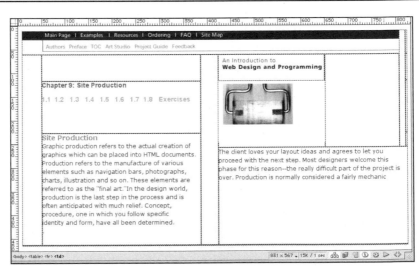

Figure 11.34   LAYOUT CONVERTED TO A TABLE IN DREAMWEAVER

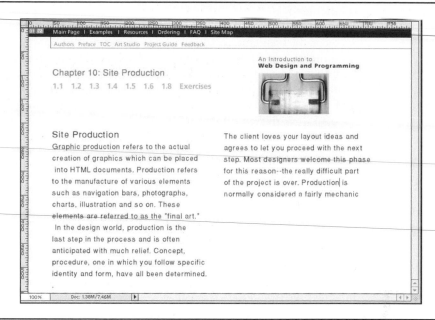

(Section 6.18). The background color and/or image can be set for the whole table, individual rows, and individual cells. The design of elastic banners and other scalable graphics will have taken this into account already. And the placement of grid guides will follow the elasticity built into the design.

- When a grid starts from the very top of the page, the `margin-top` property of the `body` element must be set to 0.

- It is a good idea for a grid to have left, right, and bottom margins to provide appropriate negative space for a page. A consistent `margin-bottom` setting for `body` is a great way to supply a consistent bottom margin for all pages. Side margins can be achieved through margin settings for the `body` element or through empty table cells. The former approach affects the entire page, whereas the latter can provide side margins where needed.

11.10 ROLLOVER NAVIGATION BARS

The navbar is often an important part of a page. The decision to use a rollover navigation bar is made at the design stage. Thus, the rollover navbar is conceived in the same spirit and conceptual context as the rest of your Web site.

The aim of all design is the integration of elements following a consistent theme.

As mentioned in Section 9.6, a rollover hyperlink usually involves three images: the base image, the mouseover image, and the page-id image. Sometimes it makes good sense to have the mouseover image perform double duty as the page-id image. In any case, a navbar consists of a good number of individual rollovers. The look and feel of a rollover navbar cannot be fully visualized just by looking at a model page. At the design stage, we need to construct page visuals with the rollover navbar in its different states to ensure that the images have good readability and combine well. Furthermore, the whole navbar must remain compatible with the page design.

A rollover navbar involves much more than swapping individual images. It presents a kind of mouse-triggered animation that provides feedback to the user to enhance the feeling of responsive navigation control. Thus, the designer must be mindful of the dynamic aspect of the navbar and its purpose of making navigation easier. Design details for a rollover navbar may not always come together in the original thumbnails or first draft comprehensive layouts. For many, the dynamics of the navbar may only become clear through experimentation.

Take the WDP Web site navbar as an example. The first series of layouts strove to achieve simplicity by using clean geometric lines (Figure 11.35). The Frutiger typeface contrasted well with these simple forms. The navbar is at the top of a fluid layout that shifts with window size, leaving a generous left margin and allowing for the full bleed of the bar on the right.

For the rollover effect, experiments were conducted to test shape compatibility (Figure 11.36) and readability through color and value adjustments (Figure 11.37).

Several ideas later, the final navbar was born. It has defined rectangles at the top and simple words below, reversed on a black bar and separated by bullets. Futura bold replaced Frutiger for increased readability and better

Figure 11.35   **INITIAL NAVIGATION BAR DESIGN**

Figure 11.36   **NAVBAR OPTION: TABS**

Figure 11.37   **TRIAL ROLLOVER COLORS**

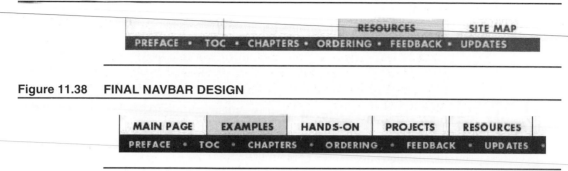

Figure 11.38   **FINAL NAVBAR DESIGN**

display in the black bar. In this example, each rollover involves two images with the mouseover image doubling as the page-id image.

In testing the animation or dynamics of the navbar, we look for the feel of navigation clarity and control following the mouse. An image should appear "armed" or "charged" on mouseover and "unarmed" or "discharged" on mouseout. The image for the current page must never appear armed under the mouse. The rollover images must be aligned precisely to avoid unwanted movements in the navbar. Careful attention to type size, kerning, and value goes a long way to ensure that your rollovers assist rather than distract the viewer. In the final design, the WDP Web site navbar is set in Futura bold with 25 points of kerning added so that the letters did not appear too close together. An additional 75 points of kerning was added to the reversed type in the bottom bar to create the same effect. Thorough testing of the rollover feature is critical to ensuring success in the navigation bar.

Rollovers in Dreamweaver

Tools such as Dreamweaver can help create HTML and JavaScript code for rollovers and rollover navbars. To create a basic rollover in Dreamweaver, choose

Insert>Interactive Images>Rollover Image

This opens a dialog where you can specify the Original Image, Rollover Image, Alternate Text, and the target URL. To make a complete navbar, choose

Insert>Interactive Images>Navigation Bar

This will insert your rollovers in a layout table. In the Insert Navigation Bar dialog, you have have more options that include naming each element and choosing the Up Image (base), Over Image (mouseover), Down Image (clicked), Over While Down Image (mousedown). You also have the option to preload images (Section 9.5) for faster loading.

It is often the case that the code produced by Dreamweaver must be hand-tuned to conform to XHTML and to have the desired dynamic effects. Designers and programmers on the project team must work together closely to achieve the best results.

11.11   CREATING CSS IN DREAMWEAVER

Creating CSS in Dreamweaver is easy and logical. You can begin by requesting a style file (File>New>CSS Style Sheets), or you can work on any page such as a template or HTML page and attach a new CSS to that. It is always best to link CSS pages to all your documents instead of to a single page. In that way, you can update all pages in your site globally.

Dreamweaver lets you style HTML tags, make custom styles, or use the CSS selector. If you style HTML tags, you will make the changes to your site almost instantly. Dreamweaver also lets you make your own custom tags, which can be combined with HTML tags for a comprehensive CSS. This is highly recommended.

Dreamweaver allows you to specify many CSS declarations, such as `background-color`, `font-family`, and `margin-top`. If you need all of these choices, fill in your preferences. If not, it is best to leave options blank so that your code does not become congested. Specify pagewide styles such as `color`, `background-color`, `font-family`, `font-size`, and margins once for the `body`. The color and font styles will be inherited by tags contained in the `body`. Or they can specify their own styles. Chapter 6 presents CSS at length.

In general, you will have minimal hand-coding in the new MX Version of Dreamweaver. The code is clean and easy to understand. Attaching the style sheets to various pages in your site is easy. Just select Attach Style Sheet in the bottom right corner of your CSS dialog box and find the file. Styles will be automatically updated in every HTML document that has the CSS link.

Creating a Style

Create a CSS style to automate the formatting of HTML tags or a range of text identified by a class attribute. To create a CSS style:

- Choose Window>CSS Styles and in the CSS Styles panel, right-click (Windows) or control-click (Macintosh), and choose New Style from the pop-up menu. You can also click the New Style icon found at the bottom of the CSS Styles panel.
- Choose from the following CSS style options:
    Custom Style (Class) creates a style that can be applied as a class attribute to a range or block of text.

Redefine HTML Tag redefines the default style of a specified HTML tag. Keep in mind that you can alter the layout of many pages when you redefine a tag.

Use CSS Selector to define the formatting for a particular combination of tags or for all tags that contain a specific id attribute.

- Enter a name, tag, or selector for the new style:

Custom style (class) names must begin with a period. If you don't enter the period yourself, Dreamweaver enters it for you. These names can contain any combination of letters and numbers, but a letter must follow the period. An example is .myhead1.

To redefine an HTML tag style, enter an HTML tag or choose one from the pop-up menu. For a CSS selector, enter any valid criteria for a selector (Section 6.4) or choose a selector from the pop-up menu. The selectors available from the menu are a:active, a:hover, a:link, and a:visited.

Select the location in which the style will be defined: New Style Sheet File (external) or This Document Only.

Click OK. The Style Definition dialog box appears.

Choose the formatting settings for the new CSS style. Leave attributes empty if they are not important to the style.

Attributes that do not appear in the Document window are marked with an asterisk (*) in the Style Definition dialog box. Some of the CSS style attributes that you can set with Dreamweaver appear differently in Microsoft Internet Explorer 4.0 and Netscape Navigator 4.0, and some are not currently supported by any browser.

Click OK or Apply.

When you create a custom (class) style, it appears in the CSS Styles panel and in the Text>CSS Styles submenu. HTML tag styles and CSS selector styles do not appear in the CSS Styles panel because they cannot be applied; they are reflected in the Document window automatically wherever the tag or selector occurs.

Dreamweaver recognizes styles in all existing documents as long as they follow the CSS guidelines. CSS works in 4.0 and later browsers. IE 3.0 recognizes some CSS, but most earlier browsers do not.

There are three types of CSS in Dreamweaver (Figure 11.39):

- Custom CSS styles—For specifying the style attribute of individual HTML elements. Use this only for special cases or exceptions to the overall page styles.

- HTML tag styles—For attaching style rules to HTML elements with HTML tag-name selectors such as body, h1, p.

- CSS selector styles—For more complicated style rules involving other forms of CSS selectors (Section 6.4) you wish to specify.

Dreamweaver also allows you to create and link to external style files.

Figure 11.39 CSS IN DREAMWEAVER

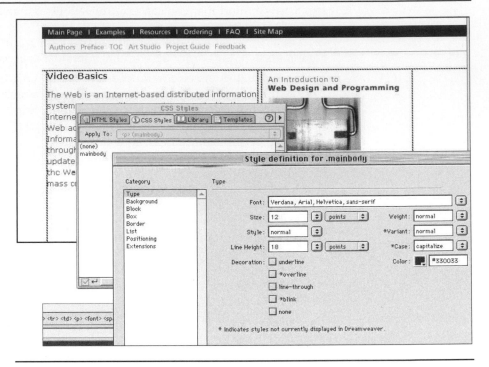

11.12 PAGE TEMPLATE PRODUCTION

A template is a skeleton HTML file that can be edited to easily produce a set of unified Web pages. Code generation tools such as Dreamweaver support the creation and use of templates for producing Web pages.

Before beginning template production, you should know the following:

- Know what the layout will look like. Know how the space will be used, such as the placement of text and images, headers, footers, and all margins. Look at your document in Photoshop. Place guides to indicate where the image will be cut into pieces that go into cells of the HTML layout table.

- Know how you will treat text. Decide on font (Helvetica, Times, Verdona, etc.), style (bold, italic, underline, etc.), alignment, and color of text. Be sure to do that for all the text such as body copy, headlines, subheads, photo captions, and copyrights.

- Know ahead of time which texts will be graphics based (e.g. in GIF) instead of being simple text strings in HTML. Keep in mind that texts as graphics are cumbersome to edit and change. Use them sparingly.

- Determine how the layout will convert into a table. Strive to use the space as economically as possible, omitting unreasonable cell breaks without altering original layout.

- Know which elements will remain constant and which will be variable, such as the headers, copyrights, images, rollovers, and so on. This is vital in template creation because designating fixed areas is the cornerstone of template creation. Templates are crucial in building consistency throughout the site.

The Objective of Template Production

The main objective of templates is to help you create unified, consistent layouts. In Dreamweaver, for example, you can create a set of templates (.dwt files) that can be used as a foundation for building your entire site. Templates make it easy to build Web sites because you can edit the same template to produce pages that are all similar.

The two most important things you should know when creating a template is which elements remain constant (noneditable) and which can be changed. For example, if you are publishing an online magazine, the master head probably won't change, but the title and content of the feature story will change with every issue. To indicate the style and location of the feature story, you can use placeholder text and define it as an editable region. To add a new feature article, the writer selects the placeholder text and types the article over it. You can modify a template even after you have used it to create documents. Then, when you update documents that use the template, the locked (noneditable) sections of those documents are updated to match the changes to the template.

Designer-Programmer Interactions

Does it make sense for designers to generate HTML and .gif files and then turn the files over to programmers to hand-tune the HTML, fit the graphics, and test the result on multiple browsers? Is it possible then for templates to be revised, allowing designers to produce more graphics within the revised code? What really works in practice?

There are no steadfast rules for creating templates. There are some designers who are more sensitive to programming issues and are quite competent when it comes to cleaning up code in Dreamweaver. There are programmers who are sensitive to layout issues and will use discretion when cutting images and placing them in appropriate spaces. As a general guideline, however, Dreamweaver generates fairly clean code, and most designers can create their own templates, logically constructing the various levels of pages for the site. It is strongly suggested that programmers review this work and clean up inefficiencies and discrepancies in the code. There's little doubt that this step can save programmers time on the project. This step is also important because it helps to convey a designer's choices, which can sometimes be difficult to explain, thereby aiding in communication. More complex code, beyond HTML and simple rollovers, as well as CGI, forms, and dynamic content should be created by programmers. After the programmers have revised the template, it can go back to the designers who may continue to develop subsequent pages. Extensive testing in all major browsers is still a must and should be standard procedure regardless of who creates the templates.

In general, the latest version of Dreamweaver, Dreamweaver MX, creates fairly clean code. However, you need to be careful when constructing templates because hard returns or inaccurate layers converted into tables will show up in your code. For the best results, it is advisable that you continually examine your code when creating pages. Remain in both code and layout view at the same time. When in doubt, change the code to obtain the desired results.

Creating Templates with Dreamweaver

Open a new document and be sure to specify that it is a template. Dreamweaver will automatically generate basic code for a template that resembles Figure 11.40.

Create your tables as you would any other HTML document. Then, specify repeating regions that will appear throughout the site and regions that can be edited (Figure 11.41).

Figure 11.42 shows the example.html page produced from our level-one template. The presentation style is defined in several style files (Ex: **BookStyle**).

Figure 11.40   DREAMWEAVER-GENERATED CODE

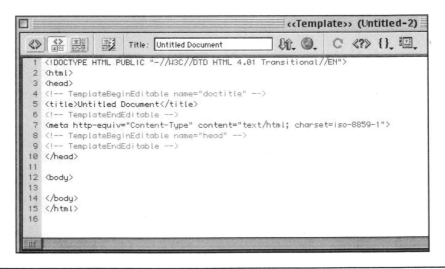

Figure 11.41   DREAMWEAVER-GENERATED CODE AND LAYOUT

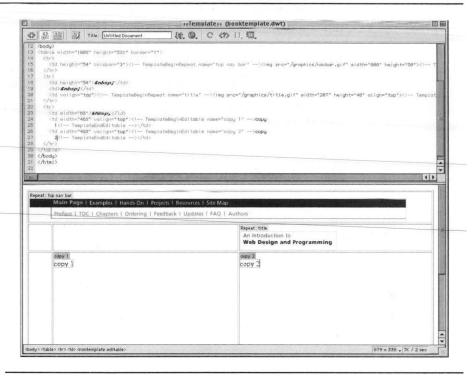

The abbreviated style sheet is as follows. (See Ex: **BookStyle** for the complete CSS code.)

```
body
{  font: small Verdana, Geneva, Arial, helvetica, sans-serif;
   color: black;    border: none;
   background-color: white;
   background-image: none;
   margin: 0px  0px  30px  0px;      /* bottom margin set */
}

input, button, menu, select, menu, option
{ line-height: 120%; }

h1, h2, h3, p, li { line-height: 150%; }

h2                                   /* in-page heading   */
{  font-weight: bold;
   text-transform: capitalize;
```

Figure 11.42   TEMPLATE-PRODUCED PAGE

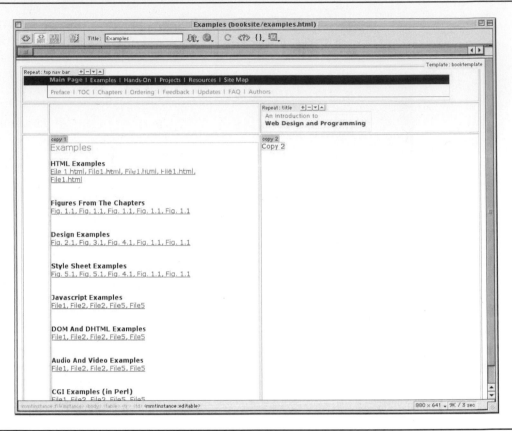

```
        color: #666;
        font-size: medium;
}

h2.red {  color: #933; }              /* page-top heading */

strong.heading                        /* subhead          */
{ font-weight: bold; display: block; }

img.anchor {  border-style: none;  }
```

Because IE does not handle line-height inheritance correctly, we needed to add the line labeled for IE.

The level-one template (Ex: **TemplateOne**), generated with the help of Dreamweaver MX, is used to produce the code for main.html. To make this an

XHTML template, we have added the required initial lines (lines 1 and 2). In the template source, editable parts are marked between begin and end editable comments. For example, the page title should be entered for each new page created from the template (lines 3 and 4). The content description and keywords, robot instructions (Section 3.14), file names for style sheets (Section 6.1), and JavaScript program (Section 9.2) to include can be edited appropriately for each page to be produced (lines 5 and 6). The page body preloads navbar images (line 7).

A four-column table (line 8) implementing a fluid layout grid follows. The first table row provides the left margin (for the entire page A) and the top rollover navbar.

The left margin for the page is 10 percent of the available space but at least 60 pixels (line 9). The page begins with a rollover navbar (575 pixels) composed in the first two table rows (lines 10 and 11). The right margin is set at 35 percent, and a black bar continues the navbar through the full bleed of the page (line 12).

The fluidness of the rollover banner comes from the percentage widths of the columns and the use of background images for the table cells. For example, bg.gif is a tiny 2 by 39 image that, when repeated horizontally, produces the end of the banner. Using this image as the background for the middle and right cells ensures seamless display as the browser window changes size or resolution.

```
<?xml version="1.0" encoding="UTF-8" ?>                     (1)
<!DOCTYPE html PUBLIC "-//W3C//DTD XHTML 1.0 Strict//EN"
    "DTD/xhtml1-strict.dtd">
<html xmlns="http://www.w3.org/1999/xhtml"
      xml:lang="en" lang="en">                             (2)
<head>
<!-- TemplateBeginEditable name="Page Title" -->           (3)
<title>Main Page-Web Design and Programming Textbook</title>
<!-- TemplateEndEditable -->                               (4)
<meta http-equiv="Content-Type"
      content="text/html; charset=utf-8" />
<!-- TemplateBeginEditable name="Style Sheet" -->          (5)
<meta name="description"  content="content description" />
<meta name="keywords"  content="keyword1, keyword2,..." />
<meta name="robots"  content="index, follow" />
<!-- <meta name="robots"  content="noindex, nofollow" />
-->
<link href="bookstyle.css" rel="stylesheet"
      type="text/css" />
<script type="text/javascript" src="filename.js"></script>
<!-- TemplateEndEditable -->                               (6)
</head>
```

```
<body onload="preloadImages();">                                    (7)
<table width="100%" border="0" cellpadding="0" cellspacing="0"> (8)
<tbody><tr valign="top" style="line-height: 0px;">
<!-- page left margin begin -->
<td style="width: 10%; height: 21px" rowspan="5">               (9)
<hr style="width:60px; height:10px; color: white;
    border-style: none" /></td>
<!-- page left margin end -->
<!-- navbar begin -->
<!-- top bar begin -->
<td colspan="2" style="width:575px; height: 21px;             (10)
    white-space: nowrap"> (one row table of rollovers) </td>
<td style="width:35%; height: 21px"> </td></tr>
<!-- top bar end -->
<!-- bottom bar begin -->
<tr valign="top">                                             (11)
<td colspan="2" style="width:575px; white-space: nowrap;
    background-image: none; background-color: black">
(one row table of rollovers)</td>
<td style="width:35%; background-image: none;
    background-color: black"> </td></tr>                 (12)
<!-- bottom bar end -->
<!-- book title begin -->                                      (13)
<tr valign="top">
<td style="width:445px"><img src="white.gif" width="445"
    height="10" alt="spacing" /></td><td style=
    "height:35px; width:189px" align="right"><a class="imglink"
    href="index.html"><img class="anchor" src="tt.gif" width="189"
    height="26" alt="Intro to WDP"/></a></td>
<td style="width:30%"></td>
</tr>                                                          (14)
<!-- book title end -->
<!-- Page title begin -->
<tr><td style="width:445px" valign="bottom">
<!-- InstanceBeginEditable name="Page title" -->              (15)
<h2 class="red" style="display: inline; vertical-align: bottom">
1st-level Page Title</h2>
<!-- InstanceEndEditable --></td>
<td valign="bottom" style="height:80px">
<!-- InstanceBeginEditable name="Page image" -->              (16)
<img src="img/hands.jpg">
<!-- InstanceEndEditable -->
</td><td></td></tr>
<!-- Page title end -->
<tr valign="top">
<td colspan="2"><div class="pagecontent"><br />
```

```
<!-- Page content begin -->
<!-- InstanceBeginEditable name="Page Content" -->        (17)
<p>page text page text page text</p>
<p>...</p>
<!-- InstanceEndEditable --></td>                         (18)
<!-- Page text end -->
</div><td style="width:30%" valign="top"></td></tr>
</tbody></table></body></html>
```

The second table row displays the book title on the right side just below the top banner (lines 13 and 14). The third table row contains the editable page title (line 15) and page identification image (line 16). The last table row is for the page content. You edit the editable part (lines 17 and 18) to enter the content for any particular page.

Furthermore, notice that the template contains fixed parts. If you make many pages from this template, you are better off putting the fixed parts in separate files and including them using SSI or PHP (Section 3.19).

Producing an effective and clean template requires a high degree of integration between design and programming.

Grids, Tables, and Templates

We discussed layout grids in Chapter 5. How does template production relate to grid design? Which comes first? What are the interactions between these two steps? Grids are determined in the layout process and then produced the way they were conceived in the production process. It is the underlying grid that becomes part of the table. Grids come before tables. One would not create a table and force the elements in the layout into a table. Rather, the grid is part of the overall design for the site. It works with the home page as well as all the subsequent pages in the site. Therefore, a designer will set up tables in Photoshop as part of the production process and align the elements on that grid. When transferring the grid to Dreamweaver, designers follow the same grid into another program. The only difference is that sometimes these grids have to be adjusted to be compliant with cells inside the tables. It would be unreasonable to divide the table into little "chopped up" pieces simply because a designer wishes to move the image over 0.5 pica. Some concessions will have to be made for the sake of efficiency. Ultimately, though, good designers will reconcile the differences without sacrificing aesthetics or the integrity of the design.

11.13   SAVING ORIGINAL FILES AND WORKING GRAPHICS

As you develop your graphics and convert them into JPGs and GIFs, keep in mind that Web sites are modified and updated frequently. New links, new graphics, new pages, and new content may be added during the life of a site, which you or someone else may be doing. You need to save all original Photoshop files, as well as any other Dreamweaver or FreeHand files, and retain adequate documentation for efficient upkeep. For example, you need to know such things as the font family, size, and the exact background colors used. Here are a few key points to note:

- Keep all original files in one folder and name it something like Working Graphics or Original Files.
- When working in Photoshop, keep all layers intact, especially the layers that provide type information such as font name, style, size, leading, tracking, color, and anti-alias.
- Be sure to keep all the original scans and images that contain the RGB color and hexadecimal equivalents. Be able to identify the colors used in your images. In this way, if you need to match any colors to background and type, you will be able to do so easily.
- When combining imagery to make one composite graphic, be sure to keep the original components of that graphic. If clients change their minds and request newly constructed graphics, you will be able to rebuild the new image with all the necessary parts.
- Keep all the original tool-produced files such as Dreamweaver and FreeHand (Section 11.4) files.
- Keep all the templates and style sheets.
- Do not save over the originals. Save As or make a duplicate file before opening to ensure that you don't accidentally rewrite over the original files.
- Document the locations and purposes for the saved files. Create a Readme.txt file for each folder where such files are saved.

11.14 SITE DEPLOYMENT

The graphics production efforts are based on the site information architecture, the content-only pages, the artistic design, and layout grids. The results of graphics production are individual graphics, images, and HTML page templates together with associated style sheets.

Site production then proceeds to apply the templates and generate individual pages for the site. Fixed parts, such as page headers and footers, common to many pages are placed in separate files to be included in actual pages (Section 3.19). The resulting page prototypes are placed on the draft site, replacing the content-only or rough layout pages.

Client-side and server-side programming are now integrated with the pages. The draft pages are reviewed on different platforms using different browsers and window sizes/resolutions. Unforeseen problems with font size, image and background colors, and layout grids may be exposed at this point. Adjustments are made accordingly.

Extensive testing of the draft site comes next. The XHTML and CSS code can be validated (Sections 3.22 and 6.23). Hyperlinks can be checked with a tool such as `linklint` (www.linklint.org), which exposes incorrect and broken links in a site, or an online service such as that at NetMechanic (www.netmechanic.com). Spelling checks, proofreading, testing of form operations and JavaScript code, and measuring and improving page loading speed are also tasks to perform.

The final draft site is presented to the client for review and comments. Any revisions and adjustments are made.

Once done, the draft site can be uploaded to the actual Web site for deployment. Once deployed, registration with major search engines is done immediately. It can take a few weeks for your registration to take effect. Also ensure the `description` and `keyword meta` tags (Section 3.14) are completed appropriately to help Internet search engines classify your site.

When maintaining and updating the site, the changes are first applied to the draft site, reviewed, and tested. The final revised pages can then be uploaded from the draft site to the deployed site. It is important to keep the draft site synchronized with the actual site. The draft site also serves as a backup site.

11.15   SUMMARY

Web site production can be a challenging and rewarding process. It is exciting to see the pages come together and displayed in the browser. The process is the result of collaboration among programmers, designers, and other team members to make this happen. Effective communication among all team members is vital for success.

Web site production is a combination of programming and graphics creation. It produces pages for building the desired site. The production process implements and integrates the site design and layout, information architecture, navigation structure, graphics, pictures, and perhaps other media content.

Image processing tools, such as Photoshop, and page generation tools such as Dreamweaver, help the site production task. Concrete results include image files, HTML files, and style sheet files. For larger sites, template files can be produced first. The templates can then be used and edited to include page content for various pages in the site. Results of this production phase will then be integrated with client-side scripting (JavaScript) and server-side programming to make the site fully dynamic and functional.

Results from the production process described in this chapter can be tested and then combined with client-side and server-side programming to complete the site development. The work requires close cooperation of designers, programmers, and other team members.

Be sure to make the files produced well-documented and easy to maintain and update. After all, you may be the person who will be doing this work. So invest the time initially and do it right.

EXERCISES

Review Questions

1. How do you scan a printed image? How is it different from scanning continuous tone photographs? What are continuous tone photographs? What is a Moiré pattern? How does it occur? Try scanning a printed image. See if you can follow the steps outlined in this chapter to minimize the Moiré pattern.

2. What is the difference between Exact Palette, Web Palette, and Uniform Palette in Index Color? Why is this important?

3. What is anti-aliasing? Why is it significant in making images for the Web?

4. What are transparent-background GIFs? Why are they important and how do you make one in Photoshop?

5. What does it mean to resample an image in Photoshop? Why is this significant when making images for the Web?

6. How do you match a color in Photoshop?

7. What is the best way to re-create a raster image as a vector graphic? What program would be most appropriate for this task? What is the best way to create an exact duplicate logo? List the steps you would take to do that.

8. What is the difference between a photograph and an illustration? In what instance would you choose to use an illustration?

9. List the steps you would take in getting images from a digital camera into your computer.

10. What is the difference between Auto Contrast and Brightness and Contrast adjustment in Photoshop?

11. What is the difference between using Levels and Curves in Photoshop?

12. What are midtones? What are shadows and highlights?

13. In balancing color in photographs, it is sometimes suggested to add a complementary color. Why?

14. What are the steps in isolating an image from the background in Photoshop? Why would you need to do that?

15. What is Quick Mask mode in Photoshop and how is it commonly used?

16. What are layers in Photoshop? Why are they significant? How do you place images into layers?

17. What does it mean to have a transparent background in Photoshop? Why is this important?

18. What does it mean to Preserve Transparency in Photoshop?

19. What are Clipping Groups in Photoshop? What do you do with them? How can you tell if layers have Clipping Groups?

20. What is the relationship between designers and programmers in Web design?

21. What are templates in Web design? Why are they important?

22. What is the primary objective for creating templates?

23. Summarize the steps in template production.

24. What is the relationship between grids, tables, and templates in Web design? In what order would you create each one and why?

25. How do you cut images in Photoshop to place inside tables? Explain the steps in this process.

26. What steps do you take to get an image from Photoshop to Dreamweaver?

27. What are layers in Dreamweaver? How are they helpful in creating tables? How can they be edited?

28. What steps do you take to create CSS in Dreamweaver?

Assignments

1. Try scanning a few ordinary objects on the scanner such as a magnifying glass, a plate, matches, or a pocketknife. Open the files in Photoshop and combine them in an interesting way. Experiment with color, layers, filters, and other features.

2. Take an image and adjust color and tone using options such as Auto Contrast, Brightness and Contrast Levels, and Curves and Color Balance.

3. Try resizing and adding borders to an existing JPG or GIF image.

4. Take a poorly scanned photograph and apply tonal adjustments to improve the quality of the image. Take note of the changes in your image. Notice how each type of adjustment affects the image in a different way.

5. Take a black-and-white image or remove color from a color photograph. Try adding color using adjustment layers.

6. Take a finished design and layout in a tool such as Photoshop and transfer it to Dreamweaver for generating HTML code and the associated style sheets. Record the steps you have to go through and show the intermediate and final results.

7. Refine the process you used for Assignment 6 and produce an XHTML template for all similar pages instead of the HTML code for a single page. How much can a tool such as Dreamweaver help? How much hand-tuning of the automatically generated code is needed?

8. Use the template you produced in Assignment 7 and generate XHTML pages with it. How useful is the template? List any improvements in the template you find. Refine your template production process to produce templates with the improvements in the first place.

CHAPTER 12

Audio and Video

A Web page can be far more than text and images. Audio, video, animation, and other media content can be added to make the Web a very versatile and effective communications medium.

Serving audio and video on the Web involves understanding digital encoding formats, file compression, clip delivery, and embedding in Web pages. Delivering original content also involves creating, editing, and preparing the media files. Creating audio, video, animation, and other multimedia content requires skills and professional training, much of which is beyond the scope of this text. However, we do provide some material for producing simple audio and video files. We also show how to make Flash animations, an effective way to bring a new dimension to your Web sites.

The material here introduces these topics, allows you to deliver audio, video, and animation on your site, and provides a foundation for further studies in this exciting direction.

12.1 A BRIEF HISTORY OF AUDIO AND VIDEO ON THE WEB

The Web is a brand new communication medium, but throughout history, humans have been using many different kinds of media to convey messages and exchange ideas. Prehistoric humans painted images on the walls of their caves (including a narrative composition) in the Grotte de Lascaux, France (15,000–13,000 B.C.). From the invention of early relief printing by the Chinese (third century B.C.) to the first publishing on the Web (1990s), it has been a long and winding journey.

During the 1980s, the Graphics Interchange Format (GIF) for images was made popular by the company Compuserve. Before this period, most of the information transmitted between computers was text. In the mid-1980s, the MP3 sound format was introduced by Fraunhofer Institute in Germany, and a few years later, it became part of the MPEG standard. In 1995, RealAudio brought streaming audio to Web users. Streaming video soon followed. Now many audio and video file formats exist, and standards are being developed as well.

More recently, systems have been developed for delivering a combination of text, pictures, audio, and video/animation to provide a *multimedia* experience on the Web. The Synchronized Multimedia Integration Language (SMIL) at the W3C and Flash from Macromedia are at the forefront. Flash uses vector graphics to make animation faster and enjoys popularity among many Web developers.

Who can predict what the Web will be like 50 to 100 years from now? Two things seem clear: It will be hardly recognizable by today's view, and it will completely integrate technology and programming with design and art.

12.2 DESIGNING MULTIMEDIA

Audio and video are just two more design elements that can help support your message on the Web. As with any other components, such as text and graphics, sound and moving images can add another dimension to your site. However, before you begin adding multimedia, ask yourself a few important questions:

- Why am I adding audio and video to my site?
- Do I need either one to deliver my message?
- Did my client ask for it? Why?
- Will multimedia make my message more stimulating or do I simply want motion on my site?

There are many practical reasons for wanting to use multimedia on your site. You may want to show how something works or demonstrate a function that can best be done with video. Entertainment and news sites obviously rely on multimedia to deliver their content. For commercial sites that require maximum speed and efficiency, enhancing the look with motion and sound may not necessarily be the best solution. However, if you do decide to include a video clip or a sound clip in your Web site, here are some basics.

12.3 AUDIO ON THE WEB

Sound adds another dimension to a Web site. The advent of the highly compressed but high-quality MP3 format has led to an explosion of music sites on the Web. Used appropriately, voice and other audio effects can make a site more functional and attractive.

Technically, audio refers to sound within the human hearing range. An audio signal is naturally a continuous wave of frequency and amplitude. Thus, most audio is analog and must be digitized to be played back on a computer. A continuous audio signal (e.g., coming from a microphone) can be digitized by *sampling* and *quantization*. The continuous sound wave is sampled at regular time intervals, and the values at each sampling point are quantized to discrete levels. The data are stored in binary format as a digital audio file. The higher the sample rate and the greater the bit depth (number of quantization levels), the higher the sound fidelity and the larger the file size.

12.4   SAMPLING AND QUANTIZATION

Figure 12.1 shows the meaning of audio sampling. Assume the audio signal has the highest frequency F. To represent the signal faithfully, the sampling rate must be at least $2F$. This is the so-called *sampling theorem*. Human hearing is limited to a range of 20 to 20K Hz (cycles per second). Thus, the CD-quality sampling rate is often 44.1K Hz. Human speech is limited from 20 Hz to 3K Hz. An 8K Hz sampling frequency is high enough for telephony quality audio.

Figure 12.2 shows the most basic *pulse code modulation* (PCM) encoding using 4-bit data for amplitudes. CD-quality audio uses 16-bit amplitude. Hence, CD-quality sound requires, for each stereo channel, 44.1K × 16 bps (bits per second). Telephone quality sound needs only 8K × 8 bps, less than 0.05 the size of CD-quality sound file sizes.

Figure 12.1   AUDIO SAMPLING

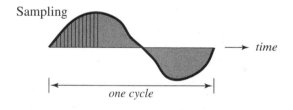

Figure 12.2   AUDIO QUANTIZATION

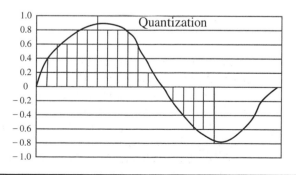

12.5 AUDIO COMPRESSION AND FILE FORMATS

Audio files can be large and time-consuming to transmit over the Web. Reducing the sampling rate and/or bit depth can shrink the file size. Many audio files found on the Web are mono rather than stereo and have a low sampling rate. Such techniques reduce the file size by degrading sound quality.

Various *compression schemes* have been devised to reduce file size while preserving sound quality. The uniform PCM uses a fixed or linear quantization step. A-law (U.S. ISDN) and μ-law (European ISDN) compression use a logarithmically increasing step achieving four-sevenths compression over linear PCM. *The Adoptive Delta PCM* represents changes in amplitudes achieving one-half compression over A-law or μ-law PCM. These schemes are often used in telephone and teleconferencing applications. There are many different audio *codec* (compression-decompression) schemes resulting in various file formats (Table 12.1). Before the time of MP3, Real Audio, and other modern audio formats, AU, AIFF, WAV, and MIDI accounted for most of the sound files on the Web.

- AU (Sun/NeXT audio)—A common compressed file format originally developed on UNIX systems.

- AIFF (Audio Interchange File Format)—A common audio format used by the Mac OS. The format does not support compression and tends to produce large files.

- MIDI (Musical Instrument Digital Interface)—A format for instrumental music. The format does not contain sound wave data. Instead, the file contains instructions for sound cards to reproduce notes from different musical instruments. Hence, MIDI files are tiny when compared to standard audio files.

- WAV (RIFF WAVE)—A format developed by IBM and Microsoft. It is a common audio file format for Windows and the Web. WAV files may be

Table 12.1 AUDIO FILE FORMATS

Filename Suffix, Format	Type	Origin
.au or .snd	audio/basic	NeXT, Sun
.aif(f), AIFF AIFC	audio/x-aiff	Apple, SGI
.mid, MIDI	audio/midi	For musical instruments
.mp2, .mp3	audio/mpeg	MPEG standard
.ra or .rm, Real Audio	audio/x-realaudio	Real Networks
.wav, WAVE	audio/x-wav	Microsoft
.wma, Windows Media Audio	audio/x-wma	Microsoft

compressed or uncompressed. But file sizes can be relatively large even when compressed.

- WMA (Windows Media Audio)—Part of Microsoft's Windows Media Technologies. This proprietary audio format claims to be half the size of comparable MP3 files.

We look at MP3 next.

12.6   WHAT IS MP3?

MP3 is the audio compression standard ISO-MPEG Audio Layer-3 (IS 11172-3 and IS 13818-3). MP3 is very popular and widely used for songs and music on the Web.

In 1987, the Fraunhofer Institute (Germany) in cooperation with University of Erlangen devised an audio compression algorithm based on *perceptual audio*, sounds that can be perceived by the human ear. Basically, MP3 compression eliminates sound data beyond human hearing. By exploiting stereo effects (data duplication between the stereo channels) and by limiting the audio bandwidth, audio files can be further compressed. The effort resulted in the MP3 standard. For stereo sound, a CD requires 1.4 Mbps (megabits per second). MP3 achieves CD-quality stereo at 112–128 Kbps, near CD-quality stereo at 96 Kbps, and FM radio-quality stereo at 56–64 Kbps. In all international listening tests, MPEG Layer-3 impressively proved its superior performance, maintaining the original sound quality at a data rate of around 64 Kbps per audio channel.

MP3 is part of the MPEG audio/video compression standards. MPEG is the Moving Pictures Experts Group, under the joint sponsorship of the International Organization for Standardization (ISO) and the International Electro-Technical Commission (IEC). MPEG works on standards for the encoding of moving pictures and audio. See the MPEG home page (www.mpeg.org) for further information.

MPEG compression has gained wide acceptance across industries. MP3 is the third and most advanced audio compression layer in the MPEG suite of audio codecs:

- MP1—designed for digital compact cassette with a target bit rate of 384 Kbps (stereo)
- MP2—designed as a compromise between complexity and performance with a target bit rate of 256–192 Kbps (stereo)
- MP3—designed for CD-quality sound with a target bit rate of 128–112 Kbps (stereo)

Each audio layer extends the features of the preceding layer. A Layer 3 decoder will be able to decode Layer 1 or 2 bit streams.

12.7 SOUND IN WEB PAGES

Sound can be included in a Web page in a number of ways. One way is by a hyperlink to the desired audio file. When the user clicks such a link, the sound file will be downloaded, and a suitable player will be used to play the sound file. Commonly linked audio formats include AU, WAV, RA, MIDI, and MP3.

Which plug-in or helper application to use for an audio or other media file depends on the browser, its configuration, and plug-ins installed. Basically, browsers use the Content-Type information in the HTTP response to determine which plug-in or helper application to invoke for handling the downloaded file. Figure 12.3 shows an audio link whose source code (Ex: **MlkLink**) is:

```
<p> Martin Luther King's "I Have a Dream" speech:
<a href="mlk.html">Full text</a>,
<a href="mlk.wav">Audio clip</a>.</p>
```

In a page, you may also embed sound that plays either onload or on demand. The situation is entirely similar to images: A linked image requires clicking, but an inline image (img tag) loads automatically. With XHTML, the object element is for embedding audio, video, and other media types in Web pages.

Figure 12.4 shows the playing and played display of an embedded audio object. The HTML code (Ex: **MlkObj**) is:

```
<a href="mlk.html">
Full text of Martin Luther King's "I Have a Dream" speech</a>
<object data="mlk.wav" type="audio/x-wav"               (1)
    width="45" height="25"                               (2)
    id="mlkspeech" title="I Have a Dream Speech"
    style="vertical-align: middle; margin-left: 1em">
  <param name="src" value="mlk.wav" />                   (3)
  <param name="autostart" value="true" />                (4)
  <param name="controls" value="PlayButton" />           (5)
</object>
```

Figure 12.3   AN AUDIO LINK

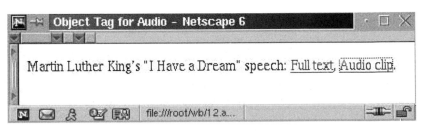

Figure 12.4   EMBEDDED AUDIO

sound playing

Full text of Martin Luther King's "I Have a Dream" speech

sound played

Full text of Martin Luther King's "I Have a Dream" speech

The `type` attribute specifies the MIME content type of the object, `audio/x-wav` in this case (line 1). The `width` and `height` give the display area dimensions (line 2). In this case, the display is the Play/Stop button audio control (line 5). If the `width` and `height` are set to zero, then the Play button will be hidden. The parameters given inside the `object` element depend on the object and the player/handler for that object. The `src` parameter gives the URL of the audio file (line 3). By setting the `autostart` parameter to `true` (line 4), the audio clip will play onload. If `autostart` is `false`, the clip will not play onload. The user can also play or pause the sound clip with the Play button. The preceding code will work for modern browsers.

Some browsers, including NN, do not support the standard `object` tag. The alternative is the `embed` tag, which is not part of XHTML. The equivalent embed code for the preceding example is:

```
<embed type="audio/x-wav" src="mlk.wav"
       width="45" height="25"
       controls="PlayButton" autostart="true"
       style="vertical-align: middle; margin-left: 1em">
</embed>
```

By setting the `loop` parameter to `true`, you can cause the clip to play repeatedly. Unless this is some soothing background sound, it is usually ill-advised to play a clip nonstop.

To ensure your audio clip code will work for different browsers, you can place the `embed` inside the `object` code immediately before the closing tag `</object>` as follows (Ex: **MlkObjEmbed**):

```
<object data="mlk.wav" type="audio/x-wav"
    width="45" height="25"
    id="mlkspeech" title="I Have a Dream Speech"
    style="vertical-align: middle; margin-left: 1em">
    <param name="src" value="mlk.wav" />
    <param name="autostart" value="true" />
    <param name="controls" value="PlayButton" />
<embed type="audio/x-wav" src="mlk.wav"
```

Figure 12.5 INLINE AUDIO CONTROLS

<u>Full text of Martin Luther King's "I Have a Dream" speech</u>

```
        width="45" height="25"
        controls="PlayButton" autostart="true"
        style="vertical-align: middle; margin-left: 1em">
</embed>
</object>
```

If we omit the `controls="PlayButton"` setting and allow more width and height, then a more complete control console is displayed inline for playing the audio (Figure 12.5).

12.8 SERVING UP MP3

Theoretically, the simple hyperlink works for MP3 files just like `.wav` or other types of audio files. The sound clip is downloaded and then played by the correct plug-in or helper application. But because MP3 files are usually complete songs taking more than 3 minutes to download even on a fast Internet connection, it is impractical to deliver MP3 songs with hyperlinks.

A good solution is the so-called *HTTP streaming*. The idea is to hand the URL of the sound file to an appropriate player, such as RealOne or QuickTime. The player can retrieve the sound file from the Web server and play can begin as soon as enough data have been buffered in the memory of the player. Play will usually begin within a few seconds. Because the songs are delivered by a Web server using the HTTP protocol, this technique is known as HTTP streaming.

If you use the embedding technique (Section 12.7), the song will usually be played with HTTP streaming. Often, embedding single music pieces is not enough. In this case, we can place one or more hyperlinks to MP3 files in a *playlist* (a text file) that has a special suffix (`.m3u`) and content type (`audio/mpegurl`). Files containing a list of media links are sometimes known as *metafiles*. The browser will download this short song list metafile very quickly and hand its content to an appropriate player. The player plays the songs identified by the links one by one with HTTP streaming.

For example, the `dion.m3u` file contains the single line

```
http://horse.cs.kent.edu/WEB2/sound/dion.mp3
```

When someone retrieves the file `dion.m3u` with a browser, a player will play the song as soon as enough is buffered.

Figure 12.6   A SONG PAGE

Songs

- Celine Dion – My Heart Will Go On Love Theme From Titanic
- Crouching Tiger, Hidden Dragon – A Love Before Time
- Crouching Tiger, Hidden Dragon – Yearning of the Sword
- Crouching Tiger, Hidden Dragon – Theme

Here is part of a Web page (Figure 12.6) that offers songs (Ex: **Mp3Songs**):

```
<ul>
<li><a href="dion.m3u">
Celine Dion - My Heart Will Go On Love Theme From Titanic</a></li>
<li><a href="cocolee.m3u">
Crouching Tiger, Hidden Dragon - A Love Before Time</a></li>
<li><a href="sword.m3u">
Crouching Tiger, Hidden Dragon - Yearning of the Sword</a></li>
<li><a href="cthd.m3u">
Crouching Tiger, Hidden Dragon - Theme</a></li>
</ul>
```

In this example, each playlist (.m3u file) contains a single MP3 song. It is possible to put more songs into a single playlist for continuous playing.

HTTP streaming is sometimes called pseudostreaming because HTTP does not control the rate of delivery or pay attention to the speed of the connection used by the client. A streaming protocol has these and other features and requires a specialized server to deliver the data stream.

The preceding material deals with MP3. But the ideas are the same for delivering other audio (or media) formats. For example, you can place links to RealAudio clips (.ra) in a playlist called a RealAudio Meta file (.ram) for streaming. In a .ram file, a line

```
http://host/directory/file.ra
```

would HTTP stream *file*.ra, whereas a line

```
pnm://host/directory/file.ra
```

would use the pnm server to stream the same audio clip.

12.9 HOW TO OBTAIN, PRODUCE, AND EDIT AUDIO

Any sound that you can hear or obtain on a music CD can be digitized, manipulated, and saved for use on the Web. Be sure to observe all laws before using copyrighted sounds and music.

Capturing Sound into Your Computer

Recording audio is as easy as using a microphone connected to a multimedia computer. Audio cards that capture audio are good places to start. Both Windows and Macs can record off a microphone easily. Windows users can record speech using Sound Recorder, the standard Windows audio player and recorder. Connect your microphone, press the Record button, and talk. Recording music works in the same way. Simply change your input device to accept your CD-ROM and press Record. Mac users can record through SimpleText, which is available with every Mac computer. Open SimpleText, select Sound>Record and speak into the microphone. Your sound will be saved for use later. SimpleText will also allow you to digitize sound from a CD ROM. Here are the steps:

- Insert music CD into drive
- File>Open
- Click CD>Track #
- Select Convert
- Options>Play>Select
- Select Start and End time of track
- Choose from these settings: Rate: 44.100 kHz, 22.050 kHz, or 11.025 kHz. Size: 8 bit or 16 bit. Use: Mono or Stereo
- Save file as Movie Player document

This file can now be used in any audio and video editing software.

Recording and Editing Audio

Capturing sound is easy, but in most cases, you will need to edit your sound files, cutting and changing to get the desired results. Most video editors will edit audio as well, but if you're strictly working with audio, then it may be best to use audio-only editing software. Much audio editing software lets you record your audio, but the big advantage over microphone recordings is that you can record from a wider variety of sources such as CD-ROM or your audio card. Connect any analog audio device, such as a CD player, cassette player, digital audio tape player, or microphone, to your computer's audio "in" socket. Capture audio at the highest quality available (44.1K Hz, 16-bit stereo). Later, you can convert the file to a smaller sample rate or remove a track to make it mono.

Audio Editing Software

Most reputable audio editing software performs basic tasks like cutting and pasting, raising the volume, removing pauses, and changing the properties of the audio file. In addition, most have sound effects that you can control such as echo, distortion, doppler, reverse, reverb, and delay. Some support MIDI controls so that you can synchronize sound, and most good programs will also convert files into streaming format. Here is a short list of both Mac and Windows programs:

- SoundEdit 16 by Macromedia (www.macromedia.com). Mac sound editor with multitrack editing and many codecs (Figure 12.7).

- Peak by Bias (www.bias-inc.com/peak.html). Macintosh-based audio editing package. Fully OS X native compatible but runs fine under Mac OS 8.6 through 9.2. Program can stitch together songs from sections taken from various takes, rearrange songs, dialog editing, sample editing, and sound design.

- Sound Forge by Sonic Foundry (www.sfoundry.com). This sound editor is for Windows 32-bit computers. Records and edits many types of audio such as RealAudio, NetShow, and TrueSpeech files.

- GoldWave by GoldWave (www.goldwave.com). This shareware program for Windows 3.x, Windows 95, and NT has multitrack audio editing. Plays and converts many different audio formats.

- CoolEdit by Syntrillium (www.syntrillium.com). This shareware program performs as professional program for Windows 3.1, Windows 95, and NT. CoolEdit Pro is an advanced version of the same program.

Figure 12.7   SOUNDEDIT 16 INTERFACE

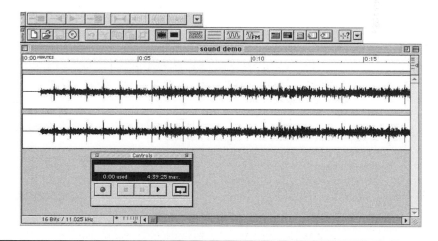

Figure 12.8 SOUNDEDIT 16: EDITING SOUND

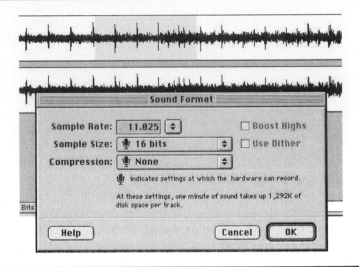

Editing Sound

Editing sound on the Mac is straightforward. The procedure involves opening a file and selecting the part of the file you want to edit (Figure 12.8). Then apply effects, cut, paste, or rearrange the sections or save to a different format.

Typical tasks that you may need to perform in sound editing programs are cutting extra noise or silence out of beginnings or endings of sounds (Figure 12.9). Another task is a fade-in and fade-out at the beginning and the end. This is also done by selecting a section and applying the fade (Figure 12.10).

Figure 12.9 CUTTING A SILENT PAUSE AT THE BEGINNING OF A SONG

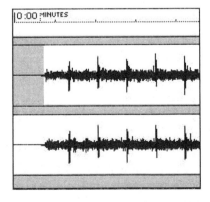

Figure 12.10   CREATING A FADE-OUT IN SOUND

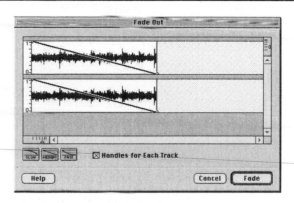

Deleting tracks to convert to 8-bit mono instead of 16-bit stereo may be another function you may need to perform for Web sounds to reduce file sizes. Saving in different sound formats is another easy thing to do in sound editing. Simply Save As and then choose from a variety of options such as Audio IFF, Weve, or QuickTime Movie. One point to keep in mind when saving files for the Web is to make the file as small as possible without a noticeable loss of quality.

12.10   VIDEO ON THE WEB

A video is a sequence of images displayed in rapid succession. For smooth motion, a rate of 30 frames per second (fps) is needed.

Analog video formats include Beta, HI-8, VHS, S-VHS, and others. Digital video formats include DVCPRO, Digital-S, DVCAM, Betacam SX, DVD, and others. For video on the Web, widely used formats include:

- MPEG—A suite of standard audio and video compression formats from the Moving Pictures Experts Group (content type video/mpeg; file suffix mpeg, mpg)

- AVI—Audio Video Interleaved format from Microsoft (content type video/x-msvideo; file suffix avi)

- QuickTime—An audio and video format from Apple (content type video/quicktime; file suffix mov, qt)

- RealVideo—An audio and video format by Real Networks. For historical reasons, it uses the seemingly incorrect content type audio/x-pn-realaudio and the file suffix rm.

Most Web video formats support 320 × 240-pixel resolution at 30 fps.

A video clip can be downloaded first and then played. But this can be very slow because video files are huge. Video clip, or live video, frames can be streamed at an acceptable rate and played at the client end as they are received. Video can be streamed with HTTP or with a specialized protocol such as RTP (Real-Time Protocol) or RTSP (Real-Time Streaming Protocol).

12.11 DIGITAL VIDEO COMPRESSION

Many compression algorithms and file formats exit. Generally speaking, video compression uses various ways to eliminate redundant data within one frame and between frames. Apple's QuickTime is one of the most popular digital video formats. It uses the *wavelet compression* technique. RealVideo from Real Networks uses the *fractal compression* technique. The ISO MPEG1 uses *motion prediction* coupled with *discrete cosine transform* (DCT) to achieve good compression.

In *motion prediction compression*, a complex mathematical formula breaks the video into frames. Each frame is broken into moving and static components. For each moving object, compression software predicts where it will be in the next frame. By refreshing only the moving components of a frame and recycling the static, data size is drastically reduced.

If the camera is panning, zooming, or moving in any way, the whole image is in motion, leaving nothing to recycle and little room for motion prediction compression.

12.12 VIDEO IN WEB PAGES

Similar to audio in Web pages, you may include a video clip by a hyperlink to a video file. This will cause the file to finish downloading before play starts. Because video files are huge (a 2-minute clip can be over 10 Mb), this is not a practical option in many cases. Embedding a video clip in a Web page can add to the attractiveness of a page and play can begin as soon as enough data are buffered. The HTML code for the QuickTime movie (Ex: **CthdQt**) in Figure 12.11 is as follows:

```
<object classid="clsid:02BF25D5-8C17-4B23-BC80-D3488ABDDC6B"      (1)
        codebase="http://www.apple.com/qtactivex/qtplugin.cab"    (2)
        type="video/quicktime" width="320" height="256">
  <param name="src"
        value="video/ct_us_big.mov" />                            (3)
  <param name="controller" value="TRUE" />                        (4)
  <param name="autoplay" value="TRUE" />                          (5)
  <param name="pluginspage"
        value="http://www.apple.com/quicktime/download/" />       (6)
  <embed src="video/ct_us_big.mov"                                (7)
        width="320" height="256" type="video/quicktime"
```

Figure 12.11   WEB PAGE WITH VIDEO CLIP

```
      pluginspage="http://www.apple.com/quicktime/download/"
      controller="TRUE" autoplay="TRUE">
  </embed>
</object>
```

The classid attribute gives the *ActiveX controls* id of the plug-in to use for playing the video clip (line 1). The URL of the plug-in is given as the codebase (line 2). The video clip URL is given as the value of the src parameter (line 3). The player controller will be displayed (line 4), and play will begin automatically (line 5). If the plug-in has not been installed, the information for the pluginspage can be used. The optional information given on line 2 helps Windows systems to retrieve the plug-in on the fly.

The embed tag presents much of the same information in its own format (line 7). Note that the values are case sensitive.

Follow this example to include your video clips. If you use RealVideo clips (Ex: **CthdReal**), the classid is

```
classid="clsid:CFCDAA03-8BE4-11cf-B84B-0020AFBBCCFA"
```

If you use other video formats, the Web developer's resource section on the format supplier's Web site will specify the classid to use, usually with full examples.

Correct object code can also be generated from HTML generation tools such as Macromedia Dreamweaver.

12.13 VIDEO STREAMING

With HTTP streaming, the Web server just sends the file. The player at the browser end will do the buffering and playing. Full-fledged video streaming requires a streaming server. This is especially true for on-Web broadcasting of live events. The entire streaming process consists of capturing, editing, producing (bit-rate-specific streaming encoding), network transport, receiving, buffering, and playback (Figure 12.12).

Three popular video players are available freely:

- Apple QuickTime and QuickTime Pro
- Microsoft Windows Media Player
- RealNetworks RealOne Player

RealOne Player handles audio, video, animation, still images, and text. It is almost a multimedia browser.

The RealOne Player and the RealNetworks streaming server together support Synchronized Multimedia Integration Language (SMIL), a W3C standard based on XML.

Figure 12.12   VIDEO STREAMING OVERVIEW

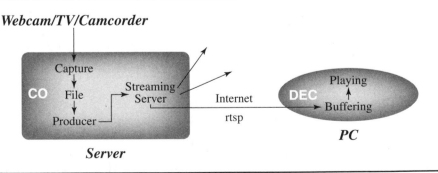

With real-time streaming, the viewer can jump to any location in the video clip, which always resides on the server. Video encoded for real-time streaming generally tries to keep pace with the user's connection speed to minimize interruptions and stalling.

Real-time streaming is best suited for longer videos, such as live event broadcasts, presentations, training videos, and lectures. Viewers can skip ahead to other parts of the clip at will, and there is no huge video file to download. It can also offer protection for the content because it can't be downloaded.

Let's look at how to serve prerecorded video by real-time streaming. We'll consider, for example, video streamed with Real-Time Streaming Protocol (RTSP) using the RealNetworks server:

1. Create the video clip file to be delivered. Save the file with a name `myclip.rm`. Make sure it is world readable.

2. Place `myclip.rm` in the *content directory* of the server.

3. Create a `.ram` (or `.rmm`) file containing a URL in the form:

   `rtsp://server.com/video/myclip.rm`

4. Place a hyperlink to the `.ram` file in your Web page. Clicking this link will start RealOne Player to play the clip (Ex: **RealLinks**). The user can use the play-position control to jump to different places in the video clip. If the `.ram` or `.rmm` file is served as an embedded `object`, then a browser plug-in is used to play the streaming media (Ex: **Angels** and Ex: **Lindbergh**).

12.14 HOW TO OBTAIN, PRODUCE, AND EDIT VIDEO

Video can be defined as a series of pictures displayed quickly to create the illusion of motion. When discussing digital video files, we first need to be familiar with three basic variables: resolution, color depth, and frame rate.

- *Resolution* refers to the number of pixels in a video frame. Picture resolution is expressed as width multiplied by height, such as 800×600 and $1,024 \times 768$. Full-screen video is 640×480 pixels. Two common video sizes are Common Intermediate Format (CIF), 352×288 and Quarter Common Intermediate Format (QCIF), 176×144.

- *Color depth* is the number of colors used in a video file. Color depth usually comes in 8-bit (256 colors), 16-bit (thousands of colors), and 24-bit (16 million colors). File size is contingent upon color depth, so the higher the color depth, the larger the file.

- *Frame rate* is the rate at which frames are shown on the screen, represented in frames per second. Television and movies are shown at 30 fps (frames per second), and most Web video is shown at 15 fps.

Video files can get quite large, and you will need plenty of RAM to work with them on your desktop. Storing these files will also take space on your hard drive, so be prepared before starting a project. For example, a 320 × 240, 24-bit file at 15 fps is 207 MB for 1 minute. To reduce the size of your files, you will need to compress (Section 12.11) them using one of the popular video formats (Section 12.10).

Capturing Video into Your Computer

Video capture means getting video into your computer. To get professional looking video results on Windows, you will need to have internal capture cards. Mac users have it the easiest when it comes to capture devices. Most Macs come with audio and video capability built into the computer. Any Power Mac will have this capability, but users can install MPEG cards to capture higher frame rates with higher resolutions. Windows users must choose a capture device, install it, and then choose and buy video editing capturing software.

If you have an iMac and DV camera, the process is even easier because you can capture and edit movies in one integrated package. You plug in *FireWire* and capture the video into iMovie. FireWire is a way to connect devices to your computer and transfer data back and forth between the computer and peripheral devices at high speeds. FireWire transmits data at 100 MB per second and can reach speeds of 1 GB per second with no loss of quality. It is by far the easiest and the most efficient way to capture video into your computer.

The goal of video capture is to get the best video possible with the fewest number of lost or dropped frames. Capture video at full motion 30 fps even if you don't intend to use it at that size. You can always resample later. Choose a window size appropriate for your content. Most people use 320 × 240 for Web video.

Video Editing Software

Once you have the video on your computer, you will need an editor to create your movies. Most video editors use nonlinear editing, which means that you aren't editing every line sequentially. Instead, you can move around and go back and forth during the editing process. Basic editing programs are able to add titles, make transitions, edit frames, compress files, and control start and stop capture times with frames or by time-code locations. High-end programs allow you to create and edit streaming file formats, have good built-in audio editing features, and in general, have more flexibility and sophistication. One of the most popular and most professional products on the market today is Final Cut Pro by Apple. It is a Mac-only product and is widely used. Others include:

- Premiere by Adobe (www.adobe.com). Both Mac and Windows video editor (Figure 12.13).
- iMovie by Apple (www.apple.com). Mac-only program.

Figure 12.13   ADOBE PREMIERE AND ITS TIMELINE INTERFACE

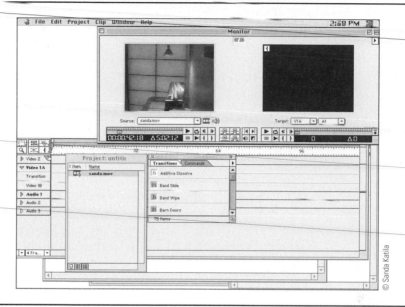

© Sanda Katila

Editing Video

Even though you may have captured great video footage, you won't be able to use it without some basic editing. Postcapture editing usually involves clipping frames from the beginning or the end of the video. This is similar to editing audio, discussed earlier in the chapter. You may need to move clips from one location to another and add titles, transitions, or special effects such as color and motion filters.

- *Transitions* are effects that lead from one scene to another. These transitions come in many different varieties, ranging from a simple cut to wipes, blends, fades, and dissolves. Keep your transitions simple. Don't choose the most distracting one in the bunch. Nothing says "amateur video editor" like a "cheesy" looking transition.

- *Special Effects.* Most programs come with many special effects ranging from color correction, tint, brightness, fading to black, warping and going into motion blurs, and simulated camera pans. Some can be effective in achieving the effect you want; others are distracting and should be used with discretion.

- *Titles, Graphics, and Chromakey.* Adding titles and graphics is a basic capability of most editors, and they are relatively simple to use. *Chromakey* is a technique that uses a blue or green screen to superimpose a scene on a background. An example of this technique would be the weather forecaster on TV who shows us the rain pattern on a map. The forecaster is really videotaped on a blue background. The map is later imposed over the blue screen to give us this special visual effect. This same effect can be used in video editing programs.

12.15   INTRODUCTION TO FLASH

Flash, originally conceived as the *Future Splash Animator* for creating and animating vector graphics, was purchased in 1997 by Macromedia, which changed its name to Flash. Macromedia began marketing this new product as a tool for creating graphics on the Web. Since then, Web sites have not been the same. Flash opened up a whole new world to designers as well as programmers, while it evolved with each new version as a highly sophisticated tool. Although it is just one program, it contains tools for many different functions. Flash's primary focus is on Web site creation, but its wide range of other capabilities makes it a powerful toolbox for multiple functions.

- It can deliver vector images, text, sound, and animation over the Web.
- It uses vector images that are small and scalable.
- It has streaming capability.
- It can create graphics using Bezier curves, but it also provides natural drawing tools without manipulating curve handles or special points on a line, which appeals to artists and nonartists alike.
- It can animate graphics such as icons, navigation buttons, and menus.
- It is not limited to the Web. You can distribute content on CD-ROMs or create stand-alone projects to distribute over email or on disk.
- You can export to other formats such as QuickTime, RealSystem, or Windows AVI.
- It uses ActionScript, an easy scripting language that even beginners can use. More advanced script writers appreciate its sophisticated capabilities.
- It provides HTML generation tools to place Flash in Web pages.

Flash's other advantage as a superior tool is its single platform target, which is the Macromedia Flash Player. Most browsers come with Flash Player already installed, but you can always download the player from macromedia.com. Unlike DHTML, which requires testing of run time and rendering inconsistencies on different browsers, Flash MX lets you focus on design because the interface will look and perform exactly as the designer intended.

Flash from a Designer's Perspective

We've already reviewed Flash's advantages and know it is a robust, popular program on the Web. Many designers have become enamored of Flash for the bells and whistles it can produce, and many have gone on to produce all-Flash Web sites. Enticing as that may be to some, keep in mind several key points.

An all-Flash site breaks the model of the Web that relies on XHTML to make pages widely accessible. You can send HTML pages in emails, for example. You can transmit them to cell phones, to browsers for the hearing or vision impaired, and for printing. Tools convert HTML pages to .txt, MS Word, or other formats. A Flash-only site has all .swf files, which are not HTML and are not processed by anything other than the Flash plug-in for browsers. Flash sites are not searchable. Flash typography has received much criticism for being too small and unreadable, which is something readers, at least for now, can't control.

So with all that said, why would you use Flash? Flash, like any other design element such as color, line, image, and typography, is just one option to consider when designing Web sites. Using Flash just to make things move on the screen seems rather pointless, unless that is the point of your site.

There are times when you may want to use Flash. Sound and animation can capture the viewer's attention quickly. Unlike HTML, Flash-based animation is smooth and responsive. Flash offers faster interaction with the user by executing on the local host and avoiding networking delays. Flash can dazzle the viewer, but before you launch the program, be sure to ask yourself these questions:

- Why am I using Flash?

- Can I solve the problem without Flash?

- Am I using Flash for me or for my audience?

- Is Flash in the best interest of my client?

- Will Flash assist or confuse the user?

- Is Flash the most effective solution?

Many usability experts that would argue that any professional site wishing to reach a wide target audience should not use Flash, period. On the other hand, proponents such as Chris MacGregor, a User Interface interaction designer with Intuitive Homes in Houston, Texas, argues that Flash creates faster, easier interfaces than HTML. According to MacGregor, knowing when and how to use Flash effectively leads to intuitive and better designed sites (www.flazoom.com/news/running1_11202002.shtml).

Our advice on Flash is to use discretion. If you want to capture viewers' attention, illustrate a process in motion, or present information that can't be done in HTML, go ahead and make part of your site with Flash. If it is an entry page, be sure to include a "skip" option for repeat visitors. Keep in mind its limitations, capitalize on its strength, keep the file sizes small, and don't alienate your target audience. Remember that usability means easy to use for your audience.

12.16 FLASH OVERVIEW

Flash allows you to create a variety of elements that go beyond the creation and animation of vector graphics. You can create movies that contain applications for the Web, imported video, bitmap graphics, and sound. Flash movies incorporate interactivity to permit input from viewers, and nonlinear movies can interact with other Web applications. Designers use Flash to create navigation controls, animated logos, and long-form animations with synchronized sound in addition to creating Web sites.

Flash documents use an .fla file name, but these are not the movies that Flash Player displays. Instead, you publish your FLA documents as Flash movies, which have the .swf file name extension and contain only the information needed to display the movie.

The following subsections are designed to provide an overview on some of the major concepts in Flash. They are intended to highlight some of the options available when working in Flash.

Design Process in Flash

Design process in Flash begins like any other design process: with your idea and message. Once you have a good reason for using Flash, you need to know how you're going to express your ideas visually. Be sure that your Flash movies fit aesthetically and conceptually into your Web site and they help support the overall communication and marketing strategies.

Before you begin creating graphics in Photoshop, Flash, or any other program, sketch your ideas on paper. This can be done in pencil or marker on layout paper. This drawing process is similar to creating thumbnails, but instead of drawing layouts, you draw sample frames showing motion. These types of sketches are called storyboards. Storyboards are important because they allow you to see your ideas on paper all at once. Storyboards don't have to be expertly drawn; they only need to convey the basic direction of your ideas.

Figure 12.14 FLASH TYPE SEQUENCE

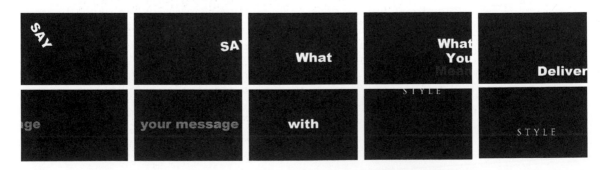

You also don't need to draw every frame but only the key frames indicating main ideas and shifts in motion. Often, it is easiest to create simple type animations such as the one shown in Figure 12.14. Be sure to get client approval on storyboards before creating graphics and movies in Flash.

Once the storyboards are completed, you're ready to create graphics. You can do this in Photoshop, in Flash, or in any combination of programs you wish (Figure 12.15). Typically, you would manipulate, scale, and create raster images in Photoshop and create your vector graphics in Flash. If you have files from other sources, such as sound and video, you can import those as well and assemble everything in Flash.

Stage

When you first launch Flash, you will see various tool palettes, a timeline, and a *Stage* (Figure 12.16). This is where you compose the content for individual frames in the movie, drawing artwork on it directly, arranging imported artwork, and adding text, sound, and user interface components.

Timeline

Timeline consists of layers, frames, and playhead. Timeline organizes and controls a movie's content over time in layers and frames, which represent a segment of time. Layers are like multiple film sections stacked on top of one

Figure 12.15   FLASH: ASSEMBLING FILES

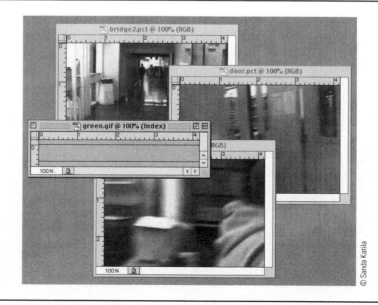

© Sanda Katila

Figure 12.16 FLASH: STAGE AREA

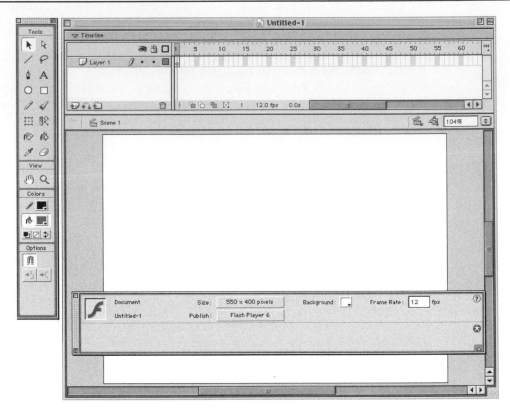

another, each containing a different image that appears on the Stage. A play-head tells you the current frame that is displayed on the Stage.

Frames in Flash

Frames appear in the timeline (Figure 12.17) in the order they will playback in your movie. Like video, Flash movies divide lengths of time into frames and measure animation speed by frames per second. However, in Flash, the speed of frames, or *frame rate*, is contingent upon the speed of the computer you're using for playback. The frame rate is specified once, at the beginning of the document, for the entire movie in the Property Inspector. A frame rate of 12 frames per second (fps) usually produces good results on the screen. Be sure to test your movies on several computers before posting to the Web, checking playback speeds on different processors.

Figure 12.17   FLASH: TIMELINE

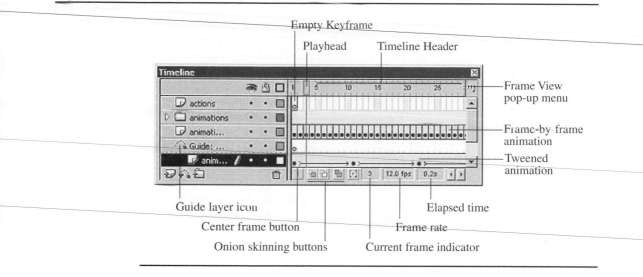

Flash also has a *keyframe*, which is a frame that you insert into the timeline if you want a change in animation or want to include frame actions to modify a movie. There is more on actions later in this chapter. Keyframes are used in a popular animation technique called *tweening*.

Keyframes are used to change the size of objects, create fade-in or fade-out, rotate an object, and so on. You would insert a keyframe at the beginning and the end of the animation to indicate beginning of animation and the end of that sequence.

Animation in Flash can be created using tween animation or *frame-by-frame* animation. With tween animation, you create the start and end of animation, and Flash fills in frames in between. With frame-by-frame animation, you create a different image in every frame. This process is more time-consuming than tweening.

To simplify the process of tweened animation, you can distribute multiple objects to separate *layers*. There is more on layers later in this section.

Drawing and Painting Tools

Flash gives you an excellent range of tools for painting (Figure 12.18), drawing, and working with both vector and raster images. It would take a whole chapter to tell you all about these various features. In this subsection, we only outline some of the major tools and show you their functions.

In Flash MX, *graphic objects* are items on the Stage. Here you can move, copy, delete, transform, stack, align, and group graphic objects. You can also link a graphic object to a URL. Graphic objects should not be confused with

Figure 12.18   FLASH: GRAPHICS DRAWING AREA

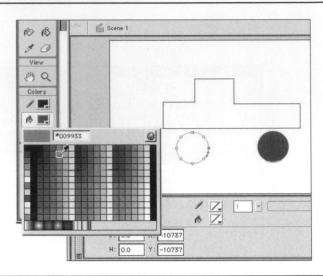

ActionScript objects, which are part of a program or script. ActionScript objects and object-oriented scripting are discussed later in this section.

For drawing, you can use any number of tools such as pen (Figure 12.19) or brush, and you can modify and group geometric shapes. When you select an object, the Property Inspector displays the object's stroke and fill, its pixels dimensions, and the *x* and *y* coordinates of the object's transformation point (Figure 12.20). You can hand-draw an object, and it can remain in that form

Figure 12.19   FLASH: PEN TOOL FOR CREATING SHAPES

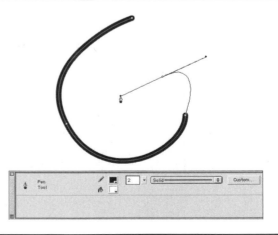

Figure 12.20 **FLASH: DRAWING GEOMETRIC OBJECTS**

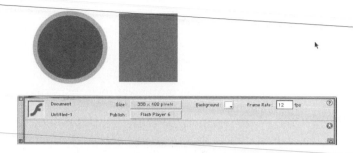

Figure 12.21 **FLASH: HAND-DRAWN SHAPES**

or you can select Smooth in the Tool Palette and your hand-drawn object will be converted into a clean geometric shape (Figure 12.21). Reshaping lines and shape outlines are easy. Fills and strokes are treated as separate objects, so they can be modified independently.

When you use most Flash tools, you will notice that the Property Inspector changes to show you the settings associated with that tool. In Figure 12.22, we see how the inspector displays text properties. Property Inspector is useful for making editing changes quickly.

Figure 12.22 **FLASH: PROPERTY INSPECTOR WINDOW**

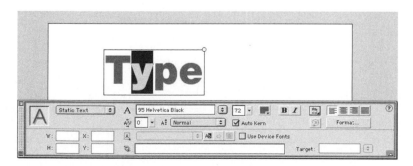

Working with Text

Flash gives you many options for working with text (Figure 12.23). As with most vector graphic programs, you have various features for manipulating fonts, point sizes, style, color, tracking, and so on. Transforming text, object rotating, scaling, skewing, breaking text apart, and reshaping text into objects are also options.

In addition to typical text functions, you can include text in your movies in three ways. First, you can create static text that you manipulate and determine when you create the movie. Second, you can design dynamic text fields that can update such things as dates and numbers on your site. Third, you can create input text fields that allow users to enter text in places such as forms and surveys. You can also create scrolling text fields. Fonts can be converted into symbols and exported as part of a shared library, so viewers can view the files exactly the way you intended.

Text fields don't have their own timelines, but instances of text fields are ActionScript objects that have properties and methods.

Figure 12.23 FLASH: TYPE OPTIONS

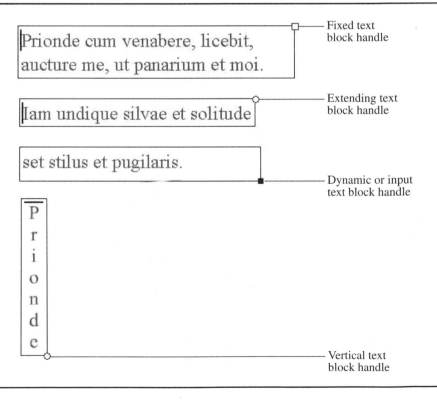

Working with Layers

In some respects, Flash layers (Figure 12.24) work much like layers in Photoshop. They can be stacked on top of one another, they are transparent, they help you to organize your artwork in documents, and you can work in one layer without affecting the other layers.

When you first create a new document, it will contain just one layer. As you begin to add images, sound, and animation, you will want to add layers to organize your project. The number of layers you can create is limited only by your computer's memory, and layers do not increase the file size of your published movie. You can hide, lock, or rearrange layers.

You can draw, paint, and modify layers by selecting them to make them active. A pencil icon next to a layer or folder name indicates that the layer or folder is active. Only one layer can be active at a time (although more than one layer can be selected at a time). Working on each layer individually is preferable because each layer may contain numerous objects. Layer folders can be created to help organize layers into logical groups that you can expand and collapse to view as you work on different parts of the project.

You can also organize and manage layers by creating layer folders and placing layers in them. You can expand or collapse layers in the timeline without affecting what you see on the Stage. It's a good idea to use separate layers or folders for sound files, actions, frame labels, and frame comments. This helps you find these items quickly when you need to edit them. Typically, the background layer contains static artwork, and each additional layer contains one separate animated object.

Figure 12.24   FLASH: LAYERS

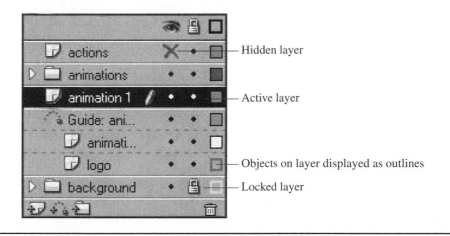

Working with Scenes

In Flash, movies are organized by *scenes*. Scenes allow you to logically organize the project by sections such as introduction, body, and ending. During playback, scenes play in the order they are listed in the Scene panel in your document (Figure 12.25). Frames in the movie are numbered consecutively through scenes. For example, if a movie contains two scenes with 10 frames each, the frames in Scene 2 are numbered 11–20.

Scenes are quite versatile. You can add, delete, duplicate, rename, and change the order of scenes. Typically, most Flash documents contain at least several scenes with multiple layers.

Working with Symbols

A *symbol* is a graphic, button, or movie clip that you create once and reuse throughout your movie or in other movies. A symbol can include artwork that you import from another application. Any symbol you create automatically becomes part of the library for the current document.

Using symbols in your movies dramatically reduces file size; using several instances of a symbol requires less storage space than saving multiple copies of the contents of the symbol. For example, you can reduce the file size of your movies if you convert static graphics such as background images into symbols that you then reuse. Using symbols can also speed movie playback because a symbol needs to be downloaded to the Flash Player only once.

Figure 12.25   FLASH: SCENE PANEL

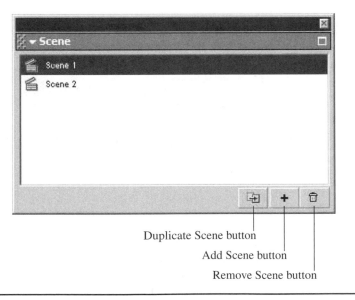

Duplicate Scene button

Add Scene button

Remove Scene button

Figure 12.26   **FLASH: SYMBOL PROPERTIES WINDOW**

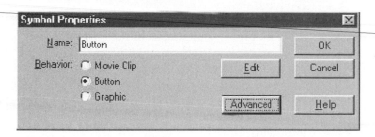

You can share symbols among Flash movies as run-time or author-time shared library assets. For run-time shared assets, you can link assets in a source movie to any number of destination movies, without importing the assets into the destination movies. For author-time shared assets, you can update or replace a symbol with any other symbol available on your local network.

Each symbol has a unique timeline and Stage, complete with layers. When you create a symbol, you choose the symbol type depending on how you want to use the symbol in the movie (see Figure 12.26). Use graphic symbols for static images and to create reusable pieces of animation that are tied to the timeline of the main movie. Graphic symbols operate in sync with the movie's timeline. Interactive controls and sounds won't work in a graphic symbol's animation sequence.

Working with Instances

Once you've created a symbol, you can create *instances* of that symbol wherever you like throughout the movie, including inside other symbols. When you modify the symbol, all instances of the symbol are updated.

An instance is a copy of a symbol located on the Stage or nested inside another symbol. An instance can be very different from its symbol in color, size, and function. Editing the symbol updates all of its instances, but applying effects to an instance of a symbol updates only that instance.

Instances are given default names when you create them. You can apply custom names to instances in the Property Inspector.

Using the Library

The library in Flash is a file that stores ready-made symbols created in Flash, plus imported files such as video clips, sound clips, bitmaps, and imported vector artwork. The Library panel displays a scroll list with the names of all items in the library, allowing you to view and organize these elements as you work. An icon next to an item's name in the Library panel indicates the item's file type.

You can open any library while you are working in Flash and select items from that library file to use in the current document.

You can create permanent libraries in your Flash application that will be available whenever you launch Flash. Flash also includes several sample libraries containing buttons, graphics, movie clips, and sounds that you can add to your own Flash documents. The sample Flash libraries and permanent libraries that you create are listed in the Window>Common Libraries submenu.

Adding Sound to Movies

Flash MX offers several options for using sound in your movies. Sound can play continuously, independent of the timeline; it can be synchronized with animation in a soundtrack; sound can be added to interactive buttons; and sounds can fade in or fade out.

Flash has two types of sounds: *event sounds* and *stream sounds*. An event sound downloads completely before it begins playing, and it continues playing until it is given direction to stop. Stream sounds begin playing as the first few frames have been downloaded; stream sounds are synchronized to the timeline for playing on a Web site.

Sound stored in a library can be shared and linked to several movies. You can also use the ActionScript onSoundComplete event to trigger an event based on the completion of a sound. Sounds can also be loaded dynamically through ActionScripts.

Adding Video to Movies

Adding video to your Flash movies is simple. You will need QuickTime 4 or later for Windows or Macintosh or DirectX 7 or later, in Windows only, installed on your system. Flash can import video in MOV, AVI, or MPEG format. Additional formats may be supported for import depending on your system. Video clips may be imported as linked or embedded files. Movies can be published as SWF files or QuickTime movies.

Embedded video clips become part of the movie, just like any artwork file. You can synchronize the frame rate of an embedded video to match the frame rate of the main movie timeline. You may want to do this to prevent "skipping" effects throughout the movie. If the clip you've embedded is 30 fps and your overall Flash movie is 12 fps, this may be a problem depending on the effect that you want. To drop frames from the video clip and synchronize the two movies, select Synchronize Video to Macromedia Flash Movie Frame Rate.

Editing original video in another application such as Adobe Premiere of Final Cut Pro is another option. You can also assign a different symbol to an instance of a video clip. Assigning a different symbol to an instance displays a different instance on the Stage but leaves all the original instance properties (e.g., color, rotation, etc.) intact.

You can create a video object on the Stage by dragging an instance of an imported video clip from the Library panel onto the Stage. As with symbols, you can create multiple instances of an imported video clip without adding to the Flash movie file size.

ActionScripts

ActionScript is the official scripting language of Macromedia Flash MX, which lets you add interactivity to movies. The ActionScript syntax and style closely resemble JavaScript, but ActionScript uses its own rules of syntax, reserves keywords, provides operators, and allows you to use variables to store and retrieve information. ActionScript includes built-in objects and functions, allowing you to create your own objects and functions. Flash MX will also read scripts written in any previous version of Flash.

Figure 12.27   FLASH: ACTIONSCRIPT DIALOG WINDOW

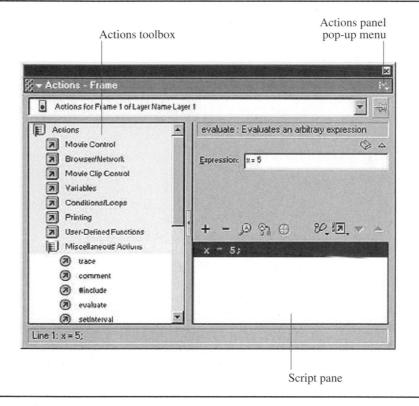

Script pane

ActionScript is an object-oriented language that uses elements such as actions, operators, and objects that you assemble in scripts, and they instruct your movies to do certain things. These elements can be set up so that navigation buttons trigger events such as starting or stopping movies.

You don't have to be a programmer to use ActionScript commands, though. In your Actions panel, you can build scripts by choosing options from menus and lists (see Figure 12.27). If you're already familiar with programming, you can work in the expert editing mode in the Script panel. Both expert and novice mode give you code hints to help you complete actions and insert properties and events. Once the script is completed, it can then be attached to any button, movie clip, or frame. Flash's built-in Help files are great for teaching you how to use ActionScripts. They introduce you to ActionScript and provide an informative overview of basic programming concepts such as functions, variables, statements, operators, conditionals, and loops. They also deconstruct sample scripts so that you can begin to understand ActionScript syntax.

12.17 PUBLISHING FLASH MOVIES

When you have completed your movie, you're ready to publish a Macromedia Flash MX document (FLA file) to the Web. By default, the Publish command creates the Flash SWF file and an HTML document that inserts your Flash movie in a browser window. You can also save your movies as GIF, JPEG, PNG, and QuickTime formats if you do not want to view the movie in the Flash Player. This allows you to edit your movies in other applications and export a movie directly into a single format. You can export an entire movie as a Flash movie; as a series of bitmap images; as a single frame or image file; and as moving and still images in various formats, including GIF, JPEG, PNG, BMP, PICT, QuickTime, or AVI.

You can also create your own HTML documents with required tags to display Flash movies instead of using the Publish command. Before publishing any movie, be sure to test it in all major browsers to check its performance.

If you're working in Macromedia Dreamweaver, you can easily add Flash movies to your Web site. Dreamweaver generates all the needed HTML code, and you can launch and edit Flash from within Dreamweaver to update the Flash movie.

You can also create your own HTML documents with required tags to display Flash movies instead of using the Publish command. To do this, include the following object code in your HTML/XHTML file (Ex: **FlashObjTag**):

```
<object classid="clsid:D27CDB6E-AE6D-11cf-96B8-444553540000"
  codebase="http://download.macromedia.com/pub/shockwave/
            cabs/flash/swflash.cab#version=6,0,40,0"            (1)
  width="550" height="400" id="myMovieName">
  <param name="movie" value="myFlashMovie.swf" />
```

```
    <param name="quality" value="high" />
    <param name="bgcolor" value="#fff" />
    <embed src="myFlashMovie.swf" quality="high"              (2)
        bgcolor="#fff" width="550" height="400"
        name="myMovieName" align=""
        type="application/x-shockwave-flash"
        pluginspage="http://www.macromedia.com/go/getflashplayer">
</embed>
</object>
```

Of course, you need to edit the code to reflect your parameter settings such as
.swf file name, width, height, and id. Note the codebase value must be on one
line. (It is displayed on two lines here to fit the width of the book page.) The
embed tag is included for the benefit of older browsers.

Often, a Web site will use a Flash entry page. The visitor is directed to the
Flash or non-Flash entry page depending on the browser used. The following
JavaScript code can check browser support for Flash and load the appropriate
entry page automatically:

```
function My_checkPlugin(plugin, theURL, altURL)
{ if ((navigator.plugins && navigator.plugins[plugin])     // (A)
      ||   // or if IE later than Mozilla/3.1
      (  navigator.appName.indexOf('Microsoft') != -1 &&    // (B)
         parseFloat(navigator.appVersion) > 3.1 ))

   {
       if (theURL.length>2)
           window.location = theURL; // flash entry
   }
   else
   {
       if (altURL.length>2)
           window.location = altURL; // non-flash entry
   }
   document.My_returnValue = false;
}
```

If the browser has the desired plugin (line A) or is an IE version after Mozilla/
3.1 (line B), then we go to the Flash entry. Otherwise, we go to the non-Flash
entry page.

The function My_checkPlugin is called onload:

```
<body onload=
    "My_checkPlugin('Shockwave Flash', 'entry.html', 'index1.html');
    return document.My_returnValue">
```

Note that the same checking scheme can be used for other types of media
plugins.

12.18 FLASH MOVIE EXAMPLE

To really understand how Flash works, you need to see at least several movie example files. You can view these files on the book's site, but for now, it may be helpful to see one movie development.

This movie (Ex: `GreenBlackBars`) began as a simple idea conveying the beginning, middle, and ending in visual communication. A storyboard was sketched out on paper first. A more advanced storyboard was created in Photoshop, where most of the graphics were created. A film loop of colored lines moving from top to bottom of the screen was done in Flash to create rhythm and pace. Sound was added to further enrich this rhythm and dramatize the message.

This movie was developed on a Power Mac. An overview of the process looks like this:

- Concept—Demonstrate the beginning, middle, and end of idea in visual communication. The idea is to enter, communicate, focus, gracefully, and then exit.
- Storyboard sketch—Hand-drawn in marker on layout paper (Figure 12.28).

Figure 12.28 STORYBOARD SKETCH ON PAPER

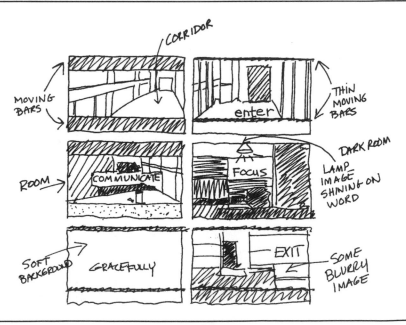

- Storyboard for client—Created in Photoshop to actual size of movie (Figure 12.29), which is 300 pixels wide × 200 pixels high.
- Photos—Background photos were taken from single frames originally created in a QuickTime movie. The initial movie was taken with a digital camera and imported into iMovie, where it was edited and saved in QuickTime format.
- Type—All typography for the movie was created in Flash.
- Moving bar graphics—This was a movie clip created in Flash.
- Sound—Sound was digitized from a CD and imported into Macromedia Peak, where it was edited and saved as an Audio IFF (44.1K Hz, 16-bit stereo) file.

Creating Movie Clips

As stated in the overview (Section 12.16), movie clips have their own time-lines, which allow you to create little movies inside movies. In the case of our sample movie, we created four different movie clips, all based on the same movement. Although the graphics are similar, there are differences in each clip. Clips were placed into a timeline and tweened, so they move from top to

Figure 12.29   FLASH EXAMPLE: PHOTOSHOP STORYBOARD

© Sanda Katila

Figure 12.30   MOVIE CLIP TIMELINE

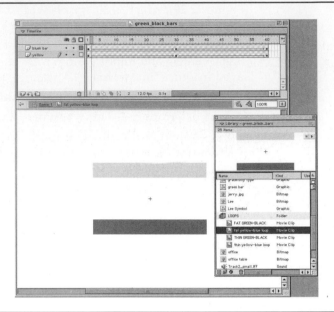

bottom. As they move, they fade in and fade out. The movement is created by inserting keyframes on changing frames. The black and green lines are shown in Figure 12.30. Same graphics were used in the blue and yellow clip. The clip was duplicated and the colors were changed for a varied effect.

Inserting Photos and Type

All photos were placed in one layer and all text in another to keep the two organized. Keyframes were inserted at each point where the words and images changed. All photos were sized to 300 × 200 in Photoshop, saved as JPGs, and imported into Flash.

All the words on the screen were created in Flash and converted to a symbol so that they could be used repeatedly without enlarging the movie file. Red guides were inserted in the layer to help align text on the screen (Figure 12.31).

As stated earlier, sound for our sample movie was digitized from a CD and imported into Macromedia Peak, where it was edited and saved as an Audio IFF (44.1K Hz, 16-bit stereo) file. The sound could have been compressed further in SoundEdit to 22.1K Hz, 8-bit mono for the Web. The other option is to have Flash compress the sound with the rest of the movie at the final publishing stage. This publishing stage is where you can further decide compression, bit rate, and quality options.

Figure 12.31   CREATING TYPE AND USING GUIDES

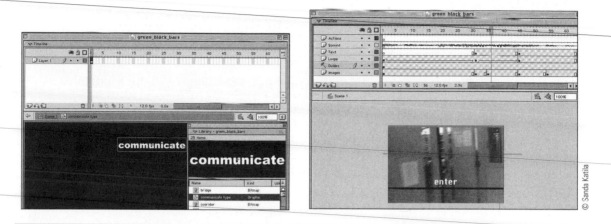

12.19 SUMMARY

Audio, video, and animation can bring additional dimensions to a Web site and, when used appropriately, can be very effective in communicating the intended messages. Multimedia content also adds liveliness and variety to a site.

Multiple compression and decompression algorithms compete to make digital files small and to preserve the quality of the audio and video delivered. On the Web, MP3 is a widely used format for sound, music, and songs. QuickTime and Real Audio/Video are widely used formats for both audio and video.

Direct links to audio/video files cause the files to download completely before being played. The object tag is the W3C and XHTML standard for embedding sound, video, and other media files in Web pages. The older embed tag is nonstandard and not to be used if you wish to conform to XHTML.

When audio/video clips are embedded or when metafiles containing playlists are used, HTTP-based streaming can take place and significantly reduce the delay in media delivery. Specialized streaming protocols provide different data rates to suit various connection bandwidths and allow client-side players to control the streaming server for data delivery.

Flash synchronizes vector graphics and textual content with sound to produce good-quality animation in relatively small file sizes. Hyperlinks are also supported within a Flash file. Appropriate use of Flash animation can increase the effectiveness of a site.

EXERCISES

Review Questions

1. How is analog audio digitized? What is sampling? What is bit depth?

2. What are the principles for reducing audio file size?

3. Name and explain the common audio file formats on the Web.

4. How do you get sound into your computer?

5. What are some sound editing programs?

6. How do you get video into your computer on Windows? On the Mac?

7. What are transitions in video editing?

8. Where would you apply special effects to video?

9. What is a chromakey? Why would you use a chromakey?

10. What is a .swf file? How do you make one?

11. What are typical video frame rates and resolutions for the Web?

12. Describe the design process in Flash.

13. Why would you use Flash movies in your Web site?

14. What is a storyboard?

15. Why do you need a storyboard?

16. In Flash, what is a Stage? What is a timeline?

17. What does frame rate mean in Flash?

18. What are keyframes in Flash?

19. How are keyframes different from regular frames?

20. What is tweening and why is it important?

21. In Flash, what are movie clips and what is unique about them?

22. Describe three different ways of working with text in Flash.

23. How are Photoshop layers different from Flash layers?

24. How would you use scenes in Flash?

25. What are symbols in Flash?

26. How are symbols different from graphics in Flash?

27. What are instances in Flash?

28. What is ActionScript?

29. What are some options for saving your files in Flash?

30. Name and explain the common video formats on the Web.

31. What are MP3 and MPEG? Why is MP3 so popular?

32. What are the ways to include sound in Web pages?

33. What are the ways to include video in Web pages?

34. What is the difference between the `embed` tag and the `object` tag? Is `embed` allowed in XHTML?

35. What causes the entire audio/video file to download completely before play begins?

36. What is HTTP-based streaming? What is special-protocol-based streaming? What is the difference?

Assignments

1. Look on the Web for audio clips (e.g., search for Audio `WAV`). Click links to audio files and see how your browser plays the audio files.

2. Digitize your own voice on the computer. Save the file and open it in sound editing software. Apply a special effect such as an echo or a fade-out to the file.

3. Take the sound file and try sampling it at different rates. Convert a file from 44.1K Hz, 16-bit stereo to a lower rate. Listen to the difference.

4. Capture short video footage with a digital camera. Your college AV services may be able to loan you one. Import the video into your computer. Edit a few seconds of the video and save the results. Save it in different formats for the Web.

5. Try embedding personal video footage into your HTML code.

6. Create a few simple geometric shapes in Flash. Try to make each shape move across the Stage with motion tweening.

7. Try to create a shape tween in Flash.

8. Create a basic button in Flash and program it to go to the last frame.

9. Scan an image in Photoshop. Import it into Flash and animate the image.

10. Draw a short storyboard illustrating a simple concept such as "motion." See if you can work with type, symbols, photos, and sound to illustrate this in Flash.

11. Make a Web page with an embedded audio clip in three ways: with the `embed` tag, with the `object` tag, and with `object` combined with `embed`.

12. Do the previous assignment for a video clip.

13. Deliver an audio file by using a JavaScript function that detects the browser version and generates either an `object` or an `embed` tag.

14. Deliver a video clip by using a JavaScript function that detects the browser and its available plug-ins and generates the correct embedding code.

15. Make a "My Favorite Songs" page and a song list using MP3 metafiles (`.m3u`).

16. Make a "My Favorite Movies" page and a list of video clips.

## CHAPTER 13

Perl and Common Gateway Interface Programming

We have seen some Perl programs in Chapter 8, where we introduced HTML forms and their connection to server-side support programs. But we presented only a cursory coverage of Perl and its support for Common Gateway Interface (CGI) programming.

Perl is a popular language to script CGI programs. This chapter introduces important Perl features to help you write better CGI programs. Perl variables, conditionals, I/O, loops, function definition, patterns, the taint mode, and more are described. Enough information is included for you to use Perl comfortably for CGI programming.

The CGI.pm module and how it helps CGI programming are emphasized. Cookies and their application in multistep user transactions are explained and demonstrated with examples.

Materials presented here give a concise and practical introduction to Perl and CGI programming. With this background, you can learn more about Perl and CGI with ease.

13.1 WHAT IS PERL?

Perl is the Practical Extraction and Report Language and is freely available for downloading from the Comprehensive Perl Archive Network (www.perl.com/CPAN/). Perl is a portable, command-line driven, interpreted programming/scripting language. Written properly, the same Perl code will run identically on UNIX, Windows, and Mac operating systems.

A Perl program (or script) consists of a sequence of commands, and the source code file can be named arbitrarily but usually uses the .pl suffix. A Perl interpreter reads the source file and executes the commands in the order given. You may use any text editor to create Perl scripts. These scripts will work on any platform where the Perl interpreter has been installed.

The Perl scripting language is usually used in the following application areas:

- Web CGI programming
- DOS and UNIX shell command scripts
- text input parsing
- report generation
- text file transformations and conversions

Although Perl is not Web specific, our coverage of Perl is focused on its application in Web CGI programming.

13.2   A BRIEF HISTORY OF PERL

Perl was created in the UNIX tradition of open source software. Perl 1.0 was released December 18, 1987 by Larry Hall with the following description:

> Perl is an interpreted language optimized for scanning arbitrary text files, extracting information from those text files, and printing reports based on that information. It's also a good language for many system management tasks. The language is intended to be practical (easy to use, efficient, complete) rather than beautiful (tiny, elegant, minimal). It combines (in the author's opinion, anyway) some of the best features of C, sed, awk, and sh, so people familiar with those languages should have little difficulty with it. (Language historians will also note some vestiges of csh, Pascal, and even BASIC—PLUS.) Expression syntax corresponds quite closely to C expression syntax. If you have a problem that would ordinarily use sed or awk or sh, but it exceeds their capabilities or must run a little faster, and you don't want to write the silly thing in C, then Perl may be for you. . . .

In 1989, Perl 3.0 was released and distributed for the first time under the GNU Public License with its now well-known *copy left* philosophy. Perl 5.0 was released in 1994, a complete rewrite of Perl adding objects and a modular organization. The modular structure makes it easy for everyone to develop *Perl modules* to extend the functionalities of Perl. CGI.pm (CGI Perl Module) is just such a library (1995 by Lincoln Stein). This module makes CGI programming in Perl much easier and more powerful.

Many other Perl modules have been created. The Comprehensive Perl Archive Network (CPAN; www.cpan.org) was established to store and distribute Perl and Perl-related software.

Because of its text processing ease, wide availability (it runs on all major platforms), and CGI programming abilities, Perl has became one of the most popular languages for CGI programming.

13.3   PERL PROGRAMMING ABC

To create a Perl program, you may use your favorite text editor. The very first line, before any other characters in the source code file, indicates the command to invoke the Perl interpreter. For example,

```
#!/usr/local/bin/perl
```

It indicates the location of the Perl interpreter, which will execute the rest of the file. This line can be different on different computers because the **perl** command can be installed anywhere on the hard disk. To move a Perl program to another computer, make sure the first line is adjusted to reflect the installation location of **perl**. This line may also specify any options, such as -T (*taint mode*; Section 13.18), for the **perl** command.

The Perl program file must be executable. On UNIX, use

```
chmod a+rx program_name
```

On Windows, run Perl programs from the MS-DOS prompt. As a Web CGI program, a Perl script must be placed in special cgi-bin directories configured by the Web server. In a Perl script:

- Comments start with the # character and continue to the end of the line.
- Each Perl statement ends with a semicolon (;).
- Statements are executed sequentially.
- The statement exit(0); (exit(1);) terminates the program normally (abnormally).

To run a Perl program, use either of the following:

```
program_name arg1 arg2 ...
perl program_name arg1 arg2 ...
```

As a CGI script, it must be placed in the Web server's cgi-bin.

Here is a short Perl program (Ex: **PerlCmdLine**) that displays the command-line arguments:

```
#!/usr/bin/perl
###  displaying the command line                    ## (a)

print "@ARGV\n";                                     ## (b)
print "First arg: $ARGV[0]\n";                       ## (c)
print "Second arg: $ARGV[1]\n";
print "Third arg: $ARGV[2]\n";                       ## (d)
```

The mandatory first line is usually followed by one or more comments (line a) documenting the purpose, usage, author, and other key information for the program.

The first statement (line b) calls the print function with a string that is the value of the built-in array variable @ARGV followed by the NEWLINE character (\n). The print function outputs strings to *standard output* or to specified destinations. The standard output is normally the terminal screen but becomes the Web server when the program executes under CGI. Array subscripting is used to display the first three command-line arguments (lines c and d).

On a UNIX system, enter this program into the file cmdline.pl and enter

chmod a+rx cmdline.pl

to make it executable. Then issue the command

./cmdline.pl a b c d e

to run the program, which is in the current directory (./). You should see the display

```
a b c d e
First arg: a
Second arg: b
Third  arg: c
```

You can run Perl programs similarly under MS/DOS. Remember to use the backslash \ as the directory separator.

Web CGI programs usually do not depend on command-line arguments and instead use form data sent via HTTP POST or GET requests. Or a CGI program can be invoked directly by a hyperlink independent of HTML forms. The general form of a CGI-invoking URL is shown in Figure 13.1:

1. The *cgi-path* usually starts with a prefix cgi-bin, which indicates a server-defined directory for placing CGI programs. The remainder is a path, relative to the cgi-bin, leading to the CGI program.

2. The optional *path-info* is a UNIX-style file pathname given by first placing a / after item 1. This value is transmitted to the CGI program via the PATH_INFO environment variable.

3. The optional *query-string* is given after first placing a question mark. It is a url-encoded string. If *query-string* contains no =, then it is transmitted to the CGI program as command-line arguments. Otherwise, it becomes the value of the QUERY_STRING environment variable.

Figure 13.1 CGI URL FORMAT

```
                         2
                    ⎧‾‾‾‾‾‾‾⎫
http://host:port/cgi-path/path-info?query-string
                 ⎩‾‾‾‾‾‾‾‾⎭          ⎩‾‾‾‾‾‾‾‾‾‾‾⎭
                     1                    3
```

Accessing a CGI program directly via such a URL is supported by the HTTP GET query.

Let's take a closer look at Perl before returning to CGI programming.

13.4   PERL VARIABLES

Perl provides three types of variables: *scalar*, *array* (list), and *association array* (hash).

Scalars

A scalar variable has a $ prefix and can take on any string or numerical values. For example,

```
$var = 'a string';        ## a quoted string
$n = length $var;         ## is 8
$x = 12;
$abc = "$var$x";          ## a string12   (A)
```

Characters enclosed in single quotation marks are taken literally, whereas variables are meaningful inside double quotation marks (line A).

Arrays

The Perl array variable uses the @ prefix. For example (Ex: **PerlArray**),

```
#!/usr/bin/perl

@arr = ("aa", "bb", "cc", "dd");   ## creating an array
print "$arr[0]\n";                 ## first array element is aa (B)
$arr[2]=7;                         ## third element set to 7      (C)
$m = $#arr;                        ## 3, last index of @arr       (D)
$n = @arr;                         ## n is 4 length of @arr       (E)
print "@arr\n";                    ## aa bb 7 dd                  (F)

push(@arr, "xyz");                 ## put on end of array         (G)
print "@arr\n";                    ## aa bb 7 dd xyz
$last = pop(@arr);                 ## pop off end of array        (H)
print "@arr\n";                    ## aa bb 7 dd
```

Note that we use the scalar notation to retrieve or set values on an array using indexing (lines B and C). The special prefix $# returns the index of the last array element (line D) and -1 if the array has no elements. Hence, $#arr+1 is the array length. Assigning an array to a scalar produces its length (line E). Displaying the entire array is as easy as printing it (line F).

Use the Perl built-in function push to append a new element to the end of the array (line G) and the pop function to remove the last element from the array (line H). The function shift (unshift) deletes (adds) an element at the beginning of an array.

Executing this program produces the following output:

```
aa
aa bb 7 dd
aa bb 7 dd xyz
aa bb 7 dd
```

Association Arrays

An association array, also known as a *hash array,* is an array with an even number of elements. Elements come in pairs: a *key* and a *value.* You can create hash arrays with the notation:

```
( key1 => value1, key2 => value2, ... )
```

The keys serve as symbolic indexes for the corresponding values on the association array.

Perl association array variables use the % prefix. For example (Ex: **PerlAsso**),

```
%asso = ( "a" => 7, "b" => 11 );   ##                    (1)
print "$asso{'a'}\n";              ## displays 7         (2)
print "$asso{'b'}\n";              ## displays 11        (3)
print "@asso{'a', 'b'}\n";         ## displays 7, 11     (4)
```

The symbol => (line 1) makes the association perfectly clear. But a comma works just as well.

```
%asso = ( "a", 7, "b", 11 );
```

To retrieve a value from an association array, use its key (lines 2 and 3). Note that the $ prefix is used with the key enclosed in curly braces ({}). To obtain a list of values from an association list, the @ prefix can be used (line 4). Use a nonexistent key or a value as a key (e.g., $asso{'z'}, $asso{7}), and you'll get an undefined value (undef).

Assign a new value with a similar assignment where the key may or may not already be on the association array:

```
$asso{'c'} = 13;
```

To remove key-value pairs from a hash, use calls like:

```
delete( $asso{'c'} );          (deletes one pair)
delete( @asso{'a', 'c'} );     (deletes a list of pairs)
```

The keys (values) function produces an array of keys (values) of a given hash:

```
@all_keys = keys( %asso )         ## ('a', 'b', 'c')
@all_values = values ( %asso )    ## (7, 11, 13)
```

You may turn a hash into a regular array (line 5) and use numerical indexing (lines 6 and 7):

```
@myarr = %asso;                   ##              (5)
print "$myarr[0]\n";              ## a            (6)
print "$myarr[1]\n";              ## 7
print "$myarr[2]\n";              ## b            (7)
```

The built-in association array %ENV contains all the environment variables transmitted to the Perl program. We have already seen how %ENV is used to access CGI-related environment values (Section 8.18).

13.5 ARITHMETIC AND STRING OPERATORS

Perl arithmetic operators are similar to those in C:

```
$a = 1 + 2;      # adds 1 and 2 and stores in $a
$a = 3 - 4;      # subtracts 4 from 3 and stores in $a
$a = 5 * 6;      # multiplies 5 and 6
$a = 7 / 8;      # divides 7 by 8 to give 0.875
$a = 2 ** 8;     # raises 2 to the power 8 (not in C)
$a = 5 % 2;      # gets remainder of 5 divided by 2
++$a;            # increments $a and then returns it
$a++;            # returns $a and then increments it
--$a;            # decrements $a and then returns it
$a--;            # returns $a and then decrements it
```

Perl strings can be easily concatenated:

```
$a = $b . $c;    # Dot operator concatenates $b and $c
$a = $b x $c;    # x operator repeats $b $c times
```

The usual assignment operations are supported:

```
$a = $b;              # assigns $b to $a
$a += $b;             # same as $a = $a + $b
$a -= $b;             # same as $a = $a - $b
$a .= $b;             # same as $a = $a . $b

($a, $b) = ($c, $d);  # same as $a=$c; $b=$d;
($a, $b) = @food;     # same as $a = $food[0]; $b = $food[1]
```

13.6 TRUE OR FALSE

In Perl Boolean values are scalar values interpreted in the Boolean context. The numerical zero, empty string, and undefined value are Boolean false. All other scalar values are Boolean true.

We test *logical conditions* with *relational operators*:

```
$a == $b      ## is $a numerically equal to $b?
              ##    also >, <, >=, <=
$a != $b      ## is $a numerically unequal to $b?

$a eq $b      ## are $a and $b equal as strings?
$a ne $b      ## are $a and $b unequal as strings?

($a && $b)    ## are both $a and $b true?
($a || $b)    ## is either $a or $b true?
!($a)         ## is $a false?
```

Also any nonzero number and any nonempty string are considered true. The number zero, the string "0", and the empty string are considered false.

13.7 AUTOMATIC DATA CONTEXT

Perl makes programming easier by detecting the context within which a variable is used and automatically converts its value appropriately. For example, you can use strings as numbers, and vice versa.

```
$str1 = "12.5";
$str2 = "2.5";
$sum = $str1 + $str2;      ## adding as numbers  (A)
print "$sum\n";            ## displaying         (B)
```

We used the strings as numbers on line A and the $sum, which is a number, as a string on line B.

The assignment $len = @arr uses @arr in a scalar context and turns its value to the length of the array. The automatic conversion of a hash to an array on line 5 is another example.

In a CGI program, the need to convert strings to numbers arises often. For example:

```
$total = param('payment');    ## a string representing a number
if ( $total > 50 )            ## number context
{   ...   }
```

The variable $total gets the string associated to the HTML form input payment. And we can compare it directly with the number 50. Converting a string that

does not represent a number to a number results in the number 0. Thus, if
$str != 0 is true, then $str is a valid nonzero number.

13.8   CONDITIONAL STATEMENTS

True or false tests are used in conditional statements that execute statements
only when specified conditions are met:

```
if ( test )
{   ... }
else          ## optional
{   ... }
```

The elsif is also available as part of an if statement:

```
if ( test )
{   ... }
elsif ( test2 ) ## note spelling
{   ... }
else    ## Everything before was false
{   ... }
```

By adding a *modifier* at the end of a statement, you can make its execution
conditional.

```
statement if ( test );
statement unless ( test );
```

13.9   PERL I/O

Standard I/O

In Perl, the *file handles* STDIN, STDOUT, and STDERR stand for the standard input
(from keyboard), standard output (to screen), and standard error output (to
screen, no buffering). When running as a CGI program, a Perl script receives
posted form data by reading STDIN. The code

```
if ( $ENV{'REQUEST_METHOD'} eq "POST" )
{   read(STDIN, $input, $ENV{'CONTENT_LENGTH'}); }
elsif ( $ENV{'REQUEST_METHOD'} eq "GET" )
{   $input = $ENV{'QUERY_STRING'}; }
else
{   $input = ""; }
```

detects the request method and sets $input to the form data.

The notation *<input-source>* is handy to read lines from an input source. For example,

```
$line = <STDIN>;    /* or simply $line = <> */
```

reads one line from standard input. Repeated execution of this statement will let you read line by line. The value of $line has the line termination character at the end. A handy function to remove any line terminator is the Perl built-in function chomp:

```
$str = chomp($line);
```

File I/O

The following program opens a file on the local file system for input, reads it, prints the data read to standard output, and closes the input file (Ex: **PerlCat**):

```
$file = $ARGV[0];                                # file name, a string
open(IN, $file) || die("can't open $file:$!"); # opens or fails
@lines = <IN>;                                   # reads into an array
close(IN);                                       # closes input file
print @lines;                                    # outputs the array
```

The file handle IN is set up by open to be used for I/O to the file. The function die prints a message before terminating the program. It is executed if open does not return true (failed). The special variable $! is the system error string.

Once the handle IN has been opened, you may use

```
read(IN, $input, 20});     # Reads 20 characters
$line = <IN>;              # Reads one line
@lines = <IN>;             # Reads whole file into array
```

to read in a specific number of characters, to read in one line, or to read in the whole file.

To open a file for output, use one of the following:

```
open(OUT, ">$file");       # opens file for output
open(OUT, ">>$file");      # opens file for appending
```

Now you can send output to the file with

```
print OUT "This line goes to the file.\n";
```

Again, you may close the output with

```
close(OUT);                     # closes the output file
```

Let $f be a file name or file handle. You can use the checks listed in Table 13.1 before opening it for reading or writing.

Table 13.1   FILE CHECKS

Check	Meaning	Check	Meaning
if ((-f $f))	is a plain file	if ((-d $f))	is a directory
if ((-r $f))	is readable	if ((-w $f))	is writable
if ((-x $f))	is executable	if ((-T $f))	is a text file
if ((-e $f))	exists	if ((-z $f))	is empty (zero size)
if ((-s $f))	is file size not 0	if ((-l $f))	is a symbolic link

Interprocess I/O

From a Perl program, you can execute any shell-level command (as another process on the same computer) and obtain its output with

```
$result = `command string`
```

where the *command string* is enclosed in BACKQUOTES (`` ` ``). For example,

```
$files = `ls -l`;
```

You can open another process for reading or writing. For example,

```
open(MAIL, "| /usr/sbin/sendmail") || die("fork failed") ;
```

gives MAIL for writing to the sendmail process. We have seen such uses in Section 8.17.
The code

```
open(RESULT, "| ls -l") || die("fork failed") ;
```

allows you to read the results from ls -l.

13.10   PERL ITERATIONS

An iteration is the repeated execution of a set of statements. Powerful programs often require iterations to perform tasks. Perl iteration constructs include foreach, while, do-while, and for.

The foreach Loop

The syntax is:

```
foreach $var ( @array )
{    statements    }
```

In a CGI program, we can display the name and value of each environment variable (Figure 13.2) with this iteration:

```
@keys = keys(%ENV);
$n = @keys;
print "<h2>Environment Values: $n</h2>";
print "<p style=\"font-size: larger\"><code>";
foreach  $key ( @keys )
{   print "$key = <span style=\"color: #c33\">
        $ENV{$key}</span><br />";
}
print "</code></p>";
```

You can list the names of all .html files with the following:

```
print "<ul>";
foreach $file ( <*.html> )        ## file name matching
{     print "<li>$file</li>";
}
print "</ul>";
```

The notation <*.html> allows UNIX shell-like file matching.

The while Loop

The while iteration has the general form:

```
while ( test condition )
{     statements
}
```

Figure 13.2   DISPLAYING CGI ENVIRONMENTAL VARIABLES

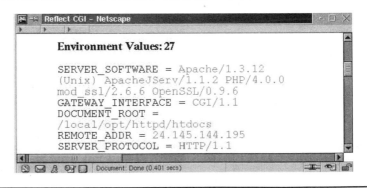

The while loop tests a condition and, if true, executes a set of statements. The cycle is repeated until the test condition becomes false. If the condition is false in the beginning, the body of while may not be executed even once.

Let amounts.txt be a file with one amount figure per line. This while loop computes the total:

```
$sum = 0;
open(IN, "amounts.txt");        # opens file for reading
while ( defined($amt = <IN>) )  # reads one line    (A)
{    $sum += $amt;   }
print "$amt\n";
```

The condition (line A) becomes false only after all lines are read from the file.

To iterate over an associative array, use

```
while ( ($person, $grade) = each(%grades) )
{     ...     }
```

The Perl function each returns the next two-element list of a hash for each iteration.

The do-while Loop

The do-while is very similar to while, but it executes the enclosed statements before checking the condition for loop continuation:

```
do
{

     statements

} while ( condition );
```

The for Loop

The while, do-while, and for loops all follow the C language. Here is an example of a for loop:

```
for ($i = 0; $i < 10; ++$i)       # starts with $i = 0
                                  # continues while $i < 10
                                  # increments $i before repeating
{    print "$i\n";    }
```

Loop Control

In a loop, the commands

```
next      (starts the next iteration)
last      (breaks out of the loop)
```

can be used. The command `next` (`last`) is like the `continue` (`break`) operator in C/C++.

If you put a label, in the form *label*:, in front of a loop, then `next` *label* and `last` *label* affect the indicated loop. These are useful in nested loops. Without a label, `next` and `last` refer only to the immediate enclosing loop.

13.11 DEFINING FUNCTIONS

Most serious programs require the definition of functions that can be called from anywhere. You define functions with the `sub` keyword. A function can be placed anywhere in your Perl source code file. Usually, all functions are placed at the end of the file. For substantial programming, functions and objects can be placed in separate *packages* or *modules* and then imported into a program with the `use` statement (Section 13.19).

The general form of a function is:

```
sub functionName
{
     a sequence of statements
}
```

A call to the preceding may take any of these forms:

```
functionName();          ## no arg
functionName($a);        ## one arg
functionName($aa, $bb);  ## two args
functionName(@arr);      ## array elements as args
functionName($aa, @arr); ## $aa and array elements as args
```

A function gets incoming arguments in the special array `@_`. In a function definition, the notations `$_[0]`, `$_[1]`, and `$_[2]` are used to access the individual arguments.

Arguments, scalars, arrays, and hashes in a function call are passed to the receiving function as a *flat list*. Consider the function call

```
myfunc($total, @toys)
```

In myfun, $_[0] is $x; $_[1] is $toys[0]; $_[2] is $toys[1], and so on. Furthermore, each $_[i] is a reference to the argument passed, and modifying it will alter the data in the calling program.

To obtain a local copy of the passed arguments, you can use

```
sub myfun
{    my($a, $b, $c) = @_;          // $a, $b, $c local to myfun
     ...                           // and have copies of passed data
}
```

Here $a gets a copy of $_[0], $b gets a copy of $_[1], and so on.

Use return value; to return a value for a function. If a function returns without executing a return, then the value is that of the last statement.

Sometimes you need to include arrays and hashes in a function call *un-flattened*. This can be done by passing *references* to the arrays and hashes. In general, a *reference* is a symbol that leads to the construct to which it refers (like a pointer). References are scalars and are passed in function calls as such.

References are not hard to understand. The following points will help:

- Put a \ in front of a variable to obtain a reference: $ref_x = \$x, ref_x = \@x, or ref_x = \%x.
- Now $ref_x is a reference and can be used just like the symbol x to which it refers.
- The notation $$ref_x is the same as $x, @$ref_x is the same as @x, and %$ref_x is the same as %x.

The following Perl program (Ex: **PerlRef**) shows a scalar $x, an array @arr, a hash %asso, and how their references are obtained and used:

```
#!/usr/bin/perl
my $x = 3.1416, @arr = ("a", "b");
my %asso = ("one" => 7, "two" => 11);

my $ref_x = \$x;              // three references
my $ref_foo = \@arr;
my $ref_bar = \%asso;

// using references
print "$$ref_x\n";            // 3.1416
print "$$ref_foo[1]\n";       // b
print "$$ref_bar{'two'}\n";   // 11
```

When references are passed in function calls, they can be used in the called function exactly the same way.

Local Variables in Functions

In Perl, all variables are global within their module (source code file) unless declared local. In a subroutine, local variables are declared with either of the keywords my or local.

- local(var1, var2, ...); (dynamic nesting)
- my(var1, var2, ...); (static lexical scoping)

A variable declared by my is known only within the function or source code file in the same sense as local variables in C, C++, or Java. A variable declared by local is known within the function and other function it calls at run time in the same sense as prog variables in Common LISP. For most purposes, the my declaration will suffice.

As an example, let's write a function htmlBegin. This can be a handy CGI utility that sends out the leading part of the HTML code for an HTTP response (Ex: **HtmlBegin**).

The function receives two arguments: the name of a page title and a file name $frontfile. The $frontfile is a partial HTML template that can be customized for the look and feel of a particular Web site.

```
sub htmlBegin
{    my $title=$_[0];         ##  page title
     my $frontfile=$_[1];     ##  HTML template
     my $line;
     print "Content-type: text/html\r\n\r\n";
     if ( defined($frontfile) )
     {   open(IN, $frontfile) || die "Can't open $frontfile";
         while ( $line=<IN> )
         {   if ( $line =~ /XYZZZ/ )
             {   $line =~ s/XYZZZ/$title/;  }              ## (1)
             if  ( $line =~ /XHTMLFRONT/ )
             {   $line =~ s/XHTMLFRONT/$xhtml_front/;  }  ## (2)
             print  $line;
         }
         close(IN);
     }
     else
     {   print ( "$xhtml_front"                           ## (3)
                 . "<head><title>$title</title>"
                 . "</head><body>\n" );
     }
}
```

The variable $xhtml_front is set to the first lines needed for an XHTML file earlier in this program.

A sample call to this function is

```
htmlBegin("Request Confirmation", "webtong front");
```

where the page title and an "HTML template" are supplied. The file `webtong.front`

```
XHTMLFRONT
<head><title>Webtong - XYZZZ</title>
<base href="http://www.webtong.com/feedback.html" />
<link rel="stylesheet" type="text/css" href="webtong.css" />
</head><body>
<table class="layout" border="0" cellspacing="0"
        cellpadding="0" width="100%">
<!-- top banner begin -->
   ...
<!-- top banner end -->
<h2>XYZZZ</h2></tr><tr>
<!-- left nav bar begin -->
   ...
<!-- left nav bar end -->

<td class="content">
<!-- CONTENT BEGIN -->
```

is an HTML fragment for the style and layout of a Web site with XYZZZ and XHTMLFRONT as parts to be replaced by the `htmlBegin` function. Perl pattern matching is used (lines 1 and 2) to make the replacement. (See Section 13.13 for a description of Perl patterns.) In case $frontfile is not defined, a generic HTML opening is used (line 3).

13.12 A FORM TO MAIL PROGRAM

For many Web sites, forms are used to collect information for offline processing. Such forms can be supported by a well-designed server-side program that takes the form-collected data and sends email to designated persons. Furthermore, such a program can be made to serve forms located on various authorized sites. Hidden fields in the form can be used to customize and control the behavior of the program to suit diverse needs (Ex: **FormToMail**). As early as 1995, such a CGI program was created and placed on the Web by Matt Wright. The **FormToMail** program described here has many new features and is also simpler because it uses the Perl CGI module. Figure 13.3 shows the FormToMail architecture. The form-supplied configuration parameters (dashed arrow) control how the CGI program works. The form-supplied email content (solid arrow) is sent to the target recipient and reflected in the confirmation response page.

Figure 13.3   FORMTOMAIL ARCHITECTURE

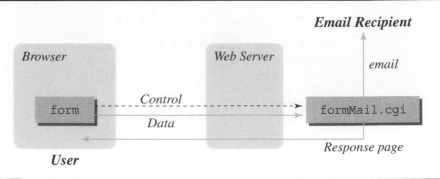

Program Configuration

Our CGI program (Ex: **FormToMail**) begins with the customization part:

```
#!/usr/bin/perl
### formToMail.cgi
use CGI qw(:standard);                  ## uses CGI
my $formid, $front, $back, $recipient;  ## global vars


#### Customization begin
$mailprog = '/usr/lib/sendmail -t';     ## location of sendmail

my @referrers = ();                     ## (1)
#### Customization end
```

The variable `mailprog` indicates the location of the *sendmail* command used for sending email. The array `@referrers` (line 1) lists all domains (or domain prefixes) whose Web site may deploy forms to access this program. Example settings are:

```
my @referrers = ("symbolicnet.org", "131.123.35.90");
my @referrers =
    ('sofpower.com', 'cs.kent.edu', 'rooster.localdomain');
```

To avoid illegitimate use of the email program, we insist on forms placed on known hosts (the referrers) and requests via the POST method. Checking is done by the function `checkReferrer`:

```
sub checkReferrer
{   if ( $ENV{'REQUEST_METHOD'} eq "GET" ) // disallowed
    {   error('get request not allowed');   }
    my $url= $ENV{'HTTP_REFERER'};                         # (2)
    if ( $url )
    {   foreach $referrer (@referrers)
```

```
   {   if ($url =~ m|https?://([^/0-9]*)$referrer|i) # (3)
       { return; }
   }
  }
  error('bad_referrer');                                    # (4)
}
```

If the URL given by the environment variable HTTP_REFERER (line 2) does not contain any domain or domain prefix listed on @referrers (line 3), an error results (line 4). The *pattern matching* used on line 3 is discussed in Section 13.13.

The Config associative array lists keys and some default values used in the formMail.cgi program. Values for these keys can be supplied by input fields in the form:

```
## Configuration values
my %Config=('formid' => '', 'sender_name' => '',
            'email' => '',   'subject' => 'Form Email',
            'redirect' => '', 'sort' => '',
            'print_blank_fields' => '',
            'page_title' => 'Thank You',
            'required' => 'formid,email,sender_name');   # (5)
```

Form-supplied values are required for the first three keys: formid identifies the HTML form, sender_name gives the name who filled out the form, and email is the sender's email address. The variable required lists form keys whose values must be supplied. Its initial value lists three items (line 5). But the submitting form can name other required form entries. The email subject and reply page_title default to Form Email and Thank You, respectively.

The form can also elect to redirect to a different response page, to request ordering of form entries in the response and in the email listing, and to list or ignore empty form fields.

Each valid *formid* has a recipient list $Recipient{$formid} and an optional email cc list defined by the configuration association lists:

```
my %Recipient=('webtong_hosting' => 'sales@webtong.com',  # (6)
              'webtong' => 'info@webtong.com',
              'wdp_MailForm' => 'test');

my %Cc = ( 'webtong_hosting' => 'DomainMaster@webtong.com' );
```

Thus, the program works only for predefined *formid*s (three here in line 6) and hard-coded recipients.

Each *formid* can also be associated with two optional files

```
$Config{'formid'}.front
$Config{'formid'}.back
```

used to build a customized response page for a particular form.

Let's take a look at the HTML form before returning to the rest of the Perl program.

Form for FormToMail

A Web hosting form, for example, may supply these values by hidden form fields:

```
<form method="post" action="/cgi-bin/formMail.cgi">
<input type="hidden" name="formid" value="webtong_hosting" />
<input type="hidden" name="subject" value="Web Hosting" />
<input type="hidden" name="page_title"
       value="Hosting Request Received" />
<input type="hidden" name="required"
       value="domain,phone,email,sender_name" />

...

</form>
```

Other values such as email and sender_name are input fields to be filled by the user.

The form must be placed on the correct referrer site and indicate the correct formid to work. An email will only be sent to recipients prescribed in the CGI program.

The CGI Program

The program formMail.cgi follows a few steps to achieve results:

```
checkReferrer();      # checks referring URL
$date = getDate();    # retrieves current date
formData();           # obtains data sent from form
checkData();          # checks data for required fields etc.
sendMail();           # sends email
response();           # returns response or redirects
exit(0);              # terminates program
```

Calling getDate() sets up a well-formatted date and time string used in the email and response page as a time stamp.

The formData() function retrieves the form-supplied data and sets values in the Config and Form associative arrays for later use. The call param() (line A) gives all keys sent by the form:

```
sub formData
{  my ($name, $value);
   foreach $name ( param() )    # for each name-value pair    (A)
```

```
{    $value = param($name);
     if (defined($Config{$name}))   ## set Config values
     {  if ($name eq 'required')
        {   $Config{$name} = $Config{$name} . "," . $value;  }
        else
        {   $Config{$name} = $value;   }
        if ($name eq 'email' || $name eq 'sender_name')   # (B)
        {    push(@Field_Order,$name);
             $Form{$name} = $value;
        }
     }
     else                                      ## set Form values
     {  if ($Form{$name} && $value)
        {
             $Form{$name} = "$Form{$name}, $value";
        }
        elsif ($value)
        {   push(@Field_Order,$name);
            $Form{$name} = $value;
        }
     }
  }
  ## removes white spaces and obtains required fields
  $Config{'required'} =~ s/(\s+|\n)?,(\s+|\n)?/,/g;          # (C)
  $Config{'required'} =~ s/(\s+)?\n+(\s+)?//g;
  @Required = split(/,/,$Config{'required'});               # (D)
}
```

Each form value is obtained and stored in either the Config or the Form associative array. The sender_name and email are set in both (line B). The required
Form and Config values are set up in the @Required array (lines C and D). The
checkData function sets up global variables (lines E and F) and uses @Required
to check for all required fields.

```
sub checkData
{    my ($require, @error, $formid);
     $formid = $Config{'formid'};           ## formid                (E)
     $recipient=$Recipient{$formid};        ## mail recipient
     if ( (-e "$formid.front") && (-e "$formid.back") )
     {  $front="$formid.front";   ## response front file
        $back ="$formid.back";    ## response back file             (F)
     }
     if (!$recipient) { error('no_recipient') }
     foreach $require (@Required)
     {   # email address must be valid
         if ($require eq 'email' )
```

```
        {   if ( !checkEmail($Config{$require}))
            { push(@error,$require); }
        }

        # check required config values
        elsif (defined($Config{$require}))
        {   if (!$Config{$require})
            { push(@error,$require); }
        }
        # check required form data
        elsif (!$Form{$require})
        { push(@error,$require); }
    }
    # If error
    if (@error) { error('missing_fields', @error) }
}
```

After user input has been received and checked, the program proceeds to send email and produce an HTTP response. The function sendMail sends email:

```
sub sendMail
{   if ( $recipient eq "test" ) { return; }
    open(MAIL,"|$mailprog")                      # opens mail program (G)
        || die("open $mailprog failed") ;
    mailHeaders();                               # email headers      (H)
    print MAIL "This is a message from the " .
                "$Config{'site'}.  It was submitted by\n";
    print MAIL "$Config{'sender_name'} " .
                "($Config{'email'}) on $date\n";
    print MAIL "-" x 75 . "\n\n";                #                    (I)

    if ($Config{'sort'} eq 'alphabetic')   # alphabetical order (J)
    {   mailFields(sort keys %Form); }
    elsif( getOrder() )                          # specific order
    {   mailFields(@sorted_fields); }
    else                                         # no ordering
    {   mailFields(@Field_Order); }
    print MAIL "-" x 75 . "\n\n";
    close (MAIL);
}
```

It opens the mail program (line G) and sends output to it with the print function. The mailHeaders function (line H) sends the To:, From:, Subject:, and Cc: headers. A confirmation copy is sent to the form sender at the given email address. The `"-"` x 75 is Perl notation to get 75 consecutive dashes, and the Perl operator `.` concatenates strings (line I). The form fields are sent on separate lines in three different possible orderings (line J) controlled by the `Config{'sort'}` value.

The `formMail` program also uses the `htmlBegin` (Section 13.11) and a similar `htmlEnd` function to allow easy site integration:

```
sub htmlBegin
{    my $title-$_[0];
     my $ln;
     print "Content-type: text/html\n\n";
     if ( defined($front) && $front ne ""
          && open(FF, $front) )                ## front file
     {    while ( $ln=<FF> )
          {  if ( $ln =~ /XYZZZ/ )
               {    $ln =~ s/XYZZZ/$title/;   }  ## page title
               print  $ln;
          }
          close(FF);
     }
     else
     {    print ("<html><head><title>$title</title>" .
               "</head><body bgcolor=white>\n");
     }
}
```

The function `htmlBegin` is called as follows:

```
htmlBegin("$Config{'page_title'}");
```

The program also contains `getDate` and other functions, including several for email checking to ensure the email address of the user is well-formed. The complete `formMail.cgi` program is available in the example package.

13.13 PATTERN MATCHING IN PERL

Matching string patterns is important in practice. This is especially true for both client-side JavaScript and Perl CGI programming. We have seen some patterns and pattern matching in JavaScript (Section 9.10) already. This is a big boost for pattern matching in Perl because almost identical regular expression notations are used. In fact, JavaScript has borrowed the Perl regular expression syntax and semantics almost without change because Perl has excellent support for pattern matching and related manipulations.

The Perl relational operators =~ (match) and !~ (nonmatch) are used for pattern matching. In Perl, patterns are specified as *extended regular expressions* similar to those used for JavaScript and the UNIX **egrep** utility.

The following are some simple matching examples involving the string $line:

```
if ( $line =~ /kent/ )    ## contains kent

if ( $line =~ /Kent/ )    ## contains Kent

if ( $line =~ /Kent/i )   ## contains kent, ignoring case

if ( $line =~ /^Kent/ )   ## Kent at beginning of line

if ( $line =~ /Kent$/ )   ## Kent at end of line
```

Note that patterns are given inside /s (the pattern delimiter). If the pattern contains /, then it is convenient to use a leading m, which allows you to use any nonalphanumeric character as the pattern delimiter:

```
if ( $url =~ m|http://| )              #(A)
```

Or you can use \ to escape the / in the pattern:

```
if ( $url =~ /http:\/\// )             #(Same as A)
```

Table 9.2 (Chapter 9) illustrates the use of patterns.

The following is a pattern we applied in Ex: **FormToMail**:

```
if ($url =~ m|https?://([^/0-9]*)$referrer|i)          (B)
```

The pattern starts with http, then an optional s, followed by the three characters ://, followed by zero or more characters each not a digit or the /, ending at the $referrer string. The i at the end (line B) is a *match option* indicating *case-insensitive* matching.

Special characters in Perl patterns include:

\n	A newline
\t	A tab
\w	Any alphanumeric (word) character. The same as [a-zA-Z0-9_]
\W	Any nonword character. The same as [^a-zA-Z0-9_]
\d	Any digit. The same as [0-9]
\D	Any nondigit. The same as [^0-9]
\s	Any white-space character: space, \t, \n, etc.
\S	Any non-white-space character
\b	A word boundary, outside [] only
\B	No word boundary
\x	escapes x

13.14   SUBSTITUTIONS

Often we look for a pattern in a string for the purpose of replacing it. This can be done easily with the string matching operator =~:

- $line =~ s/http/HTTP/;—Replaces first occurrence of http in $line by HTTP.
- $line =~ s/http/HTTP/g;—Replaces all occurrences *globally* in $line.
- $line =~ s/http/HTTP/gi;—Ignores case in global matching.
- $line =~ s/*pattern*/*cmd*/e;—Uses the replacement string obtained by executing *cmd*.

Pattern Matching Memory

You can store the parts of the string that matches parts of a pattern and use these matched parts in substitutions or for other purposes.

You use parentheses in a pattern to call for memory. Matched strings get remembered in the variables $1,...,$9. These strings can also be used in the same regular expression (or substitution) by using the alternative codes \1,...,\9. For example:

- /(\w)\1/—Matches repeated words.
- /(['"]).*\1/—Words within single or double quotes,
- s/(Art)/$1s/—Art becomes Arts.

Perl automatically uses the built-in variables $` (string before the matched string), $& (the matched string), $' (string after the matched string) to remember the three parts for a match. Thus, the following works:

s/Art/$&s/   Art becomes Arts

Let's look at some substitution examples. If $line is

$line = 'BB   MM   GG   LL';

then

```
$line =~ s/(\S+)\s+(\S+)/\2 \1/;   ## switches BB with MM
$line =~ s/s+(\S+)\s+(\S+)/\2 \1/; ## switches BB with GG
$line =~ s/(\S+)\s+(\S+)/$2 $1/g;  ## switches first two,
                                   ##   then next two ...
```

The flag g matches the pattern repeatedly.

The flag e allows you to execute a Perl expression and use the result of that expression as the substitution string. The following statement

$form_data =~ s/%(..)/pack("C", hex($1))/ge;

decodes the hex codes in the URL-encoded $form_data. The built-in function hex turns a string into a hex number, and the built-in function pack turns a hex number into a corresponding ASCII character.

13.15 SIMPLE PAGE SEARCH

Let's see how string manipulation, file I/O, function definition, and pattern matching can be put to use in a CGI program.

The Web site SymbolicNet.org has an email directory for people in *symbolic computation*, an area of research. The email directory page offers a page-search function (Ex: **PageSearch**) that allows users to enter a text string to obtain all email listings matching the given string. Figure 13.4 shows the form at the beginning of the email directory page (listing.html).

The HTML source code for the form is:

```
<p>To look for email entries in this page,
   please enter text to find.</p>
<form method="post"
      action="/cgi-bin/pagesearch.pl">        <!-- a -->
  <input type="hidden" name="page"
         value="/email/listing.html" />        <!-- b -->
  <p>Find text:<br />
  <input name="pattern" size="20" />  
  <input type="submit" value="Find All" /> </p>
</form>
```

The CGI program pagesearch.pl (line a) receives the location of the file to search via a hidden form field (line b).

The program pagesearch.pl performs these tasks:

- Opens a given email listing page
- Looks for the form-supplied pattern in each line of the page

Figure 13.4 EMAIL DIRECTORY SEARCH

- Remembers all matching lines
- Outputs the count of lines matched followed by all matching lines
- Reports errors when something is wrong

This CGI program also sends the content length conforming to HTTP 1.1. Let's look at the source code of pagesearch.pl.

The CGI.pm module (line 1) is used. The variable $sn_root (line 2) is the file path of the document root for SymbolicNet. The string $reply is the search result, and $error is for error messages (line 3). The actual page to search ($page) is now retrieved from the value of the form parameter page (line 4). If $page is not set, a message is appended to $error (line 5).

The program proceeds to open the file to be searched (line 6). If that file fails to open, a message is added to $error (line 7). Note the use of the Perl operator or, which can also be written as ||. If open fails, its value is false, which causes the right operand of or to be evaluated. If open succeeds, its value is true and the right operand of or will not be evaluated.

```perl
#!/usr/bin/perl
##   search email listing
use CGI qw(:standard);                          ## (1)

my $sn_root="/home/httpd/htdocs";               ## (2)
my $reply="", $error = "", $file;               ## (3)
my $page = param('page');                        ## (4)

if ( $page eq "" )
{  $error .=
     "<p>Page to search not specified!</p>";     ## (5)
}
else
{  $file = $sn_root . $page;
   open(listing, "$file") or                     ## (6)
     $error .= "<p>Can not open $file!</p>";      ## (7)
}

$pt = param('pattern');                          ## (8)

if ( $pt eq "" )
{  $error .= "<p>You didn\'t " .                 ## (9)
       "submit any text to find.</p>";
}

if ( $error )
{  errorReply($error); exit(1); }               ## (10)
```

```
### construct reply
outputFile("frontfile");                              ## (11)

### find matching entries
my $count = 0, $match="";
while ( defined($line=<listing>) )                    ## (12)
{   if ( $line =~ /$pt/i )                             ## (13)
    {   $count++;                                      ## (14)
        $match .= $line;                               ## (15)
    }
}
close(listing);   ## done with listing

$reply .= "<h3 style=\"margin-top: 16px\">
          Found $count entries matching
          <code>$pt</code>:</h3>";                     ## (16)

if ( $count > 0 )
{   $reply .= "<ol> $match </ol>"; }                   ## (17)

outputFile("backfile");                                ## (18)
sendPage($reply);                                      ## (19)
exit(0);                                               ## (20)
```

With `listing` opened (line 6), we now obtain the pattern to match (line 8), handling the missing-pattern error in a similar way. If any error has been detected (line 10), the `errorReply` function is called to display the $error and the program terminates.

Detecting no error, the program begins to construct the $reply string. The `frontfile` is added to $reply first (line 11).

The `while` loop (line 12) reads each line (in the form of an `<li>` element) from `listing` and, if the line contains the pattern (line 13), increments the *match count* (line 14) and concatenates the line to the variable $match (line 15).

The number of matching entries found is appended to $reply (line 16) as a level-three heading. And if there are any matching entries, they are displayed in a numbered list (line 17). The program terminates (line 20) after adding the `backfile` and sending the response page (line 19).

The functions used are at the end of the program. The `front()` function puts out the `Content-type` header and two line terminators (line 20). It then calls `outputFile` (line 22) to send out the front part of the HTML code.

```
sub outputFile                                         ## (21)
{   my($ln, $f);
    $f = $_[0];                                        ## (22)
    open(FF, $f) ||
      errMail("failed to open the file $f.");          ## (23)
```

```
    while ( $line=<FF> ) {   $reply .= "$line"; }
    close(FF);
}
```

The `outputFile` function (line 21) takes a file name argument (line 22). The notation $\_[0]$ refers to the first argument passed to a function.

The `frontfile` and `backfile` are fixed HTML codes that put the CGI-generated content in the presentation style of the SymbolicNet site. Thus, the CGI response is integrated with the SymbolicNet site (Figure 13.5). A unified look and feel is important for both static and dynamic pages.

Code in `frontfile` and `backfile` usually contain hyperlinks relative to the location of the HTML form rather than the location of the CGI program. We can make those links work for the CGI reply page by adding to the base element

```
<base href="URL-of-correct-location" />
```

The `sendPage` function takes the page content argument and sends it out under HTTP 1.1 protocol. By sending the content length (line 24), the server and client can keep their connection alive for better networking efficiency.

```
sub sendPage
{   my $content=$_[0];
    my $length=length($content);
    print "Content-type: text/html\r\n";
    print "Content-length: $length\r\n\r\n";                    ## (24)
    print $content;
}

sub errorReply
{   my $msg=$_[0];
    outputFile("front");
```

Figure 13.5   MATCHING EMAIL ENTRIES

```
        $reply .= "<h3 style=\"margin-top: 16px\">
                Error encountered:</h3> $msg";
        $reply .= "<p>Please go back and submit your
                request again.</p>";
        outputFile("backfile");
        sendPage($reply);
}
```

The errorReply function (called on line 10) displays $error and then terminates the program. Figure 13.6 shows a sample error page.

The errMail function is called (line 23) when frontfile or backfile cannot be opened. This internal error won't happen if these two files have been placed in the cgi-bin together with pagesearch.pl with read access opened.

chmod o+r frontfile backfile

When called, the errMail function sends the internal error information to the Webmaster of SymbolicNet.

```
sub errMail
{  my $mailer;
   $mailer = "/lib/sendmail -t";                          ## (25)
   $msg = $_[0];
   if ( open(MAIL, "| $mailer " ) )
   {  print MAIL "Subject: $ENV{'SCRIPT_NAME'} Error\n";
      print MAIL "To: $ENV{'SERVER_ADMIN'}\n";            ## (26)
      print MAIL "From: SymbolicNet\n";
      print MAIL "Script error: $msg";
      close (MAIL);
   }
   else
   {  print STDERR "mail failed\n"; }
```

Figure 13.6   ERROR DISPLAY

```
    exit(1);
}
```

The **sendmail** command (line 25) is the most basic email program located at /lib/sendmail on most UNIX systems. The email address of the server administrator is obtained from the environment variable SERVER_ADMIN (line 26).

13.16   PERL BUILT-IN FUNCTIONS

Perl Documentation

In both Chapter 8 and this chapter, we have seen many built-in functions in action. Many more built-in functions are available in Perl, making it a powerful tool. You can find complete coverage of all functions in the Perl documentation. On UNIX systems, the shell command

man perl

shows the Perl overview and the list of topics you can access with the **man** command. In particular

man perlfunc	built-in functions
man perlsub	defining your own functions
man perlre	regular expressions

and so on. On the Web, Perl documentation can be found at www.perldoc.com.

Generally, a built-in function takes either one scalar argument or an argument list. In the latter case, a function call looks like

functionName(arg1, arg2, ... , argn)

Each argument can be scalar, array, or hash. And the arguments are passed as a flat list, as described in Section 13.11.

Let's describe a few more useful functions. The function join(*$str*, *$list*) forms a single string by joining all the elements on *list* separated by the given string *str*. The function substr(*$str*, *$offset*, *$length*) obtains a substring of *str*. The last argument is optional. The function index(*$str*, *$substr*) returns a zero-based index of the position of *substr* in *str*.

The tr function performs character-by-character translation:

$var =~ tr/chars/replacements/

For example,

```
$var = "name=John+J+Doe";
$var =~ tr/+/ /;                    (becomes name=John J Doe)
```

translates each + to a SPACE in $var, whereas

```
$sentence =~ tr/abc/ABC/
```

replaces a by A, b by B, and so on. The following replaces all lowercase characters with uppercase ones:

```
$var =~ tr/a-z/A-Z/;      becomes NAME=JOHN+J+DOE
```

The `split` function is used to split a string into parts. The parts are returned in an array. For example,

```
$info = "Caine:Michael:Actor:14, Leafy Drive";
@personal = split(/:/, $info);
```

Then @personal becomes

```
("Caine", "Michael", "Actor", "14, Leafy Drive")
```

If `split` is given only one argument (a string), and then it is split at white-space characters.

The function `eval` can be given a string, and it will execute that string as a Perl statement.

Numerical functions in Perl include `abs` (absolute value), `cos` (cosine), `exp` (exponentiation), `hex` (hex value), `int`, `log` (natural logarithm), `oct` (octal value), `rand` (random number generation), `sin` (sine), `sqrt` (square root), and `srand` (sets seed for `rand()`).

13.17 HANDLING PASSWORDS

Putting some of the functions to use, let's look at a Perl program `unixpw.pl`. This example (Ex: **UnixPW**) is a complete Perl program that produces an encrypted password using the UNIX crypt method. The shell-level command

unixpw.pl catandmouse 9i

produces the output

```
catandmouse --> 9iYuNF9nj2vm.
```

displaying the password in clear and encrypted text.

The 9i is a *salt*, a random two-character string from the character set `[./0-9A-Za-z]`, to make the encrypted password more secure.

```
#!/usr/bin/perl
## unixpw.pl generates a Unix encrypted Password

use strict;

my $salt='';
my $encrypted='';
my $password='';
my $use = 'usage: unixpw password [salt]';
```

```perl
my @saltchars=('.', '/', 0..9, 'A'..'Z', 'a'..'z');
my $args=length(@ARGV);

if ( $args < 1 || $args > 2 )                    ## (1)
{   print "$use\n";                              ## (2)
    exit;
}

$password=$ARGV[0];

if ( $args == 1 )                                ## (3)
{   $salt = join('',@saltchars[rand(64),
            rand(64)]);
}
else                                             ## (4)
{   $salt=$ARGV[1];
}

$encrypted=crypt($password,$salt);       ## (5)
print "$password --> $encrypted\n";
```

The number of command-line arguments is checked (line 1), and if incorrect, the program usage is displayed (line 2). If only one argument is supplied (line 3), a salt value is generated randomly by calling the rand and join functions. The password and salt are then passed to the crypt function to produce the encrypted password (line 5).

A password checking program can use

```perl
if ( crypt($password, $encrypted) eq $encrypted )
```

to check if a user-supplied $password is correct by using an $encrypted string from a password file.

13.18   TAINT MODE

CGI programs sometimes use form data in shell-level or system-level commands. This presents a security problem if the user data are not well-formed or even intentionally set to break the security of the server.

One good way to lock out security bugs in Perl code is to turn on *taint mode*. Taint mode causes a Perl script to automatically treat all user-supplied input as tainted and dangerous unless the programmer explicitly OKs the data.

To turn on taint mode, you add the -T option to the Perl interpreter:

```perl
#!/usr/bin/perl -T
```

In taint mode, Perl does not allow the use of tainted data in potentially unsafe operations (guarded operations). These include shell commands with BACK-QUOTEs (`` ` ``), any system or piped open() calls, opening files for output, and deleting or renaming files. Perl first ensures that the command search PATH and command-related values on the ENV are correct. In taint mode, the Perl program must explicitly set $ENV{'PATH'} and delete unneeded values on %ENV:

```
$ENV{'PATH'}='/usr/sbin:/sbin:/bin:/usr/bin';
delete @ENV{qw(IFS CDPATH ENV BASH_ENV)};
```

The formMail program will run under taint mode if you add the preceding two lines to the program.

A program must also check the correctness of user-supplied data. Correct user data can be untainted before being used in guarded operations. For example,

```
$email = param('email');       ## email address from user
if ( checkEmail($email) )       ## check correctness
{   $email = untaint($email);  ## untainting
    sendMail($email);           ## function uses guarded operation
}
```

The function checkEmail is a Perl version of the email checking program described in Section 9.15.

The untaint function is:

```
sub untaint
{   $_[0] =~ /(.+)/;            ## pattern matching
    return $1;
}
```

Any result from pattern matching, $1 here, becomes untainted and usable in guarded operations.

Let's look at a simple but complete example (Ex: **UnTaint**) of a taint-mode Perl script. It can serve as a guide for writing your own taint-mode scripts.

```
#!/usr/bin/perl -T
use CGI qw(:standard);

$ENV{'PATH'}='/usr/sbin:/sbin:/bin:/usr/bin';   ## (A)
delete @ENV{qw(IFS CDPATH ENV BASH_ENV)};        ## (B)

$file = noSpecial(param('filename'));            ## (C)
open($FH, ">$file");                             ## (D)
print $FH "a text line\n";
close($FH);

sub noSpecial                                    ## (E)
```

```
{    $_[0] =~ s/([^a-zA-Z0-9_@,.-])/\\$1/g;
     untaint($_[0]);
}
```

```
sub untaint
{    $_[0] =~ /(.+)/;
     return $1;
}
```

The program first takes care of PATH and @ENV (lines A and B). Then it checks and untaints the file name supplied by the user before using it to create a new file (line D). If the file name is not untainted, the guarded operation open will fail.

The function noSpecial adds the escape character \ in front of any UNIX shell special characters and then untaints the argument string (line E). See the security section of the Perl manual (perlsec) for more information.

13.19   THE PERL CGI MODULE

CGI.pm is a *Perl module* that we have been using informally since Chapter 8. It is time to provide a description of Perl modules and an overview of the CGI module.

What Is a Perl Module?

Perl modules are packages of Perl functions that perform particular tasks. Module files are named *module_name*.pm. For example, CGI.pm is for writing CGI programs for the Web, and LWP.pm is for making HTTP requests from Perl programs.

A module is a package that provides a separate name space where all its identifiers have the *module_name*:: prefix when used from outside the module.

Standard modules, such as CGI.pm, come with the Perl distribution. Additional modules can be downloaded for free, and new ones are being developed all the time. See www.cpan.org/modules for a listing and how to install or update Perl modules. The command

perl -MCPAN -e shell

loads Perl modules with a high degree of automation.

Using Perl Modules

To use the functions and variables defined in a *module*, you put one of the lines

```
use module              (e.g., use CGI)
use module feature_list (e.g., use CGI qw(:standard))
```

at the beginning of your Perl program. The first line imports all features of *module*. The second line imports only the listed features. Usually, this means a number of functions and variables defined in *module* are now directly usable in your program. For example, use CGI qw(:standard) makes the param function available.

The use operator locates the required module on directories listed in the special variable @INC, where Perl looks for headers and modules to include.

To load a module without importing its symbols, use

use *module* ()   (e.g., use CGI ())

In this case, you can access features with the CGI:: prefix (e.g., CGI::param('email')).

The CGI Module

CGI.pm makes Web CGI programming easy. It can

- receive and parse incoming form data
- create forms with initial values derived from user input
- generate simple HTML
- support file upload, cookies, cascading style sheets, server push, and frames

Some of these features are explained here. On UNIX systems, use **man** CGI to see the manual page for CGI.pm. You can find the latest version, as well as an introduction and complete documentation, at

stein.cshl.org/WWW/software/CGI/cgi_docs.html

With CGI.pm, form data can be obtained easily with the param function.

```
$value = param('email');        ## value for email
@value = param('sports');       ## array of values

@names = param();               ## all param names
foreach $name ( @names )
{   $value = param( $name );
    ...
}
```

A CGI program using CGI.pm can generate its own forms on the fly and make submit-again forms based on user-supplied values and flagged errors. Such a CGI program follows this structure:

1. If there is no input data (if (! param())), a blank form to be submitted to the program itself is generated.
2. If there is form input, then the correctness of input is checked. A submit-again form is generated if errors are detected.

3. For correct input, the input data are processed, and success is confirmed. The program may also invite a new request with a blank form.

HTML Code Generation

CGI.pm has a set of functions for HTML code generation. They produce strings that can be sent as output. These functions have obvious names and work as you might expect. Table 13.2 shows the general code generation call syntax that makes producing tags, attributes, and enclosed content easy.

For example (Ex: **CodeGen**), the code

```
print( h3('Survey'),                                    ## (1)
       start_form(-action=>"/cgi-bin/gen.pl"),          ## (2)
       span({-style=>'font-weight: bold'},
           "Your name: "),                              ## (3)
       textfield('name'),                               ## (4)
       p("What's your favorite color? ",                ## (5)
          popup_menu(-name=>'color',
             -values=>['red','green','blue']),
        ),
       submit(-name=>"send", -value="Send"),            ## (6)
       end_form;                                        ## (7)
    )
```

is a print call where the arguments are code generation functions. The lines in the following code are labeled to indicate how they are generated:

```
<h3>Survey</h3>                                         (from 1)
<form method="post" action="/cgi-bin/gen.pl"            (from 2)
       enctype="application/x-www-form-urlencoded">
  <span style="font-weight: bold">Your name: </span>    (from 3)
  <input type="text" name="name"  />                    (from 4)
<p>What's your favorite color?                          (from 5)
<select name="color">
```

Table 13.2   CODE GENERATION CALL SYNTAX

Call	HTML Code
p()	<p>
p("text")	<p>text</p>
p({'-class'=>'fine'})	<p class="fine">
p({'-class'=>'fine'}, "text")	<p class="fine">text</p>

```
               <option  value="red">red</option>
               <option  value="green">green</option>
               <option  value="blue">blue</option>
           </select>
           </p>                                             (from 5)
           <input type="submit" name="send" value="Send" />   (from 6)
           </form>                                           (from 7)
```

HTTP Header Generation

HTTP header generation is also done with `CGI.pm` using the `header` function. If it is called with no arguments

```
header()
```

it will return a `Date` header and the default content type header.

```
"Content-Type: text/html; charset=ISO-8859-1\n\n"
```

Use something like `header(-type=>img/gif)` to produce a different content type and something like `-charset=>'UTF-8'` if the page contains characters outside Latin-1 (ISO 8859-1).

If `header` is called with one or more *-Name=>str* arguments, then the specified headers will be returned together with the appropriate default headers.

```
header(-Name=>str,          -Name2=>str2,
       ...)
```

Any underscore in the name part will become a hyphen (-) in the generated header name. For example,

```
print header(-Content_length=>"990", -charset=>'UTF-8');
```

outputs these lines

```
Date: Tue, 17 Sep 2004 02:22:28 GMT
Content-length: 2990
Content-Type: text/html; charset=UTF-8
<empty line>
```

13.20 HANDLING FILE UPLOADING

In Section 8.7, we described the HTML form to upload a file. But we still need a server-side program that can handle the uploaded file. With `CGI.pm`, the following code can retrieve the uploaded file and store it in a prearranged directory:

```
$FH = upload('file_name');}                    (A)
binmode(FH); binmode(OUT);                      (B)
while ( <$FH> ) {       print OUT;      }
```

The CGI.pm function upload (line A) when given the name attribute of the file input field (file_name) returns a file handle for reading the uploaded file. To store the file, we use binary mode I/O (line B).

The content type and length of the uploaded file can be retrieved by the calls

```
$type = uploadInfo($FH)->{'Content-Type'};
$len = uploadInfo($FH)->{'Content-Length'};
```

A file-upload handler will usually check the userid and password supplied to limit file uploading to authorized users.

13.21   TESTING AND DEBUGGING CGI.pm SCRIPTS

CGI.pm makes it easy to test and debug Perl scripts. You can employ the -debug feature

```
use CGI qw/:standard -debug/;
```

for testing and debugging. In this mode, you can test your CGI scripts from the command line. You can supply, from the keyboard or a redirected file, name-value pairs in one line or on separate lines. The code

```
CGI_Script_Name < data_in
```

tests a CGI script with the prepared form data in the file data_in. The Dump() function call also produces an HTML list of all the input form data.

For general Perl debugging, you can run a Perl program interactively with the debugging option:

```
perl -d program_file arguments
```

You can also run Perl interactively and experiment with Perl constructs using

```
perl -de 7       Runs Perl interactively
```

The e 7 simply gives something for Perl to execute at the beginning. This allows you to type in Perl statements and have them executed immediately. When you are finished, type q to quit.

13.22   SESSION CONTROL

HTTP is a protocol that treats each request-response transaction between a client and a server independently. Consequently, a server normally cannot tell if two requests are from the same client. Hence, a CGI usually handles each incoming request as new business not related to anything before. Thus, a CGI program does not remember anything from a previous request because there is no need. This model is fine for simple data retrieval such as getting weather reports, obtaining stock quotes, and listing movies from a local cinema.

But more complicated operations such as airline reservations, shopping, credit card purchases, and membership services are difficult because they require a sequence in which later steps depend on previous ones. Using HTTP, multistep operations require a sequence of transactions (a *session*) to complete. To perform multistep operations, we must find a way to track requests from the same user that belong to the same session. This is not quite possible for a server-side program to do under HTTP. But it is possible to do something close: track all requests from the same client browser. This *session tracking* ability allows server-side agents such as CGI programs to give acceptable support to multistep operations.

13.23   SESSIONS UNDER HTTP

With HTTP, a server-side program does not have an easy way to tell the difference between a follow-up request and a new request. Thus, if you send your billing information in a prior request and then send your shipping information in a subsequent request, the server-side program has no easy way to associate the shipping information with the earlier billing information. The lack of memory of prior requests is known as the *stateless* property of the HTTP protocol.

To maintain sessions, a server-side program must *maintain session state* by remembering the effects of prior requests and be able to tell which new incoming request belongs to which session.

There are several ways to get around the stateless HTTP and achieve session control:

- Hidden form fields—A CGI program generates forms for subsequent steps of a session. Each generated form contains hidden form fields with values from all prior requests. This method essentially makes a multistep process into a single-step process behind the scenes. Because forms are subject to alteration by users, this method is not at all secure or efficient.

- URL rewriting—Instead of hidden fields, the information can be stored in the action URL as extra path-info or command-line parameters. This method has the same drawback as hidden form fields and may conflict with programming or actual form fields.

- Cookies—A way for servers to store information in browsers to be sent to target server-side programs together with future requests. This is perhaps the best way for session tracking under HTTP.

13.24 WHAT IS A COOKIE?

A *cookie* is a `name=value` pair that a Web server sends to a browser. The browser stores the cookie received and will return it in well-defined future requests to the same server (Figure 13.7).

A browser may accept or reject a cookie with the approval of the Web surfer. A browser will record cookies accepted and send the appropriate cookies in future requests to servers. The cookie technique was first devised by Netscape and has now become part of HTTP.

HTTP Cookie Headers

A CGI program can send a cookie to a browser with the `Set-Cookie` header in an HTTP response. The `Set-Cookie` header takes the following general form:

```
Set-Cookie: name=value; expires=date;
path=path; domain=domain_name; secure
```

In addition to the required `name=value` pair, a cookie has the following optional attributes:

Expiration time: A time/date string, in a special format (*Wdy, DD-Mon-YYYY HH:MM:SS GMT*), to indicate the expiration time of the cookie. A browser will return the cookie until the expiration time is reached even if the user exits the browser and restarts it. Omit this attribute and the cookie will remain active until the browser is closed.

Domain: A domain name or prefix for which the cookie is valid. The browser will return the cookie to any host that matches the specified domain.

Figure 13.7   UNDERSTANDING COOKIES

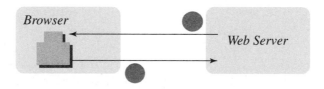

Thus, if the cookie domain is `.webtong.com`, then the browser will return the cookie to Web servers on any of the hosts `www.webtong.com`, `control.webtong.com`, and so on. A cookie domain must contain at least two periods to avoid matching on top-level domains like `.com`. The default domain is the host where the cookie originates.

Path: If the `path` attribute is set, the browser will return the cookie only with requests with a URL matching the path. For example, if the path is `/cgi-bin`, then the cookie will only be returned to every script in the `cgi-bin` directory. The default path is `/`.

The `secure` *flag*: If the word `secure` is included, the cookie will only be sent with requests via a secure channel, such as SSL[1] (a URL that starts with `https`).

Browsers return a cookie with the `Cookie` header:

```
Cookie: name1=value1; name2=value2; ...
```

Consider the following scenario:

1. A Web client requests a document and receives in the response:

   ```
   Set-Cookie: Customer=Joe_Smith; path=/cgi-bin/;
       expires=Monday, 09-Nov-2000 23:12:40 GMT
   ```

2. Later, when the client sends to this server a request whose URL starts with `/cgi-bin/`, the request will include the `Cookie` header:

   ```
   Cookie: Customer=Joe_Smith
   ```

3. The client now receives from the same server a response that contains another cookie:

   ```
   Set-Cookie: SessionID=AbX0017e; path=/cgi-bin/;
       expires=Monday, 09-Nov-2000 23:12:40 GMT
   ```

4. Future requests from the client (to this server whose URL starts with `/`) will include the `Cookie` header:

   ```
   Cookie: Customer=Joe_Smith SessionID=AbX0017e;
   ```

The following points are worth noting when using cookies:

- Cookies for different domains or paths are distinct, even if they have the same name.
- A cookie with a current or past expiration time will be discarded by the browser and will no longer be included in requests.
- Cookies can help server-side programs maintain session state through multiple HTTP transactions with the same client (browser).

---

[1]Secure Sockets Layer.

- Cookies coming back from user agents are available in the CGI environment variable HTTP_COOKIE.

13.25   COOKIES IN CGI PROGRAMS

Let's see how cookies are set and received in a CGI program. To set a cookie, a CGI program can send a Set-Cookie header:

```
print "Set-Cookie: Customer=Joe_Smith; ";
print "path=/cgi-bin/; "
print "expires=Monday, 16-Oct-2000 09:00:40 GMT\n";
print "Content-type: text/html\n\n
```

To receive cookies, a CGI program uses the value of the HTTP_COOKIE environment variable:

```
$cookies = $ENV{'HTTP_COOKIE'};
if ( $cookies ne "" )
{   print "HTTP_COOKIE: $cookies"; }
else
{   print "No HTTP_COOKIE"; }
```

CGI.pm offers several functions to make cookie handling easy. The cookie function creates a cookie

```
$myCookie =
    cookie(-name=>'SessionID',          ## cookie name
           -value=>'AbX0017e',          ## cookie value
           -expires=>'+1h',             ## cookie expiration time (A)
           -path=>'/cgi-bin/member/',   ## cookie path
           -domain=>'.webtong.com',     ## cookie domain
           -secure=>1);                 ## cookie secure flag
```

and the header function can set any HTTP response header, including Set-Cookie:

```
print header(-cookie=>$myCookie);
```

Be sure to set all headers before any output to STDOUT.

With CGI.pm, you receive incoming cookies (from browsers) with a simple call:

```
$value = cookie('name');
```

If the cookie stored a Perl hash array value, then you can recover that hash array with

```
%arr = cookie('name');
```

The expiration time (line A) is set with strings in the following forms:

```
"now"   -- expire immediately    "+180s" -- in 180 seconds
"+2m"   -- in 2 minutes          "+12h"  -- in 12 hours
"+1d"   -- in 1 day              "+3M"   -- in 3 months
"+2y"   -- in 2 years            "-3m"   -- 3 minutes ago(!)
```

13.26   CGI.pm COOKIE EXAMPLE

For an application of cookies for session control, let's look at a Perl script to check the availability of domain names for registration (Ex: **DomainCheck**). The HTML form (Figure 13.8) is:

```
<p><b>Check Domain Name Availability</b></p>
<form method="post" action="/cgi-bin/wb/domaincheck.pl">
<p>Check <input name="dn" size="16" />
   .com, .net, and .org  
<input type="submit" value=" go " /></p>
</form>
```

The CGI program remembers the domain names checked and lists the ones that are available and unavailable as the user continues to check new possibilities (Figure 13.9).

The **whois** command is used to check if a domain name is taken already (lines 1 and 6). The hash %recover receives (line 2) a Perl hash saved as a cookie (lines 7-8). Values on the hash are separated into the available $namelist and the unavailable $takenlist (line 3).

```
#!/usr/bin/perl -T
use CGI qw(:standard);
$ENV{'PATH'}='/usr/sbin:/sbin:/bin:/usr/bin';
delete @ENV{qw(IFS CDPATH ENV BASH_ENV)};

## script values
```

Figure 13.8   DOMAIN NAME AVAILABILITY FORM

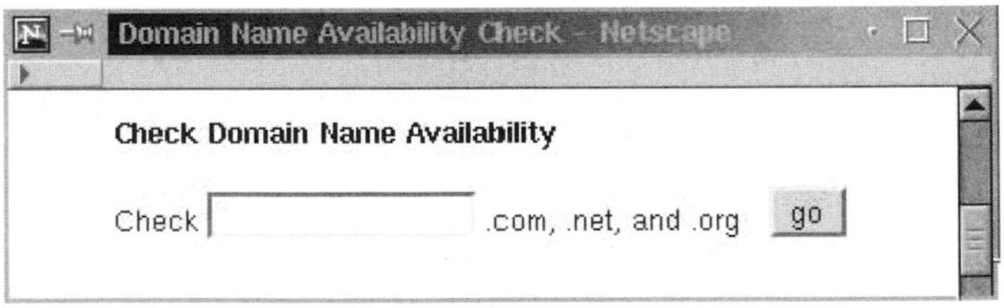

Figure 13.9   **DOMAIN CHECK RESULTS**

```
$cookie_path = '/cgi-bin/wb/domaincheck.pl';
$front_file="domain.front";
$back_file="domain.back";
@tld_list=(".com", ".net", ".org");
$found="", $reply="";
$found_not="";
$whois="/usr/bin/whois";                                 ## (1)
##### in-script configuration values END

# Get previously found domain names from the cookie:
%recover=cookie('tlds');                                 ## (2)

foreach $key (sort keys %recover)                        ## (3)
{  if ( $recover{$key} == 1 )
   {  push(@namelist, $key);  }
   else
   {  push(@takenlist, $key);  }
}

## check domain names
$name=param('dn');    ## fresh domain name to check      ## (4)

if ( $name )
{  foreach $top ( @tld_list )                            ## (5)
   { $try= "$name$top";
     if ( $recover{$try} < 1 )
```

```
          {  $try = noSpecial($try);
             if ( $top eq ".org" )
             {  $t = "$try" . "\@whois.pir.org"; }   ### .org whois server
             else
             {   $t = $try;  }

             $result=`$whois $t |
                  /bin/grep -i "No match\|NOT FOUND"`;          ## (6)

             if ( $result ne "" )     ## available
             {   push(@namelist, $try);
                 $found .= "  $try";
                 $recover{$try}=1;
             }
             else                       ## unavailable
             {   push(@takenlist, $try);
                 $found_not .= "  $try";
                 $recover{$try}=2;
             }
}}}
## set cookie
$the_cookie = cookie(-name=>'tlds', -value=>\%recover,   ## (7)
                  -expires=>'+1h', -path=>$cookie_path);

# Print the cookie header with expiration date
print header(-cookie=>$the_cookie, -charset=>'UTF-8');   ## (8)
```

The new domain name possibility is obtained from input form data (line 4) and checked in a list of top-level domains (line 5). The UNIX grep command looks for No Match or Not Found in the **whois** result, which indicates an available domain (line 6). A checked domain name joins $namelist or takenlist and is placed in %recover that is stored via the cookie for the next step (lines 7-8).

The program is now ready to construct and send the response page to the client. The reply page lists available and unavailable domains checked so far (lines 9-10) and invites the user to try another possibility:

```
##### send HTML page
outputFile("$front_file");

$reply .= '<table><tr><td style="width: 10px">
           </td><td>';

if ($found ne "")    ## available
{  $reply .= '<p style="font-size: larger">Congratulations:
        we found<code style="font-weight: bold">'
       . "$found</code></p><p>available.</p>";
}
```

```
elsif ( $found_not  ne "" )
{ $reply .= '<p style="font-size: larger">Unfortunately:
        </p><p><code style="font-weight: bold">' .
        "$found_not</code></p><p>are not available.</p>";
}

$reply .= '<p>So far, the following domain names have
        been checked:</p><table><tr><th>Available</th>
        <th style="width:30px"> </th><th>Unavailable
        </th></tr><tr><td align="left" valign="top">';

if (@namelist)                                         ## (9)
{   foreach $name(@namelist)
    { $reply .= "<code>$name</code><br />\n"; }
}

$reply .= '</td><td style="width:30px"> </td>
        <td align="left" valign="top">';

if (@takenlist)                                        ## (10)
{   foreach $name(@takenlist)
    { $reply .= "<code>$name</code><br />\n"; }
}
$reply .= "</td></tr></table></td></tr></table>";
outputFile("$back_file");
sendPage($reply);
exit;
```

The domaincheck.pl program makes use of several functions we have defined
before in this chapter. The complete source code for this practical application
can be found in the example package.

13.27 SUMMARY

Perl derives its syntax from C and the UNIX shell. Perl scalar, array, and
hash variables use the $, @, and % prefixes, respectively. Arrays use zero-based
indexing, and hashes access values by keys. Strings can be concatenated with
the . operator. Perl uses values in a context-dependent way. One result is that
numbers and their string representations can be used interchangeably.

Perl functions are defined with the notation

```
sub functionName{ ... }
```

Scalar, array, and hash arguments are passed in a flat list that is accessed in the
called function by the array @_, whose elements $_[0], $_[1], . . . are references
to the arguments. You can avoid the "flattening" by passing references.

The construct `'shell command'` executes the shell command and returns its output. Perl and JavaScript use almost identical regular expressions. The `=~` operator is used for string matching and substitution. A pattern is specified as `/pattern string/` or `m|pattern string|`, which allows you to pick the pattern delimiter (`|`). Use STDIN and STDOUT for standard I/O and the open function to create file handles for I/O to and from files and processes.

It is good to turn on the taint mode to add security to CGI programs. Tainted user input causes guarded operations to fail. This forces the program to check and untaint user input before using them in guarded operations.

A Perl module provides a separate name space. You import a Perl module with `use module qw( features )` to access its functions and data directly. The CGI.pm module provides good facilities for writing CGI scripts, including HTML generation, HTTP header generation, form data access and modification, and cookie and debugging support.

The HTTP cookie is a mechanism to get around the statelessness of the HTTP protocol. Server-side programs can set cookies for browsers (client-side agents) to return them in future requests. CGI.pm supports cookie usage with simple functions to set and retrieve cookies.

EXERCISES

Review Questions

1. What is the form of the very first line of a Perl program? What does this line do? How does this line change if you move the program to a different computer?

2. Where can you find Perl documentation? On UNIX systems? On the Web?

3. How do you make a Perl program executable as a regular program? As a CGI script? How do you invoke a Perl program from the command line? Describe the URL used to access a CGI program.

4. Identify and explain the three types of variables in Perl. What is the difference between using double quotation marks and single quotation marks to form strings in Perl? What is the difference between these two constructs:

   ```
   $var = "$filename.$suffix";
   $var = "$filename" . "$suffix";
   ```

5. Consider Perl arrays. How do you form an array? Access and set array elements? Obtain array length? Add and delete elements at the beginning or end of the array? Display an array?

6. Consider Perl hashes. How do you form a hash? Access and set hash elements? Obtain keys and values? Add and delete pairs? Display a hash?

7. In Perl, how do you find the length of a string? Join two strings? Obtain substrings? Find if a character is on a string?

8. How do you declare variables in JavaScript? In Perl?

9. In Perl, what is true? What is false?

10. What is a file handle? How do you open a file handle? Name the handles for standard I/O.

11. How do you define a function in Perl? How does such a function receive arguments?

12. Compare pattern matching in JavaScript with that in Perl and state their similarities and differences.

13. List the special pattern characters in Perl.

14. What is taint mode for Perl? Why is it important for CGI programs?

15. How does CGI.pm help CGI script testing and debugging?

16. What is session control under HTTP? Why is there a need for it?

17. What is a cookie? How are cookies used to maintain session state?

18. Identify and explain the HTTP headers for setting and returning cookies.

Assignments

1. Deploy the Perl program Ex: **PerlCmdLine** in Section 13.3 on your system and make it run.

2. Write a Perl script that takes what you type on standard input into a file whose name is given as a command-line argument.

3. Write a Perl script that displays a file whose name is given on the command line.

4. Take the htmlBegin function (Section 13.11) and the file it uses and deploy them in your cgi-bin and experiment with them from the Web.

5. Take the formMail.cgi program (Ex: **FormToMail** Section 13.12) and deploy it in your Web space. Make it work.

6. Continue from the previous assignment and make formMail.cgi run in taint mode.

7. Write a Perl script to look for the pattern /
/ in a file and create a transformed file replacing <br> with <br />.

8. Take the password handling code in Section 13.17 and implement a password checking CGI program.

9. Make the join.cgi program in Section 8.17 run in taint mode.

10. Make the Ex: **PageSearch** (Section 13.15) program run in taint mode.

11. Take the email address checking program in JavaScript (Section 9.15) and translate it into Perl.

12. Connect the club joining example (Ex: **JoinClub**; Section 8.17) to the formMail.cgi code in Chapter 13. Make sure the email checking is deployed with JavaScript in the form and in Perl in the CGI program.

13. Take the example in Section 13.26 (Ex: **DomainCheck**) and make it into a complete program accessible from the Web. Use it to check domain name availability.

14. Implement an on-Web *Imagemap Code Generation* facility:

    a. The user uploads any Web-supported image for the image map (Section 2.19).

    b. A page is displayed where the user can enter a rectangle, a circle, or a polygon with mouse operations. The user can also supply a URL as the target for the selected area.

    c. After each completed area, the program displays the additional area code for the map element being constructed.

    d. When the user is finished, the completed map code is displayed.

15. Follow the model given in Section 10.21 to construct a time clock service consisting of

    a. A server-side CGI program that reports the time in a standard time zone.

    b. A client-side DHTML to access the CGI service and display the time by ticking the seconds forward for a reasonable length of time (e.g., 15 seconds).

Photos

Index